CLEANING UP
THE BOMB FACTORY

WEYERHAEUSER ENVIRONMENTAL BOOKS

Paul S. Sutter, Editor

Weyerhaeuser Environmental Books explore human relationships with natural environments in all their variety and complexity. They seek to cast new light on the ways that natural systems affect human communities, the ways that people affect the environments of which they are a part, and the ways that different cultural conceptions of nature profoundly shape our sense of the world around us. A complete list of the books in the series appears at the end of this book.

CASEY A. HUEGEL

CLEANING UP THE BOMB FACTORY

Grassroots Activism and Nuclear Waste in the Midwest

University of Washington Press *Seattle*

Cleaning Up the Bomb Factory is published with the assistance of a grant from the Weyerhaeuser Environmental Books Endowment, established by the Weyerhaeuser Company Foundation, members of the Weyerhaeuser family, and Janet and Jack Creighton.

Copyright © 2024 by the University of Washington Press
Design by Mindy Basinger Hill. Composed in Minion Pro.

All rights reserved. No part of this publication may be reproduced or transmitted in any form or by any means, electronic or mechanical, including photocopy, recording, or any information storage or retrieval system, without permission in writing from the publisher.

UNIVERSITY OF WASHINGTON PRESS *uwapress.uw.edu*

Cataloging information is available from the Library of Congress
Library of Congress Control Number: 2024906507
ISBN 9780295752549 (hardcover)
ISBN 9780295752556 (paperback)
ISBN 9780295752563 (ebook)

∞ This paper meets the requirements of ANSI/NISO z39.48-1992 (Permanence of Paper).

FOR MY PARENTS,
DARREN AND CATHY HUEGEL

CONTENTS

- ix — Foreword by Paul S. Sutter
- xv — Acknowledgments
- xviii — Maps

- 1 — Introduction
- 13 — *One.* Atomic Farmlands
- 33 — *Two.* Trinity Day
- 58 — *Three.* FRESH Activism
- 85 — *Four.* The Strike
- 107 — *Five.* Going National
- 132 — *Six.* "America's Worst Polluter"
- 159 — *Seven.* FUTURESITE
- 185 — *Eight.* Grassroots Cleanup
- 207 — Conclusion

- 221 — Notes
- 271 — Bibliography
- 289 — Index

Paul S. Sutter

FOREWORD A Fresh Look at Antinuclear Activism

I set off for the Fernald Preserve on a gorgeous spring morning, a brief diversion from an otherwise mundane three-day drive across the country. I had stayed the prior night in a nondescript hotel just off I-74, northwest of Cincinnati, but it didn't take long to get away from the commercial world of the interstate and into the bucolic, undulating Ohio countryside. I passed through the small town of New Haven, where American flags decorated the main street, saluting the nation from every power pole. Many more adorned the modest but well-kept houses that lined the road to Fernald. Memorial Day was a week away, and I wondered if the town was preparing for a celebration. Or perhaps the flags were a permanent feature of the place. Either way, it felt like archetypal rural America: patriotic, working-class, and, if true to the drift of Ohio politics, conservative as well. It seemed an unlikely place to have hosted one of the most important environmental mobilizations of the late twentieth century.

As I entered the preserve, I stopped briefly at Lodge Pond, where ducks dabbled, dragonflies hovered, swallows darted across the surface of the water, and a pair of Canada geese doted on their goslings. I drove on to the main parking lot. It was early, and the visitor center was closed, but I happily headed out on the extensive trail network, binoculars in hand. I strolled through grasslands pocked with small ponds and depressional wetlands and into an extensive stand of maturing forest. I must have been there during peak spring migration, for the woods were positively alive with birds. Fernald has a reputation as a birding hot spot, so this was not surprising, but I was heartened nonetheless, because I knew what the place had been before its reincarnation as a nature preserve.

From 1951 until 1989, the Fernald Preserve was the site of the Feed Materials Production Center, a uranium processing plant that was a critical node in the Department of Energy's national network of nuclear weapons production facilities. The end of the Cold War had coincided with the end of uranium production at Fernald, and it prompted a larger reckoning with the extraordinarily hazardous legacies of the nuclear arms race. During subsequent decades, the DOE and its various partners had cleaned up the highly polluted facility, a Superfund site, in what was then one of the largest environmental remediation and ecological restoration efforts ever undertaken. But the signs of Fernald's past life were everywhere: in the interpretive placards explaining that the various ponds and wetlands had been dug as part of the cleanup; in the fenced-off groundwater treatment facility that is the last operating remnant of the remediation effort; in the "Weapons to Wetlands Grove" of trees dedicated to "honoring the leaders behind the Fernald cleanup"; in the "authorized personnel only" signs that proscribed public access to parts of the preserve; in the On-Site Disposal Facility, a massive, treeless mound looming on the east side of the preserve that entombs millions of cubic yards of contaminated soil and debris; and in the very fact that Fernald is a nature preserve managed by the Department of Energy, under the aegis of its euphemistically named Office of Legacy Management. Even the frogs in one of the ponds sounded suspiciously like Geiger counters registering the hidden hazards that remain at Fernald.

In *Cleaning Up the Bomb Factory*, Casey Huegel unpacks Fernald's remarkable history as a place of Cold War production, worker and resident activism, and environmental remediation. In some ways, the Fernald story will be familiar to those who know the history of antitoxics activism in the United States. It was led mostly by working-class women who, when confronted with powerful threats to their families and community, worked tirelessly to mobilize their fellow citizens to oppose polluting industries and seek redress. Think Lois Gibbs of Love Canal fame, or Karen Silkwood, the union activist who took on dangerous working conditions at one of Kerr-McGee's Oklahoma nuclear plants, or Erin Brockovich, who sued PG&E over the polluting of groundwater in Hinkley, California.

But Huegel also pushes that familiar storyline, the stuff of Hollywood films, in new and fruitful directions. One great virtue of Huegel's treatment is his careful attention to the local milieu, and to the complexities of mobilizing and managing an environmental campaign in this rural part of Ohio at a time when environmentalism had become a source of partisan polarization. The activists at the center of Huegel's story brilliantly managed various actors: antinuclear peace activists, organized labor, the DOE, corporate contractors, national environmental groups, local residents, and state and national politicians. In the process, they orchestrated a pragmatic and democratic brand of environmental activism that balanced progressive goals with the conservative values of the local community.

The Feed Materials Production Center, like the rest of the nation's nuclear weapons infrastructure, was born in relative secrecy during the early Cold War. DOE representatives came to Southwest Ohio in 1951 and abruptly informed a group of farmers that they would need to sell their land or face eminent domain proceedings. Soon the facility, which combined uranium milling, refining, and smelting in one location, was up and running, with National Lead of Ohio (NLO) the contractor in charge. From its earliest days, Huegel argues, the DOE and NLO prioritized production over worker health and environmental safety, abetted by the fact that federal law exempted the DOE from environmental oversight. As a result, those who worked in and lived around the Fernald plant had only a limited sense of the risks that the plant posed.

During the era of détente, production at Fernald slowed, but it ramped up again during the Reagan years, when the demands of a renewed nuclear arms race met the reality of Fernald's aging physical plant. In the wake of the Three Mile Island accident in 1979, a group of antinuclear activists from the greater Cincinnati area "discovered" Fernald, a nuclear weapons facility in their own backyard, and began to build a case that it was a threat to local environmental health and safety. Meanwhile, Fernald's workforce, organized in the Fernald Atomic Trades and Labor Council (FATLC), pushed for more careful government studies of worker health and safety at the plant. Together, though not initially in cooperation with each other, activists and workers began amassing evidence to show that Fernald was not as safe as officials made it out to be. In 1981, the

Ohio Environmental Protection Agency discovered radioactive contamination in several wells that adjoined Fernald, including one that served the home of Lisa and Ken Crawford, though they would not be apprised of that discovery for several years. Then, in 1984, after a major uranium leak at the plant, investigations revealed that Fernald was indeed both a hazardous working environment and a potential threat to the larger community. In response, workers and community members mobilized to hold NLO and the DOE accountable.

The most prominent face of the local movement was Fernald Residents for Environmental Safety and Health, better known by its acronym FRESH. Radicalized by the belated discovery of her poisoned well, Lisa Crawford became FRESH's most vocal leader. But from its inception, FRESH was also pragmatic and inclusive. Its leaders quickly built cordial relations with FATLC leadership and made worker health and safety a central issue of their campaign, something that earlier peace activists who had targeted the plant failed to do. They also set themselves apart from the antinuclear movement by opposing the closure of Fernald, a move that also endeared them to Fernald's workers and the larger community.

FRESH faced a federal government that was newly hostile to environmental regulations and had gutted enforcement, so it turned to the state, and to cultivating the support of state and national representatives. As Huegel observes, "FRESH's carefully crafted image as a labor-friendly environmental organization of concerned mothers" secured it the support of important political allies. Despite its local orientation, FRESH built national connections — most importantly through an organization called the Military Production Network, founded in Colorado in 1987 — that linked it with environmental activists at other nuclear production sites around the country. It also embraced the logic of a burgeoning environmental justice movement and resisted the worst aspects of the era's NIMBYism. As Huegel shows, FRESH activists accepted that Fernald was part of their backyard, they supported the plant's larger Cold War mission, and they recognized the local economic benefits that came with it. But they were uncompromising in their insistence that the DOE and its contractors had behaved badly, and that they needed to protect worker and resident health and safety.

FRESH filed a class action lawsuit against NLO for its mismanagement of the Fernald plant and won a major settlement from the DOE. It also motivated the DOE to remove NLO as Fernald's contractor, and, along with the FATLC, it forced the federal government to finally study workplace and community health at Fernald. More than that, though, by demanding that it admit to its mistakes, FRESH helped to transform the DOE from one of the nation's premier Cold War era polluters to an agency on the cutting edge of environmental remediation. This careful attention to the institutional history and cultural transformation of the DOE is another signature achievement of *Cleaning Up the Bomb Factory*.

FRESH and its many allies were less successful at keeping Fernald open—the DOE shut it down in 1989—but it continued to advocate for workers as production gave way to the multibillion-dollar cleanup project. Fernald activists were also instrumental in the passage of the Federal Facilities Compliance Act (FFCA), which ended the immunity from environmental oversight that DOE facilities enjoyed. Theirs was a vibrant local movement with profound national consequences.

Fernald activists did not decamp once the facility closed. Serving as members of the Fernald Citizens Task Force, local activists had an important voice during the remediation process, and they again showed their pragmatism. They accepted a risk-based approach to cleanup that balanced benefits with costs, they accepted that compromise was a part of the process, and they recognized that they would always be living with a level of risk. Few decisions better captured this spirit than their acceptance of the On-Site Disposal Facility, where Fernald's low-level nuclear waste is interred, as part of their responsibility. Activists, having lived with the hazards of Fernald and influenced by the claims of the environmental justice movement, were unwilling to foist these wastes on others. While it would be easy to criticize this pragmatic approach as too willing to compromise with the government agencies and corporate contractors whose negligence had, for decades, magnified the hazards of the place, it was also an approach that held those responsible to account, empowered local people as decision makers, and was true to local values. In the end, Huegel asks us to assess the Fernald campaign on the local activists' own terms. And on those terms, it would be difficult to see their grassroots mobilization, and the dramatic results they achieved, as anything but a far-reaching success.

As I was leaving the Fernald Preserve that spring morning, I noticed an engraved stone, shaded beneath some bushes, dated May 8, 2001. It read: "Fifty years ago, at the onset of the Cold War, the United States government began construction of a uranium processing facility on this land. This marker is dedicated to the families who originally lived on this property, the people of the surrounding communities, and the patriotic men and women who contributed to the operation and environmental remediation of the Fernald site." Placed there by the DOE and Fluor Fernald, the contractor in charge of the remediation effort, it was a succinct summary of the site's remarkable history, one tinged with a strange mix of pride, duty, sacrifice, regret, and the constraints of a bygone era. It betrayed no conflict between those displaced by the plant, those who lived in its shadow, those who worked there, and those who strove tirelessly to clean up the mess. There was a stoic quality to the message that obscured as much as it revealed, hiding the complexity of Fernald's history behind the veil of patriotism. Still, knowing Fernald's history as I now do, and having seen firsthand the beauty and life of the Fernald Preserve, there was also something fitting about a dedication that gave honor to all parties involved. It was an outcome that local activists would have wanted, one that spoke to the strengths of their inclusive and pragmatic approach.

In the end, then, *Cleaning Up the Bomb Factory* is not only a compelling history of a unique and highly effective environmental mobilization; it is also a blueprint for how to mobilize to solve environmental problems in a divided world. As Casey Huegel aptly concludes: "Fernald's environmental movement serves as a powerful reminder that rapid institutional change for the sake of environmental protection is possible even in a polarized political environment."

ACKNOWLEDGMENTS

Nine years ago, I went for my first hike at the Fernald Preserve in Southwest Ohio. As I walked the park's trails, read the interpretive signs, and explored the visitor center's exhibits, I learned that this beautiful park was once an extraordinarily contaminated uranium metals production facility and part of the massive Cold War nuclear weapons complex. Reading about this physical transformation from nuclear wasteland to nature preserve was shocking. I imagine most first-time visitors to Fernald—including myself—begin with the same simple question: How did this happen? This book is my best explanation.

Publishing with the University of Washington's Weyerhaeuser Environmental Books series has been a wonderful experience. Past titles in this series inspired my early fascination with environmental history, and its new books continue to expand and challenge my own interpretations. Thank you to acquisitions editor Mike Baccam and series editor Paul Sutter for believing in my manuscript's potential. Mike has been a patient, knowledgeable, and supportive guide throughout this process. Paul, as well as two peer reviewers, provided excellent feedback that identified my manuscript's weaknesses, encouraged its strengths, and undoubtedly made this book better. I also want to thank project editor Jennifer Comeau for carefully overseeing production, Ben Pease for creating these wonderful maps, Richard Isaac for the skillful copyediting, assistant editor/acquisitions fellow Marcella Landri, publicity manager Molly Woolbright, marketing manager Benny Sisson, acquisitions assistant Ishita Shahi, and everyone at the University of Washington Press who made this book possible.

In between that first hike at Fernald and this book's publication, I had the privilege of earning my PhD in history at the University of Cincinnati. For six years, I studied environmental activism with my advisor, mentor, and friend, David Stradling. David supported and encouraged this project from an idea to a dissertation and, finally, a book. I am deeply grateful for the time and energy David has dedicated to my intellectual growth. I am also most appreciative of my dissertation committee, including Jason Krupar, Tracy Teslow, and Drew Swanson, whose thoughtful comments guided the first revisions to my manuscript. Drew also invited me to write a post for the Agricultural History Society's blog, *The Short Rows*, which challenged me to strengthen my arguments about Fernald. I also want to thank Alyssa McClanahan, Anne Delano Steinert, and Rob Gioielli from the UC community. Alyssa shared her excellent manuscript on antinuclear activism in Cincinnati and read draft chapters from this book. Anne shared her knowledge of local history and helped connect me to the Fernald community. Rob has always been generous with his time to talk environmental history.

I have had the pleasure of meeting numerous historical actors in this book, as well as those who work hard to share Fernald's history with the public. Lisa Crawford, Tom Carpenter, Don and Kathy Meyer, and James Werner all sat for interviews. Linda Musmeci Kimball and Dave Fankhauser provided extensive documentation, which made this book possible. Joyce Bentle shared her documentaries. Stephen Depoe directed me to the Fernald Living History Project. Graham Mitchell and the rest of the Fernald Community Alliance opened their meetings for conversation. Penny Borgman provided invaluable research support, and Frances Boyens, Shirlyn Myles, and Heidi Palombo helped with numerous image requests.

Two timely lecture opportunities, one local and one national, helped clarify my thoughts on Fernald's grassroots environmental movement. Thank you to Alyssa Fernbach and everyone at the Ross Township Historical Society for hosting me and promoting community history. I also had the opportunity to make a presentation for Princeton University's Program on Science and Global Security. Thank you to codirector Zia Mian for the invitation, Igor Moric for setting up the discussion, and everyone in attendance for their kind words, fascinating stories, and engaging questions.

Many other scholars and archivists also made this book possible. Public Policy Archivist Carly Dearborn at The Ohio State University Libraries was particularly helpful with John Glenn's Senate papers. Although we never met in person, nuclear historian Bill Knoblauch's encouragement over email was inspiring. Finally, Ed Roach, Carol Engelhardt Herringer, and Dawne Dewey helped get me started in this field and have supported my scholarship and public history work over many years.

This book is dedicated to my parents, Darren and Cathy Huegel. I cannot thank them enough for their many sacrifices and endless support throughout my life. I also never could have written this book without learning my father's work ethic and my mother's communication skills. Thank you both for these great gifts. I also want to thank my brother, Alex Huegel, for his support and interest in my work. Finally, I am deeply indebted to my wife and life partner, Mindy Huegel. In one way or another, I have been working on this book since we met in 2016. Although Fernald has remained a constant in our lives, so much else has changed, and it has been a beautiful and rewarding journey to grow together. Your love, support, and encouragement made this book possible, and I appreciate your understanding that when I am buried in books and lost in writing at my desk that I am truly happy. Thank you!

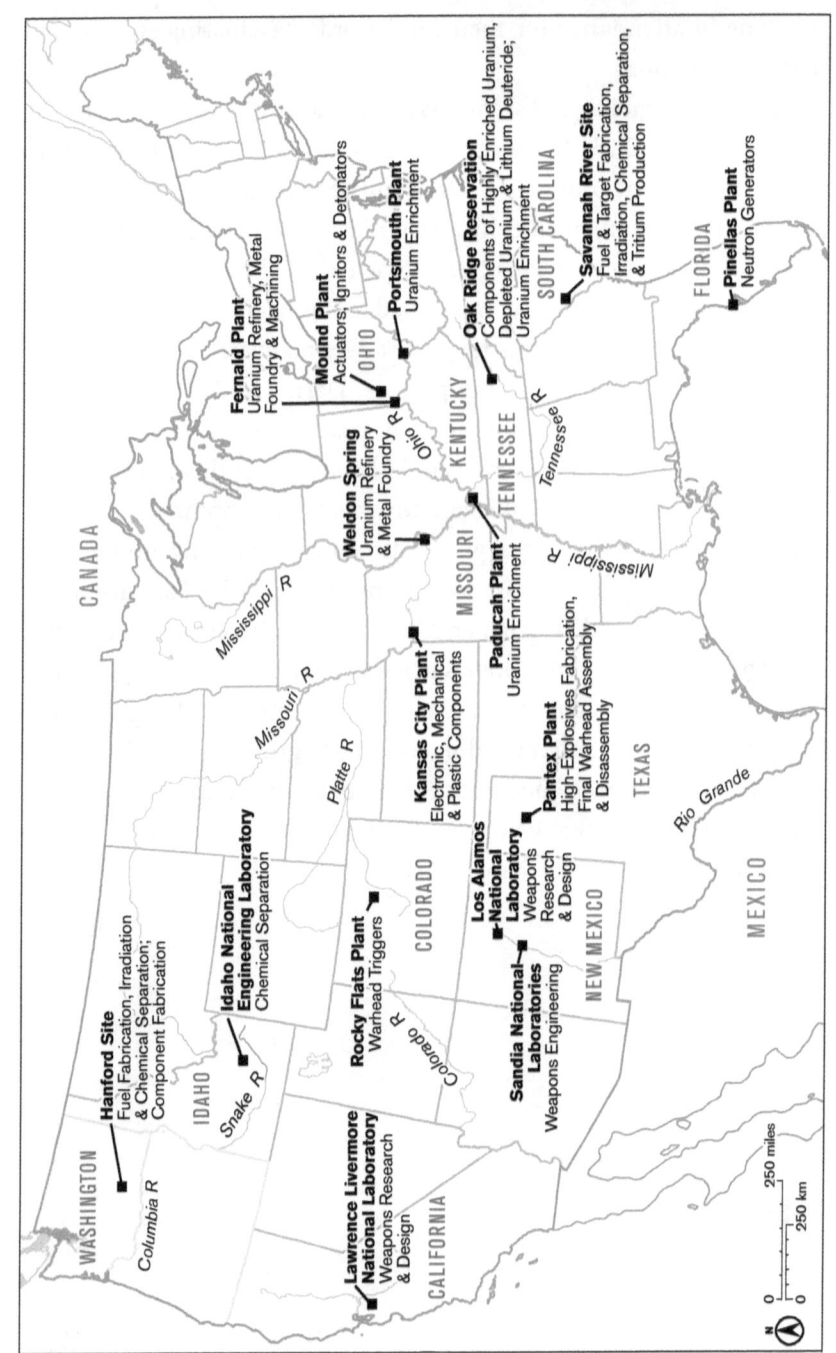

MAP 1. US Cold War Nuclear Weapons Production Facilities

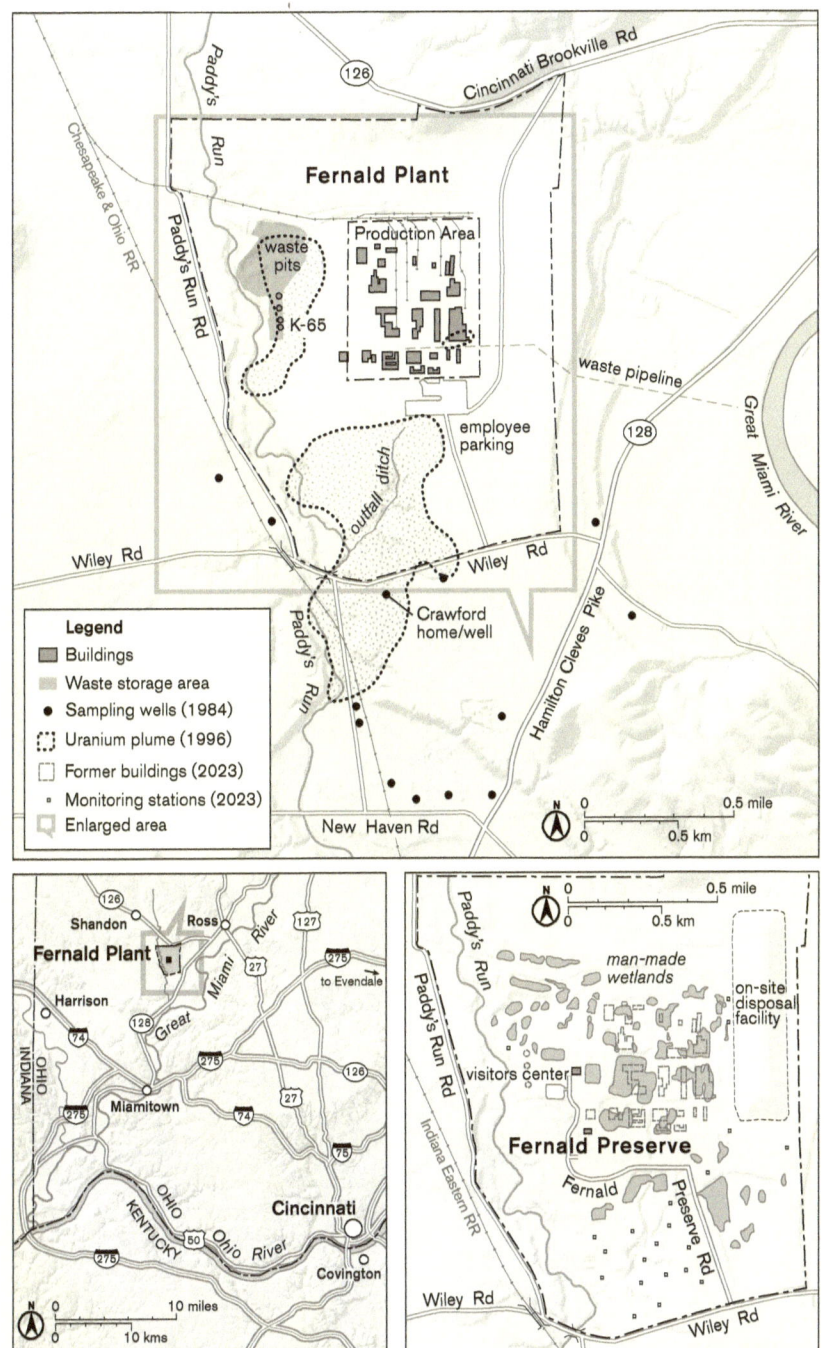

MAP 2. Fernald Plant and Vicinity

**CLEANING UP
THE BOMB FACTORY**

INTRODUCTION

On November 19, 1984, an alarm sounded in Plant 9, the Special Products Plant, at the Feed Materials Production Center—better known as Fernald—a Department of Energy (DOE)-owned uranium processing facility located about eighteen miles northwest of Cincinnati, Ohio. Plant 9's industrial processes produced air pollutants, which were drawn into a dust collection system before the air was released up a sixty-foot stack. When functioning properly, the dust collector captured about 130 pounds of uranium each day, but the Geiger counter stack monitor alarm had indicated that uranium was escaping directly into the environment. During inspection, a technician from the Industrial Health and Radiation Department replaced the stack filter and sent it to the lab for analysis, which confirmed a release of about fifty-four pounds of uranium over the previous three days. As part of daily procedures, an employee had visually inspected the baghouse but did not observe any "stray dust" indicative of a torn, loose, or disconnected dust collection bag. The Geiger counter's sensitivity, as a result, was decreased by a factor of ten, so that it would no longer trigger the alarm and disrupt production.[1]

Production was king during the Cold War, and a disruption at Fernald would have reverberated throughout the sprawling nuclear weapons complex. Inside Plant 9, workers contracted through National Lead of Ohio (NLO) machined uranium metal products and cast uranium ingots, which measured up to twenty-five inches long and thirteen inches in diameter, and weighed nearly two thousand pounds. As part of the next step in the nuclear assembly line, trucks drove these ingots three hundred miles northeast to Reactive Metals Inc. in Ashtabula, Ohio, for further processing before railcars carried them across the country to Hanford in

Washington State to fuel the N Reactor, which generated electricity, and, most importantly, produced plutonium for America's nuclear arsenal. At Fernald, production workers transformed uranium ore and uranium-bearing scrap into essential feed materials. As the "first link" in the nuclear weapons production complex, it was easier to ignore an alarm than disrupt the entire bomb making process.[2]

Fernald's small uranium release was no nuclear disaster. Instead, the dust settled rather harmlessly on Fernald's 1,050-acre property and garnered no immediate media attention.[3] Historians of the Atomic Age have chronicled many more severe accidents in nuclear weapons and nuclear power, including Castle Bravo, Kyshtym, Windscale, Chernobyl, and Fukushima, which devastated human bodies and environments on massive scales; or, in the case of Three Mile Island, a gut-wrenching near miss.[4] "The main reason for continuing mistrust of the nuclear industry and the governments that promote it," historian Serhii Plokhy wrote, "is the series of accidents that have dogged the industry in its military and civil incarnations since the 1950s."[5]

There was no singular moment at Fernald, however, such as a mushroom cloud or reactor meltdown, to signal that something had gone terribly wrong. Instead, the "slow violence" of uranium metals production and nuclear waste disposal accumulated gradually.[6] By the mid-1980s, this comparatively small and largely forgotten uranium plant was widely recognized as the "third largest radioactive waste dump in the United States," trailing only the astronomically larger Hanford and Savannah River sites (360,000 and 192,000 acres, respectively).[7] For much of the Cold War, small releases of uranium to the air and water were considered ordinary events, an insignificant price to pay in a global power struggle between the United States and the Soviet Union.[8] Over time, however, these small releases from the processing of about five hundred thousand metric tons of uranium created a nuclear wasteland at Fernald and stirred up anger and mistrust in the community equivalent to any of history's more dramatic and infamous nuclear disasters.[9]

From mid-September to December 7, 1984, about 275 pounds of uranium had escaped the Plant 9 dust collector through loose dust collection bags, which were hidden from workers' view in the baghouse during

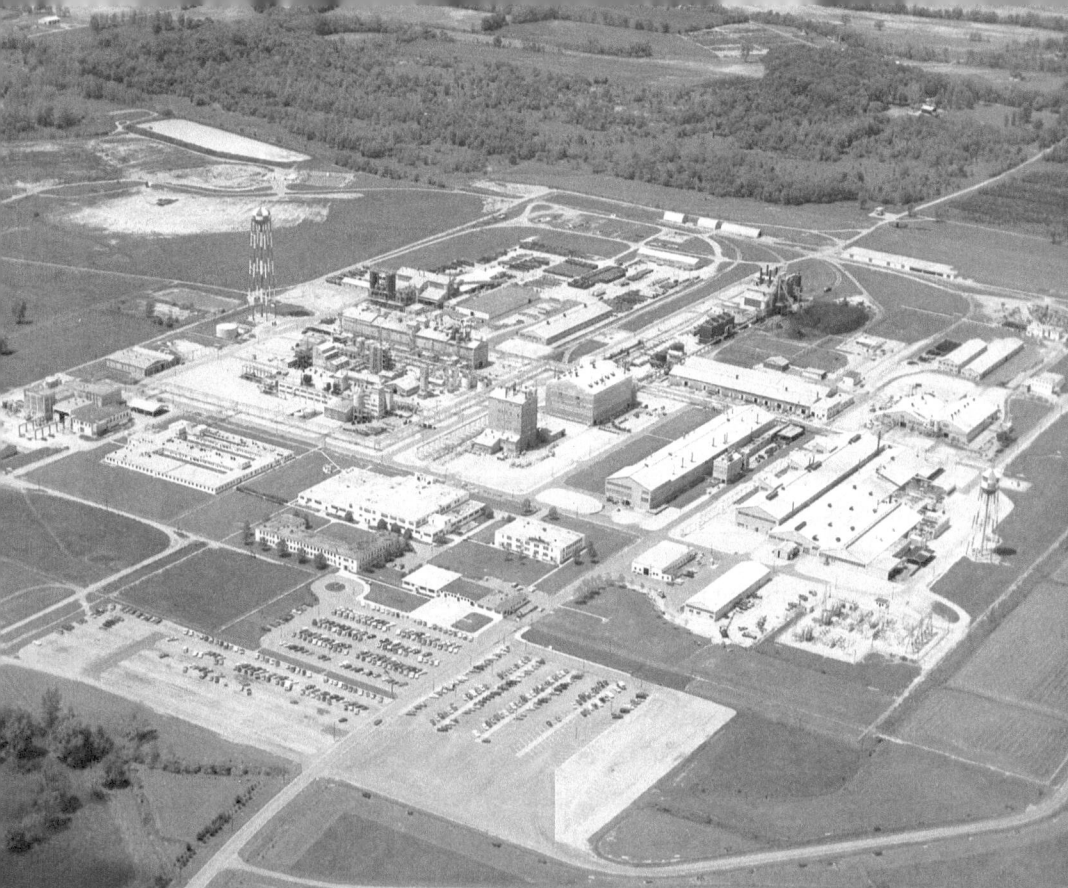

FIGURE 1. Aerial view of the Feed Materials Production Center, better known as Fernald, 1986. Courtesy of the US Department of Energy.

inspections.[10] Though modest in terms of radiation, the aftermath of this event—known as Fernald's "uranium leak"—transformed the map of nuclear weapons production in the United States as well as grassroots environmental activism. On December 11, 1984, *Cincinnati Enquirer* environmental beat reporter Ben Kaufman published a front-page article titled "NLO Checking Possible Uranium Leak." The headline captured the initial uncertainty of what had happened. Still, the DOE was nervous and dispatched expert bureaucrats from Oak Ridge, Tennessee, to host a public meeting at the nearby Crosby Elementary School. Although DOE and NLO representatives assured the public that there was "no immediate risk," they were greeted with hostility by a packed crowd of plant neighbors and workers.[11] In contrast to other nuclear disasters, Fernald's public meeting did not launch a national debate about humanity's gamble with the atom, or even pose a challenge to America's nuclear deterrent. Instead, the attendees wondered why NLO had silenced the stack monitor alarm and not shut down Plant 9. Why had it made similar decisions again and again for decades? These choices demonstrated to an angry public that the DOE prioritized uranium metals production over public health and the environment.

In the weeks following the public meeting, the community organized Fernald Residents for Environmental Safety and Health (FRESH) to hold the DOE accountable for polluting Fernald's backyard. Led by a reformed "quiet little housewife," Lisa Crawford, FRESH succeeded where countless—and undoubtedly more experienced environmental activists—had failed.[12] It tailored its locally focused, but nationally connected movement to fit the interests of working people.[13] In recognition of the rural and traditionally patriotic values of Fernald's surrounding communities, as well as the economic stakes and personal pride of union workers in the Fernald Atomic Trades and Labor Council (FATLC), FRESH fought to clean up but never close Fernald.[14] This was a shrewd decision, which led to the development of a powerful grassroots coalition of residents, workers, and moderate politicians, including Ohio's Democratic senator and former Project Mercury astronaut John Glenn, who transformed Fernald's uranium leak into a symbol for the environmental health and safety crisis plaguing the nuclear weapons complex.[15] FRESH's efforts forced the DOE to reimagine its Cold War mass production model for nuclear weapons, comply with environmental laws and protect public health, pull back the curtain on nuclear secrecy, and launch a national environmental remediation program of unprecedented scale to clean up the radioactive legacy of the nuclear arms race.

GRASSROOTS ACTIVISM DURING THE COLD WAR'S END

Cleaning Up the Bomb Factory explores environmental activism in the polarized decades of the 1980s and 1990s, a tipping point and maturation period for the movement. The inauguration of President Ronald Reagan in 1981 began what historians James Morton Turner and Andrew C. Isenberg called "the Republican Reversal," an era in which conservatives started the process of dismantling the bipartisan spirit of environmental legislating during the 1960s and 1970s in favor of probusiness policies and widespread assaults on science and the regulatory state.[16] Perhaps the most infamous appointment from the Reversal's beginnings was Reagan's selection of Colorado-based lawyer and politician Ann Gorsuch to lead the Environmental Protection Agency (EPA). Known as a member of "the crazies" in the Colorado House of Representatives for espousing what were at the time extreme libertarian views, Gorsuch spearheaded the Reagan administration's efforts to weaken the agency from within. Although scandal forced Gorsuch to resign less than two years into her appointment, the administration's gutting of the agency hampered its effectiveness for years to come.[17]

While conservatives weaponized the budget to bleed regulatory agencies like the EPA dry, they bankrolled the DOE and Department of Defense (DOD) as part of the largest peacetime military buildup in American history. Now engaged in a renewed nuclear arms race with the Soviet Union, the Reagan administration also ramped up its anticommunist rhetoric to a point where nuclear war seemed right around the corner.[18] After years of quiet operations with a skeleton crew during détente (a period of improved diplomacy between the United States and the Soviet Union during the late 1960s and 1970s), Fernald was suddenly producing quantities of uranium metal unmatched since the Lyndon B. Johnson administration.[19]

Increased production posed two significant challenges for Fernald. Three decades into the Cold War, the plant's equipment had fallen into disrepair after the DOE and its predecessor agencies the Atomic Energy Commission and the Energy Research and Development Administration refused to invest in the plant as the threat of nuclear war declined during the 1970s.[20] The Atomic Energy Act also ensured that the DOE self-regulated its radioactive materials, which conflicted with changing American attitudes toward industry and the environment during the Cold War.[21] In part, this explains the community's anger toward the DOE and NLO. In the wake of the environmental movement's legislative victories during the 1960s and 1970s, the public expected the federal government, including the EPA and the Occupational Safety and Health Administration, to regulate polluting industries at a time when most Americans accepted a clean environment as a basic human right.[22] During the 1980s and 1990s, however, environmentalists discovered that nuclear weapons production plants were shockingly contaminated landscapes that somehow slipped through the cracks of the regulatory state.[23] Fernald poses a powerful case study of the first decades of the Republican Reversal, in which FRESH and their allies successfully fought against the federal government for a cleaner environment.

Environmental historians focus heavily on national politics, particularly the bipartisan "golden age" of environmental policy reform between the passage of the Wilderness Act of 1964 and the establishment of the Superfund program in 1980.[24] From this legislative perspective, conservative politicians have dominated the environmental agenda since Reagan's election.[25] *Cleaning Up the Bomb Factory* challenges this interpretation in several important ways. By focusing on local, nonprofessional activists instead of national organizations, this book brings into focus the diverse goals of grassroots environmentalism. During the 1980s and 1990s, grassroots activists were just as interested in remaking environmentalism as they were local environments. Two well-known environmental movements illustrate this point. After leading the successful relocation of homeowners out of the nation's most infamous toxic community, Love Canal, Lois Gibbs created the Citizens Clearinghouse for Hazardous Waste (CCHW) in 1981 to support and network local grassroots organizations across the country. Gibbs made the CCHW into the organization that she wished had existed only a few years earlier, when the rediscovery of Hooker Chemical's wastes turned Love Canal residents' lives upside down.[26] Led by seasoned civil rights activists, including Rev. Dr. Benjamin Chavis, and inspired by activism against a PCB landfill in Warren County, North Carolina, the United Church of Christ published *Toxic Wastes and Race in the United States* in 1987 to document environmental racism on a national scale and challenge mainstream environmentalism's long-held belief that regulation benefited all segments of society equally.[27] Both efforts posed important structural challenges to the nationally focused, and socially homogeneous, mainstream model of environmentalism.

FRESH's experience in the Military Production Network (MPN), a coalition of national peace and environmental organizations, as well as local groups from nuclear weapons production communities, adds to our understanding of this grassroots project to remake environmental activism. Through the MPN, FRESH courted new allies, learned new skills, and gained access to resources and expertise, but at the same time engaged in a power struggle to preserve its autonomy in the context of national environmental politics. Carving out an equitable balance between the local and the national was part of the environmental movement's struggle with its own history of exclusion based on race, class, and gender, in addition to the broader movement's consolidation of power in Washington, DC, which was particularly significant for FRESH's Southwest Ohio–based environmental movement.[28] During the Clinton administration, some basic tenets of environmental justice were adopted into national environmental policy, including in the DOE.[29] Despite the quick spread of the environmental justice movement's ideas, however, some activists of color in the MPN still felt marginalized compared to their white allies.[30]

"Many of today's problems," environmental leaders wrote in 1985, "are global in scope and make local, regional, or even national solutions difficult." Considering the urgent threats of nuclear war and chemical contamination, as well as the looming threat of global warming during the polarized Reagan years, there were many reasons for concern about political gridlock.[31] The popular perspective of national organizations, however, obscures how the grassroots operated, which was first and foremost by fighting for environmental justice in their own neighborhoods. During the late 1970s and early 1980s, peace and environmental activists increasingly challenged the global nuclear arms race locally.[32] The problem with protesting a hypothetical nuclear apocalypse was its intangible nature. Nuclear weapons production facilities, however, were physical spaces that could be disrupted, reimagined, or even dismantled. During the early 1980s, peace activists called for a "freeze" to the nuclear arms race, but by the end of the decade, activists, journalists, and politicians overwhelmingly discussed the bomb in terms of environmental health and safety.[33] This was local thinking and local action transforming a global environmental issue. By cleaning up their own backyard, Fernald's environmental movement helped clean up everyone's.

GREENING THE DEPARTMENT OF ENERGY

In its follow-up investigation to Fernald's 1984 uranium leak, the DOE determined that poor communication, inadequate inspections, indifference toward radiation exposures, deteriorated equipment, and most importantly, "a pride of accomplishment which centers upon production" prolonged and normalized the contamination. Any number of documented mishaps during these months—the stack monitor alarm, a lack of replacement filtration bags, numerous contaminated filters, a fire that inhibited environmental monitoring capabilities, the exposure of four workers to a "puff" of uranium oxide—were all valid reasons to shut down operations, but NLO's plant managers decided to keep going despite these red flags.[34] In this report, the DOE finally had to reconcile itself with Fernald's dangerous culture of production, which the department had nurtured throughout the Cold War. It was a tedious process that got worse before it got better, but beginning in the early 1990s, the DOE took concrete steps toward its new mission of modernizing the nuclear weapons complex and cleaning up the Cold War's radioactive legacy. By mid-decade, the DOE was already funding 20 percent of the world's environmental remediation market.[35] It was challenging bureaucratically, as well as from a public relations perspective, to "green" the DOE in the budget-slashing context of Speaker of the House Newt Gingrich's Contract with America and amid shocking revelations about the Cold War's human radiation experiments.[36] Still, a physical survey of former and remediated nuclear weapons production facilities now stewarded by the DOE's Office of Legacy Management offers hard physical evidence of meaningful environmental change over time.[37]

If sweeping legislative reform continues to be the barometer for all environmental movements, it will also be difficult to study them in their specific historical contexts. Fernald's movement did support the passage of federal legislation in the form of the Federal Facilities Compliance Act of 1992, which filled an important regulatory gap by forcing the DOE's nuclear weapons production facilities and the DOD's military bases to comply with national, state, and even local hazardous waste laws. This law's passage, however, represents only part of the success of Fernald's environmental activists. As historian James Morton Turner argued, there are currents of "antimodernism" running through environmentalism, including a "discomfort with large-scale human activity."[38] This explains, perhaps, why little has been written on the complex alliance between federal and state governments, powerful corporations, blue-collar workers, and grassroots environmental activists that cleaned up the nuclear weapons complex as part of "the largest environmental cleanup program in the world," according to the DOE.[39] This long-term program has cost tens of billions of dollars spread across four decades, including Republican and Democratic administrations, and continues to the present day. Even as one of the DOE's smaller facilities, Fernald's environmental remediation

FIGURE 2. Three workers standing in Fernald's scrap pile, January 5, 1956. This scene captures the Department of Energy's culture of production that created radioactive backyards across the country during the Cold War. Courtesy of the US Department of Energy.

program was nothing short of a decade-long megaproject, which cost $4.4 billion (excluding ongoing environmental stewardship activities) and relied upon the expertise and resources of global corporations as well as local contractors.[40] Such environmental challenges would be impossible to solve with the decentralized and small-scale appropriate technology movement of 1970s environmentalism.[41]

Today, the Feed Materials Production Center is the Fernald Preserve, a 1,050-acre park featuring seven miles of hiking trails through wetlands, forest, and fields, which, following ecological restoration, are alive with wildlife.[42] The backdrop to this renewed landscape, however, is the On-Site Disposal Facility, which contains almost three million cubic yards of radioactive contaminated soil and building debris from Fernald's cleanup.[43] This imperfect juxtaposition of natural beauty and environmental hazards is a fitting symbol for environmental politics during the Cold War's end, when activists fought to diversify the movement, develop new strategies, and strike compromise in an increasingly partisan era. Through cleanup, FRESH accomplished its main goal of staving off the site's abandonment as a "national sacrifice zone," and an innovative DOE public participation program ensured that residents and workers had direct access to technical experts and environmental health and safety data throughout the process.[44] Fernald's transformation into a park also meant a cheaper price tag for taxpayers and more lingering contamination for area residents.[45] This reflects, in part, the antienvironmental agenda of the Republican Congress at the time but also a bipartisan transition toward risk-based problem-solving and the influence of environmental justice on the politics of radioactive waste disposal. At Fernald, grassroots activists understood that if the radioactive waste in their own community did not stay there, it was going to be shipped across the country to pollute somebody else's.[46] Fernald's On-Site Disposal Facility stands as a physical symbol for grassroots solidarity in the supposedly selfish era of not-in-my-backyard environmental activism.[47]

FERNALD'S RADIOACTIVE BACKYARD

Cleaning Up the Bomb Factory uses Fernald's radioactive backyard as a vehicle for understanding the challenges, conflicts, and triumphs of grassroots environmental activism in the 1980s and 1990s. Chapter 1 begins at the dawn of the Cold War, when Fernald was an agricultural community. In the aftermath of the Soviet Union's first atomic test in 1949, however, the federal government seized farmlands in the area and constructed an industrial landscape in their place. Over the following decades, the DOE's culture of production polluted the Fernald area, but the nuclear secrecy that enabled this process ultimately backfired when public distrust eroded the Cold War consensus.[48] Chapter 2 explores the greater Cincinnati peace movement's 1983 "Trinity Day" protest at Fernald, which confronted the bomb's environmental legacy and reintroduced the plant to the public but also disrupted union workers' own activism to make their workplace safer. This conflict highlights competing interpretations of backyards in grassroots environmental activism. Chapter 3 focuses on Fernald's uranium leak and the formation of FRESH, which, through skillful organizing, avoided a similar conflict by supporting moderate political goals that overlapped with the interests of Fernald's unions. These tactics led to the development of a powerful statewide alliance of activists, workers, politicians, and regulators to cleanup Fernald's radioactivity.

Chapter 4 begins with the FATLC's 1985 strike, which secured unprecedented rights to environmental health and safety during the union-busting Reagan years. The strike also helped bridge any lingering divide between local activists and workers. By cleaning up their workplace, workers also cleaned up the surrounding community. Chapter 5 picks up with FRESH joining the MPN during the late 1980s to forge a national environmental movement for nuclear weapons cleanup. This movement represents collective thinking about local environmental issues. If everyone at Fernald, Hanford, and Rocky Flats, for example, pitched in and cleaned up their radioactive zones, the crisis of America's nuclear wastelands would be solved. Chapter 6 explores FRESH's lawsuit against the DOE. As this courtroom narrative demonstrates, such local battles over backyards can be just as confrontational and influential as any case study in national environmental politics.

In the aftermath of the community's settlement, the time had finally come to clean up Fernald. Through the development of citizen advisory boards at DOE sites, Chapter 7 examines how a broad group of stakeholders came together to reimagine Fernald's formerly secretive and radioactive landscape as a shared space, which required compromise.[49] Instrumental to this process was a board game called FUTURESITE, which enabled players to simulate the challenges and tradeoffs of radioactive waste management.[50] Chapter 8 explores the monumental undertaking that was Fernald's cleanup, directed by the DOE's technical experts, executed through corporate power and the sweat of blue-collar workers, and overseen by environmental regulators and grassroots activists. Through this cooperative effort, the Fernald community remade a radioactive backyard and unlocked new possibilities for large-scale environmental problem-solving.

ONE Atomic Farmlands

On March 30, 1951, Ellen Reidy of the Atomic Energy Commission (AEC) got off the train in Cincinnati, Ohio, after reassignment from the Brookhaven National Laboratory on Long Island, New York. She set up her office in the Faller Building at the intersection of Eighth and Walnut Streets. The following day, as Reidy got acquainted with the Queen City, government agents from the US Army Corps of Engineers went knocking on doors in Fernald, a small farming community about eighteen miles northwest of the city, to inform residents that their land was being seized by the federal government. The AEC had recently selected Fernald's productive farmlands as the site for the Feed Materials Production Center, a uranium processing facility that would serve the rapidly expanding Cold War nuclear weapons complex, and the landowners were given between thirty and sixty days to buy new farms, pack up their belongings, move their equipment and livestock, and vacate the premises.[1]

While the AEC was able to purchase eight properties outright, a handful of farmers who owned about half of the future plant's 1,050 acres, including Arthur and May Fuchs, Raymond and Clara Irwin, and Henry Knollman, refused, arguing that the federal government's offers of between $375 and $672 per acre were not fair compensation. Their farms were, after all, built upon rich soil with convenient access to markets, including the Cincinnati milkshed, biscuit and feed companies, grain oil processors, and distilleries. The federal government refused, however, and initiated condemnation proceedings against the farmers in US District Court.[2] On April 24, US District Court judge John H. Druffel signed a decree in Cincinnati granting the AEC "immediate possession" of the properties on the city's outskirts.[3] With the stroke of a pen, Fernald the rural farming community became Fernald the uranium processing plant. Instead of farmers producing corn, hay, and wheat to feed people and livestock, nuclear workers would now produce uranium metals to feed plutonium reactors.[4] Despite their best efforts, Fernald's rural residents had little hope of beating a powerful federal agency engaged in winning a cold war. It would take decades, a uranium leak, and the development of a powerful grassroots environmental movement to make the bomb makers budge.

The physical transformation of Fernald's landscape from bucolic to atomic was made possible through the AEC's unparalleled power, which was tacitly supported by the public's faith in experts and institutions.[5] "The best indicator of the esteem in which experts and administrative agency were held," historian Brian Balogh argued, "was the extraordinary degree of autonomy that the Atomic Energy Commission initially was granted."[6] While the Fernald community's relocated farmers had sold their goods on the open market, the AEC generated its own demand for feed materials and managed them in a closed political system.[7] Knowledge about Fernald's radioactive backyard, as a result, was strictly limited, through nuclear secrecy, to an elite group of decision-makers in the AEC, government contractors in the nuclear industry, scientists on the General Advisory Committee, and legislators on the Joint Committee on Atomic Energy.[8] Fernald's construction, as a result, roped this small farming community into a global Cold War while at the same time isolating the plant from its closest neighbors.

The AEC was legally required, as well as highly motivated by the urgency of the nuclear arms race, to prioritize the production of nuclear weapons and fissionable materials.[9] This meant that all of the AEC's subordinate missions, including the development of civilian nuclear power, managing radioactive waste, and workplace environmental health and safety, took a back seat to the bomb's development.[10] During the early Cold War, the public found this arrangement to be justified, as the threat of nuclear war loomed as the greatest threat to American lives. During the late 1950s and early 1960s, however, activist-scientists Barry Commoner and Rachel Carson demonstrated that nuclear fallout from AEC nuclear weapons tests and DDT from federal pesticide spraying programs posed more immediate risks to public health.[11] The environmental movement that followed in the 1960s and 1970s transformed American society in two important ways: federal environmental laws significantly cleaned up America's polluted rivers and smoke-filled skies, and the public widely embraced regulatory agencies like the Environmental Protection Agency (EPA) and Occupational Safety and Health Administration (OSHA) as powerful checks on polluting industries.[12] At the same time, however, the environmental movement's relentless attacks on the federal government, no matter how justified, also contributed to the public's declining trust in expertise and institutions.[13]

After Fernald's construction, the AEC transformed the plant's 1,050 acres into a radioactive waste dump through digging waste pits, piling radioactive scrap metals, stacking tens of thousands of barrels of chemical and radioactive wastes, storing the nation's thorium supply, and, most dangerously, constructing the K-65 silos.[14] These byproducts of production would contaminate Fernald's former farmlands indefinitely, but even as these materials piled up, the Atomic Energy Act shielded the AEC from external oversight and broader changes in American society.[15] Its deeply engrained culture of production also nurtured an arrogance that Fernald's radioactive landscape was a static environment under its complete control, despite a growing body of evidence to the contrary.[16] By the time greater Cincinnati's peace movement rediscovered Fernald in the early 1980s, residents in surrounding communities were already growing increasingly suspicious of their secretive and nuclear neighbor.

THE NUCLEAR ARMS RACE

Fernald-area farmers had mixed feelings about the seizure of their lands. Clayton Cone, for example, was not bitter. Like most Americans, he understood the gravity of the Atomic Age and wanted to do his part, but spring "is a bad time of the year for a farmer to be moving," because it was too late in the season to replant crops elsewhere.[17] Some were downright angry at what they saw as the AEC's abuse of federal power. "We're just simple farmers, and all we want is to be left alone," said Cecelia Minges, "but it seems the important people can do anything they like."[18] Minges had a point. Fernald was not the first community uprooted to make room for the Atomic Age. During the Manhattan Project—America's top-secret program to develop the atomic bomb—lands were also seized in Hanford, Washington, and Oak Ridge, Tennessee, for major production facilities.[19] The dropping of atomic bombs on Hiroshima and Nagasaki and the shocking end of World War II, however, could not return a sense of normalcy to the home front. The Cold War and nuclear arms race between the United States and the Soviet Union had already blurred the lines between war and peace.[20]

In 1949, the Soviet Union detonated its first atomic bomb, which caught American intelligence agencies off guard, broke the short-lived US atomic monopoly after World War II, and launched the nuclear arms race.[21] The following year, President Harry Truman ordered the National Security Council to reevaluate American geopolitical strategy in a world with two nuclear powers. Its report, "National Security Council Resolution 68 (NSC-68)," asserted that considering the Soviet Union's larger and better-equipped military, the United States needed "overwhelming atomic superiority" and "command of the air" to deter Soviet aggression.[22] NSC-68 generated a rush to develop and stockpile thermonuclear weapons. During the early 1950s, the AEC dramatically scaled up its production capabilities to meet this demand by constructing industrial facilities in Fernald, Rocky Flats in Colorado, Savannah River in South Carolina, and the Pantex Plant in Texas.[23] This nationwide buildup mobilized as many as 150,000 workers and placed the bomb at the center of American military and political strategy for decades.[24]

The domestic implications were also enormous. As historian Sarah E. Robey has argued, "the tension of being simultaneously at war and not at war defined American life in the postwar years."[25] At Fernald, this contradiction helped seize lands for the AEC and mobilize a patriotic workforce to battle the Soviet Union through nuclear weapons production. At the same time, this wartime mentality justified the exclusion of workers and plant neighbors from the protections of environmental and occupational safety laws on the grounds of national security. During the 1970s, the environmental movement made significant strides in regulating industry to protect workers and the public, including the creation of the EPA and

OSHA, along with the passage of the National Environmental Policy Act, Clean Air Act and Clean Water Act amendments, the Toxic Substances Control Act, and the Resource Conservation and Recovery Act.[26] Inside Fernald's gates, however, the Atomic Energy Act trumped them all and permitted the AEC, and later the Department of Energy (DOE), to self-regulate its radioactive materials, its workspaces, and even its employees' bodies.[27] As Americans increasingly embraced environmentalism during the late twentieth century and supported external oversight of polluting industries, the Atomic Energy Act froze Fernald in the insulated Cold War culture that built the plant.

FARM TO FACTORY

In May 1951, Reidy and James F. Chandler, whom the AEC recruited from the Army Corps of Engineers to serve as its area manager, abandoned their offices in downtown Cincinnati to construct Fernald in the countryside.[28] Several factors guided the AEC's selection of the location, which straddled the borders of Crosby Township in northern Hamilton County and Ross and Morgan Townships in southern Butler County near the villages of Ross and Shandon.[29] Southwest Ohio's interior geography kept Fernald out of reach of Soviet bombers and was centrally located between uranium ore delivery ports in New York and New Orleans, as well as the plutonium reactors at Hanford and Savannah River, which served as the plant's primary customers for feed materials. Its proximity to Cincinnati offered attractive housing markets, a strong labor force, and vital infrastructure, including an energy supplier in Cincinnati Gas & Electric, multiple highways, and the Chesapeake and Ohio Railway, which passed through Fernald on its way to Chicago. Finally, there was plentiful water from the Great Miami Aquifer, and, despite its proximity to Cincinnati's western suburbs, Fernald was secluded enough to offer privacy and cheap property values.[30]

Reidy and Chandler were two of the last outsiders to witness Fernald as a quiet farming community. "It was very enjoyable in the beautiful countryside," Reidy recalled, but it did not last long. After they "moved the heavy equipment in and started tearing up everything," Reidy continued, "things were a mess. When it rained, there was nothing but mud. When it didn't rain, there was nothing but dust."[31] The AEC contracted the Catalytic Construction Company of Philadelphia to design the plant, the George A. Fuller Company of New York to build it, and National Lead of Ohio (NLO) — which was better known for its Dutch Boy brand paint but was also a leader in metallurgy — to operate it.[32] Using bulldozers and other heavy equipment, hundreds of Fuller's workers moved 2,600,000 cubic yards of earth to prepare Fernald's farmlands for the atomic plant. While farmers suffered from displacement, job opportunities and wages increased for construction workers in Hamilton County. Local businessman Paul Fiehrer also capitalized on the opportunity. Catalytic Construction rented office space from Fiehrer, who helped relay phone messages back to the job site, and most importantly, fed the thousands of construction workers at his restaurant the Venice Pavilion in nearby Ross, whose population in 1950 was only three hundred.[33] The Cold War brought hardship as well as prosperity to Southwest Ohio's countryside.

Fernald's primary technological innovation was consolidating several uranium milling, refining, and smelting techniques into one government-owned facility. During the Manhattan Project and the early postwar years, the AEC's uranium process was widely dispersed: ore sampling at the New Brunswick Laboratory in New Jersey; brown oxide production at the Mallinckrodt Chemical Works in St. Louis, Missouri; green salt production at the Harshaw Chemical Works in Cleveland, Ohio; and finally, uranium metal conversion at Union Carbide's Electro-Met division in Niagara Falls, New York.[34] At Fernald, these processes were replicated and refined in nine primary buildings. In Plant 1, the Sampling Plant, workers received and sampled uranium ore concentrates and uranium-bearing scrap, and dried, crushed, milled, and ground these materials for processing. Plant 2/3, the Refinery, received these uranium-bearing products and digested them in nitric acid. This process created a solution of uranyl nitrate, which was chemically converted into orange oxide. Plant 4, the Green Salt Plant, reduced the orange oxide to brown oxide by cooking it around 550 degrees Celsius in stainless steel fluid bed reactors. The brown oxide was then pushed through three ribbon screw reactors to mix with anhydrous hydrogen fluoride to create green salt. As the pivotal

FIGURE 3. A machinist/tool operator removes a finished uranium fuel core in Plant 6 (the Metals Fabrication Plant) at Fernald, January 1, 1980. Courtesy of the US Department of Energy.

intermediate compound in feed materials production, green salt could be converted into pure uranium metal for plutonium production or uranium hexafluoride for highly enriched uranium production.[35]

In Plant 5, the Metals Production Plant, green salt and magnesium granules were blended in a steel pot and heated in a Rockwell furnace. After three to four hours, the green salt reacted with the magnesium, and the contents of the pot skyrocketed to a temperature of 1,649 degrees Celsius. This process created uranium metal derbies, which were named for their resemblance to the hat. Next, the derbies and pure uranium scrap were remelted in vacuum induction furnaces and cast into ingots, which workers sawed and cropped to specified lengths to produce billets. In Plant 9, the Special Products Plant (next in the flow of material), workers cast irregular-sized uranium metals, along with machined billets. Plant 6, the Metals Fabrication Plant, strengthened machined billets by treating them in a saltwater bath. Plant 8, the Scrap Recovery Plant, processed recycled materials and treated waste products. (More on Plant 7, which was shut down after eighteen months, later on.) The unnumbered Pilot Plant produced green salt from uranium hexafluoride tailings, which were byproducts left over from production at the DOE's gaseous diffusion plants.[36]

As the Pilot Plant demonstrates, Fernald's designers followed progressive engineering principles to reduce waste in feed materials production.[37] This was particularly important during the early Cold War, when the raw materials of nuclear weapons production were scarce.[38] Air filters captured particulates, wastewater treatment collected uranium, workers recycled solvents, and technicians monitored the environment to assess the plant's containment. These practices also protected workers, but the system's logic was more rooted in industrial efficiency than environmental health and safety.[39] Fernald's technologies were sophisticated and dirty. They produced "the highest purity uranium that's ever been generated in the world" but, according to longtime workers, also resembled "black art and witchcraft."[40] In other words, feed materials production required a complex interplay between man, machine, and uranium.

The production plants were supported by two dozen administrative, service, and laboratory buildings, including a hospital, water treatment plant, and sewage disposal plant, and interconnected by twenty-four acres of paved roads and four miles of railroad tracks.[41] (In comparison to Fernald's modern infrastructure, the plant's neighbors drank well water or rainwater collected in a cistern.[42]) The bulk of construction was completed in 1954, but Fernald's workforce peaked two years later during plant expansion. At 2,891 employees, the working population was nearly triple the size of Crosby Township, which encompassed about 90 percent of the plant's acreage.[43] The urgency of the Cold War quickened the pace of life in surrounding communities as workers, automobiles, and trains shuttled in and out each day.[44] "Life in Ross," geographer James Ray Wilson observed in 1956, "was almost completely disrupted by the traffic, of which it received the bulk because of its location on the most direct route to the cities of Hamilton and Cincinnati."[45] For better or worse, Fernald was now a vital link in a nuclear weapons production network that stretched from coast to coast.

ATOMIC MIGRATIONS

With industrial development came industrial workers, who flipped the suburban commuting pattern on its head. Fernald's workforce overwhelmingly lived in urban areas, including 694 from Cincinnati, 555 from Hamilton, and 239 from Harrison, Ohio, and 201 from Lawrenceburg and 142 from Aurora, Indiana. Each day these workers drove from the city to the country for work.[46] At a time when the prospect of nuclear energy promised material abundance for the middle class, Fernald's production plants promised economic security for the working class.[47]

Gene Branham, who later served as president of the Fernald Atomic Trades and Labor Council (FATLC), illustrates this point. Branham's journey to Fernald began in the small eastern Kentucky coal-mining town of Wayland.[48] When money got tight for his family, he was forced to quit school and go to work at the mines. He was too young to go underground, so Branham and others his age would "trim timbers" for the adults to haul down the mine shaft after blasting with dynamite.[49] During the early 1950s, however, the Wayland mine shut down, putting Branham and his family out of work. A former mine supervisor named Johnny Walsh recommended Fernald, so in October 1952, Branham and his father traveled to the plant and were hired. Fernald eventually employed Braham; his father, uncle, brother, and son; and dozens of friends and former coal miners.[50] Coming from coal country, Branham and his father were "amazed" by Fernald: the pay was competitive, workers changed clothes and showered twice a day, and the production area appeared spotless.[51]

Born in the coalfields of Summerly, West Virginia, Gene Sneed was another Appalachian migrant who built a career for himself at Fernald. When Sneed was young, his father died in a mining accident, so his older brother bought a home and relocated the family to Hamilton, Ohio, in search of better job opportunities in Southwest Ohio's factories. After serving in the Korean War, Sneed accepted a position at Fernald in 1956. It was not easy, particularly in the plant's early years. As an African American, racism limited Sneed's early career prospects to "porter," janitorial work, or laundry. The jobsite was also plagued by interunion conflict and occasional racial violence.⁵² In May 1952, for example, a jurisdictional dispute over the construction of scaffolding erupted in fighting between white carpenters in the Ohio Valley Carpenters District Council and Black laborers in the Hod Carriers and Building Laborers Union, which resulted in several injuries, including a laborer being struck with a hammer. The following day, police seized numerous weapons, including guns, knives, and clubs, from workers trying to enter the plant at the same time hundreds more failed to report for work.⁵³

Sneed was also a catalyst for change at Fernald. He was part of a group of African American porters who were trained as chemical operators, which was significant, because it shattered the color line on production work. In the short-term, this meant a pay bump for Sneed, but it was also symbolically important for workers of color to cut through the anticommunist hysteria of the Cold War and serve on the front lines of the nuclear arms race. Sneed continued to learn new trades and enjoyed a successful career at Fernald spanning nearly four decades. It is important to remember that for production workers, including the significant numbers from Appalachia, Fernald provided an opportunity to support their families and achieve the American dream, and, despite the dangerous and hard physical labor expected of them, feed materials production still seemed to be safer, cleaner, and more consistent work than the coal industry.⁵⁴

The AEC and NLO, however, exploited this blue-collar reality for many of Fernald's production workers. As Sneed recalled, "most of the guys were young" and "a lot of them [were] from Indiana, West Virginia, Kentucky," adding, "We weren't interested in the intellectual side of it, the production side of it; we were just doing a job."⁵⁵ Fernald's production workers prided themselves on putting in a hard day's work, supporting their families, and contributing to the Cold War. The downside to this mentality, as Sneed suggested, was that many of these young men were not prepared to question authority when it came to their long-term health and safety. While you cannot miss the soot on a coal miner's face and dirty clothes, some of Fernald's radioactive hazards were invisible. With a monopoly on atomic knowledge, the AEC ensured that Fernald's unions never fully grasped the dangers to workers' health.

MAKING A RADIOACTIVE BACKYARD

Fernald's radioactive byproducts contaminated human bodies and environments through administrative indifference and the strict control of information. Throughout the Cold War, this indifference came from the top of the AEC, which informed the work as well as tied the hands of government contractors at Fernald.[56] On November 9, 1962, less than two weeks after the thirteen harrowing days of the Cuban Missile Crisis, AEC chairman Glenn T. Seaborg visited Fernald.[57] Seaborg was a Nobel Prize–winning chemist, best known for leading the researchers at the University of California that discovered plutonium in 1941. During the Manhattan Project, he worked on chemical extraction and purification processes for plutonium at the Metallurgical Laboratory at the University of Chicago, which was scaled up for industrial production at Hanford.[58] Flying out of Andrews Air Force Base in Maryland, Seaborg arrived in Cincinnati at 11:40 a.m. and was greeted by the local AEC office's C. L. Karl, who drove Seaborg to Fernald for lunch and a tour of the production process with plant managers. Afterward, Karl and Seaborg drove east to nearby Evendale for a tour of General Electric's Materials High Temperature Laboratory, which was developing a gas-cooled maritime reactor for the Navy and a fast gas-cooled compact reactor "for space applications."[59] Instead of studying the earthly pollution in Fernald's radioactive backyard, Seaborg and the AEC turned their attention to military superiority in the depths of the oceans and the outer reaches of space.

Later that evening at the Netherland-Hilton Hotel, Seaborg lectured on "Atomic Power in Space" before an audience of five hundred people at the annual meeting of the Cincinnati post of the American Ordnance Association. "A compact, high-powered nuclear reactor," Seaborg stated, "must provide the electrical power required in the electrical propulsion concepts being developed by NASA and the Department of Defense."[60] While Seaborg rubbed elbows with military contractors at black-tie affairs, the chemist was far more dismissive toward the academic scientists who criticized the AEC. During the early 1960s, the AEC began "distancing itself" from geologists in the National Academy of Sciences who called

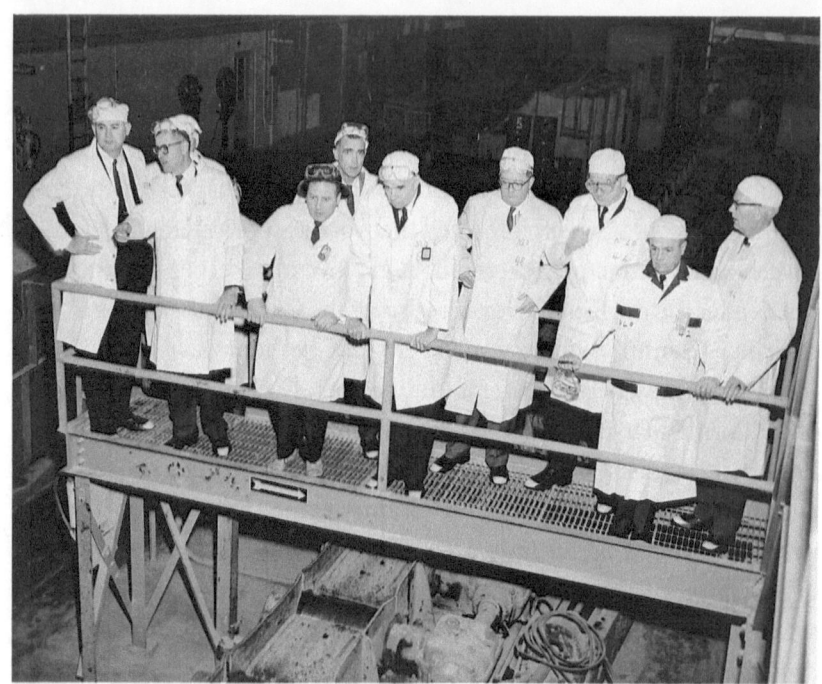

FIGURE 4. Atomic Energy Commission Chairman and former Manhattan Project chemist Glenn T. Seaborg watches the uranium metals rolling process on a tour of Fernald with AEC and National Lead of Ohio management, November 9, 1962. Left to right: Colonel James H. Hill, W. T. Warner, Robert M. Spenceley, McDonald S. Nelson, Glenn T. Seaborg, Shadburn Marshall, Arnold R. Fritsch, C. L. Karl, J. H. Noyes. Courtesy of the US Department of Energy.

for long-range planning in the AEC's radioactive waste disposal program. Geologists viewed the AEC as an "operating agency," which focused on short-term production at the expense of future risks to public health. From a geological perspective, radioactive waste was a long-term and fluid environmental problem, which required frequent data collection and careful planning for its inevitable migration in the environment. This was particularly important, because substantial quantities of low- and intermediate-level waste were buried in unlined pits and trenches, which was dangerous, because the AEC's largest nuclear weapons production facilities were also located over some of the nation's largest aquifers, which served growing metropolitan centers. Seaborg was defensive toward these critiques. In a letter to National Academy president Frederick Seitz, Seaborg claimed that the AEC "has always considered the satisfactory treatment and permanent disposal of all waste materials as a prime requisite for all program activities." Enclosed with Seaborg's letter was an internal AEC report, which was "self-congratulatory," according to historian Jacob Darwin Hamblin, and concluded that its own radioactive waste disposal program was satisfactory.[61] This disagreement captures the irony of science in the AEC, which was led by one of the world's most accomplished chemists in Seaborg but, in pursuit of developing ever bigger and better bombs, insulated itself from the larger scientific community and excluded itself from the scientific method.

It was also beneficial, however, for the AEC to appear open when it served its own interests. While the Manhattan Project was top-secret, Fernald's development as part of the Cold War nuclear arms race was widely covered in Cincinnati's newspapers, which largely praised the economic opportunities created by the plant. During construction, the *Cincinnati Enquirer* highlighted Fernald's positive local impact through hiring, subcontracts, and supply orders. Area Manager James F. Chandler was even forthcoming that "waste products from the Fernald plant will be stored on the site." Chandler reassured readers, however, that there "will not be any undesirable health environment, either to the workers or to the community."[62] During the early 1950s, when the public's faith in expertise was high, this promise was satisfactory. Since it was made in a closed political system, however, there was never an ongoing dialogue with surrounding communities as the AEC transformed Fernald into a radioactive waste dump.

Fernald's production process was messy. For every pound of high-purity uranium metal produced, ten pounds of waste were generated, which over time filled six pits with six hundred thousand cubic yards of radioactive and chemical waste, as well as tens of thousands of drums.[63] Fernald also became a dumping ground for the larger nuclear weapons complex. The most dangerous materials stored at the plant were the K-65 residues. Leftover from uranium processing at the Mallinckrodt Chemical Works in St. Louis during the Manhattan Project, the K-65 waste was shipped to Fernald in the 1950s, stored in temporary and quickly deteriorating concrete silos, and years later determined to be the world's largest point source of radon gas.⁶⁴ Two decades later, the DOE transferred 2.5 million pounds of thorium to Fernald from Gulf General Atomic in Youngsville, North Carolina, which was stored in corroding bins and drums.⁶⁵ Although nuclear waste disposal would largely become associated with the American West after the Yucca Mountain controversy in the 1980s and 1990s, this was not always the case.⁶⁶ During the Cold War, the AEC, and later the DOE, applied temporary solutions to storing dangerous and long-lived radioactive materials across the eastern United States, including at Fernald, Oak Ridge, and Savannah River.⁶⁷

Even as the AEC experimented with public relations after World War II, it still inherited a strict national security program from the Manhattan Project.⁶⁸ Fernald was physically and socially separated from the surrounding community, including by gates and armed security guards.⁶⁹ Workers underwent intensive background investigations by the FBI to obtain a Q clearance, which the AEC had to approve to grant employees access to restricted data, including the production process.⁷⁰ NLO's security director, Clyde Bingham, a former intelligence officer during World War II, delivered security orientations and swore new hires to secrecy about Fernald's business under threat of a $10,000 fine or ten years in prison. "You was kind of afraid to talk," recalled Fernald worker Paul Davies, "so you just didn't."⁷¹ Through the military strategy of compartmentalization, workers were confined to certain spaces and, therefore, limited in their technological knowledge about the plant.⁷² Workplace injuries were preferably treated on-site, but it was also common for NLO doctors to supervise cases at local hospitals.⁷³ Everyone knew Fernald played an important role in America's national security, but it took time for the public to piece together exactly what that mission entailed.

Fernald-area residents who grew up during the early Cold War generally knew about the plant's nuclear mission. "We always called it the bomb factory as kids," recalled Crosby Township trustee Jane Harper.⁷⁴ When the AEC released information, however, it was often carefully crafted press releases that guaranteed public safety and promoted confidence in nuclear weapons programs. At Fernald, these narratives stressed the importance of the plant's national security mission and downplayed concerns over environmental health and safety.⁷⁵ Sometimes this strategy required collaborations with journalists. Beginning with *New York Times* science reporter William "Atomic Bill" Laurence's exclusive coverage of Trinity—the first nuclear weapons test as part of the Manhattan Project—the AEC learned to manipulate the media to its advantage.⁷⁶ In the 1950s, the *Cincinnati Post*'s Si Cornell went "inside the fence" at Fernald to write two favorable reviews on the plant's safety as well as its abundant wildlife, which supposedly thrived in the hundreds of acres of buffer zone surrounding the production area. Two decades later, the *Cincinnati Enquirer*'s John Chace wrote a similar piece on Fernald's positive contributions to the community, with its only complaint from neighbors being "annoying noise," which NLO had remedied by planting more trees on the property.⁷⁷ As late as 1981, the *Cincinnati Post*'s Dick Perry interviewed Fernald's assistant plant manager, Weldon Adams, to dispel "rumors" at the plant.⁷⁸ Through the skillful control of information, the DOE and its predecessor agencies successfully projected a positive image of Fernald for decades.

Beginning in the late 1960s, the threat of nuclear war declined during a decade of increased diplomacy between the United States and Soviet Union called *détente*, which is French for "relaxation."⁷⁹ After the near miss of a nuclear war during the Cuban Missile Crisis, détente was a welcome reprieve for both superpowers, which were preoccupied with invasions in Vietnam and Czechoslovakia and, according to historian Odd Arne Westad, "feeling the sting of military expenditure."⁸⁰ Peace was good for people but bad for the nuclear industry.⁸¹ As the demand for uranium metals declined during the 1960s and 1970s, Fernald's boosters were forced to scramble for alternative contracts to halt the plant's closure, such as the production of uranium penetrators to pierce armored vehicles for the US Army. Cincinnati-area Democratic congressman Tom Luken, who later became one of the plant's biggest critics, led this pork-barrel campaign to slow the hemorrhaging of jobs from the plant, whose workforce bottomed out at 538 employees in 1979.⁸² At a time when the DOE should have been making environmental health and safety upgrades and increasing oversight to conform with the spirit—if not the letter—of

1970s environmental laws, DOE managers actually decreased oversight, ceased research and development, and left Fernald struggling to survive.[83]

THE ANTIEXPERT ERA

As Cincinnati suburbanized in the postwar years, families moving to the Fernald area hoped to escape the busyness of an increasingly sprawling metropolis.[84] That the AEC would have placed a nuclear weapons production plant in Southwest Ohio's quiet farmlands simply did not register for most people. Fernald was never a secret, though. Newspapers sporadically covered the plant's happenings in the 1970s, even items like the receipt of 5,600 barrels of thorium, which would have caused an uproar only a decade later.[85] As Cold War tensions dissipated, however, so did public knowledge of Fernald, even as it remained partially operational. For new arrivals, its name—the Feed Materials Production Center—was confusing. Since it was surrounded by farmlands and with cattle grazing on its property, it is not surprising that many wondered if it produced ag-

FIGURE 5. Dairy cows grazing at Fernald with the Purina-esque red-and-white checkerboard water tower in the background, August 4, 1965. Courtesy of the US Department of Energy.

ricultural supplies.[86] One of the most noticeable parts of Fernald's skyline was also not its production plants but its red-and-white checkerboard water tower, which to many so closely resembled the Purina Company's logo that they assumed that the plant made dog food.[87] Finally, NLO's logo — the Dutch Boy — was best known for its association with lead paint and provided yet another rumor about the plant's purpose.[88] Although "feed materials" was simply AEC jargon and the water tower was painted red and white to alert low-flying aircraft, activists later associated these early Cold War artifacts with blatant government deception.[89]

Few Americans, even among the fifty people uprooted to build Fernald, would have questioned the importance of the plant's mission in the 1950s and early 1960s.[90] Professional activists in the postwar decades, however, increasingly challenged the public's faith in technology, expertise, and government by drawing their attention to the explosion of industrial pollutants that infiltrated local environments and human bodies as the American economy boomed after World War II.[91] Part of this boom in pollutants came from actual explosions. Between 1945 and 1963, the United States, the Soviet Union, and the United Kingdom collectively detonated 435 nuclear weapons in the open environment, which emitted radioactive gases, dust, and debris that swirled in the atmosphere, swam the oceans' currents, and fell to the earth as radioactive fallout.[92] In the AEC's proving grounds in the Pacific and the American West, nuclear tests demonstrated that increasingly powerful thermonuclear detonations were unpredictable, particularly because experts struggled to estimate explosive yields and calculate changes in wind direction. On March 1, 1954, the fifteen-megaton Castle Bravo test in the Bikini Atoll of the Marshall Islands, whose radioactive plume forced the evacuation of eighty-two Rongelap Atoll islanders and poisoned the Japanese fishing crew aboard the *Lucky Dragon*, demonstrated how a couple of miscalculations could threaten human life and the environment, even in the middle of an ocean. Despite this disaster, the AEC continued to assert that the risks posed to the public by nuclear fallout were negligible and exaggerated.[93]

Beginning in the late 1950s, Washington University in St. Louis biologist Barry Commoner led a science information movement against the AEC's atmospheric nuclear weapons testing program. His best-known campaign was the Committee for Nuclear Information's Baby Tooth Survey, which collected tens of thousands of baby teeth from concerned mothers in St. Louis, linked the widespread absorption of strontium-90 in infants to nuclear fallout, and demonstrated that the AEC was gambling with the lives of America's children for a leg up in the nuclear arms race.[94] In 1962, US Bureau of Fisheries biologist turned professional writer Rachel Carson published *Silent Spring*, a best-selling critique of toxic pesticides, their threat to humans and wildlife, and the federal government's complicit role in their gross overuse.[95] Carson's editor, Paul Brooks, believed that the public's concern over nuclear fallout prepared readers to receive Carson's terrifying message in *Silent Spring* about DDT and other persistent toxic chemicals. The spread of man-made radioactivity through nuclear fallout, and particularly the detection of strontium-90 in cow's milk and baby teeth, laid the intellectual foundation for the larger environmental movement against the dangers of industrial production.[96] Despite these popular critiques of government, federal legislation remained the most powerful tool available to protect public health and the environment.

In the wake of Commoner's and Carson's work, highly publicized industrial accidents, including the 1969 Santa Barbara oil spill and the burning Cuyahoga River in downtown Cleveland that same year, helped mobilize for the first time a cohesive environmental movement around Earth Day 1970. Earth Day's influence was so enduring, according to historian Adam Rome, because it united formerly separate issues, such as suburban sprawl, nuclear fallout, and toxic pesticides, into a single fight against a broad "environmental crisis."[97] During this sweeping moment of environmental policy reform, a bipartisan coalition built the modern environmental regulatory state.[98]

But this bipartisan moment would not last. Devastating public scandals, including Watergate and the leak of the Pentagon Papers, revealed corruption in both the Republican and Democratic Parties. Ralph Nader's liberal public-interest movement waged an unflinching war throughout the 1970s against all things big, including big government, big business, and big organized labor. By the early 1980s, the New Right's antigovernment brand of populism—which became known as the Sagebrush Rebellion in the American West—had risen to power and blamed regulations for rolling back the American economy during the previous decade.[99] In light of an explosion in environmental hazards, shocking political scandals, and hostile challenges to authority on the left and the right, it is not surprising that many Fernald-area residents believed that the federal government would paint a Purina-esque water tower to exploit them as the Cold War's human guinea pigs. Continuing revelations about Fernald's radioactive contamination throughout the 1980s only confirmed their worst fears.

THE SEEDS OF FERNALD'S DESTRUCTION

The nuclear landscape crisis was set in motion when what is known as "the Second Cold War" (1979–85) collided with the dilapidated Fernald plant. Its accidental architect, Ronald Reagan, was elected president in 1980 on the promise to roll back the environmental regulations that had supposedly hamstrung American businesses. Reagan unapologetically solicited industry for guidance and appointed critics of the environmental movement to positions of power, including Ann Gorsuch as administrator of the EPA and James Watt as the secretary of the interior.[100] At the same time as these well-known attacks on regulators and public lands, the Reagan administration also orchestrated the largest peacetime military buildup in American history.[101] Backed up with fierce anticommunist rhetoric, such as President Reagan's "Evil Empire" speech in 1983, this Second Cold War had enormous implications for production facilities like Fernald.[102] After nearly closing during détente, Fernald's production output nearly tripled from 1979 to 1984, its workforce nearly doubled, and it was slated for $70 million in capital improvements, which was the largest investment in the plant in three decades.[103] But Reagan's revitalized nuclear arms race also planted the seeds of its own destruction. Fernald was physically worn out, run by NLO managers out of step with society's environmental values, and poorly regulated by the DOE. The early Cold War's mass production model for the bomb seemed like a relic to a public that distrusted experts, demanded government accountability, and valued the work of ecologists over the physicists who pioneered the Atomic Age.[104]

At the dawn of the Cold War, the public trusted AEC experts to safely manage Fernald and genuinely believed its feed materials would help preserve American democracy. Beginning with Barry Commoner and Rachel Carson, however, activist-scientists demonstrated that the federal government was also willing to wage another kind of war on its own people through invisible hazards like radioactive fallout and toxic pesticides. The red-and-white checkerboard pattern on Fernald's water tower symbolizes these diverging views of risks, which were on a collision course by the 1980s.[105] For Fernald's employees and longtime area residents, the circulating rumors about a water tower conspiracy seemed laughable. "It was still the atomic plant," thought area resident Dan Finfrock. "These people don't know what's going on."[106] But the plant's critics were also on to something. Through nuclear secrecy and a workplace culture obsessed with production, Fernald's managers were deceptive and willing to take risks with environmental health and safety to extract more uranium metals out of workers and the plant's aging technology. Although Fernald's neighbors were never the DOE's human guinea pigs, their decisions did contaminate the environment and human bodies through administrative indifference. For the moment, Fernald's radioactive backyard remained a secret, but greater Cincinnati's peace movement was working hard behind the scenes to expose it.

TWO Trinity Day

On July 16, 1983, about a hundred peace activists gathered at Fernald to protest the nuclear weapons complex in Ohio with songs, speeches, and signs.[1] It was the thirty-eighth anniversary of the Trinity test, the world's first nuclear explosion in Alamogordo, New Mexico, part of the top-secret Manhattan Project.[2] Organized by Oxford Citizens for Peace (OCP), the Ohio Nuclear Weapons Freeze Campaign, and the American Friends Service Committee (AFSC), the protest was coordinated with "Ohio Nuclear Weapons Awareness Day," or "Trinity Day," a collection of demonstrations at eight sites connected to nuclear weapons production across Ohio: Fernald, Mound Laboratory in Miamisburg, Portsmouth Gaseous Diffusion Plant in Piketon, Newark Air Force Station, Rockwell International in Columbus, Reactive Metals Inc. in Ashtabula, and Goodyear in Akron.[3] At Fernald, activists memorialized atomic bomb victims in Japan, stood in solidarity with fellow peacemakers across the state, demanded the plant's conversion from military to peaceful uses, and spread awareness of the dangers of nuclear weapons production.[4]

Pauline Brokaw, dressed in light clothing and a large sun hat for protection from the summer heat, stood at the Wiley Road entrance to Fernald with five other peace activists. At sixty-six years old, Brokaw could have easily been the mother or even grandmother of her twenty- and thirty-something companions, Amy Griten, Kathy Freese, Leslie Clayton, Gary Skitt, and Thaddeus Coffin. Considering the group's plans for civil disobedience, however, the younger activists looked to the experienced Brokaw for leadership.[5]

During the 1940s, Brokaw converted to Quakerism while attending Ball

State Teachers College in Muncie, Indiana, where she fought for racial integration on campus, and she later founded the Committee to End the War in Vietnam in Cincinnati with her husband Amos.[6] As a Quaker, Brokaw was a pacifist whose activism was spiritually guided. Quakers express their faith in God through personal choices and deeds, which are called "testimonies." Inspired by the divine, their goal is to manifest a more peaceful and equitable world.[7]

Standing in front of the activists and separated by barricades was a formation of twenty helmeted sheriff's deputies. The police knew what was coming, but they still offered the protesters a chance to turn back. The activists refused. After stepping across the barricades, they were arrested for criminal trespassing on federal property.[8]

National Lead of Ohio (NLO) plant manager Robert Spenceley was pleased that the demonstration was nonviolent and thanked the police for guarding the plant's entrance. He reassured reporters that Fernald was safe, noting that NLO did not assemble nuclear bombs or handle plutonium, a man-made radioactive element that scientists first isolated and weighed in measurable quantities at the University of Chicago in 1942 for the Manhattan Project.[9] Fernald processed uranium, a naturally occurring and comparatively mild radioactive element buried in ores around the world, including the American West.[10] According to Spenceley, "The very small quantities of uranium we have lost over the past 32 years of operation have not significantly increased total uranium concentration in the soils, water and rock in the area."[11] Spenceley's words followed the longtime public relations strategy of the Department of Energy (DOE) and its predecessor agencies of reaffirming safety and downplaying the public health and environmental risks of low-level radiation releases from nuclear weapons tests, nuclear weapons production, and radioactive waste disposal.[12] Based on the information they possessed, however, peace activists believed that Fernald was far more contaminated than Spenceley claimed. Now they needed to prove it.

After processing the arrests, Hamilton County Sheriff Lincoln Stokes offered to release the protesters on their own recognizance, but again, the activists refused. The point was to raise awareness, and each day spent in jail provided an opportunity to teach others about the dangers of the nuclear arms race. "Ohio has more factories contributing to the bomb than any other state," Brokaw stated. The public needed to pay attention because "the nuclear situation is life-and-death, not just for you and me, but for the earth." Getting arrested was a critical tool for activists because "it takes a strong measure to make people aware of the danger of nuclear weaponry, and I can't think of any stronger measure than putting my body on the line."[13] Refusing to pay the $100 fine, Brokaw remained in jail for eleven days.[14] She had plenty of support, however. Fellow peace activists held a vigil outside the Hamilton County Workhouse in her honor.[15] Brokaw's act of civil disobedience provided the capstone to Trinity Day and received significant media coverage across the state.[16]

Through skillful organizing, the peace movement highlighted Ohio's deep economic ties to nuclear weapons production. Beginning with the Manhattan Project, Charles A. Thomas of Monsanto's Central Research Department directed a top-secret program on polonium triggers for the atomic bomb in Dayton. Shortly after the war, Monsanto's polonium research continued when the Atomic Energy Commission (AEC) developed Mound Laboratory.[17] During the early Cold War, the AEC's nuclear buildup continued with Fernald and the Portsmouth Gaseous Diffusion Plant.[18] For the peace movement, funding weapons over human needs was a moral failing, but these political priorities could be transformed through political action. With "more key nuclear weapons facilities than any other state," said Ohio Nuclear Weapons Freeze Campaign director Sara Kirschenbaum, "if Ohioans can turn it around, it would end the arms race."[19] For activists, Trinity Day was about building a more peaceful world for everyone.

The geographic distribution of Ohio's nuclear weapons production facilities also demonstrated that countless Ohioans were potentially being exposed to radioactive materials in their own vicinity. This was an important argument for the antinuclear movement. Since there have been no nuclear weapons deployed in warfare since World War II, peace activists have largely battled what-if scenarios regarding nuclear war. This opened the door for criticism within peace circles as activists debated the most effective means to draw the public's attention to the Reagan administration's renewed nuclear arms race. Tony Webb of the Foundation for

National Progress, which published the progressive magazine *Mother Jones*, argued that the Nuclear Weapons Freeze Campaign—the most successful American antinuclear group of the early 1980s—focused "on weapons and hardware instead of people." This technical, even abstract approach ignored how the bomb affects human beings. According to Webb, a "backyard" strategy, alluding to the widespread success of locally driven, not-in-my-backyard (NIMBY) environmental activism, would do much better to drive "the issue home."[20]

As part of a larger movement to localize the nuclear threat, greater Cincinnati's peace movement found its backyard at Fernald. Beginning with local concerns about the development of a commercial nuclear power plant in Cincinnati, as well as national connections to protests at the Rocky Flats nuclear weapons plant in Colorado, peace activists uncovered the first body of evidence to publicly challenge Fernald's claims to safe nuclear weapons production and expose potential environmental hazards at the plant. By the 1980s, Fernald's mission was largely forgotten outside of Ohio's nuclear workforce, particularly as the tenser moments of the early Cold War—such as the detonation of the Soviet Union's first atomic bomb in 1949 and the Cuban Missile Crisis in 1962—faded into history. The peace movement's awakening of the greater Cincinnati area to the bombmaker in their backyard was a pivotal moment, as a result, in the DOE's dramatic transformation from the 1980s to the 2000s, when an insulated and dangerous culture of production slowly adopted the tenets of environmentalism.[21]

If Fernald was the greater Cincinnati peace movement's backyard, however, it was Fernald production workers' living room. As peace activists publicly planned Trinity Day, Fernald's unions—the population most directly exposed to the plant's toxic and radioactive byproducts—requested an industrial health study of their workspace by the National Institute for Occupational Safety and Health (NIOSH), which conflicted with the peace movement's efforts to halt the nuclear arms race as quickly as possible.[22] This conflict demonstrates how backyards were contested spaces in environmental history, not only between industry and activists or managers and workers but between local movements. Ultimately, the peace movement's inattention to union workers' campaigns for environmental health and safety at Fernald alienated itself from a conservative community where many already viewed its activists as outsiders.

THE MAKING OF AN ACTIVIST

Tom Carpenter, like countless Americans before and since, was first exposed to environmentalism after reading Rachel Carson's 1962 book *Silent Spring* in college. In it, Carson warned against the abuse of science and technology for profit, as corporations marketed increasingly dangerous synthetic pesticides to the public in the wake of World War II. Even worse, the government not only left these materials unregulated but actively encouraged their use across the nation—despite knowledge of their toxicity—without the public's consent.[23] In the late 1970s, inspired by Carson's book, Carpenter joined the Cincinnati Food Co-Op, located in the basement of a Methodist church in Clifton. It was a logical first step for the young environmentalist. The organic food movement paralleled the rise of synthetic pesticides, as Americans feeling powerless against the rise of industrial agriculture increasingly turned to local farmers and organic markets to challenge the status quo with their purchasing power.[24]

At this working co-op, members were required to perform a job as part of their membership dues. Carpenter, who recalled his younger self as "lazier than most people," happily accepted the easygoing role of education coordinator. As such, Carpenter was tasked with recruiting monthly speakers.[25] For a time, Carpenter was spared the trouble of stocking heavy boxes of produce or providing customer service as a cashier. In the long run, however, the position started Carpenter on a lifelong journey of challenging work on nuclear issues.

In 1978, one of Carpenter's speakers lectured on the historical connections between nuclear weapons production and the nuclear power industry, a relationship long suppressed through government propaganda.[26] Beginning with President Dwight Eisenhower's "Atoms for Peace" speech to the United Nations in 1953, the United States forcefully promoted civilian nuclear power both domestically and internationally. On the surface, "Atoms for Peace" supported the idea that America took disarmament, along with the welfare of developing nations, seriously. "Ironically," wrote historian Jacob Darwin Hamblin, "the peaceful proposal was designed to mitigate the political damage from what the United States really intended—to integrate nuclear weapons more fully into American and allied military plans and to embark on an extraordinary series of atmospheric nuclear weapons tests."[27] Throughout the 1970s, peace activists and environmentalists mobilized to confront the reemerging threat of nuclear war, the safety of nuclear power plants, and the dangers of radioactive waste disposal and exposures to low levels of radiation.[28]

The antinuclear movement sought to remedy the mistakes of the Vietnam era by building more of a grassroots base. According to leading activist Sam Lovejoy, "One of the problems of the antiwar movement was that we didn't have much of a base at home other than college towns," and "the movement always cut off its nose to spite its face by going to Washington and ranting." "The difference between the war movement and the nuke movement," Lovejoy continued, was that "the Vietnam War was 15,000 miles away" while "the nuke is in my backyard."[29] From Seabrook in New Hampshire to Diablo Canyon in California, a locally based but nationally networked movement developed to fight the construction of nuclear power plants and protect public health.[30] Before Carpenter could fight the nuclear power plant in his own community, however, he needed some training. The Cincinnati Food Co-op's speaker invited the group to an upcoming demonstration at Rocky Flats, a nuclear weapons production facility located sixteen miles northwest of Denver, Colorado. Deeply inspired by the lecture, Carpenter packed his bags for the protest.[31]

In the foothills of the Front Range of the Rocky Mountains, the AEC built Rocky Flats during the early 1950s as part of its massive expansion of the nuclear weapons complex. For much of the Cold War, its primary mission was producing plutonium "pits," or "triggers," which served as the explosive detonators for hydrogen bombs. On Mother's Day, May 11, 1969, specks of plutonium spontaneously ignited an oily rag in the bottom of a glove box in Building 776, which spiraled out of control into an extremely dangerous fire in a radioactive environment. Firefighters and workers courageously put out the blaze, but not without significant personal risk and numerous exposures to radiation. After reports of the fire appeared in Denver and Boulder newspapers, local scientists, citizens, and journalists started questioning the safety of Rocky Flats.[32]

Ed Martell, a fifty-one-year-old experimental chemist at the National Center for Atmospheric Research laboratory in Boulder and member of the Colorado Committee for Environmental Information, led a study of undisturbed soils around Rocky Flats. Martell and his radiochemical assistant Stuart Poet discovered plutonium to the east of the plant, which the Colorado Committee attributed to the Mother's Day fire. Despite the AEC's denial, Martell's study "localized the threat," according to environmental journalist Len Ackland, which significantly raised public awareness about Rocky Flats beyond the small group of peace activists who occasionally protested outside the plant. Activists in Citizens Concerned about Radiation Pollution built upon Martell's work by going door-to-door to collect dirt samples from people's yards, labeling them in plastic bags, and delivering them to congressional candidates at public meetings. Judy Danielson of Concerned Citizens recalled telling candidates, "This is in our backyard. What are you going to do about it?"[33]

Activism at Rocky Flats continued to grow. In 1974, Danielson and her colleague Pam Solo—both now at the AFSC—founded a coalition of peace activists and environmentalists called the Rocky Flats Action Group. In a collaboration between national peace and environmental organizations, they helped organize two major protests in April 1978, one at Rocky Flats and another at a nuclear reprocessing plant under construction in Barnwell, South Carolina. The goal was to attack the nuclear industry on both fronts, including weapons and civilian power. Five thousand people, including Tom Carpenter, attended the Rocky Flats protest on April 29. Daniel Ellsberg, the former Rand Corporation employee who leaked the Pentagon Papers to the press during the Vietnam War, was one of several nationally known speakers at the demonstration.[34]

The following day, Ellsberg led dozens of protesters in an act of civil disobedience by blocking the railroad tracks at Rocky Flats. Danielson and Solo anticipated the civil disobedience to be symbolic—to simply prove to the DOE that bodies could physically halt the movement of radioactive materials, and therefore shut down the nuclear weapons production complex—but activists calling themselves the "Truth Force" refused to budge. Supporters brought camping equipment, food, and ponchos to keep the activists comfortable. Danielson and Solo were frustrated with the movement's radical turn, because it threatened to undermine years of careful dialogue with union leadership at Rocky Flats. The media also did them a disservice by stressing the "hippie" image of the carefree youths leading the blockade, ignoring years of cautious planning. None of this mattered. The protest was a huge success and swelled the ranks of the peace movement. Carpenter was deeply inspired by the courage of those getting arrested for the antinuclear cause and received training in Denver that prepared him for future work in Cincinnati, including political organizing, writing press releases, and chartering an antinuclear group.[35] Carpenter left for Denver as a passionate youth but returned to Cincinnati an activist.

Back in Ohio, Carpenter reached out to Polly Brokaw to help launch an antinuclear group. Brokaw, already a member of the Ohio Valley Citizens Concerned about Nuclear Pollution, readily agreed. They chose the name Citizens Against a Radioactive Environment (CARE) and set off to challenge the construction of the William H. Zimmer Nuclear Power Station on the Ohio River, twenty-four miles southeast of the city.[36] Carpenter recalled that Brokaw "taught me a lot," so he listened when she instructed him that people "gravitate toward action."[37] CARE, as a result, began its work as a direct-action organization that was unrepentant in its opposition to all forms of nuclear energy.[38]

CARE employed a variety of protest tactics. Members met biweekly, often with a large cohort of University of Cincinnati students, lectured throughout the community about the dangers of nuclear power, held direct-action protests at the Zimmer plant, and launched a media campaign against its development. One advertisement in the *Cincinnati Enquirer* claimed that Zimmer was "The Most Dangerous Idea to Ever Hit the Midwest."[39] In another theatrical display, activists released balloons to illustrate where the wind would blow radiation after an accident at Zimmer.[40] Balloon releases were popularized in the early 1960s by the Association to Preserve Bodega Head, an antinuclear organization in California, to associate nuclear reactors with the radioactive fallout from nuclear weapons testing. These symbolic protests, mimicked across the country and spanning multiple decades, helped establish a link in the public's mind between nuclear weapons production and the civilian nuclear power industry.[41]

While activists in CARE were successful in raising awareness, nothing could educate the public on the dangers of nuclear power quite like the real thing. On March 28, 1979, a series of minor mechanical failures and operator errors at the Three Mile Island nuclear power plant in Harrisburg, Pennsylvania, spiraled from a repairable situation into an unprecedented emergency over the following days. Although engineering safeguards succeeded in preventing a disastrous release of radiation, the panic and confusion generated during the event terrified surrounding communities and pushed many Americans to oppose the construction of new nuclear power plants. For antinuclear activists, the meltdown at Three Mile Island confirmed their worst suspicions that complex technological systems were destined to fail, with potentially deadly consequences for the public.[42]

After Three Mile Island, attendance at CARE's meetings skyrocketed from dozens to hundreds of people. Carpenter was extremely busy during this period, with his days "eaten up by research and talks and meetings." Then everything changed. While working on Zimmer, Carpenter stumbled across an article in the *Cincinnati Enquirer* discussing the expansion of a nuclear waste program near Cincinnati that tipped him off to another, and potentially even more dangerous, plant called Fernald. Carpenter was shocked to learn that a link in the nuclear weapons complex was located only eighteen miles northwest of the city.[43] After Fernald's rapid buildup in the 1950s, newspaper coverage of the facility slowed in the 1960s and 1970s as production dipped and the plant declined as a regionally significant employer. During this period of the Cold War, commonly known as détente, Hanford and Savannah River produced a plutonium surplus, AEC facilities aged toward obsolescence, and international disarmament treaties relaxed tensions between the United States and the Soviet Union.[44] For the young and predominantly urban activists in CARE who were not old enough to remember the fearful beginnings of the Cold War, Fernald had always been invisible.

A NEW GENERATION DISCOVERS FERNALD

After Carpenter's newspaper discovery, several CARE members drove to Fernald to investigate. Like activists at Rocky Flats, they took matters into their own hands. Instead of collecting soil, however, they took water samples from Paddy's Run, a stream that flows through the plant before emptying into the Great Miami River, a tributary of the Ohio River.[45] One sample was sent to a laboratory in Richmond, California, which measured ten picocuries per liter of alpha radioactivity in the water. This was a small dose, which the Environmental Protection Agency (EPA) would still consider to be a safe level for drinking water, but it was evidence of uranium escaping the facility, just like the plutonium had at Rocky Flats. Further, this was one sample from a moving stream. What if the uranium concentrated somewhere, such as a family's well water? Fearful over possible uranium contamination and distrustful of the DOE, Carpenter reached out to the Ohio EPA to conduct a formal search for elevated levels of radioactivity. The agency hesitated, however, which raised further suspicions for peace activists already skeptical of government.[46]

In January 1980, CARE hosted a teach-in at the University of Cincinnati to share its findings with the community and discuss the dangers of the nuclear industry.[47] (First popularized by the peace movement during the Vietnam War, teach-ins spread to environmentalism through the youth-led and decentralized structure of Earth Day 1970.[48]) After visiting Fernald, Carpenter and his colleagues could now visualize how radionuclides might travel from the plant into the bodies of Cincinnati's residents, including the one hundred or so people in the audience. There was milk from the cows grazing in the surrounding grasslands to worry about and, even more frightening, sources of drinking water. Frustrated, Carpenter challenged the Ohio EPA's objectivity. "I think we have enough evidence for an independent investigation," Carpenter said, but "we have had no cooperation from the Ohio EPA. They pass the buck."[49] Carpenter's distrust of regulators was common in the aftermath of the partial meltdown at Three Mile Island. While safety systems prevented a dangerous release of radiation, activists were suspicious of regulators in the Nuclear Regulatory Commission (NRC) who downplayed their fears and personal experiences of the event and appeared to serve the interests of industry more so than the public.[50] Still, as a state agency, the Ohio EPA could develop into an important ally in a fight against a federal nuclear weapons plant.

Established in 1972, two years after President Nixon created the federal EPA, the Ohio EPA unified the state's weak regulatory programs to meet the public's growing demands for outdoor recreation, safe and livable cities, and compliance with new federal environmental laws. During this period, Ohio had a terrible reputation for pollution. Steubenville and the surrounding upper Ohio Valley contained some of the worst air pollution in the country. Agricultural runoff created massive algal blooms that suffocated Lake Erie. Most infamously, on June 22, 1969, an oil slick on the Cuyahoga River caught fire—which had been a common occurrence throughout the twentieth century—but intense media coverage of the fire transformed Cleveland into a symbol for America's urban and environmental crises in the lead-up to Earth Day in 1970.[51] The collision between decades of untethered industrial capitalism and federal environmental laws created the demand for a statewide regulatory agency as well as a new generation of regulators.

America's colleges and universities were essential to battling the environmental crisis. In the years surrounding the first Earth Day, interdisciplinary environmental science programs spread in popularity across the country.[52] One of these new departments was Miami University's Institute for Environmental Sciences in Oxford, Ohio, which welcomed its first class of students in the fall of 1971. In the spirit of the times, emphasis was placed on hands-on, ecological problem-solving—the kind of work required to purify America's rivers and clean its smoke-filled skies. Students were required to design a project for potential employers, such as a health department, municipal service, or state agency, and according to director C. E. Barthel, the program was in high demand even during its first year.[53] Graham Mitchell, a Miami University master's in environmental science graduate, went to work for the Ohio EPA in 1977 and became the manager of its surface water surveillance program in Southwest Ohio.[54]

The Ohio EPA sent Mitchell to investigate CARE's findings. Mitchell sampled one low point and one high point of Paddy's Run, finding no traces of radioactivity.[55] For NLO and the Ohio EPA, CARE's report of radioactivity in Paddy's Run was not nearly as unsettling, because there had been an environmental monitoring program at the site for decades. Beginning in the 1950s, NLO collected air quality samples on gummed paper placed around the plant and tested the water at various points along the Great Miami River, and the results were reported to the Ohio Department of Health (ODH) and published in regular reports.[56] Since 1976, NLO also reported to the EPA under a National Pollution Discharge Emission System (NPDES) permit.[57] Mitchell's results, which were reported in the *Cincinnati Enquirer*, quieted local fears over water pollution for a time. Along with this relieving news, however, the *Cincinnati Post* revealed to its readers that Fernald was one of the largest dumping sites for radioactive waste in the country.[58] For these reasons, Mitchell's work at Fernald was just getting started.

Finding no evidence in the water, Carpenter looked to the archives to uncover Fernald's secrets. In 1979, he filed a Freedom of Information Act (FOIA) request, an increasingly important tool for antinuclear activists, for any accident reports at Fernald.[59] On the heels of the Pentagon Papers and Watergate scandals, FOIA was strengthened through a series of amendments that imposed tighter deadlines on federal agencies and permitted federal judges to review classified material. In the late 1970s, these amendments aided military veterans seeking compensation for exposure to radiation during atmospheric nuclear weapons tests, which helped renew public interest in the potential dangers of low-level radiation.[60]

A couple of months later, the boxes of FOIA documents arrived. These carbon copies of typewritten reports were censored by hand, so the classified information was simply crossed out with a marker. To beat this unsophisticated classification system, Carpenter cleverly held the pages up to light to read the blacked-out text.[61] The documents were worth the wait. On June 15, CARE published its revelatory findings. "Twelve separate documents," CARE began, "expose equipment failure and human error that has led to the release of more than seven thousand pounds of radioactive materials, mostly enriched uranium, to the air and to the Great Miami River."[62] This information was extracted from twelve documents covering 120 pages and spanning the years 1962 to 1979, including letters, reports, and a press release. The largest documented accident occurred in 1966, after a worker broke the valve of a heated cylinder of uranium hexafluoride, releasing 3,844 pounds of radioactive gas into the environment. Six workers were hospitalized out of precaution from the incident.[63]

Most recently, in 1979, a few pounds of uranium escaped through the storm sewer into the Great Miami River.[64] NLO and the DOE would normally consider this level of release to be a harmless byproduct of uranium processing.[65] Management was concerned, however, because the origins of the uranium leak could not be traced. The best hypothesis was that "a pool of uranium-bearing solution is contained under the Plant 6 concrete floor and that a break exists in the Storm Sewer drainage line."[66] For CARE, the settling of radioactive waste underneath the site was disturbing, because Fernald sat above the Great Miami Aquifer, a source of drinking water for nearby communities. To spread the word about the contamination, copies of these records were made accessible through the Quaker meetinghouse and offered to newspaper editors at no charge.[67] While CARE worried that Cincinnati faced a potentially catastrophic nuclear meltdown from Zimmer, FOIA documents revealed that Fernald's hazards more closely resembled a slow poisoning.[68]

CARE: FROM ANTINUCLEAR TO NUCLEAR SAFETY

For the next few years, Fernald remained in the shadows as CARE focused its political energies on Zimmer after a whistleblower came forward and altered the course of Tom Carpenter's life. In December 1979, Zimmer's operator, Cincinnati Gas and Electric (CG&E), hired a private inspector, Thomas Applegate, who stumbled across illegal guns sales between Zimmer employees while working on another case and contacted the company. CG&E tasked Applegate with a much narrower mission: to investigate time theft—paying employees for hours they did not actually work—at the plant. For six weeks, Applegate worked undercover as a cost accounting engineer, observing construction, interviewing workers and union leaders, and reviewing plant records. Applegate's investigation revealed a litany of problematic behaviors that were far more serious than fraudulent time cards, including stolen construction materials, the possession of illegal firearms, drunkenness, and lax security. Not surprisingly, this poor workplace culture impacted the development of critical safety systems at Zimmer. Applegate documented inadequate fire detection, poor quality control, and cracked safety welds that had been covered up. Applegate brought his findings to CG&E's leadership, hoping to make a difference.[69]

CG&E ignored Applegate's more serious accusations and only demonstrated interest in time theft. Then the company worked to silence anyone threatening to stall the plant's construction. CG&E asked Applegate to find a reason to fire Peabody Magnaflux, the contractor performing radiography services for CG&E's quality assurance department. Radiography, a noninvasive method of inspecting plant components, was just the kind of test capable of detecting faulty construction at Zimmer. Applegate refused, however, after watching Peabody Magnaflux's employees working diligently on the project. CG&E fired Applegate, the radiographers, and all workers documented to be cheating on their time cards, who also happened to be CG&E's most vocal critics.[70]

Applegate believed that CG&E's actions warranted criminal charges, so on February 15, 1980, he phoned the NRC, the federal agency responsible for oversight of the civilian nuclear power industry, to report his findings. He also shared them with the FBI and the US Attorney's Office in Cincinnati. The NRC met with Applegate but did so "reluctantly." After reviewing the investigation, the NRC found Applegate's evidence to be "unsubstantiated."[71] Although the federal government downplayed his complaints, Applegate refused to give up. Next, he turned to Tom Carpenter.[72]

To give the NRC some credit, Applegate did display erratic behavior. Before meeting with Carpenter at CARE, Applegate broke into its offices to determine if the organization could be trusted. He also carried a loaded gun after learning about the mysterious death of nuclear worker turned whistleblower Karen Silkwood. That did not mean, however, that Applegate was a fraud. Together, Applegate and Carpenter reviewed boxes of evidence and tape-recorded conservations of Zimmer workers, which revealed that twenty percent of Zimmer's steel came from a junkyard. This evidence was too big for CARE to handle alone. In June 1980, Applegate and Carpenter drove to Washington, DC, and met with representatives of a nonprofit law firm called the Government Accountability Project (GAP). Developed in 1976 as part of the liberal think tank the Institute for Policy Studies, GAP offered legal counsel for corporate and government whistleblowers.[73] It was a perfect match for someone in Applegate's situation.

GAP's legal director, Tom Devine, was a rising star in the profession. During his undergraduate years at Georgetown University, he interned at Ralph Nader's antinuclear organization, the Critical Mass Energy Project. While attending Antioch School of Law, Devine worked as a research assistant for a public interest law firm investigating "the Saturday Night Massacre," President Richard Nixon's attempt to purge members of the Justice Department during the Watergate scandal, including then Deputy Attorney General William Ruckelshaus, the first administrator of the EPA.[74] Deeply inspired by efforts to expose corruption, Devine established a whistleblower's law clinic at Antioch and was hired by GAP after graduating. Devine's background, which combined antinuclear activism and whistleblower protection, all came together at Zimmer.[75]

After interviewing Carpenter and Applegate, Devine agreed to take on the case and recruited Carpenter to serve as a local point of contact for GAP.[76] Devine explained his strategy to the young activist and whistleblower. The plan was to use all the legal tools at GAP's disposal to challenge the plant's safety record through whistleblower evidence and subpoenaed NRC documents, which would delay the licensing process and raise costs for CG&E. Devine's legal precision inspired Carpenter to reconsider CARE's role at Zimmer. After returning to Cincinnati, he called a CARE meeting and urged its membership to fight alongside GAP by shifting from an antinuclear group to a nuclear safety organization. Brokaw and several colleagues disagreed, preferring the moral power of mass movements and the urgency of direct actions to transform society. After much discussion, however, the group sided with Carpenter. The change in tactics was reflected in CARE's new name: the Cincinnati Alliance for Responsible Energy.[77]

Brokaw's and Carpenter's competing visions for CARE represented a generational shift in American activism. Brokaw came of age during the civil rights movement and Vietnam War, an era dedicated to nonviolent civil disobedience. Although Carpenter was always sorry to have missed the excitement of the 1960s, the environmental movement had demonstrated through a sweeping set of legislative victories in the 1970s that society could be transformed within the system. During this period, activists traded in the streets for offices in Washington, DC, as the movement focused its efforts on holding polluters accountable through lawsuits and constructing the environmental regulatory state.[78]

Devine's leadership paid off. After revisiting Applegate's case against CG&E, the NRC's Office of Inspector and Auditor acknowledged that it had erred in its initial investigation of mismanagement at Zimmer. NRC regulators never inspected faulty welding, overlooked critical documents, and generally failed to follow through on the investigation. Following this report, the NRC fined CG&E $200,000, which was the largest penalty ever placed on a nuclear plant that was still under construction. Over the next several years, whistleblower reports and safety violations, rising construction costs, public anger over consumer rate hikes, and the growing fear of nuclear power in the aftermath of Three Mile Island halted the plant's momentum. On January 21, 1984, staring down a $3.5 billion price tag for nuclear power, CG&E announced Zimmer's conversion to coal.[79]

THE NATIONAL PEACE MOVEMENT

Protests at Zimmer and Fernald were part of a nationwide resurgence in antinuclear activism. While environmentalists rallied around Three Mile Island, it was the Carter administration's approval of the MX, a new generation of intercontinental ballistic missiles, that sparked a resurgence in the peace movement. Then the Reagan administration's hardline anticommunist rhetoric and unprecedented arms buildup poured gasoline on the flames. This renewed energy revived Physicians for Social Responsibility and the National Committee for a Sane Nuclear Policy (SANE), two antinuclear organizations formed during the late 1950s to combat atmospheric nuclear weapons testing.[80] It was the Nuclear Weapons Freeze Campaign, however, that carried the peace movement into the mainstream. That was the brainchild of Randall Forsberg, the director of the Institute for Defense and Disarmament Studies, a think tank in Brookline, Massachusetts. Forsberg learned about nuclear weapons issues while working as a staffer at the Stockholm International Peace Research Institute, and she later coined a simple message—"freeze" the nuclear arms race—as a unifying concept for the diverse factions of the peace movement during this era. Forsberg put her thoughts into words in the 1979 essay *A Call to Halt the Arms Race*, in which she called for a bilateral stoppage to the production, testing, and deployment of nuclear weapons.[81] This document spread like wildfire throughout the peace community.

From 1980 to 1984, the Nuclear Freeze Steering Committee worked tirelessly to inject the freeze message into mainstream politics.[82] Their efforts were realized when Massachusetts Democratic Senator Edward M. Kennedy and Oregon Republican Senator Mark O. Hatfield introduced a freeze resolution in Congress, which passed in the House of Representatives but was blocked in the Senate.[83] On June 12, 1982, activists organized a freeze rally in New York City with musical performances by Bob Dylan, Joan Baez, Bruce Springsteen, Jackson Browne, and Bonnie Raitt. With an estimated turnout of hundreds of thousands or even almost one million people, it was the largest antinuclear protest in American history.[84] Nuclear bestsellers were flying off the shelves, including Jonathon Schell's *The Fate of the Earth*, Robert Molander's *Nuclear War: What's in It for You?*, and Senators Kennedy and Hatfield's *Freeze! How You Can Help Prevent Nuclear War*. ABC's antinuclear television movie, *The Day After*, was viewed by a record-breaking audience of approximately one hundred million Americans on November 20, 1983, and scientist Carl Sagan introduced his "nuclear winter" theory in the popular *Parade* magazine. Americans now had the tools to imagine a nuclear apocalypse as a blazing inferno or frigid death. Largely out of the spotlight since the passage of the Limited Nuclear Test Ban Treaty (LTBT) in 1963, which outlawed nuclear explosions in the atmosphere, underwater, and in outer space, the bomb was back in popular culture.[85]

For all the success of the Nuclear Freeze, its simplistic message—at least on the surface—opened the movement up to criticism, both within and outside of the peace movement. Progressives worried that it catered to the mainstream and fell short of the movement's true goals, which was a reorganization of society that empowered people instead of the Pentagon.

War hawks complained that the freeze was an implausible and hysterical solution to the calculated and complex realities of the Cold War.[86]

Sometimes the message was too simple, but it was also a major asset for the Freeze. One pamphlet from the Ohio Nuclear Weapons Freeze Campaign, for example, challenged readers to consider the best way to halt the arms race with two possible solutions: "build more nuclear weapons" or "stop building nuclear weapons."[87] Commonsense was undeniably appealing. As historian William Knoblauch argued, the popularity of the Nuclear Freeze transformed the 1982 New York City rally from "a modest protest" into "the largest antinuclear demonstration in American history."[88] Much of this conversation about the Freeze's simplicity was also overblown. Even at the peak of the Nuclear Weapons Freeze Campaign, peace activists were presenting far more complex arguments on the ground than the monolithic image presented in public debate, including the bomb's environmental toll.

THE OHIO PEACE MOVEMENT

While a handful of antinuclear organizations dominated the national dialogue, the peace movement was also a local phenomenon. *The Grassroots Peace Directory: A Guide to Peace Groups and Resources: Ohio* identified almost 150 active groups across the state in 1984, including religious communities, environmentalists, university students and faculty, medical professionals, lawyers, social workers, and women's groups.[89] One such organization, Oxford Citizens for Peace was founded in 1979 in Oxford, Ohio, a college town that was home to Miami University. OCP rose from the ashes of Oxford Citizens for Peace in Vietnam, which disbanded after the war but was reborn under the leadership of Linda Musmeci Kimball during the Carter administration's ICBM buildup and Reagan's renewed nuclear arms race. While growing up in New Orleans, Kimball's witnessing the inequalities of Jim Crow and experience in the civil rights movement inspired her lifetime of activism. In 1968, she moved to Oxford, where her husband Jeffrey joined Miami University's history department and she joined the antiwar movement. In 1980, Kimball and her colleagues launched their first action as OCP, a letter to five hundred like-minded citizens about the dangers of the nuclear arms race.⁹⁰

Local groups like OCP defied the easy categorization of the national conversation on the peace movement. OCP's first action letter, for example, called for a dramatic reorganization of American priorities at home and abroad. "While $1 Billion a day is being spent on weapons of destruction and their maintenance," OCP wrote, "over half the people in the world suffer from malnutrition and lack adequate housing and medical care."⁹¹ Even with these progressive arguments, OCP also fully embraced the Nuclear Weapons Freeze Campaign, networking with other Freeze affiliates across the state, promoting their literature, and collecting signatures in support of the freeze resolutions in Congress.⁹² At the end of the day, local groups were most concerned about ending the nuclear arms race, regardless of the strategy.

Antinuclear activists have often been on the cutting edge of modern environmentalism.⁹³ In 1964, scientist and environmentalist Barry Commoner called the LTBT the first great victory of the environmental movement.⁹⁴ Though the LTBT failed to slow the nuclear arms race, by forcing nuclear tests underground, it succeeded in its secondary goal of sharply reducing the release of radioactive fallout into the environment.⁹⁵ With the revival of the peace movement in the late 1970s, activists built on this foundation. One popular technique was mapmaking. "Man-Made Radiation Hazards" by Women Strike for Peace and "Nuclear America" by the War Resisters League documented the nationwide nuclear industry from mining to disposal, including nuclear weapons plants, power plants, storage facilities, and landfills; university laboratories; and uranium tailings.⁹⁶ These maps, according to historian Kyle Harvey, "were designed to highlight for local residents the dangers in their own backyards."⁹⁷ SANE issued a "Nuclear Wastes Fact Sheet," which listed Fernald as having a nation-leading 11,450,000 cubic feet of low-level radioactive waste stored on-site. Overall, it was the third largest storage facility for nuclear waste in the country, trailing only Hanford, Washington, and Savannah River, South Carolina.⁹⁸ On Trinity Day, the environment would be a key issue for greater Cincinnati's peace movement.

FERNALD: A CONTESTED BACKYARD

As Trinity Day approached, activists readied their tactics. Tom Carpenter conducted research for a "Fernald Fact Sheet" on the plant's dangerous industrial nature. "Fernald handles as much as 50 tons of uranium per day," Carpenter wrote, and "stores 11,450,000 cubic feet of the deadly wastes onsite." According to accident reports, Fernald had released "a total of several tons of radioactive material over a period of years."[99] Meanwhile, the Quakers coordinated their act of civil disobedience, and Freeze activists crafted flyers for the event, decorated with doves, bombs stamped "Made in Ohio," and a vulture ready to feed on the remains of atomic victims. Trinity Day was a local affair, and one OCP flyer reminded its readership in Oxford to "make a peaceful presence with your neighbors at the nuclear weapons facility nearest you ... FERNALD."[100] Then all that preparation came to a screeching halt. Only five days before Trinity Day, Fernald's labor unions asked Cincinnati's peace community to call the protest off.[101]

While the AFSC communicated with Rocky Flats' union leadership leading up to the 1978 blockade, Cincinnati's peace community had failed to contact the Fernald Atomic Trades and Labor Council (FATLC), a local affiliate of the AFL-CIO. Had they done so, they would have learned that the FATLC—and nuclear workers across the country—were growing increasingly worried about routine exposures to low-level radiation. One frightening study from this era published by Dr. Thomas Najarian, a hematology fellow at the Veterans Administration hospital in Boston, determined that submarine workers at the Portsmouth Naval Shipyard in Kittery, Maine, were nearly five times as likely to die from leukemia than the public.[102] In the wake of Najarian's study and other damning reports, in 1979, the Oil, Chemical and Atomic Workers Union at the Portsmouth Gaseous Diffusion Plant requested NIOSH to conduct a radiation exposure survey. A similar cancer study was conducted at the Portsmouth Naval Shipyard. Finally, in February 1983, the International Association of Machinists and Aerospace Workers union of the FATLC requested a general study of health hazards at Fernald.[103] It was during the intense negotiations between the DOE, NIOSH, and the FATLC that Fernald's unions asked Cincinnati's peace community to stand down.[104]

DOE resistance, and complications of the federal bureaucracy, limited NIOSH's access to nuclear weapons plants. The Occupational Safety and Health Act and the Federal Mine Safety and Health Act granted NIOSH "right of entry" into private industries and mining operations, but it could not investigate federal facilities or contractor-operated federal facilities, such as Fernald, without the agency's cooperation. "In comparison with the number of epidemiologic studies we have conducted over the years in other areas of American industry," NIOSH's Philip Bierbaum testified, "our experience with nuclear facilities has been minimal."[105] Requiring special permissions from the DOE, NIOSH investigators were held up significantly at the Portsmouth Gaseous Diffusion Plant as they awaited security clearances. NIOSH worked with the FATLC, NLO, and the DOE to overcome these hurdles, and arranged for a site visit to Fernald in October.[106]

Despite the FATLC's request, Trinity Day went forward as planned. On July 16, activists gathered at the Wiley Road entrance to the plant, surrounded by Southwest Ohio's rolling farmlands with barriers separating the crowd of protesters from a formation of police. Activists held a vigil in memory of atomic bomb victims in Japan and carried signs saying "Honor Life, Dismantle a Bomb," "Taxes for Life, Not Death," and "Freeze Nuclear Weapons, Convert Fernald." They sang songs, prayed, and made speeches. Most importantly, the press was on the scene to write stories about the event, which appeared in newspapers across the state and on Ohio Public Radio.[107] "I think we touched thousands of people's lives with the deepest concerns of our hearts," said one activist. "We have spoken, and we must speak out again and again and again."[108]

Not all activists felt so sure. After Trinity Day, Tom Carpenter regretted ignoring Fernald's unions despite the substantial effort he put into the event. After all, if it were not for the testimony of working people at Zimmer, CARE never could have stopped the nuclear power plant's construction. To express his change of heart, Carpenter penned "An Open Letter to the Peace Movement" in the newsletter of the Cincinnati

Nuclear Weapons Freeze Campaign. He wrote, "I could not help but feel that we acted carelessly, first by not checking out the work being done by the unions out there." He understood "the difficulty of de-mobilizing a demonstration a mere days away. We could have done it, though." In the future, the peace movement needed to align itself with nuclear workers if it ever was to achieve "a just society free of nuclear tyranny."[109] Without the FATLC, the peace movement might be stuck outside Fernald's barricades for good.

POISON IN THE WELLS

Inspired by his collaboration with GAP, Carpenter moved to Washington, DC, in 1983 to attend Antioch School of Law, a branch of Antioch College, which was founded in 1852 in Yellow Springs, Ohio. Antioch School of Law was Tom Devine's alma mater, where the onetime Zimmer lawyer established a whistleblower's law clinic the previous decade.[110] Established in 1972, the law school was designed with a social justice model of learning through community service, particularly by providing legal counsel to the poor, and was part of Antioch College's development of satellite campuses in the decades after the civil rights movement to serve diverse communities.[111] Carpenter, who gained vital experience at Zimmer, quickly rose through the ranks. During his second year of law school, GAP hired him to run its nuclear oversight campaign.[112] This transition solidified Carpenter's belief that the law, rather than mass movements, was the most effective strategy for social change.

Although disheartened by the union conflict, Carpenter could take pride that CARE's FOIA request resuscitated a long-suppressed conversation about water contamination at Fernald. Since the 1950s, academic geologists who collaborated with the AEC criticized the agency for its poor radioactive waste disposal practices, including temporary solutions like tanks, trenches, pits, and drums, which routinely failed and leaked into the environment. The AEC's operational culture, which was later inherited by the DOE, lacked the ecological thinking of the geologists by assuming that its materials would remain on-site despite their disposal into complex environments. Even worse, several AEC sites, including

Fernald, were located above some of the largest aquifers in the United States, threatening drinking water sources for fast-growing population centers.[113] As early as 1960, AEC geologist John K. Hartsock identified hazardous waste barrels and production runoff at Fernald as a significant threat to the Great Miami Aquifer.[114] Decades later, Hartsock's fears would be proven correct.

In late 1981, the Ohio EPA discovered radioactive contamination in private wells on Fernald's southern border during an investigation of Mobil Chemical and Delta Steel, two companies located downstream along Paddy's Run. The Ohio EPA contacted NLO for assistance with this study, so the company launched its own investigation in December and confirmed that Fernald's uranium was the source of the radioactivity. The DOE then requested a study by the US Geological Survey (USGS), which took its own samples in August 1982. Three wells, assigned the numbers H108, H111, and H121, revealed uranium levels significantly above those naturally occurring in the environment. Located just south of the plant where Fernald's storm sewer emptied into Paddy's Run, H111 and H121 were used primarily for industrial operations. H108, unfortunately, provided the drinking water for Lisa and Ken Crawford and their young son, Kenny.[115]

In the early 1980s, there was no EPA maximum contaminant level for uranium in drinking water, so the regulatory measuring stick for safety was unclear. From the perspective of combined radioactivity, the Crawford's well was safely below the EPA's standard. Radioactivity, however, was not the primary concern. Uranium is toxic when ingested. The Ohio EPA contacted the federal EPA and the DOE for guidance; both agencies considered the readings significantly elevated but likely no risk to public health. The USGS measured 250 micrograms per liter in the Crawford's well. In comparison, its report noted that health physicists had recommended an interim guideline of 14.7 micrograms per liter for uranium.[116] Using this recommendation, a glass of water pumped from the Crawford's well contained uranium levels seventeen times higher than what might be considered safe.

None of this was public knowledge yet. The DOE, NLO, the Ohio EPA, and the ODH, which took over as the lead agency studying the contamination, only shared this information on a need-to-know basis. In the face of scientific uncertainty, the DOE and Ohio's regulatory agencies chose to ignore the issue. To NLO's credit, it did its part by informing the property owners. In February 1982, Fernald's plant manager, Robert Spenceley, wrote those impacted by the contamination, including the Knollmans, a dairy-farming family and the primary landowners south and east of the plant, who rented a house to the Crawfords.[117] Spenceley explained that while elevated levels of uranium were detected, everything was within safe limits.[118] This was technically true, but a little misleading, considering there was no regulatory standard for drinking uranium. The Knollmans, however, had no reason to doubt Spenceley. The family grazed their cattle on the plant's outskirts and NLO had tested their milk for decades without any unusual findings.[119] The only problem was that the Knollmans never bothered to inform the Crawfords.[120] Workers at Delta Steel were more fortunate. After receiving Spenceley's letter, the company switched its employees to bottled water.[121]

One month after the Trinity Day protest, NLO publicly admitted for the first time to a minor environmental problem at Fernald in a front-page story in the *Cincinnati Enquirer*.[122] Citing NLO documents, environmental beat reporter Ben Kaufman exposed elevated levels of radiation near two waste storage tanks on the west side of the plant, called the K-65 silos. Standing twenty-seven feet tall and eighty feet in diameter, the K-65 silos contained 9,500 tons of radioactive residues from pitchblende, a high-purity uranium ore mined in the Belgian Congo (later known as the Democratic Republic of the Congo, also Zaire) and processed at the Mallinckrodt Chemical Works in St. Louis for the Manhattan Project. These legacy wastes, which included uranium, radium, and thorium, had been stored at Fernald since the 1950s. Due to the economic value of radium-226 at the time, Belgium's Afrimet-Indussa Company retained ownership of the K-65 wastes in hopes of one day extracting the material for resale.[123] In an unusual case of atomic diplomacy, the US assumed ownership of the K-65 wastes in 1983 as part of a deal to deploy Pershing II missiles in Belgium.[124]

Spenceley again reassured the public, saying, "We do not have any concern about the integrity of these two tanks."[125] The radioactivity, according to him, was more likely surface contamination from operations—a routine part of uranium processing. The public could trust NLO to "blow the whistle on ourselves," because the company self-regulated by the strictest standards available.[126] Behind closed doors, however, NLO was concerned about the tanks. As early as 1963, the silos showed significant signs of deterioration, so it was decided to construct earthen embankments around the tanks to stabilize the pressure coming from the internal contents.[127] Even assistant plant manager Weldon Adams, a skeptic of the hazards of low-level radiation, acknowledged that the K-65 silos posed a real danger and contained "the nastiest" material on-site. After agreeing to permanently retain the K-65 wastes, NLO "protested the decision to the Department of Energy," but "they just simply ignored us."[128] With no plans to properly dispose of the K-65 wastes, the DOE decided that Fernald's backyard would remain its dumping grounds.

By framing nuclear weapons as a local issue, the peace movement had successfully spread awareness about possible contamination at Fernald from greater Cincinnati's urban and university-centered peace movement to Fernald's neighbors. In September 1983, residents of the Branch Hill Mobile Home Park, located a half-mile from the plant, requested an investigation of their water. Resident Maggie Merritt captured the community's distrust of government, telling a reporter, "The EPA says our ground water is safe, but if there is a problem, no one's going to tell the citizenry. They'll try to downplay it."[129] Located predominantly in rural America, economically struggling nuclear communities around the country felt increasingly victimized by government bureaucrats in the DOE.[130] A uranium leak would soon validate Merritt's worst fears and inspire a community-based environmental movement against Fernald that would finally hold the DOE accountable for the radioactive waste.[131] Its success, however, would require a fresh perspective on environmentalism's relationship to working people.

THREE FRESH Activism

On December 11, 1984, *Cincinnati Enquirer* reporter Ben Kaufman broke a front-page story that "unacceptably large amounts of uranium dust may have escaped from National Lead of Ohio (NLO)'s Fernald uranium processing plant in northwest Hamilton County." It was a shocking revelation for the community, which had read very little about the plant since its construction in the early 1950s. Department of Energy (DOE) and NLO representatives immediately downplayed the event and even manufactured doubt over the leak's existence. "If it really happened," said NLO spokesman George Smith, "the uranium slipped by a flawed filter and pressure monitor in a work area exhaust system for three months.... But it may not have happened," because "monitoring data are contradictory." "They're mystified," the DOE's Jim Alexander chimed in from Oak Ridge, Tennessee. "They keep scratching their heads and saying, 'Guys, *is* this a problem? We don't know." Either way, Smith and Alexander reassured the public that the uranium posed "no immediate risk" to the community.[1] Despite these statements, the DOE was in a panic behind closed doors.

To mitigate the damage, DOE officials in Oak Ridge—who oversaw Fernald's operations—dispatched investigators to Ohio to study the uranium leak and hold a community meeting. It was a public relations strategy that had recently helped smooth things over in Oak Ridge after the DOE admitted to releasing two million pounds of mercury from its Y-12 electromagnetic uranium separation plant into the environment.[2] The DOE was hopeful for a similar outcome at Fernald.

On December 12, the DOE upgraded the likelihood of the leak to "a probability" but again informed the public that Fernald's uranium was not a threat to their health because the material was "only slightly more radioactive than that found in nature."[3] Just like public relations strategists in the chemical, lead, and tobacco industries, the DOE and its contractors were experts in minimizing the dangers of low-level radiation.[4] Instead of protecting profits, however, their primary aim was protecting nuclear weapons production.

The following day at 7:30 p.m., hundreds of Fernald's neighbors and plant workers crowded into the Crosby Elementary School gymnasium for the meeting.[5] In this tense moment, the fear and anger of nurse and mother Kathy Meyer collided with the arrogance and indifference of DOE representatives and NLO managers. While the DOE hoped to smooth over any controversy and keep producing uranium metals, Meyer worried over the health of her children. These opposing forces proved irreconcilable, and a community environmental movement was born.[6] Fernald Residents for Environmental Safety and Health (FRESH) transformed the DOE's relationship to Fernald's neighbors by holding the agency accountable for decades of shortsighted radioactive dumping.

Unlike the bipartisan 1970s, FRESH organized at a time when the federal government was particularly hostile toward environmentalism.[7] To complicate matters further, the latter was also waging a renewed nuclear arms race with the Soviet Union.[8] To navigate this growing partisanship and a rise in anticommunist rhetoric, FRESH designed its movement around the interests of working people. This politically moderate approach, which challenged the DOE on environmental health and safety but not the bomb's military value, attracted influential allies, including Ohio Senator John Glenn and Cincinnati-area Representative Tom Luken in Congress, Ohio Environmental Protection Agency (EPA) regulators, Governor Richard Celeste, and Attorney General Anthony Celebrezze Jr. from the state, and eventually, leadership in the Fernald Atomic Trades and Labor Council (FATLC). With the decimation of environmental leadership at the top of the federal government, the State of Ohio stepped in to fill the void on nuclear cleanup.

THE PLANT 9 DUST COLLECTOR

The uranium leak from the Plant 9 (Special Products Plant) dust collector was not a catastrophic event. It was more accurately a series of failures involving outdated equipment, inadequate inspections and oversight, and communication breakdowns, as well as, most importantly, the prioritization of nuclear weapons production over environmental health and safety at Fernald. The polarized perceptions of environmental risk between NLO management and the community created a public relations disaster that snowballed from greater Cincinnati into a national conversation on nuclear cleanup across the DOE's production complex.

It all started on September 4, when the dust collector was serviced. Technicians replaced forty-five filtration bags and repaired a ring blower on the machine, which was originally installed in the 1960s. The aging dust collector, which captured uranium particulates from the remelt furnaces and returned the material back into the production process, significantly lowered radiation exposure for workers. On average, it removed ninety-seven pounds of uranium from the air per day and, when serviced properly, could function as high as 99.8–99.9 percent efficiency.[9] Two decades into its lifespan, however, it was starting to show its age.

On October 10, NLO workers first observed a problem. During the monthly inspection of the stack sampler, which measures emissions from the baghouse up a sixty-foot stack, workers detected a small quantity of uranium. This discovery suggested that uranium was escaping the filtration system. No action was taken. On November 5, production increased in Plant 9 from a twenty-four-hour, five-days-per-week schedule to a round-the-clock, seven-days-per-week operation. During this boom, the differential pressure gauge was running high, which indicated that the filtration bags were now saturated with uranium. A maintenance team discovered torn rubber seals, which prevented the reverse air flow system from functioning properly. The following day, the Industrial Hygiene and Radiation (IH&R) department reinspected the stack sampler and found its filter contaminated. On November 9, millwrights were sent to work in the baghouse to perform dangerous repairs in its cramped and contaminated interior. To reduce radiation exposures, they wore respirators and were permitted to work in this space for only a few minutes at a time. By November 12, the maintenance team had replaced the damaged components and production resumed.[10]

Four days later, IH&R workers inspected the stack filter and found it caked with uranium. Their analysis determined that between September 11 and November 16, about eighty-four pounds of uranium escaped the stack, which was reported to Plant 9 leadership. The following day, an inspection of the baghouse revealed no issues, so operations continued as usual. On November 19, a Geiger counter connected to the stack system sounded its alarm. IH&R workers analyzed another filter and measured a loss of about fifty-four pounds of uranium into the environment during the previous three days. An inspection revealed no observable damage in the baghouse, so instead of digging deeper into the uranium leak's origins, the Geiger counter's sensitivity was decreased to prevent it from sounding again.[11] Alarms, after all, were a nuisance to production.

On November 26, the uranium losses continued, later determined to be about forty-nine pounds. Instrumentation also signaled that uranium was actively escaping, but during a visual inspection of the baghouse from the access door, no obvious problems were recognized. Production continued as usual. At 6:30 a.m. the following day, a fire broke out in the vacuum generator of the dust collection system. IH&R workers later determined that about twenty-eight pounds of uranium were lost over the previous two days. Even though the vacuum generator was inoperable and the ability to monitor emissions was down, production continued in Plant 9. At 6:00 p.m. on November 29, the workers—who were not wearing respirators—repairing the vacuum were exposed to a burst of four pounds of uranium oxide trapped in the system. On December 7, which was coincidentally Pearl Harbor Day, the department superintendent finally made the decision to shut down operations. During this three-month period, about 273 pounds of uranium had escaped the Plant 9 dust collector into the environment.[12]

After learning of the continuous uranium leaks, Fernald's plant manager, Robert Spenceley, called and left a message for Oak Ridge's technical representative, Malcolm Theisen, who was, unfortunately, out of the office that day. Spenceley and the assistant plant manager, Weldon

FIGURE 6. The failed Plant 9 (Special Products Plant) dust collector, December 7, 1984. Courtesy of the US Department of Energy.

Adams, were frustrated it had taken so long to hear about this enduring problem, but they also believed that the uranium posed no risk to workers, the public, or the environment. December 7 also happened to be NLO's holiday party, so Spenceley and Adams left to prepare for the festivities. The IH&R department's Bob Weidner was perhaps the last manager at the plant when he received a call from Oak Ridge. At the party, Spenceley and Adams were only able to relax for about twenty minutes before Weidner frantically informed them that "all hell has broken loose at Oak Ridge over the Plant 9 dust collector release."[13] For the former superintendent of Fernald's chemical plants, Don Dunaway, the uranium leak "turned out to be sort of the Pearl Harbor for Fernald." "Although it was a much bigger picture," Dunaway recalled, "than what any of us realized at the time."[14] For the DOE, it was also "a date which will live in infamy," because production at Fernald and the rest of the nuclear weapons complex would never be the same.[15]

The federal environmental laws of the 1970s transformed how most government agencies conducted their business. After President Richard Nixon signed the National Environmental Policy Act into law in 1970, all federal or federally funded projects were required to consider the environment before breaking ground. The Army Corps of Engineers, for example, was suddenly accountable to environmental organizations, which served as watchdogs over the agency's Environmental Impact Statements for development projects.[16] Things worked differently for the DOE. The Atomic Energy Act, which concealed restricted data on nuclear weapons production for national security purposes, provided a veil of secrecy that delayed the influence of the environmental regulatory state on the DOE's nuclear weapons program.[17] This regulatory monopoly started to crumble toward the end of the decade, however. In 1978, President Carter first granted the EPA authority to conduct special investigations into nuclear weapons production facilities.[18] After the discovery of mercury releases at Oak Ridge, the Natural Resources Defense Council and the Legal Environmental Assistance Foundation (LEAF) sued the DOE over the contamination. On April 13, 1984, Judge Robert Taylor ruled that the DOE's mercury releases violated the Resource Conservation and Recovery Act (RCRA). *LEAF v. Hodel* established a precedent that the DOE was accountable to federal environmental laws, which directly influenced how Oak Ridge approached Fernald's uranium leak later that year.[19] In compliance with the Comprehensive Environmental Response, Compensation, and Liability Act (CERCLA), better known as Superfund, Oak Ridge reported the uranium leak to the National Response Center, the Ohio EPA, the Ohio Department of Health (ODH), and the Ohio Disaster Services Agency, and it even tasked NLO with drafting a press release to inform the public.[20] The only problem was that the press release was much more confusing than informative.

NLO's top managers, Spenceley and Adams, viewed the uranium leak much differently than did DOE leadership at Oak Ridge. Spenceley started his career during Fernald's construction in 1951 as a technical assistant, and Adams was hired two years later as an instrument engineer.[21] Adams recalled telling his father, who worked at Champion Paper in nearby Hamilton, that Fernald "is the cleanest, safest plant I've ever been in."[22] Since Fernald's uranium emissions were substantially higher in the 1950s and 1960s, Spenceley and Adams both viewed its environmental record as a story of progress.[23] These attitudes, which were also shared by the IH&R team, had fallen out of step with the times. In Oak Ridge's investigation report into the uranium leak, the DOE criticized NLO leadership as "conditioned to tolerating large size releases because of the operational experiences of earlier years (1955–1972) when routine and upset losses were much higher than recent years."[24] Further, although NLO had experienced industrial hygienists protecting workspaces, it had no qualified health physicist dedicated to the environment.[25] Beyond Fernald's walls, universities were churning out the next generation of environmental problem-solvers to fill the EPA and other regulatory agencies.[26] While the Atomic Energy Commission (AEC) was a leader in environmental science during the 1950s, the closed system of nuclear weapons production prevented the agency from maintaining that status. By resisting external oversight, environmental compliance, and the rise of ecological ideas throughout the Cold War, the DOE was better known as a secretive and shortsighted polluter than a scientific innovator by the 1980s.[27]

NLO had rarely engaged surrounding communities, because the DOE had long maintained that its radioactive wastes were nobody else's business.[28] After Fernald's uranium leak, however, this arrangement was no longer possible. The first face-to-face meeting between NLO management, DOE representatives, and Fernald's neighbors was held on December 13, 1984, in the Crosby Elementary School gymnasium. The meeting's location only fueled the anxiety. Parents in the audience were acutely aware that the plant spewing uranium through its stacks was located only about a mile from where their children attended school.[29] In this highly stressful context, the DOE confessed to releasing about 275 pounds of uranium from Fernald.[30]

DOE biologist William Bibb and health physicist Billy Joe Davis traveled from Oak Ridge to Fernald to investigate the uranium leak and manage public relations. Bibb was familiar with this role. In the late 1960s and early 1970s, he was a "frequent pro-AEC speaker" who pushed back against its critics, including scientists calling for stricter radiation standards and citizens protesting the construction of nuclear power plants.[31] In Oak Ridge, a company town built for the Manhattan Project that largely supported the DOE, the community meeting helped calm the public's nerves over the mercury releases. In the more populated and economically diverse Cincinnati region, however, the DOE held no special clout.[32] For three hours, Bibb and Davis were heckled while they spoke to the audience. Local businessman Elmer Reide mocked NLO's monitoring program for allowing the release to continue for several months. Debbie Martins, an expectant mother, revealed that the EPA told her that her water supply was contaminated but still somehow safe to drink.[33] Martins blamed NLO and the DOE's negligence for putting her unborn child at risk. Martins's question was just one of many about public health.

But NLO and the DOE offered no answers. In part, they were silent because Oak Ridge's investigation into the uranium leak would not be complete for another two months.[34] There was also the scientific ambiguity surrounding exposures to low-level radiation, which permitted the DOE to speak in probabilities about safety, but never with certainty.[35] While these points were both true, what went unspoken was the culture of secrecy that allowed the department to control the science of low-level radiation exposures for decades. This was the primary reason that Americans in the 1980s did not know the effects of nuclear weapons testing in Nevada, for example, which spread 145 million curies of radioactive iodine to downwind communities.[36] For scientists intellectually and economically invested in the success of the DOE's nuclear programs, uncertainty was acceptable when the odds of immediate harm were negligible. Uncertainty was unacceptable, however, to angry mothers when it came to their children's long-term health. Kathy Meyer, a local nurse and mother of two, spoke on behalf of many parents that night when she said, "I am concerned for them and for their 230 classmates that are out playing every day just two blocks from Fernald."[37] Much to Meyer's surprise, the DOE put her on the spot after speaking and asked if she would be willing to serve as a liaison between Fernald and its neighbors. Meyer said yes, and with that split-second decision, she became a community activist.[38]

Spenceley and Adams were largely unmoved by the audience, not necessarily out of callousness—although they certainly appeared that way—but from decades of working closely with radioactivity. Sometimes too closely. On one occasion, Adams peered into a hopper, only to inhale a small explosion of uranium trioxide into his mouth, nose, and throat. Afterward, Adams remembered coughing up the radioactive and bright orange material while sitting out a week of work from the exposure. After literally breathing uranium into his body, Adams just could not understand the worry of people who lived a mile from the plant.[39] Managers also remembered the peak production levels of the early Cold War, which was an era when environmental controls were even less developed. Two or three hundred pounds of lost uranium was simply the cost of doing business. As Spenceley put it, uranium losses "had happened before and would happen again."[40] While the public had very little experience with radiation outside of frightening news stories or dental X-rays, radioactivity was a part of daily life for Fernald's workforce.[41]

Under attack, Spenceley and Adams maintained their composure. They knew it was false to accuse them of having no environmental monitoring. NLO had reported its emissions to regulatory agencies for decades, and the DOE possessed a sophisticated program in radiation safety.[42] Where NLO and the DOE erred most was in scoffing at the public's emotions, thinking them irrational, and downplaying the threats to public health and the environment that worried them.[43] Even at this early stage, the plant's emissions had irrefutably disrupted people's lives. In the audience, one local farmer described Fernald's uranium contaminating his water supply, including one well on his property that was shut down and another that now produced unpotable water. Brewster Rhodes, director of the Ohio Public Interest Campaign and consumer rights activist in the Zimmer movement, produced a document proving that Fernald was withholding information from the community. Through a Freedom of Information Act request, Rhodes secured the 1982 US Geological Survey report that documented uranium contamination in three local wells.[44] For the public, this confirmed their worst fears: the DOE had deadly secrets buried in its backyard. The time had come to uncover them.

A VICTORY FOR LABOR

The biggest winner of the first public meeting was union workers in the FATLC. Following the site visit by the National Institute for Occupational Safety and Health (NIOSH) in October, NLO and the DOE had delayed passing along health and safety reports requested by the agency.[45] With the heat turned up on the DOE in the Crosby Elementary School gymnasium, William Bibb assured Fernald's unions that NIOSH would be allowed to conduct its environmental health and safety investigations at the plant. According to Al O'Connor, president of District 34 of the International Association of Machinists and Aerospace Workers union, this agreement fulfilled four years of hard work against a hostile company.[46] "Exposure to this stuff—uranium and other chemicals used in the processing of uranium—is hurting people," O'Connor said. "Over the years," he continued, NLO "has convinced people that the plant is a safe place to work," but "threatened to close the plant if we raised hell."[47] Based on the latest epidemiological research, NIOSH's investigation could not come soon enough.

During the 1980s, scholars from the School of Public Health at the University of North Carolina, a member of Oak Ridge Associated Universities (ORAU), completed several important epidemiological investigations at nuclear weapons production facilities. Harvey Checkoway linked worker exposures to toxic chemicals and radiation at Oak Ridge's National Laboratory and Y-12 electromagnetic uranium separation plant to an increased risk for developing cancer.[48] Under the recommendation of Clarence Lushbaugh, chairman of the Medical and Health Sciences Division at ORAU, University of North Carolina (UNC) doctoral student Jerome Wilson—who later in his career helped found Howard University's department of epidemiology—conducted his study at Fernald. His 1983 dissertation, "An Epidemiologic Investigation of Non-Malignant Respiratory Disease among Workers at a Uranium Mill," determined that high levels of exposure to uranium dust in NLO's workforce put them at increased risk for developing nonfatal pulmonary diseases, including asthma, chronic bronchitis, emphysema, and pneumonia.[49] This vital information, which spoke directly to NLO workers' long-term health, was never shared with Fernald's unions.

Ironically, everyone knew about Wilson's study except the people getting sick. The UNC's research was funded by the DOE through ORAU, and Wilson thanked NLO managers and directors of health and safety Richard Heatherton and Mike Babcock for their "outstanding cooperation and support" in his acknowledgements.[50] NLO did not pass along Wilson's dissertation to the FATLC, claiming the findings were "preliminary." The unions, as a result, obtained their own copy through a university library.[51]

This internal brand of science—which did little for sick patients but was a powerful insulator for the DOE's nuclear weapons program—was not unique to Fernald. It was part of a much deeper history of human radiation experiments conducted without patient consent that ensured the United States could wage the Cold War. The first plutonium injection, for example, took place on April 10, 1945, and was given to an African American man named Ebb Cade, who worked as a cement mixer for an Oak Ridge construction company. Cade showed up at the Oak Ridge army hospital over two weeks earlier with serious fractures in his arm and leg from a car accident but was deemed otherwise to be in good health. Without his knowledge, the Manhattan Project medical division selected Cade to receive a plutonium injection and assigned him the number HP-12, which stood for "human product." Doctors injected Cade with 4.7 micrograms of the material, which they planned to monitor through blood samples, bone tissues, and bodily secretions over the following weeks. Cade also had fifteen teeth extracted and sampled for plutonium, but the experiment was never completed, because one day, Cade got up and left the hospital. He died of heart failure eight years later in Greensboro, North Carolina.[52]

Lushbaugh, who recommended Wilson's dissertation topic at Fernald, was also closely involved in the human radiation experiments. At Oak Ridge, he supervised a clinic, which secretly lined hotel-like rooms with radioactive cesium and cobalt to irradiate over two hundred patients who suffered from a variety of diseases, including leukemia, lymphoma, and arthritis.[53] Many historians—including the President's Advisory Committee on Human Radiation Experiments—have been careful to place these studies in their appropriate historical context, but that does not mean these physicians operated without their own political motives.[54] Lushbaugh expressed "cynical" views, according to historian Kate Brown, of epidemiological research on low-level radiation exposures in nuclear workers. In 1980, Lushbaugh confided to a colleague that these studies would produce "little 'useful' knowledge" and were only good, according to him, for reassuring the nuclear workforce, denying workers' compensation claims, and pushing back against "antinuclear propaganda."[55] Lushbaugh's comments, along with the withholding of Wilson's dissertation, demonstrate that nuclear medicine in the DOE had as much to do with social class as it did with science.[56]

Wilson's findings were extremely important for the FATLC. First, they countered the DOE's longtime downplaying of low-level radiation as a potential health hazard by exploring uranium as a complex material with both toxic and radioactive properties. Most importantly, Wilson's findings focused on the living. The few existing epidemiologic studies of chronic exposure to low-level radiation in the workplace all focused on mortality. Wilson hypothesized that an analysis of nonfatal disease—rather than death—would provide a more sensitive tool for measuring the cumulative effects of low-level radiation and industrial chemicals.[57] Much of the DOE's research agenda ignored the suffering of human bodies, and Wilson's dissertation pushed back on this trend by analyzing how chronic uranium inhalation could harm workers' quality of life before it was too late.[58]

Fernald's unions attracted the attention of Governor Richard Celeste, who supported their call for NIOSH's intervention. In a letter to Dr. J. Donald Millar at the Centers for Disease Control in Atlanta, Celeste argued that "there does not appear to be a clear, well-defined program for protecting the employees from hazards that exist in this facility."[59] As the *Cincinnati Post* observed, while "NLO does its own monitoring of its workers' health," Fernald's unions and now the state demanded external oversight.[60] This was an important break in tradition. Throughout the twentieth century, nuclear workers' bodies were treated as government property, which AEC and DOE leadership used to extract knowledge about radiation for military application and to justify the nuclear arms race.[61] Opening Fernald's doors to NIOSH regulators was the first step for workers to reclaim their bodies as their own.

Following the uranium leak, NLO reversed course on its public relations strategy. Instead of denying Fernald's dangers, assistant plant manager Adams claimed that the plant was so outdated and underfunded that NLO could not meet the Reagan administration's production demands for uranium metals or produce these materials in compliance with contemporary environmental regulations. To remediate the situation, the DOE would have to foot the bill for $284 million in upgrades. Faced with this criticism, the DOE was finished with NLO's cavalier managers. From their perspective, NLO botched the uranium controversy, failed to report to Oak Ridge in a timely fashion, and tolerated too much environmental contamination. In December, the DOE rescinded NLO's contract extension.[62] For the first time in Fernald's history, the plant would come under new management.

The DOE's criticism of NLO's leadership was fair, and Fernald's unions did not trust them either. At the end of the day, however, the DOE was responsible for oversight of its nuclear weapons production facilities, including their radioactive wastes. The DOE permitted Fernald to fall into disrepair before the renewal of the nuclear arms race.[63] In the late 1970s, NLO had requested dust filtration and other environmental improvements at Fernald, which the DOE denied because it felt that investments in environmental health and safety were not worth the money.[64] NLO's managers were lax on uranium releases, but the DOE's hands-off managerial system was its own design. Since the Manhattan Project, the DOE and its predecessor agencies relied heavily on corporate contractors to operate its facilities, which only increased with time. In the 1960s, for every federal employee in the nuclear weapons complex, there were twenty-five corporate or university contractors. During the Carter and Reagan administrations, caps on federal hiring made oversight even harder. At its worst, according to historian Rodney P. Carlisle, this strain encouraged collusion between DOE field office staff and operating contractors.[65] At

Fernald specifically, the DOE removed its last on-site supervisor in 1973.⁶⁶ The collapse of environmental health and safety in the nuclear weapons complex was a top-down failure.

But somebody needed to take the fall at Fernald, and NLO's biggest failing was its inexperience with public relations. The DOE understood that environmental activism threatened nuclear weapons production and needed to be addressed with tact. Never had a DOE facility been under such intense criticism from its closest neighbors, and with more than three decades of momentum behind the Cold War nuclear arms race, halting Fernald's operations was still unthinkable for the department.⁶⁷ Ohio's elected officials had also taken an activist stance toward Fernald's emerging environmental crisis. Representative Tom Luken, whom Kathy Meyer's husband Don knew from Democratic politics, called for a congressional investigation into the uranium leak. Attorney General Anthony Celebrezze Jr., announced the State of Ohio's lawsuit against the DOE over hazardous waste violations at Fernald.⁶⁸ By firing NLO, the DOE thought it could neutralize these attacks. That was before they met Lisa Crawford.

ORGANIZING FRESH

On Christmas Eve 1984, Lisa Crawford was baking cookies for the holiday when a reporter knocked on the door and asked for a comment about the uranium dust releases at Fernald, which was located directly across the street. Crawford turned the reporter away, because, at the time, she knew nothing about it.⁶⁹

Lisa and Ken Crawford had moved to Crosby Township from nearby Fairfield in December 1979 to get away from the busy suburb and raise their two-year-old son in the country. Ken's family went back several generations in the area, and the Crawfords wanted to build a house on some land they had recently purchased. As they planned their dream home, the Crawfords rented an old farmhouse from the Knollmans. It was a little run-down, but they enjoyed the garden and watching their son play in its spacious yard, which made it easier to ignore the giant eyesore that was Fernald. Lisa was a full-time secretary and volunteer coordinator at a psychiatric hospital in Cincinnati, and Ken worked for

General Motors in nearby Hamilton. Between work, raising a child, and building a house, there was little time for reading newspapers or watching television.[70] Somehow the chaos developing directly across the street had spared them. At least they thought so.

On January 9, 1985, the Crawfords' bucolic dreams were turned upside down. Just before rushing out the door for a doctor's appointment, Ken answered the telephone. It was the landlord, Byron Knollman, who called with shocking news. Knollman instructed Ken not to drink the water, because the well was contaminated. This information was going to be made public soon, and Knollman wanted to tell Ken personally. Ken hung up and immediately called Lisa at work. Lisa picked up their son from the babysitter and rushed home to call Knollman herself, but she could not get any more information out of him except that everything was supposedly within safe limits. By this time, the Crawfords had grown suspicious of their water supply after coming home to find a stranger sampling the well and hearing reports of water contamination in the area. To find out that it was happening to them personally, however, was terrifying. They agonized over every glass of water, every meal they had prepared, and every bath they had given their son in that house. Every memory was now contaminated with Fernald's uranium.[71]

In the weeks after the first public meeting at Crosby Elementary School, Kathy and Don Meyer worked to organize Fernald's surrounding communities. The first meeting of what became FRESH was held at the Venice Castle in Ross Township, a restaurant and bar that was a popular hangout for Fernald's workers.[72] As an attorney, Don used his legal expertise to draft a charter and focus the mission of the organization.[73] FRESH was formed with input from citizens and workers to balance the goals of jobs and a clean environment.[74] For these reasons, it distanced itself from the disarmament goals of the peace movement, which did not represent the conservative values of the community or the Fernald workers who made their living contributing to the nuclear deterrent.[75] Instead, FRESH focused on environmental health and safety, goals with obvious overlap to those of Fernald's labor unions.[76]

On January 11, FRESH organized a second public meeting with Representative Tom Luken, whose Energy and Commerce Committee spearheaded an investigation into the uranium leak. During the meeting, Luken disclosed the US Geological Survey's 1982 report on water contamination near Fernald.[77] As the rest of the room breathed a collective sigh of relief that their water was safe, the Crawfords sat in disbelief of how the federal government could "harm a child's life this way."[78] To NLO and the DOE, the contamination was data to be measured and repurposed to improve the production process. It was also too low to cause acute damage, so there was no reason for immediate alarm.[79] For the Crawfords, though, it was far more personal. They felt betrayed by their own government for endangering their child's health. Lisa's fear turned into rage, and for the first time in her life, she spoke in public. Lisa found her voice, and even during this chaotic and uncertain moment, it was a liberating experience. After the meeting, Kathy Meyer approached Lisa and recruited her to join FRESH.[80]

Lisa Crawford and Kathy Meyer had a lot in common. Both were angry mothers, which motivated Meyer to organize FRESH and Crawford to lead the organization to national significance. Mothers, as the traditional protectors of the home, assumed leadership roles in the environmental movement throughout the twentieth century. The language of motherhood helped these women crack open traditionally masculine domains of industry and government, including nuclear weapons.[81] On November 1, 1961, for example, Women Strike for Peace organized an estimated fifty thousand women to protest nuclear weapons testing—many motivated by the detection of strontium-90 in milk supplies and baby teeth—which helped pressure the United States, the Soviet Union, and Great Britain to sign the Limited Nuclear Test Ban Treaty in 1963. Their efforts curtailed a dangerous radioactive threat to the atmosphere and vulnerable human bodies.[82]

Two decades later, Lois Gibbs and the Love Canal Homeowners Association launched an environmental movement in Niagara Falls, New York, to clean up Hooker Chemical's toxic waste that contaminated the community school and to relocate residents to safety. Like Crawford and Meyer, Gibbs was politicized by her child's exposure, and through tireless activism and self-education on complex hazardous waste issues, set an example that ordinary women could be a force in environmental politics. While Love Canal is best remembered for pushing Congress to pass the Superfund law in 1980, its influence on grassroots activism was far greater.[83]

THE NIMBY "SYNDROME"

After the toxic dust settled at Love Canal, Gibbs moved to Arlington, Virginia, and launched the Citizens Clearinghouse for Hazardous Waste (CCHW) in 1981. Through the CCHW, Gibbs developed what Love Canal residents had needed: a toolbox for communities dealing with the horrors of toxic waste, including organizing tips, legal advice, networking opportunities, and technical assistance. Its newsletter, *Everyone's Backyard*, captured the collective thinking of Gibbs and the CCHW's thousands of subscribers, who relished the opportunity to connect with the broader antitoxics movement.[84] The organization was wildly successful. By the end of the decade, the CCHW was serving five thousand local groups across the country.[85] FRESH followed in Love Canal's footsteps, carrying the banner for locally focused but nationally connected grassroots environmental activism to the DOE's nuclear weapons production complex.[86]

Despite the development of national networks, grassroots environmentalism during the 1980s was still an isolating experience. In the aftermath of Love Canal, local antitoxics groups were fiercely criticized by government and industry for spawning a national NIMBY, or not-in-my-backyard, "syndrome."[87] The NIMBY syndrome's symptoms, according to critics, were grassroots activists who stalled the siting of nuclear power plants, waste disposal facilities, or chemical incinerators, which harmed economic development. These facilities were essential, in their view, so NIMBYs were selfish for forcing their placement elsewhere.[88]

Grassroots environmentalists saw it differently. As Lois Gibbs argued, activists saying "we don't want this in our backyard" also meant "we don't want this in anybody's backyard."[89] This was Gibbs's motivation for starting the CCHW in the first place. FRESH also defied popular NIMBY criticism. Since its inception, it was sensitive to the interests of organized labor and Fernald's important role in the community as an employer and source of pride. Despite their inexperience, Fernald's community activists avoided one of the easiest pitfalls of the environmental movement: ignoring the blue-collar workers who made their living from developing the environment.[90] A closer analysis of grassroots environmental activism in the 1980s reveals that the most harmful symptoms of the NIMBY "syndrome" surfaced not in the activists themselves but in the people hostile toward the environmental movement.

In FRESH's early days, Lisa Crawford was out running errands when she pulled over to buy her son a Popsicle from the corner store. After paying and walking out, an NLO employee stopped her and asked, "You're Lisa Crawford, aren't ya?" "Yeah," she replied. "You need to go home and be pregnant and barefoot," the man said, and "keep your mouth shut."[91] Crawford successfully defused this situation, but it was the first time she was harassed for joining FRESH. It was also the least of her troubles. The Crawford family's activism led to feelings of betrayal and abandonment by former friends who gossiped behind their backs and suddenly treated them as outsiders.[92] At its worst, Crawford received several threatening voicemails at home and was even followed by a strange vehicle.[93] In later years, FRESH's critics complained that activists stirred up trouble for attention and financial gain, but realistically, they paid dearly by sacrificing their privacy and personal lives for an environmental movement that they believed in.[94] It was their critics who acted selfishly.

THE COMMUNITY LAWSUIT

Lisa and Ken Crawford were emotionally exhausted, and worst of all, they were being completely ignored by NLO and the DOE. These relationships were so hostile that on one occasion Lisa came home to find an NLO employee testing her well again, but when she approached him with questions, he refused to even speak to her.[95] At work, Ken occasionally had to find a quiet space in the plant to cry.[96] One day, Ken asked his GM coworker Marvin Clawson what he would do in his situation, to which Clawson replied, "Hunt me up the best lawyer I knew how and sue them up to high heaven."[97] Neither Ken or Marvin knew how to hire a lawyer, so Ken checked out a book on accessing legal services from the library. It turned out that one of Lisa's coworkers went to school with a lawyer named Stanley Chesley, so Lisa gave his office a call. They had nothing to lose.[98]

Of all the lawyers practicing in greater Cincinnati, it was a stroke of good fortune to find a personal connection to Stanley Chesley, who earned the nicknames "Master of Disaster" and "Prince of Torts" for his ability to settle mass tort lawsuits during his career, including $206 billion from big tobacco, $3.2 billion for silicone breast implants, and $200 million from the chemical companies that produced Agent Orange.[99] In the late 1970s, Chesley caught his break after securing $49 million for his clients in the Beverly Hills Supper Club fire in Southgate, Kentucky, which killed 165 people and injured 116. At the time, nobody wanted to touch the case, but Chesley's ambitions transformed mass tort litigation by suing not only the club owners but entire industries related to the fire, including wiring, paneling, and upholstery manufacturers. This legal strategy, called "enterprise liability," led to improved building codes and product liability laws.[100]

In December 1984, Chesley was called to negotiate a settlement for the victims of the worst industrial accident in history. On December 2, forty-two tons of methyl isocyanate—a poisonous gas—had leaked from a Union Carbide pesticide plant in Bhopal, India, which killed almost four thousand people and littered the city with dead animals and wilted vegetation.[101] The following month, Chesley met with the Crawfords and agreed to take on their case. He warned them, however, that the coming media storm would change their lives forever.[102]

On January 23, 1985, the Crawford family and two neighbors, Michael Deitriech and Edgar Lee Roe, filed a $300 million class-action lawsuit against NLO for property damages and emotional trauma caused by uranium contamination.[103] This original lawsuit later expanded to represent fourteen thousand residents who lived within a five-mile radius of the plant.[104] Chesley argued that the "uranium leak" was more accurately a "hemorrhage," and likely just the "tip of the iceberg" of decades of NLO contaminating the soil and aquifer. To identify the extent of the contamination, the possible health effects on the community, and the emotional trauma, Chesley was going to "open the whole plant to public scrutiny" in federal court. The law was the most powerful tool available, according to him, for environmental justice.[105]

During the early 1980s, grassroots environmentalists increasingly took corporate polluters to court. After Love Canal and Superfund, the movement secured a stronger mechanism for securing accountability from industry for its toxic waste. In Woburn, Massachusetts, for example, activists in For a Cleaner Environment conducted epidemiological research with public health professionals on a childhood leukemia cluster in their community. In May 1982, after the EPA identified two plumes of contamination, eight families of leukemia victims sued W. R. Grace and Beatrice Foods for the improper disposal of industrial solvents, including trichloroethylene (TCE) and tetrachloroethylene (PCE), which contaminated drinking water in the community and sickened its residents.[106] Such cases raised important questions about who is responsible for hazardous wastes, but they often left a haze of mixed results, including conflicting emotions and community exhaustion in their wake.[107] In the case of Fernald, FRESH also faced the additional challenge of suing a longtime government contractor. It was essential, as a result, to recruit some respected political allies.

OHIO'S ENVIRONMENTAL ALLIANCE

Shortly after the second public meeting, Lisa Crawford reached out to the Ohio EPA and the ODH for advice. Within twenty-four hours, both agencies came to the Crawfords' home and tested their well. Graham Mitchell at the Ohio EPA advised Lisa and Ken to seek an alternative source of drinking water. On the other hand, the ODH, the lead agency on the water contamination study, assured them the water was safe to drink.[108] At the time, the science on uranium's toxicity in drinking water was uncertain, and no regulatory standards had been developed. By exercising caution, Mitchell demonstrated that the Ohio EPA prioritized the Crawfords' health, no matter how low the risk. By reassuring the Crawfords of the water's safety in the context of scientific uncertainty, the ODH revealed that corporate and economic interests were more important. The Crawfords chose to believe the Ohio EPA. After the DOE "sloughed us off like we were dirt," it was validating for Lisa and Ken to find a government agency they could trust.[109]

By this time, the Ohio EPA was already hot on Fernald's trail. In March 1984, regulators Donald S. Marshall and David Duell conducted an inspection of the plant in search of RCRA violations. Fernald's drum storage, which Marshall and Duell described as "in very poor condition," encapsulated the problem of the DOE's self-regulation and the unfinished business of regulating radioactive materials at nuclear weapons production facilities. Without independent oversight, many of the drums were corroded, lids were poorly secured, and some were even actively leaking. The drums were also haphazardly stacked, which made it impossible for workers to safely conduct inspections or respond to accidents with the proper equipment. NLO had not maintained an operating record of its hazardous wastes, so essential information, including the types and quantities of each hazardous waste treated, stored, or disposed of at Fernald, went undocumented.[110] For Ohio EPA regulators, it was like a reoccurring dream. This was the kind of waste disposal program—or lack thereof—that had manufactured America's toxic waste crisis at places like Love Canal and pressured Congress into passing Superfund. It also added to the growing body of evidence that the DOE prioritized producing nuclear weapons over protecting Ohio's citizens and the environment.

In early 1985, FRESH reached out to Senator Glenn, who was fresh off a disappointing 1984 presidential bid, which was so poorly managed, it derailed his once promising career. This experience left Glenn, a morally rigid and highly ambitious person, frustrated with the corporate fundraising and gamesmanship that dominated American politics. FRESH's cause reinspired Glenn. In them he found an opportunity to serve "ordinary citizens," which despite his celebrity status as a former Project Mercury astronaut during the Cold War, recalled his humble upbringing surrounded by the farmlands of New Concord, Ohio.[111] As Glenn wrote in his memoir, "A group of citizens from Fernald, Ohio, northwest of Cincinnati, came to my office to spell out their concerns about high cancer rates around the nuclear weapons plant there. . . . I suspected the claims were overblown, but when I went to Fernald [in 1985] with some committee staff members, we quickly found the group's concerns were justified." According to Glenn, "From those relatively small beginnings emerged a shocking picture of the entire network of nuclear weapons production."[112]

FRESH's carefully crafted image as a labor-friendly environmental organization of concerned mothers paid off in securing Glenn's help. As Lisa Crawford recalled, FRESH realized that if the group stormed into Glenn's office shouting "Ban the bomb!" that they would not get anywhere.[113] This was a shrewd analysis, as Glenn had supported the creation of nuclear weapons jobs in Ohio throughout his career. As early as 1977, he wrote President Carter to remind him of his campaign promise to bring centrifuge technology for uranium enrichment to Ohio's Portsmouth Gaseous Diffusion Plant in Piketon, which was estimated to bring six thousand jobs to the community for construction alone.[114] In the late 1980s, Glenn even lobbied for President Reagan's Strategic Defense Initiative, or "Star Wars" nuclear defense program—which was mocked by peace activists—to come to Piketon after the DOE partially vacated the plant in 1985 after abandoning gas centrifuge enrichment technology.[115]

Despite his nuclear boosterism, Glenn also took environmental health and safety issues seriously. In 1979, union leaders at the Portsmouth Gaseous Diffusion Plant first alerted Glenn to their fears over radiation exposures, increased cancer rates, and environmental contamination. These concerns led the senator to call for a General Accounting Office investigation, hold congressional hearings, and introduce the Radiation Protection Management Act of 1979, his first legislation intended to protect nuclear workers, their communities, and the environment.[116] By the time FRESH contacted Glenn, the senator was ready to lead on the issue.

Glenn's first step was a site visit. On the front page of the March 2, 1985, edition of the *Cincinnati Enquirer*, a photograph showed Senator Glenn and Ohio Attorney General Anthony Celebrezze Jr. wearing white coats, hard hats, and safety goggles, being led on a tour of Fernald by the DOE's manager of operations at Oak Ridge, Joe LaGrone. Although the clean, white uniforms gave the impression of a sterile scientific laboratory, most outsiders' first impression of Fernald in the 1980s was that it looked like any stereotypical and dilapidated rust-belt factory, which were a dime a dozen across the Midwest.[117] After seeing the plant up close for the first time, FRESH's Kathy Meyer told reporters, "The overall impression leads one to believe it's a very old plant. When you combine that with the fact that they are dealing with a radioactive substance, it validates the fears of the community. We need this kind of help."[118]

Glenn held a press conference that day, offering a political road map forward for FRESH and the FATLC in coordination with their activism. His plan included legislation that would overturn the DOE's ability to self-regulate, the installation of air monitors outside the plant boundary to protect the community, ensuring that health researchers at NIOSH obtained access to worker exposure histories, and turning over health and safety issues from the DOE to the Department of Health and Human Services.[119] After Glenn's speech, one labor consultant stated, "Senator Glenn has grasped the problem exactly. It's a perfect starting point."[120] In a congressional hearing the following month, the testimony of FRESH and the FATLC; the political leadership of Senator Glenn, Representative Luken, and Anthony Celebrezze Jr.; and the oversight of the Ohio EPA realized a statewide movement to transform environmental health and safety at the DOE's nuclear weapons production facilities.

On April 22, 1985, the Subcommittee on Energy, Nuclear Proliferation, and Government Processes of the Senate Committee on Governmental Affairs gathered at Cincinnati City Hall for their first hearing on Fernald's poor environmental record. Senator Glenn, who convened the hearing, set the tone for the testimony ahead. "My goal today is a simple one," he said. "It is to identify those steps that must be taken to improve the safety and health protection of Fernald workers, the environment, and the residents of surrounding communities." After decades of production, it was time for workers and the public to learn the facts about radioactive contamination. "Workers and residents alike," Glenn stated, "have a right to know what risks they've been exposed to in the past, and they have the right to know what's being done to reduce the hazards in the future." Despite Fernald's essential Cold War mission, the DOE had no right to contaminate anyone's bodies or backyards. Not in Ohio or anywhere else. "Problems similar to those at Fernald have been reported at DOE facilities all across the country," Glenn added, "including Savannah River in South Carolina, Hanford in Washington, Rocky Flats in Colorado, and

Oak Ridge in Tennessee.... Hopefully, the testimony and evidence we receive at this and future hearings on Fernald will lead to solutions that can be applied to other facilities."[121]

FRESH's Kathy Meyer told the story of the 1984 uranium releases, including the terror experienced by parents at the first two public meetings, and the shameful display of apathy by the DOE and NLO toward the community. "We are aware," Meyer said, "that dust particles released into the atmosphere did not automatically stop at the fence line.... The crux of the problem continues to be that the Department of Energy, while producing the materials that endanger our health, sets its own standards for safe levels of air, water, and soil contamination and monitors its own performance. Unless the situation changes, we can never feel safe." Finally, Meyer challenged the DOE and NLO directly with some unscripted comments: "DOE and NLO stated in their testimony that they want to be 'a good neighbor.' A good neighbor does not take thirty years to meet its neighbors, nor thirty years and outside pressure to become concerned for their health and safety.... We will not stop until we in the community are safe."[122]

Gene Branham worked at Fernald for thirty-two years. Now president of the FATLC, he spoke on behalf of fifteen unions and 627 production, maintenance, and service workers. Through a laundry list of hazardous materials, Branham made it clear just how toxic Fernald was. "We fear," he began, "the largely unmonitored exposures that we have had and we continue to receive daily," including "uranium, plutonium, radium, technetium, and thorium," as well as "nonradioactive chemicals, including asbestos, TCE, PCBs, numerous acids, numerous fluorides, solvents, and heavy metals." Branham also took NLO to task for "management incompetency and collusion," arguing that "at no time [have] safety priorities exceeded [those] of production commitments," which created a dangerous work culture in which uranium metal output was valued over human life. Despite these shortcomings, Fernald's unions placed most of the blame on the DOE, which owned the plant, after all, and allowed it to deteriorate. Even worse, the DOE "monopolized the regulation of the facility" and "erected the wall of national security for management to hide behind," which eliminated contractor liabilities, maintained monopolistic control over health studies, and locked out external regulators.¹²³ The result was a system where the DOE was only accountable to itself, and workers suffered for it.

Attorney General Celebrezze addressed the state's complex legal challenges against the DOE. According to him, "one of our serious concerns is the determination of jurisdiction over mixed hazardous wastes," or wastes containing both chemicals and radioactive materials.¹²⁴ The state wanted to force the DOE into compliance with its environmental laws, which would require the federal government to obtain permits and file reports with the Ohio EPA, granting the state regulatory power over the federal government. More difficult was the regulation of radioactive emissions at Fernald, which according to the attorney general, was the worst offender in the country. After the federal EPA withdrew its proposed regulations for atmospheric radioactive emissions in 1984, a byproduct of the Reagan administration's deregulatory agenda, the State of Ohio joined the Natural Resources Defense Council, the Environmental Defense Fund, and the Sierra Club in petitioning for the appeal of the EPA's withdrawal in federal court. Celebrezze concluded his testimony by reassuring the Fernald community that the State of Ohio would pursue every legal avenue available to enforce compliance, stop the polluting, and clean up the site.¹²⁵

DOE'S TRANSFORMATION BEGINS

Fernald's uranium leak was a public relations disaster for the DOE, with national stories appearing in the *New York Times* and *Washington Post* in 1985.¹²⁶ In the *New York Times* article, the acting executive secretary of Cincinnati's AFL-CIO Labor Council, Dan Radford, accused NLO of operating under a "veil of secrecy" at Fernald.¹²⁷ Even worse, Fernald's environmental alliance was gaining steam with local activists in FRESH and the FATLC, Governor Celeste, and Attorney General Celebrezze, and aggressive representation in Congress through Senator Glenn and Representative Luken. The DOE took notice and responded both locally and nationally. At Fernald, NLO hired its first public information officer, William "Pete" Kelley, who after eleven years of working as a journalist and editor turned to public relations. Kelley's first actions were developing an on-site reading room, establishing a site newspaper with workers serving as journalists, informing reporters of accidents instead of concealing them, and reaching out to attend FRESH's meetings.[128] For the first time in its history, Fernald's "veil of secrecy" was at least partially opened to the outside world.

The word was out that production trumped safety at the DOE. Secretary of Energy John S. Herrington, as a result, forced the agency to do some soul searching. He requested that James Kane, the former deputy director of the Office of Energy Research, write a report on the DOE's environmental health and safety program. In spring 1985, Kane released his findings to DOE leadership, which revealed the collapse of the DOE's regulatory programs during the Reagan administration's nuclear arms buildup. According to Kane, "The current state of Environment, Health, and Safety is a disgrace." The program was widely perceived as powerless compared to production goals, and employee morale was low. Kane did not hold back, referring to DOE oversight as a "toothless watchdog guarding the safety and environmental integrity of one of the potentially most hazardous undertakings in the world."[129] Importantly, Kane also made two critical recommendations that guided the DOE's future. First, the agency needed to revitalize its environmental health and safety program. Second, it needed to begin planning and budgeting for an unprecedented task: cleaning up the nuclear weapons production complex.[130]

Fernald became a major priority for the DOE. This was apparent after Secretary Herrington established the position of assistant secretary for the newly established Office of Environment, Safety, and Health. Herrington ordered it to conduct baseline environmental surveys of the DOE's nuclear weapons production facilities, and Fernald was selected as first in line for the study. The DOE also promised to more than double its annual environmental health and safety budget, from $40 to $100 million.[131] Fernald received more than its fair share. In fiscal year 1986, the DOE dedicated $21.5 million to environmental health and safety improvements at the plant, which was a massive turnaround in funding.[132]

Fernald's environmental movement made it impossible for the DOE to hide from its radioactive legacy, an unresolved issue stretching back to the Manhattan Project. With the rise of grassroots environmental activism in the 1980s, national security was no longer an acceptable excuse for pollution, even in a rural township in Southwest Ohio. Secretary Herrington knew that the DOE had fallen behind the times. "What was acceptable in 1945," he acknowledged, "is not acceptable in 1985."[133] By opening the DOE's wallet, Herrington hoped to revitalize environmental health and safety at Fernald so the plant could get back to business producing uranium metals for the nuclear arms race. Fernald's unions had other ideas.

FOUR The Strike

At 12:01 a.m. on Saturday, October 5, 1985, Fernald's union workers walked off the job, shutting down production at the plant. The Fernald Atomic Trades and Labor Council (FATLC) had gathered the previous evening at the nearby Venice Pavilion, a popular hangout for Fernald workers, and voted 432 to 148 in favor of the strike. The vote was greeted with a roar of applause. After thirty-three failed negotiation sessions over the previous two months, it was clear that the FATLC had lost all trust in National Lead of Ohio (NLO). "The contract offer is terrible," said Fernald electrician John Neumann. "We're working with toxic chemicals, toxic waste, heavy metals, and high voltage, and they keep saying, 'Everything's okay, just wear your respirator.'"[1] This was going to be a strike over "health and safety issues," according to the *Cincinnati Enquirer*, and from the FATLC's perspective, the state of the environment at Fernald was far from okay.[2]

FATLC president Gene Branham had a lot to worry about. Under his leadership, hundreds of people were going to be out of work, and there was already a rush of them dipping into their savings at the company credit union to ride out the strike. There also had not been a labor demonstration at the plant since a wildcat strike in 1969, and union politics were getting ever more complicated in the Reagan era, as the leadership remained firmly Democratic while the rank and file were increasingly being courted by the Republican Party.[3] But Branham knew that the unions were presented with a unique opportunity.[4] Demand for Fernald's uranium metals was high for the Reagan administration's renewed nuclear arms race at the same time the Department of Energy (DOE) was under unprecedented scrutiny over the plant's uranium leak. NLO was also halfway out the door, with Westinghouse scheduled to take over as operating contractor on April 1, 1986.⁵ If the FATLC was ever going to make Fernald safer for blue-collar workers, that time was now.

Both union workers and Fernald Residents for Environmental Safety and Health (FRESH) viewed NLO's management as hostile to safety. Earlier that year, during a press tour of Fernald, assistant plant manager Weldon Adams picked up a small uranium derby and asked reporters rhetorically, "You don't think I would hold it like this in my bare hands if I thought it was dangerous, do you?"⁶ Such comments were not unusual for Adams, who was also accused by workers and community activists of stating that the only hazard posed by Fernald's uranium was if it fell on your head or your foot.⁷ Similarly, labor ascribed to NLO's director of health and safety, Mike Babcock, the outrageous statement that a person would have to eat a teaspoon of uranium daily for the substance to cause any harm.⁸ Even a DOE-led investigation criticized NLO management for leaving critical safety decisions, such as the appropriate jobs for wearing respirators, to individual workers, without providing adequate safety training.⁹ Inside Fernald's gates, production workers were largely on their own.

For these reasons, worker solidarity was necessary for survival. If environmental health and safety was going to be taken seriously at Fernald, the effort needed to come from the bottom up. On October 7, about five hundred union workers attended a "solidarity rally" at the Fernald plant to highlight the class divide between salaried managers and hourly union employees, which unjustly distributed resources as well as bodily hazards. While union workers performed the most dangerous jobs at the plant, salaried managers enjoyed superior pensions and medical benefits. Wearing signs that stated, "Fernald Atomic Trades and Labor Council ON STRIKE," the union strikers spread out across both entrances to the plant at 7:30 a.m. to make a statement to managers as they filed in for work at 8:00.¹⁰ For years, according to Branham, labor negotiations at Fernald were "a game" in which NLO had "the upper hand" and the unions had "no cards."¹¹ Fernald's environmental movement reshuffled the deck. The time had come for the DOE to take seriously the FATLC's demands, including reduced annual limits for radiation exposures, a strengthened environmental monitoring program, and granting workers a voice in developing safety guidelines.¹²

FIGURE 7. Fernald Atomic Trades and Labor Council picket line at the plant's south access road, October 22, 1985.

The FATLC was not alone in its struggle. After Lisa Crawford filed the community lawsuit against NLO, some workers felt bitter toward FRESH for threatening their livelihoods. Crawford hoped to mend those relationships. One evening, after working overtime at the psychiatric hospital, Crawford brought the strikers White Castle hamburgers and coffee to show FRESH's support. The gesture earned Crawford a meeting with union leadership, and she pitched the obvious connection between the groups: both fought for environmental health and safety at Fernald, the FATLC on the inside and FRESH on the outside. They should be working together instead of against each other. The coffee-and-hamburger diplomacy proved successful. FRESH and the FATLC reached an understanding that would help green the landscape of nuclear weapons production.[13]

Local members of the Sierra Club joined the FATLC on the picket line, signaling the national environmental movement's growing interest in Fernald. The Sierra Club and the FATLC both supported Senator John Glenn and Representative Tom Luken's proposed Mixed Hazardous Waste Amendment Act of 1985, which would transfer jurisdiction on mixed radioactive and chemical wastes from the DOE to the Environmental Protection Agency (EPA).[14] A coalition of public interest and environmental organizations, including the Government Accountability Project (GAP), the Natural Resources Defense Council, FRESH, the Ohio Public Interest Campaign, the Environmental Policy Institute, the Sierra Club's local Miami Group, and the Sierra Club Radioactive Waste Campaign also called for the federal government to complete an Environmental Impact Statement for proposed upgrades at Fernald. Tom Carpenter, now with GAP, had returned to work on Fernald with his newfound legal expertise. Carpenter proclaimed that "an environmental impact statement is needed to at least slow down the government's headlong rush to increase production at a plant that already has its share of environmental concerns."[15] With a powerful environmental alliance rallying around it, the FATLC headed to the bargaining table.

Despite an increased national interest in nuclear weapons production, NLO preferred to bury its head in the sand. The FATLC had sent a letter to NLO informing it that the FATLC was bringing industrial hygienists from the AFL-CIO to the labor negotiations so that matters of environmental health and safety could "be discussed in depth." NLO ignored Branham's warning, which forced federal mediator Lou Manchise to call a three-day recess that left NLO scrambling for its own experts. According to FATLC president Gene Branham, NLO "had not anticipated us having that kind of resources and that kind of expert people within organized labor. . . . It was a weakness of National Lead" and "probably the turning point of workers' protection of safety and health."[16] In a historic victory for nuclear weapons production workers, the negotiations led to the establishment of a joint safety board with union representation—a longtime goal of unions at DOE sites—and the individual right to refuse working in a hazardous environment if an employee believed it was dangerous to his or her health.[17]

On October 23, workers were back at the Venice Pavilion, surrounded by the celebratory echoes of clinking beer glasses and billiard balls cracking across pool tables. Along with unprecedented rights to environmental health and safety, the unions secured increased medical coverage, wage increases, and the transfer of Mike Babcock—who Branham referred to as the "Eichman [sic] of the nuclear industry"—from his position as director of health and safety into a new role.[18] In a 363–146 vote, Fernald's union workers elected to accept NLO's contract and return to work.[19] It was a courageous victory, particularly during the union-busting Reagan years, which was highlighted by the breaking of the Professional Air Traffic Controllers Organization strike. This was part of a broader campaign by conservatives in government and industry to double down on their efforts to drive a wedge between blue-collar workers and environmental activists, arguing that Americans could choose between "jobs" or "the environment," but that they could never have both.[20]

For grassroots environmental activists during the 1980s, the cry of "not in my backyard" was rarely intended to be an exclusive term.[21] As Fernald's movement realized, the borders of a backyard were malleable and just as easily applied to the workplace. "If you raise health and safety standards inside the plant," said Fernald electrician John Heard, "it's going to help things outside, too."[22] The FATLC used its leverage in collective bargaining at a critical turning point in the nuclear arms race, when demand was high for uranium metals but the DOE also faced widespread criticism from a growing environmental movement. By making environmental health and safety the centerpiece of its collective bargaining agreement, the FATLC launched a new chapter of the nuclear arms race, which forced the DOE to manufacture nuclear weapons in collaboration with union workers. For Fernald's environmental movement, it was possible to have jobs *and* the environment.

MOUNTING PRESSURE IN WASHINGTON

The Reagan administration's antiregulatory politics, according to historian Ellen Griffith Spears, created "an unprecedented level of collaboration among environmental groups."[23] In 1981, national environmental organizations, including the National Audubon Society, the Sierra Club, the Izaak Walton League, the National Parks Conservation Association, the National Wildlife Federation, the Wilderness Society, the Environmental Defense Fund, the Environmental Policy Institute, Friends of the Earth, and the Natural Resources Defense Council banded together as "the Group of Ten." Leveraging their collective lobbying power, the Group of Ten dug in their heels to protect the legislative gains of the 1970s environmental movement.[24] While their defensive role was important, they also prepared for the future.

In 1985, the Group of Ten published *An Environmental Agenda for the Future*, which aimed to guide the environmental movement into the next millennium. "Many of today's problems," including human population growth, persistent toxic chemicals, and global warming caused by the burning of fossil fuels, "are global in scope and make local, regional, or even national solutions difficult," it warned. "Looming over all," the Group of Ten argued, "is the specter of nuclear war with its massive immediate death and destruction, which could be followed by the cold and dark of nuclear winter spreading climatic change throughout the world, destroying the life support systems, eliminating many species of plants and animals, and even threatening the survival of the human species."[25] At the height of the arms race, environmentalists viewed nuclear weapons—not fossil fuels—as the greatest threat facing humanity.

But the bomb's threat to our environment "is neither potential nor contingent," the Group of Ten claimed. "Its damage is being done today.... Nuclear Weapons production and testing activities," the report continued, "directly degrade the environment and continue to pose an immediate health and safety danger to employees and the general public through toxic and radioactive contamination of air, water, and food."[26] Just as the peace movement observed during the late 1970s and early 1980s, the Group of Ten recognized the arms race's dual hazards: its hypothetical, but no less planetary, risk to life on earth if used in war, and the localized "slow violence" of radioactive wastes seeping from the DOE's production plants into the environment and human bodies.[27] To solve this crisis, the Group of Ten recommended the transfer of oversight of environmental health and safety from the DOE to the National Institutes of Health, the

EPA, the Nuclear Regulatory Commission, and state governments.[28] In Congress, Senator Glenn was already working on this issue.

In April 1985, Senator Glenn requested an investigation by the General Accounting Office (GAO) into the DOE's environmental health and safety programs at three Ohio nuclear weapons production facilities: Fernald, the Portsmouth Gaseous Diffusion Plant in Piketon, and Mound Laboratory in Miamisburg. Later that year, the GAO released *Environment and Workers Could Be Better Protected at Ohio Defense Plants*, a report based on extensive interviews with DOE, EPA, Ohio EPA, Ohio Department of Health, and Ohio Attorney General's Office representatives, along with contractors, union leadership, consultants, and local officials. During the GAO's investigation, the reliability of contractors' environmental reporting came into question. "While contractor data show that the contamination is within DOE's limits," the GAO wrote, "various DOE and consultant studies, as well as both Ohio and U.S. Environmental Protection Agency officials, have questioned the reliability of the contractors' data."[29] In the coming years, the DOE's poor records management and deceptive practices were formidable obstacles in assessing the true human and environmental costs of the nuclear arms race.[30]

The GAO determined that Fernald's nonradioactive releases were generally within state limits for the previous five years, but the plant, which stored approximately five hundred thousand metric tons of radioactive contaminated waste, was out of compliance with state hazardous waste laws. Even worse, Fernald released the highest atmospheric doses of any nuclear weapons facility in 1984, on top of the second or third most from 1980 to 1983, despite processing some of the least radioactive material in the entire nuclear weapons complex. When calculated to the EPA's new standards for 1985, which were informed by the International Commission on Radiation Protection, the uranium emitted from Fernald could cause a dose of radiation to the lungs fifteen to twenty times higher than previously anticipated.[31]

The report's most significant conclusion was that self-regulation had failed. Although Fernald implemented an environmental monitoring program, Oak Ridge determined that the plant's sampling equipment "had deteriorated and that data collected by the equipment was not reliable."³² Despite Fernald's problems in environmental health and safety, the DOE still awarded NLO bonuses for meeting its production goals.³³ This cost-plus-award-fee contractual system was one of the FATLC's biggest critiques of plant management.³⁴ "Under such contracts," the GAO wrote, "an award fee is paid when the contractor's performance meets criteria that the contractor and DOE agree to prior to each contract period." Only in the wake of Fernald's highly controversial uranium leak did Oak Ridge adopt the environment as an independent criterion for measuring NLO's performance. Until that time, production was king. NLO had always received "excellent ratings" as a result, and "had little incentive" to improve its environmental health and safety program.³⁵ To restore public trust in the plant, the GAO recommended that the DOE, the State of Ohio, and Fernald's contractor implement a system for independent verification of radiological data.³⁶ The report added to a growing chorus of voices, including FRESH, the FATLC, Senator Glenn, Representative Luken, and the State of Ohio, calling for external regulation of Fernald's radioactive backyard.

A NEW OPERATING CONTRACTOR

On January 1, 1986, the Westinghouse Materials Company of Ohio (WMCO), a subsidiary of the Westinghouse Corporation, replaced NLO as operating contractor of Fernald in a five-year, nine-month deal estimated at $1 billion.³⁷ Westinghouse was one of the most experienced corporations in the nuclear industry, beginning with its construction of the first large-scale commercial power reactor in the United States in Shippingport, Pennsylvania, during the 1950s.³⁸ Its bid came at the personal request of Secretary of Energy John S. Herrington. Beginning with Fernald, Herrington tapped Westinghouse to take over several aging nuclear weapons production plants in the late 1980s, including Hanford and Savannah River, to help resolve the environmental health and safety issues plaguing the complex. If the nuclear arms race was going to continue, the DOE needed to demonstrate that production could be done safely for workers, citizens, and the environment.³⁹

NLO's departure marked a significant shift in the management of Fernald. While NLO operated in a secretive and production-driven culture with little DOE oversight, Westinghouse would be closely scrutinized on its environmental impact.[40] The DOE and Westinghouse also had to learn to share authority with the FATLC's joint safety board together with the recently established Health and Environmental Advisory Committee, whose membership included representatives of FRESH and the Sierra Club, as well as doctors, educators, and business leaders. The committee created a forum in which residents and environmental activists could discuss controversial issues at Fernald, such as radiation safety, with engineers and scientists.[41] Shortly after its hiring, Westinghouse solicited in Cincinnati and Louisville newspapers for new hires to meet its staffing needs, including engineers, a writer-editor in Fernald's "growing Communications Department," and radiological monitoring technicians to "perform radiological surveys to determine, correct, and minimize releases to the environment and employee exposure."[42] The FATLC and FRESH welcomed these changes and expressed more confidence in Westinghouse's ability to manage the plant safely. More importantly, they were glad to be rid of NLO.[43]

As manager of plant operations, Westinghouse's Bill Britton was tasked with the daunting responsibility of revitalizing Fernald, but his experience had prepared him for the moment. In 1955, Britton accepted a position at the Bettis Atomic Power Laboratory in Pennsylvania, which developed nuclear propulsion systems for the US Navy.[44] At Bettis, Britton's unit reported directly to the founding father of the nuclear Navy, Admiral Hyman Rickover, who designed the pressurized water reactor that powered the USS *Nautilus*, the world's first nuclear-powered submarine, as well as the commercial nuclear reactor at Shippingport. Rickover was "hard-working, straight-shooting, demanding, and often abrasive," according to historian Serhii Plokhy, but his demand for excellence inspired generations of nuclear engineers, from President Jimmy Carter to Westinghouse's Bill Britton.[45] Working for Rickover, according to Britton, taught him "very strict discipline of operations."[46] It is fitting that in 1986, one DOE official compared modernizing Fernald to "taking a rusty old battleship and re-outfitting it."⁴⁷ By hiring Rickover disciples, Secretary Herrington was hoping to do just that, plus instill Navy-like discipline in nuclear weapons production workers.

Although the DOE hoped Westinghouse could be its savior, the company brought its own baggage to Fernald. Early on, Britton thought his employer's "arrogance" from its extensive portfolio in the nuclear industry got in the way of building a productive working relationship with FRESH.⁴⁸ Britton's assessment was correct. Lisa Crawford and FRESH were highly skeptical of Westinghouse's intentions and did not take its public relations staff seriously.⁴⁹ Britton recognized that Westinghouse could be its own stumbling block, and he used a famous cartoon to remind himself of that. In a well-known comic designed by Walt Kelly, Pogo the Possum looks upon a landscape littered with cans, bottles, and trash and tells the reader, "We have met the enemy, and he is us."⁵⁰ Ironically, the operations manager of Fernald—at the time, a national symbol for environmental negligence—pinned one of Earth Day 1970's most widely circulated symbols to the wall of his office as a reminder to be a good neighbor.⁵¹

Luckily for Fernald's workers, there was little turnover after Westinghouse's hiring. Many grew discouraged, however, with all the critical and at times sensational publicity that cast Fernald in a negative light.⁵² Lucy Rathgens's forty-year career at the plant helps illustrate this point. After going to college in midlife, she transitioned from secretarial and accounting work to become the first female shift supervisor in the production department, a historically masculine domain. Rathgens felt "maybe even bitter" when employees were suddenly portrayed as "bad people" for doing what they genuinely believed to be a patriotic service to their country.⁵³ She had worked hard to earn a living and had broken gender barriers to make Fernald more equitable. The constant barrage in the media was hurtful.

The criticism did not let up. Less than three weeks into Westinghouse's management, another accident rattled the community. On January 19, two chemical operators noticed a smoky substance flowing out of the ventilation system and into the Pilot Plant, which the DOE had recently renovated to double its production capabilities. The workers alerted the plant manager, who immediately shut down operations and evacuated the building. The radioactive cloud contained up to 21.6 pounds of depleted uranium hexafluoride and 7.3 pounds of hydrogen fluoride. After the release, a visual inspection traced the contamination to a seven-inch crack in reaction vessel 2, where uranium hexafluoride was mixed with hydrogen at high temperatures to produce uranium tetrafluoride, or "green salt." Luckily, no workers complained of respiratory distress, but one chemical operator's urine sample revealed elevated levels of uranium contamination. An Oak Ridge appointed investigation board concluded that the vessel cracked because it had been operating at temperatures that were too high for extended periods of time.[54] In other words, the DOE's production demands taxed its equipment to the point of endangering workers no matter which company operated the plant.

The cracked reaction vessel was not an isolated incident but one of several failures in environmental health and safety during Westinghouse's early tenure. In April, subcontractors applied a weatherproof coating to newly fabricated covers for the K-65 silos, which were installed after an engineering firm determined that the silos' concrete domes were cracking and losing their structural integrity. It was a hazardous job. In only three days, several of the subcontractors neared the DOE's quarterly limit of 1,250 millirems of radioactivity. On the fourth day, radioactivity was measured at 800–850 millirems per hour, workers heard the hissing sound of radon gas building up in Silo 2, and they observed bubbling in the weatherproof coating. On April 25, without DOE approval, Westinghouse vented the radon gas to relieve pressure in the K-65 silos and allow workers to finish the job. Coincidentally, a party including US Representative Tom Kindness, fresh off launching a Senate campaign against incumbent John Glenn, was touring Fernald and drove past the silos during the venting.[55]

A DOE investigation of the radon venting concluded that Westinghouse concealed information about the release to prevent its disclosure.[56] The string of accidents kept the fire burning in the media, and Fernald received weekly if not daily coverage in Cincinnati's newspapers. It also kept the fire burning in Lisa Crawford.[57] "I find it absolutely appalling, and I am sick and tired of their lies," said Crawford. "They had better shape up their act," because the "people that live out here are angry."[58] By the time

FIGURE 8. A Department of Energy (DOE) employee collects data from the K-65 silos as part of the investigation into operating contractor Westinghouse's unauthorized venting of radon gas, May 6, 1986. Courtesy of the US Department of Energy.

of the radon venting, Kathy Meyer had left FRESH to raise her third child, and Crawford had taken over as FRESH's president. Under her leadership, FRESH was determined to turn environmental health and safety at the DOE's nuclear weapons facilities into a national issue.[59] The Fernald area was not the only community, after all, with a radioactive backyard.

OVERCOMING FEARS

Lisa Crawford had never flown in an airplane. In fact, she was terrified to fly, but on April 10, 1986, Crawford—trailed by two television networks—boarded her first airplane and flew "white-knuckled all the way" to Washington, DC, to testify before Congress on the regulation of mixed waste at Fernald and other DOE facilities.[60] Joining Crawford from Ohio was deputy director of the Ohio EPA, Virginia Aveni, whose role was to argue the state's regulatory position that mixed waste at the DOE's plants, including Fernald, Mound, and Portsmouth, were subject to the Resource Conservation and Recovery Act (RCRA) as well as state hazardous waste laws. The DOE's Assistant Secretary for Environment, Safety, and Health, Mary Walker, countered with the department's own interpretation. The DOE acknowledged that after *LEAF v. Hodel*—the landmark lawsuit following the DOE's disclosure of mercury releases at Oak Ridge—the department was subject to RCRA enforcement, but it still maintained that the lawsuit permitted dual regulation. The chemical components of mixed waste were regulated under the RCRA, but the radioactive components still fell under the Atomic Energy Act, and therefore, the DOE's control. To support this argument, the DOE had redefined "byproduct material" in its regulations from "radioactive material" to "waste substance containing radioactivity," which the department hoped would further entrench its regulatory independence.[61] The RCRA also did not apply, according to Walker, to cases that disclosed classified information or if RCRA disposal resulted in increased radiation exposure.[62] The DOE was willing to implement the RCRA and work with the states on a case-by-case basis, but it chose to fight uniform compliance at all costs.[63]

Congressional hearings are public theater, and Lisa Crawford played the most important role: to personalize the consequences of the DOE's mixed wastes.[64] For FRESH, this was about people's lives, not the legalese of environmental compliance. "For five years, my family and I drank contaminated water with uranium from a DOE facility, the Fernald Plant in Cincinnati," Crawford began. "The uranium in my water came from leakage from hazardous waste pits at Fernald and from storm water runoff." Worst of all, "Fernald officials failed to tell us that my family's drinking water was polluted, even though they had known that since 1981." Beyond the contaminated water, Fernald was also "the worst uranium dust emitter in the country," it stored "five hundred thousand tons of radioactive and chemical wastes in pits that are leaking," and it processed "some of the most dangerous materials in the world" with "antiquated" and "poorly maintained" equipment. "These are just a few of the problems," Crawford said in her rebuke, "at our friendly neighborhood DOE plant."⁶⁵ Crawford's testimony demonstrates how grassroots perspectives were essential to transforming the technical and expert-driven issue of nuclear weapons production into a relatable environmental issue for the broader public.

In the following weeks, nuclear contamination dominated the headlines both locally and internationally. On April 26, 1986, the Chernobyl nuclear power station in the Soviet Union went supercritical during a safety test. The immediate aftermath of the accident, which released 100–200 million curies of radiation into the environment, killed 31 people and sent 140 more to the hospital with acute radiation poisoning. The explosions released a radioactive plume that forced the evacuation of 130,000 people in Chernobyl's surrounding communities and drifted widely across the continent.⁶⁶

Back at Fernald, FRESH learned that the plant had waste problems beyond uranium. Since 1972, Fernald had served as the DOE's thorium repository, stuffing 2.4 million pounds of the material into silos, bins, and drums, which were temporary solutions to a long-term storage problem.⁶⁷ Westinghouse was also planning to process 168 metric tons of plutonium-contaminated uranium, a task that fell outside Fernald's normal scope of operations.⁶⁸ None of these hazards, however, could stop FRESH from taking its first tour of the plant.

On June 21, 1986, thirty-eight members of FRESH gathered at Fernald to finally see the plant that had turned their lives upside down. "The tour was described as an unprecedented event by both management and union officials," wrote the *Cincinnati Enquirer*, "because it was the first time members of the public were allowed to tour the refinery buildings with workers as guides—unrestrained by management."⁶⁹ Under new management and with unprecedented rights to environmental health and safety after the strike, the FATLC was eager to begin a safer and more democratic chapter of nuclear weapons production. "Our intent was to collectively, management and labor, demonstrate that there is an open atmosphere and attitude here now," said FATLC president Gene Branham, "unlike that of the previous operator."⁷⁰ Westinghouse had demonstrated more openness than NLO, but FRESH members were still leery of their radioactive neighbor. For an expert's perspective on the plant, they recruited University of Cincinnati Clermont College biology professor Dr. Dave Fankhauser to join them on the tour.

Fankhauser, the son of Quaker activist Polly Brokaw, had earned a PhD in genetics from Johns Hopkins University, "which is where I first became interested in genetic poisons," recalled Fankhauser.[71] Like his mother, Fankhauser was a staunch critic of the nuclear industry. Soon after returning to Ohio from Johns Hopkins, he discovered that the Zimmer Nuclear Power Station was planned for development only ten miles from his home. He worked tirelessly to shut down the plant, and eventually secured himself intervenor status in the case.[72] Fankhauser first heard about Fernald during a public debate on nuclear power with University of Cincinnati radiologist Eugene Saenger. After the Cold War, Saenger's Department of Defense–funded total-body irradiation experiments on cancer patients during the 1960s and 1970s helped fuel a controversial public reckoning with patient consent, racism, and military funding in medicine.[73] At the time, however, Saenger was still widely respected as a leading radiologist. The debate was cordial, and during the event Saenger leaned over to Fankhauser, the activist recalled, and whispered, "You shouldn't be worried about nuclear power. But you ought to take a look out at Fernald."[74] That is exactly what Fankhauser did. In August 1985, he conducted a radiological survey of Fernald's perimeter using a scintillation counter, which measures ionizing radiation. Along the plant's western boundary, Fankhauser detected a sixfold increase in gamma rays. After the scientist mapped the data, it became clear that the uptick in radiation was being emitted from the K-65 silos.[75]

Fankhauser's survey caught the Fernald community's attention. Westinghouse recruited Fankhauser to organize two environmental conferences on Fernald, which were attended by representatives of the company, the Sierra Club, and local radiation professionals.[76] Tom Carpenter at GAP filed a Freedom of Information Act request for documentation on the K-65 silos, which Fankhauser helped organize into the report *Wasting Away: A Special Report on the Governmental Neglect of the "K-65" Radioactive Waste at Fernald.*[77] Finally, Fankhauser was contacted by FRESH to lecture at one of its meetings. These connections led Fankhauser back to Fernald, but this time he was permitted inside the plant's gates.[78]

As a scientist and activist, Fankhauser knew it was critical to document what he saw that day. But as he approached the entrance, Westinghouse employees stopped him in his tracks for carrying a camera and scintillation counter. FRESH stood up for the scientist, refusing to participate with such restrictions on equipment. Westinghouse relented, because the tour was, after all, a gesture of good faith to Fernald activists and neighbors.[79] Unfortunately for the company, it was impossible to conceal decades of disrepair at Fernald.

It was not for a lack of trying. Lisa Crawford could smell the fresh paint coating Fernald, including green in the green salt area and yellow in the yellow cake area. But this superficial makeover could not conceal the fact that it was still "a very dirty, dusty, antiquated, ugly, old factory."[80] Things got much worse in Plant 5, the Metals Production Plant, where green salt was combined with magnesium in crucibles and fired in a furnace for four hours at 1,300 degrees Fahrenheit. At the end of this process, the magnesium ignites, which skyrockets temperatures in the crucible to 3,000 degrees and reduces the green salt to a uranium metal derby.[81] As FRESH discovered, it was not uncommon for these volatile reactions to blow the seal off the crucibles and release radioactive gas into the plant. An alarm sounded during the tour, but the guide reassured them that it was a common occurrence and nothing to worry about. Moments later, a worker in a white lab coat rushed in and evacuated the building.[82]

Most surprising to Fankhauser was just how "wide open the place was in terms of radioactive material slopped all over the place."[83] Green salt was caked all over the packaging equipment, including visibly on a worker's arms.[84] Hundreds of enriched uranium ingots lined the streets of the plant.[85] Thousands of corroded drums of radioactive waste were stacked outside and exposed to the elements.[86] Six thousand five hundred tons of contaminated scrap metal was piled in a field, giving the appearance of an atomic junkyard.[87] Worst of all for Fankhauser, there was no end in sight. Fernald was producing at three times the levels of the 1970s.[88] Unless the DOE drastically changed its ways, the waste was going to keep piling up.

TOWARD SAFE NUCLEAR PRODUCTION

Cleaning up Fernald was a priority for the DOE. In June, the department started its first baseline environmental health and safety survey at the plant. Even though it trailed Hanford and Savannah River as the third most polluted nuclear weapons production facility, Fernald was "no. 1 on my hit list," according to Mary Walker, the DOE's assistant secretary for Environment, Safety, and Health.[89] This was because of the horrendous conditions inside the plant. Fernald was "the DOE's most decrepit dinosaur," according to the *Seattle Times*, and "probably the worst plant in the entire DOE bomb-making system from the standpoint of safety and environmental hazards." The DOE's years of neglect caused this decline. Workplace safety was a joke. Equipment was rusted and outdated. The environment was an afterthought. "During a 15-year period, we received a total of $20 million," said former plant manager Robert Spenceley, "to maintain a plant whose current replacement value would be $1 billion."[90] While Hanford and Savannah River's plutonium reactors represented the potential for a Chernobyl-like disaster in the United States, Fernald was the symbol of the DOE's negligent environmental standards.

The following month, the DOE and the US EPA signed a federal facility compliance agreement outlining the necessary steps for Fernald to comply with the Clean Air Act, the RCRA, and the Comprehensive Environmental Response, Compensation, and Liability Act (CERCLA) — better known as Superfund — as well as a remedial investigation and feasibility study to determine the extent of contamination at the site.[91] These policies, which prioritized environmental health and safety, had come at the direction of Secretary Herrington. This was a testament to the influence of Fernald's environmental movement on the highest levels of the DOE.[92]

When testifying in support of the DOE's 1986 appropriations, Secretary Herrington had stressed the importance of environmental health and safety to this new era of safe nuclear weapons production. "I am devoting increased management attention to safety in all its dimensions, safeguards and security, environmental concerns, and our responsibility to be a good neighbor at all of our locations," he said. "Doing a good job in each of these areas of responsibility is of vital importance if we are to continue meeting the Nuclear Weapons Stockpile Memorandum requirements." For Herrington, production and the environment were two important but independent responsibilities. "The public concern for environmental health and safety matters can be treated separately," Herrington stated, "without blurring the important role of and debate on the United States nuclear deterrent in our national security and general well-being."[93] For Fernald's workers on the front lines, however, it was impossible to separate the two. Production, their bodies, and the environment had always been inextricably linked.

THE WHISTLEBLOWER

On August 13, 1986, the Government Accountability Project's Tom Carpenter stood before the House of Representatives' Committee on Energy and Commerce to introduce Daniel J. Arthur, an Army veteran from Iowa and former methods analyst/lead auditor in the Quality Assurance Department at Fernald. Arthur, who came to Fernald from the private sector, worked at the plant from May 1984 until March 1986, when he resigned to blow the whistle on the DOE and Westinghouse. The goal of quality assurance is safety and accident prevention, which was particularly important at Fernald, since the plant was at the time essentially self-regulating. Arthur was hired into a department, however, that was shockingly understaffed, with only a few employees available to complete literally hundreds of audits. Worst of all, it took orders from the production department, which always prioritized production schedules at the expense of environmental health and safety. Arthur was advised by his supervisor, as a result, to alter or even stop some of his audits.[94]

Arthur, like most newcomers to Fernald, was shocked that management could tolerate such an unhealthy environment. Production workers tracked radioactive dust throughout the plant, which seemingly settled on every surface. In the Sampling Plant, the Green Salt Plant, the Metals Production Plant, and the Special Products Plant, Arthur found layers of uranium dust, uranium saw chips, green salt, orange oxide, and magnesium fluoride all over the place. The air was so thick with uranium dust that he could barely breathe. Most alarming for the health of his coworkers, many were not wearing masks or respirators.⁹⁵

Management warned Arthur not to perform audits on the K-65 silos, the chemical waste pits, the mechanical shops, and the dust collector systems. The dust in the laboratory building grew so intolerable, however, that Arthur ignored his supervisor and inquired about changing the filtration bag. It turned out that nobody knew whose responsibility it was or the procedures to complete the task. Like any good quality assurance inspector, Arthur took it upon himself to investigate. Upon physical examination of the equipment, the filtration bag completely disintegrated, which meant that radioactive dust had been emitted directly out the stacks, and nobody knew for how long. Arthur believed that the bag had amazingly never been changed since the equipment was installed. This should not have been so surprising. During his first few months on the job, Arthur completed the first audit of maintenance procedures in the plant's history. Recordkeeping was also a complete disaster. It could take hours to find a particular maintenance file, so workers' memories were relied upon instead. Arthur found it to be "incredible that maintenance operation at a nuclear materials facility was allowed to go unchecked and unverified for over 30 years."⁹⁶ Maintenance turned out to be just the beginning of his frustrations.

Arthur took his job seriously, but it soon became obvious that his recommendations would not be implemented if they inconvenienced production. Before the DOE fired NLO, Arthur was able to audit some of its environmental monitoring procedures. In November 1984, Fernald's last month of operations before the uranium leak went public, Arthur audited the operation of the water plant, whose responsibilities included preventing uranium losses through waterways, treating drinking water, sanitary sewage disposal, testing fire pumps, and sampling chemical waste pits. During this audit, Arthur found fourteen violations of standard operating procedures (SOPs). Routine inspections, including of the chemical waste pits, were never conducted. In the most blatant violation, Arthur discovered that one test well had its pump removed and was no longer in operation because "uranium levels in the well were too high." Arthur's supervisors instructed him to omit this information from his report.⁹⁷

It turned out that Fernald's water sampling data was highly unreliable. Arthur learned that when workers collected samples from production wells, test wells, drinking fountains, the storm sewer, the sewage treatment system, chemical waste pits, the Great Miami River, and Paddy's Run, SOPs were completely ignored. The quantities of chemicals used in tests were inconsistent with established procedures. Many tests were not completed at all, and several others were completed outside of the SOPs. No records were kept on the life spans of the chemicals. There was no written guidance on how to properly mix chemicals to complete the tests. When Arthur found laboratory equipment that was supposedly sterile to be contaminated, his supervisors again instructed him to omit this information from his report.[98] In Fernald's laboratories, the practices more closely resembled alchemy than modern science.

Westinghouse showed little more integrity than NLO. In February 1986, Arthur completed a detailed audit of T-hopper shipping procedures after one of these vessels, which transported radioactive materials, arrived contaminated at Hanford after being shipped from Fernald along the Burlington Northern Railroad. This event was highly criticized by the DOE, but when the DOE and Westinghouse met to discuss solutions, Arthur's supervisors declined to share any of his findings that suggested there were still important gaps in procedures.[99] This dishonesty bothered Arthur, but it was his final audit that was the last straw. This project called for the processing of 168 tons of plutonium-contaminated uranium oxide. Fernald was a uranium plant, so it was not set up to routinely handle plutonium. Since this uranium oxide was significantly contaminated, it was considered plutonium-out-of-specification (POOS) material, which was anything containing greater than ten parts per billion of plutonium. POOS projects required enhanced safety procedures, including protective equipment and respirators, continuous air monitoring, and frequent analysis of worker exposures. In 1982, Fernald had processed plutonium-contaminated materials without any advanced safety precautions, which resulted in a highly critical report by the DOE and infuriated Fernald's unions, because workers were not informed of the plutonium by NLO management. Westinghouse was under intense pressure to get the job done, however, because a shortage of green salt threatened production schedules. Arthur was tasked with developing the procedures to process the POOS materials safely and felt that two months would be appropriate to get the job done right. Instead, Westinghouse gave him two weeks. The stress overwhelmed Arthur and the soon-to-be whistleblower resigned instead of approving POOS procedures that threatened the health and safety of his coworkers.[100]

Arthur's experience led him to conclude that Westinghouse's hiring was strictly a public relations move. If the DOE continued to value production over environmental health and safety, it really did not matter what corporation was operating the plant. Quality assurance at Fernald was, according to Arthur, "in itself a mini-model of the whole system of nuclear weapons production. Quality concerns that serve the function of protecting human health and safety are controlled by a management that has to worry about the ledger sheet."[101] In this managerial system, production would always take precedence over safety, and workers' bodies and surrounding communities would suffer for it.[102] While hourly union employees boldly voiced this perspective during their 1985 strike, Arthur was the first salaried employee to speak out against management at Fernald.[103] This class divide, which had long split the workforce on issues of environmental health and safety, was finally broken. The mass production of nuclear weapons had relied upon disposable, blue-collar bodies. Without them, an entirely new system would need to be constructed.

RELOADING THE SUPERFUND

On October 17, 1986, President Reagan signed into law the Superfund Amendments and Reauthorization Act (SARA), which replenished Superfund with $8.5 billion. Despite the Reagan administration's original intent to undermine the law, the president relented because SARA received widespread and bipartisan support for its conservative price tag, which easily could have been tens of billions more, and for balancing the share of responsibilities for toxic cleanup between government agencies and private industry.[104] SARA was a huge victory for environmentalists, because it filled important gaps in the original law. One underappreciated contribution of 1980s grassroots environmentalism, according to historian Richard S. Newman, was SARA's creation of the "first federal right-to-know law," which required corporations to share information with the public on chemical storage, uses, and releases. This concealment of toxic knowledge had no doubt contributed to environmental crises across the country, from Love Canal to Fernald, and led to a more open dialogue on hazardous waste.[105] Fernald's environmental movement's most significant contribution to SARA was Congress's waiving of the federal government's sovereign immunity and extending Superfund obligations to federal facilities.[106] The DOE would now be held to the same standards as private companies.

Fernald's environmental movement helped usher in a safer era of nuclear weapons production. Radioactive waste, for the first time in the DOE's history, was treated as an urgent problem instead of one that could be put off for the next generation to deal with. The future also looked bright for union workers, who secured unprecedented rights to environmental health and safety in their 1985 strike. Employment and production were resurgent for the renewed nuclear arms race, and the DOE planned to invest millions of dollars to upgrade the plant. As Arthur's whistleblower testimony demonstrated, however, the DOE could not so easily segregate internal production and external pollution, and it was uncertain whether a responsible brand of uranium metals production was possible in such an outdated facility. Outside Fernald's gates, FRESH carried this message to a national audience and transformed nuclear weapons production from a local threat into a national crisis. The voices of many radioactive backyards were stronger than one.

FIVE Going National

On April 24, 1987, at 10 p.m., 5.3 million American households tuned into ABC *News Closeup: The Bomb Factories*, a documentary about the Department of Energy (DOE)'s negligence in environmental health and safety at its nuclear weapons production facilities.[1] The show, based on a six-month investigation of Hanford, Rocky Flats, Savannah River, and Fernald, added a fresh perspective to the popular conversation on nuclear weapons in the United States. *The Bomb Factories*, according to ABC producer Steve Singer, was "neither pro-nuclear nor anti-nuclear. We looked at these plants as if we were dealing with a major American industry."[2] In the aftermath of the meltdown at Chernobyl in the spring of 1986, whose path of radioactive fallout carved out a 1,660-square-mile exclusion zone and contaminated at least 39,000 square miles, the nuclear threat transformed in the public's mind from the bomb and war to industry and pollution.[3] "The plants," said correspondent Richard Threlkeld in his introduction, "are an accident waiting to happen."[4]

During the early 1980s, antinuclear activists were primarily concerned with the prospect of global annihilation from nuclear war. At a time when President Ronald Reagan called the Soviet Union "the focus of evil" in the world and Vice President George H. W. Bush claimed that the United States could "win" a nuclear war, it seemed possible—if not likely—that the first use of a nuclear bomb in conflict since Nagasaki was imminent.[5] Over the next several years, however, Reagan's reelection helped sink the Nuclear Weapons Freeze Campaign, and the president and Soviet General Secretary Mikhail Gorbachev developed a productive working relationship, which significantly cooled the hostility of the Cold War arms race.[6] Just as the threat of nuclear war started to subside, Chernobyl raised the prospects of deadly accidents at nuclear facilities. For activists across the country, the problem shifted from the global and moral question of nuclear war to the local environmental hazards of deteriorating equipment, poor oversight, and a managerial system that rewarded production over environmental protection. This made America's nuclear weapons complex, according to *The Bomb Factories*, "a national disgrace" that threatened "national security" and "public safety."[7]

The Bomb Factories represented the media's shift in focus from arms control to environmental issues during the late 1980s. Toward the end of 1988, for example, the *New York Times* published 108 stories on contamination at nuclear weapons production plants, including 37 cover stories, in a little over three months.[8] With the threat of nuclear war declining and stockpile reductions underway, national peace and environmental organizations responded by joining forces with Fernald Residents for Environmental Safety and Health (FRESH) and other grassroots groups from nuclear weapons communities, which banded together as the Military Production Network (MPN) in 1987 to challenge the arms race through environmental health and safety initiatives.[9] Fernald's local pollution was suddenly a national problem, and FRESH and the MPN recognized that if everyone pitched in to clean up their radioactive backyard, they could transform the entire nuclear weapons production network.

FRESH, the Fernald Atomic Trades and Labor Council (FATLC), and their political allies had already influenced the direction of the DOE, which could no longer operate without the input of organized labor and activist neighbors. Their strategy only grew stronger when national peace and environmental groups created the Plutonium Challenge, a call for the United States to immediately halt the production of plutonium at its dangerously outdated reactors at Savannah River and Hanford.[10] This tactical shift suggests that during the late 1980s, the antinuclear movement took on the global threat of the nuclear arms race with local environmental activism. On the first anniversary of the Chernobyl disaster, for example, eleven protesters carrying buckets, mops, and brooms were arrested for trespassing onto the Hanford Nuclear Reservation to "march on N Reactor" and "begin cleaning up nuclear wastes."[11] While nuclear war and "nuclear winter" were hypothetical dangers, Fernald and Hanford's radioactive backyards were tangible landscapes. As activists localized the nuclear threat, they made it solvable.

Through the MPN and the Plutonium Challenge, activists developed a locally focused but nationally connected movement for environmental health and safety in the DOE that led to Fernald's closure and the downsizing and modernization of the nuclear weapons complex. The movement never banned the bomb, but it dramatically reduced nuclear dangers by transforming the sprawling and polluting model of nuclear weapons production into a smaller network that gradually complied with environmental laws.[12] This was a major victory for Fernald's movement, which demonstrated the power of local solutions to national—or even global—environmental problems.

GOVERNMENTAL AFFAIRS

On June 16, 1987, the Senate Committee on Governmental Affairs convened in the Dirksen Senate Office Building in Washington, DC. At 9:45 a.m., the chairman of the committee, Senator John Glenn of Ohio, called the meeting to order.[13] The committee "was not the kind of headline-grabbing vehicle that appealed to many senators," Glenn recalled, but "it could be an effective engine for improving the workings of government."[14] That day, it hoped to do just that through a discussion of the Nuclear Protections and Safety Act of 1987, which was introduced by Senator Glenn. His bill was an ambitious proposal to strengthen oversight of the DOE, including the creation of an independent safety board to oversee nuclear weapons production facilities, to apply the provisions of the Occupational Safety and Health Act to DOE workers, to empower the Environmental Protection Agency (EPA) in the regulation of nuclear waste, and to ensure scientific independence in DOE studies of radiation's effects on human beings.[15] After Chernobyl, the potential for accidents was on everyone's mind.

"The Department of Energy," Glenn began, "have [sic], since the beginning of the nuclear age, managed to avoid outside, independent oversight of their technical operations.... In recent years, it has become increasingly evident that this situation is no longer tolerable."[16] In that Washington room, Glenn took the committee on an oratorical national tour of would-be nuclear disasters at the DOE's plutonium production reactors, which the National Academy of Sciences studied at the request of Secretary of Energy Herrington in the aftermath of Chernobyl.[17] From 1979 to 1986, the DOE had operated its Savannah River plutonium production reactors at a load twenty-six percent higher than its emergency core cooling system could handle. "In other words," Glenn clarified, "we would have had an uncontrolled meltdown" if the reactors went critical.[18]

Of even greater concern was Hanford's N Reactor, a graphite-moderated reactor that closely resembled the Chernobyl RBMK design. Although the N Reactor featured several superior safety features over Chernobyl, including faster control rods, pressurized instead of boiling water, and a backup boron-carbide ball safety system, it lacked a hydrogen-monitoring system and a containment vessel, which was the last line of defense against a deadly release of radioactivity into the environment. If the N Reactor was a civilian design, it never would have passed the Nuclear Regulatory Commission's licensing requirements.[19] As Glenn pointed out, "we oversee all the commercial electrical nuclear generating plants in the country very, very carefully," but "we have not been adhering to those same standards in the Department of Energy's weapons productions processes." The Senate Committee on Armed Services, on which Glenn also served, voted to shut down the N Reactor.[20]

Then Glenn turned to the environment. "This committee," he began, "has heard extensive testimony about the environmental hazards created by unsafe waste disposal practices at the Feed Materials Production Center at Fernald, Ohio." But the problem was much bigger than Fernald. Savannah River also had "extensive on-site ground water and soil contamination," including leaking high-level waste storage tanks. "DOE facilities in Colorado, South Carolina, and Tennessee," Glenn continued, "have contaminated the ground water with solvents as much as 1,000 times above the proposed drinking water standards." Oak Ridge had polluted a stream with mercury, and Hanford had an astonishing 65 million gallons of mixed radioactive and chemical wastes buried in 170 underground storage tanks. The scope of the problem was daunting. The General Accounting Office had identified water and soil contamination at almost every DOE facility it visited.[21]

This national crisis raised important questions about environmental cleanup. As Glenn observed, a program on this scale is going to be measured "in the billions" of dollars, and much of the science and technology necessary to remediate groundwater was still undeveloped. Worst of all, he said, "we have not gotten started" on this unprecedented project. Before cleanup could begin, however, it was important to stop the problem at the source. If the nuclear arms race continued, it needed to do so without contaminating the bodies of workers and neighbors, in addition to the environment. The Nuclear Protections and Safety Act would help ensure that.[22]

More so than any of the DOE's political critics, Senator Glenn's patriotic but environmentally accountable brand of nuclear weapons production shaped the future of the department. As a former Marine fighter pilot, Cold War celebrity during Project Mercury, and booster for Ohio's nuclear weapons industry, Glenn was far from an antinuclear activist.[23] But he also believed in a nuclear deterrent that was accountable to democracy. "It does very little good to protect us from the Soviet Union with weapons production," Glenn proclaimed, "if we poison our own people in the process."[24] This style of environmentalism—which never challenged long-standing Cold War strategy but demanded the safe production of nuclear weapons—closely mirrored the beliefs of FRESH, the FATLC, and the conservative communities surrounding Fernald. It also came to represent a national movement for environmental health and safety that recognized the value of moderate arguments in matters of national security. Glenn's words were reprinted by mainstream environmental and antinuclear organizations like the Sierra Club and Physicians for Social Responsibility, as well as quoted in national publications, including the *New York Times* and *Time* magazine.[25] In activist circles, the fight to eliminate the bomb was gradually replaced with a call for environmentally responsible production.

THE PLUTONIUM CHALLENGE

On November 5, 1987, the Plutonium Challenge, with the support of the Environmental Policy Institute, the Energy Research Foundation, the Federation of American Scientists, Friends of the Earth, Greenpeace, the

Natural Resources Defense Council, Physicians for Social Responsibility, and the Union of Concerned Scientists, issued an open letter to President Reagan and Congress to identify a "historic opportunity" with "substantial economic and environmental benefits for our nation." The Plutonium Challenge called for an "immediate two-year moratorium" on plutonium production by the United States, along with the negotiation of a "bilateral, verifiable cutoff" of plutonium and highly enriched uranium production with the Soviet Union.[26] With a stockpile of twenty-five thousand nuclear weapons, the United States would only lose out on enough plutonium to produce 250 warheads, which was negligible considering the already massive arsenal that contained more than enough firepower to destroy much of life on earth. The payoff, however, was immediate, with a reduction in environmental hazards at nuclear weapons production facilities, billions of dollars in savings from limiting operations, and the establishment of a pathway to permanent arms control.[27] The letter was signed by over two dozen current and former leaders from universities, government, environmental and peace organizations, the military, and intelligence agencies.[28]

Nuclear weapons production was at a crossroads. With Reagan and Gorbachev closing in on a reduction in arsenals, the Plutonium Challenge stated, the time was ripe for a bilateral freeze on plutonium production. But instead of prioritizing the cleanup of nuclear weapons production facilities—which were already a national public health and environmental crisis—the DOE planned to invest tens of billions of dollars into new production reactors and a special isotope separation facility, which would prepare plutonium for use in nuclear warheads through laser technology.[29] It was a clear signal that at the DOE, production still trumped environmental health and safety.

The Plutonium Challenge offered a compelling argument for disarmament, which provided an off-ramp for the arms race without weakening the nuclear deterrent. With production shut down, perhaps the United States and Soviet Union could reflect on the high costs, both environmental and economic, of the arms race and find a new direction forward.[30] In many ways, it was environmentalism's version of the Nuclear Freeze. Instead of emphasizing diplomacy, however, the Plutonium Challenge's freeze was localized in physical production reactors at Hanford and Savannah River. This stressed the immediate environmental health and safety and economic benefits over a reduction in the threat of nuclear war.

If the strength of the Plutonium Challenge's open letter was the environment, however, its weakness was its inattention to labor. Nuclear weapons production was a highly interconnected network, and the ramifications of a halt or slowdown at one facility reverberated across the complex. In a document circulated within activist communities, the Plutonium Challenge noted that its proposal would impact production—and therefore jobs—at Hanford and Savannah River, as well as the plants reliant on those facilities, such as Fernald and Reactive Metals Inc. in Ashtabula, Ohio, which modified Fernald's uranium metal products into billets and tubes.[31] In the open letter, however, the Plutonium Challenge made no reference to nuclear workers' livelihoods. While national peace and environmental organizations wielded significant political power and expertise, their physical distance from nuclear weapons production communities limited their knowledge of what people's lives were like on the ground. FRESH, on the other hand, had no prior experience in activism but recognized since its inception that earning the respect of organized labor was going to be critical to its success.[32] Only days later, another organization formed that brought essential grassroots credibility to the national movement for environmental health and safety at nuclear weapons production facilities.

THE MILITARY PRODUCTION NETWORK

In November 1987, FRESH's Lisa Crawford joined representatives from twelve other national peace and environmental groups, as well as local activists from nuclear weapons production communities, at the La Foret Conference and Retreat Center in Black Forest, Colorado, to form the Military Production Network. Located fifteen miles north of Colorado Springs and owned by the Rocky Mountain Conference of the United Church of Christ, La Foret offered a peaceful and scenic refuge for the MPN's founding members to discuss the pressing dangers of radioactive contamination at nuclear weapons production facilities. MPN's founding members were Lisa Crawford of FRESH; Jen Pilcher of the American Friends Service Committee in Denver; Mary Ellen Carlow of Citizens

Against Rocky Flats Contamination; Nina Bell and Kathy Maloney of the Coalition for Safe Power in Portland, Oregon; Lisa Schultz of the Colorado Peace Network in Denver; Beck Hardy, who was unable to attend, from the Energy Research Foundation in Columbia, South Carolina; Jim Beard and Cathy Kirkham from Greenpeace; Tim Connor from the Hanford Education Action League in Spokane, Washington; Liz Paul from Life Guard Idaho; Bill Mitchell from the Northwest Nuclear Safety Campaign in Seattle; Barbara Wolf from the Ohio Public Interest Campaign; Mary Butters from the Palouse Clearwater Hanford Watch in Moscow, Idaho; and Janet Miller from Puget Sound SANE in Seattle. Their main goal was to form, out of many small activist communities, a grassroots network supported by national organizations to better challenge the DOE on several key issues of environmental health and safety.[33]

The MPN's umbrella-type structure reflected important shifts taking place in environmental activism in the 1980s. During this period, environmental organizations continued to diversify their traditional goals, such as wilderness preservation, with public health issues, including toxic and radioactive waste and urban pollution, which had a much greater impact on people's daily lives.[34] A key part of this transformation was a bottom-up redistribution of power from national organizations to grassroots communities.[35] During the late 1970s, Lois Gibbs and the Love Canal Homeowners Association had demonstrated the enormous influence that local antitoxics activists, and particularly women, could possess in American society.[36] Only a few years later, a multiracial coalition of activists in Warren County, North Carolina, protested the siting of a PCB landfill using the language and tactics of the civil rights movement, which highlighted the role of racism and classism in the distribution of environmental hazards and gave birth to what is now called "environmental justice."[37] Many grassroots activists, including women and people of color, felt ignored—if not entirely erased—from national campaigns.[38] Broad coalitions like the MPN networked and empowered local activists to speak for themselves and emerged as an alternative form of organizing to the consolidation of power in the DC-centric and exclusively male Group of Ten.[39]

Back at La Foret, the MPN's first order of business was to get to know each other. Lisa Crawford was given the floor to discuss some of FRESH's major accomplishments over the previous several years, which through dedicated and consistent organizing was recognized by the DOE as a "legitimate representative of the Fernald population."[40] Crawford explained that documents on Fernald's operations were available to researchers in a public reading room, lifting the veil of secrecy on nuclear weapons production at least partially. The installation of an emergency warning system, which would cover a two-mile radius from Fernald when fully operational, and drills for an evacuation plan (involving Westinghouse; Butler and Hamilton Counties' civil defense agencies; the Ohio Disaster Services Agency; the New Baltimore fire department; and Providence and University of Cincinnati Hospitals) better prepared the community in the event of chemical releases at Fernald.[41] FRESH's class-action lawsuit against Fernald's former operating contractor, National Lead of Ohio (NLO), and the State of Ohio's lawsuits against the DOE, NLO, and Westinghouse were all underway.[42] In Congress, Senator Glenn was leading the charge on legislating independent oversight of the DOE.[43] In a few short years, Fernald's environmental alliance had forced the DOE into being a more accountable neighbor.

After introductions, the meeting's facilitators Terry Odendahl and Richard Male of the Community Resource Center in Denver, guided the activists in developing the concept of a national movement for environmental health and safety at DOE nuclear weapons production facilities, which would stress the importance of both local and national issues. During a brainstorming session, the group fleshed out several possible goals, including shutting down plutonium production, halting the construction of new reactors, disarmament, and improved environmental health and safety. The activists also stressed the importance of diversity in the movement, including the need to fight for the interests of farmers, ranchers, low-income residents, and communities of color. Ideal outcomes for the movement included cleaning up the environment, securing compensation for victims of radioactive contamination, the implementation of epidemiological studies, the elimination of nuclear weapons, and the development of alternative economic opportunities to defense spending.[44]

To succinctly capture the MPN's mission, the group drafted a document called "Democracy before Weaponry: A Bill of Rights for Citizens in the Shadows of America's Nuclear Weapons Production Facilities," which aimed to reorganize the asymmetrical relationship of power between the DOE and ordinary citizens.[45] The "Bill of Rights" built on decades of civil rights and environmental activism, which during the 1960s and 1970s took advantage of new opportunities for participatory democracy, such as the National Environmental Policy Act; activists also chose to identify with democratic terms like "citizen" instead of "environmentalist" to legitimize and give a patriotic voice to their movement.[46] The DOE and its predecessors, according to the MPN, sacrificed the environment, public health, and institutional trust to build a massive nuclear arsenal without the consent of the ordinary citizens whose communities and bodies were contaminated by the arms race. The "Pre-Amble" to the "Bill of Rights," which skillfully articulated these concepts, read:

> Over the past four decades, the U.S. government has built and operated a nation-wide network of nuclear weapons production facilities. Yet, only recently have citizens become aware of the damage to public health and the environment that has resulted from these operations. To date, the evidence is compelling that the damage caused represents a profound breach of trust with the American people.
>
> As citizens who live in the shadows of nuclear weapons production plants, we have an active interest in the recognition and observance of our rights to public safety, environmental quality, government accountability, and due process.
>
> We insist that major reforms are required. The perpetuation of secrecy and self-regulation in the nuclear weapons production system is no longer tolerable. Without major changes in current laws and practices, the American people have no guarantee that the continued operation of nuclear weapons production facilities is in the best interest of American taxpayers, nor that public safety and the environment are being adequately protected.[47]

Later in the day, the activists developed communications strategies and paired representatives in a "buddy system" to share information and support each other "when things get tough."⁴⁸ Lisa Crawford and Cathy Kirkham from Greenpeace Chicago were matched together, establishing a presence for the MPN in the Midwest with national visibility and grassroots credibility. Bill Mitchell from the Northwest Nuclear Safety Campaign, Jim Beard from Greenpeace Seattle, Cathy Kirkham in Chicago, and Nina Bell and Kathy Maloney from the Coalition for Safe Power would also start communicating through Greenpeace's Environet, an electronic bulletin board that supported forums on nuclear disarmament, toxic waste, wildlife preservation, and sustainable living. Users could also send and receive messages, download information to support activism, and read the latest issue of the Remote Access Chemical Hazards Electronic Library's *Hazardous Waste News* by the Environmental Research Foundation.⁴⁹ At a time when corporations increasingly learned to coopt and manipulate environmentalism, Environet and other bulletin board systems provided alternative sources of information and organizing opportunities for grassroots activists as America entered the digital age.⁵⁰

The "Bill of Rights" offered a unified voice to a broad national coalition, which the MPN hoped to expand even further for the following meeting. The MPN singled out the recently formed Plutonium Challenge and more than two dozen national disarmament and environmental organizations as potential allies, including local groups near Hanford, Oak Ridge, Pantex, Rocky Flats, and Savannah River, as well as Native Americans for a Clean Environment, which was battling the Kerr-McGee Corporation over a uranium release at its Sequoyah Falls plant in Oklahoma. To make the biggest splash with the "Bill of Rights," the MPN set aside the document for a planned release at coordinated press conferences in Washington, DC, and other regional sites throughout the network the following year.⁵¹ After the meeting, Lisa Crawford returned to Ohio with significant resources, a network of allies, and a larger platform for FRESH. Most importantly, she learned the value of working locally and nationally on nuclear cleanup.

THE OHIO PEACE MARCH

On Memorial Day 1988, peace activists gathered in Portsmouth, Ohio, a community on the Ohio River and home to the DOE's Portsmouth Gaseous Diffusion Plant, to begin the summerlong Ohio Peace March for Global Nuclear Disarmament.[52] The Ohio Peace March was a statewide spin-off of the Great Peace March for Global Nuclear Disarmament, a national protest that traversed the country from Los Angeles to Washington, DC, over nine months in 1986. The Ohio march's goal was to "raise consciousness, town by town, newspaper by newspaper" across the state, but like the Great Peace March before it, it would be met with the familiar challenges of spreading the message of peace in the Midwest.[53] In the blue-collar farm and factory towns of the Buckeye State, people could be leery of marchers with the perceived economic means to step away from work for months at a time. The marchers were committed, however, to dispelling stereotypes of peace activists as naïve or elitist and hoped to demonstrate their sincerity through face-to-face conversation.[54]

From Portsmouth, the march wound north through the Appalachian foothills of eastern Ohio until they reached Cleveland, then west across the shores of Lake Erie to Toledo, south to the state capital of Columbus, and finally down to Cincinnati on the Kentucky border. Along the way, protesters managed to hold constructive dialogue with doves, war hawks, and moderates alike. "Even people who are not necessarily sympathetic," said Berta Lambert of Cincinnati, "appreciate the physical effort" of marching through the hot and humid summer and sleeping on the floors of unfamiliar houses, churches, and fire stations. The final leg of the May-to-September, seven-hundred-mile journey was a two-day march from Fountain Square in downtown Cincinnati to the gates of Fernald.[55]

About seventy-five protesters walked those last twenty-five miles. Another twenty-five activists, including Oxford Citizens for Peace (OCP), Miami University Students for Peace, and Oxford Friends Meeting, greeted them upon arrival at the plant. For six hours, the group listened to music, watched street theater, and heard speeches by University of Cincinnati Clermont College professor Dave Fankhauser, Ohio SANE/FREEZE director Barbara Fitzgerald, Ohio Public Interest Campaign director Roxanne

FIGURE 9. Peace activists protesting Fernald in coordination with the Ohio Peace March, September 9, 1988. Courtesy of the US Department of Energy.

Qualls, and Judith Janrus of the National Resource Information Center in Washington, DC. It was the Ohio peace movement's largest protest at Fernald since Trinity Day in 1983.[56]

The following day, about twenty protesters returned to Fernald for an act of civil disobedience. At 8:35 a.m., Reverend Maurice McCrackin, an eighty-two-year-old minister and longtime antiwar and civil rights activist from Cincinnati, first crossed the line onto Fernald's property. "Sir, you're trespassing on government property," said a Hamilton County sheriff's deputy, but "we'll give you a chance to leave." McCrackin refused, and *Cincinnati Post* photographer Robert Dickerson was there to capture the iconic moment that followed when two deputies, one on each arm, carried the limp and gray-haired McCrackin away to a police van.[57] McCrackin told reporters that "all possible should be done to clean up the deadly pollution that has accumulated here at Fernald, and then the plant should be closed down. There is no way that it can be made safe."[58] Six others were also arrested and charged with criminal trespassing: James Mullin from the Saint Francis Catholic Worker House in Cincinnati; Edward Bain of Pataskala, Ohio; Thomas Wilkinson of Highland Heights, Kentucky; Mark Becker of Cincinnati; Mark Stansbery of Columbus; and Berta Lambert of Cincinnati.[59] For McCrackin, who had endured hunger strikes, a police stun gun, numerous incarcerations, and even dismissal from the Presbyterian Church for refusing to pay taxes because of his pacifist beliefs, fighting the environmental contamination at Fernald was another issue worth going to jail for.[60]

While McCrackin was specific with his words to reporters, the overall message of the Ohio Peace March was less so. At the Fernald protest, Cincinnati coordinator Ray Estes told reporters that the marchers were "giving a presence to the workers arriving," which was ambiguous as to whether they stood in solidarity with Fernald's unions—and therefore the class issues that dominated internal plant politics—or lumped together blue-collar workers and managers as all part of the problem.[61] Similarly, *Cincinnati Enquirer* reporter Elizabeth Neus wrote on the multiple issues concerning Ohio peace marchers. "I'm worried about the environment and toxic waste, and I'm interested in women's rights and gay rights," said Mike Pessefall of Defiance, Ohio, because "everything's intertwined." "We figured out by listening to each other that we all work on the same issues," said Eunice Meadows of the Butler County chapter of the National Organization for Women. "The whole thing fits together. It's all about rights."[62]

Pessefall and Meadows were not alone in their concerns about human rights, the right to a clean environment, the right to equality, the right to self-expression and love. They all mattered, but the complex messaging demonstrated the Ohio peace movement's continued struggles with balancing the fight for social equality with pragmatic solutions to the arms race.[63] According to Lambert, there was no observable drop-off in activism since the 1960s, but what dramatically changed was the range of political issues receiving attention. "There are thousands of excellent ones," the activist said, "But the one that could destroy us all is nuclear war."[64]

OPEN HOUSE, EMPTY FACTORY

With the local and national spotlight on Fernald, the pressure was on Westinghouse to clean up the plant's radioactive backyard and its public image. On September 17, 1988, Fernald hosted a public "open house" to educate its neighbors about uranium processing. Westinghouse had granted FRESH, politicians, and the media tours in the past, but this was the first time in the plant's history that anybody who showed up was welcome. It was a shocking turnaround from the culture of secrecy, including fenced perimeters and armed guards, that would have greeted unwanted visitors to Fernald just a few years earlier.[65] The idea for the "open house" was born out of a successful family day for Fernald's workers, and the event offered a perfect opportunity for Westinghouse to show off recent improvements. "We are extremely proud of the tremendous progress we are making in modernizing and cleaning up the site," said Westinghouse Materials Company of Ohio president Bruce Boswell, and "we want to show our neighbors what we are doing to improve environmental, safety, and health conditions."[66] Through a bus tour of the production area, a walking tour of two uranium processing plants, and exhibits on environmental monitoring and emergency preparedness, visitors had the opportunity to see these projects for themselves, including a reduction in the inventory of low-level radioactive waste, the construction of new chemical storage facilities, and the stabilization of the K-65 silos.[67]

Less than two weeks later, on September 29, President Reagan signed the Department of Defense's fiscal year 1989 authorization bill, which formally established Senator Glenn's Defense Nuclear Facilities Safety Board.[68] It was another national victory for Fernald's environmental movement and an important step toward independent oversight of nuclear weapons production. At the same time, however, Westinghouse's relationship with the FATLC was crumbling over increased costs for medical insurance. At 12:01 a.m. on October 7, workers walked off the job for the second time in only three years.⁶⁹ But this time, the unions had almost no leverage. The meltdown at Chernobyl in the Soviet Ukraine reverberated across the American nuclear weapons complex as the DOE battled increased public scrutiny over the potential for nuclear accidents during a significant decline in Cold War tensions. After the DOE announced that Hanford's N Reactor—Fernald's largest customer for uranium metals—was going to be "mothballed" after a two-year closure for safety upgrades because of a plutonium surplus, Fernald's mission was also called into question. "It's an obsolete facility," said Robert Alvarez of the Environmental Policy Institute, and "the department is going to have to close down some of these old plants."⁷⁰ With the DOE sitting on a plutonium surplus and investing in new technology to recover more from spent nuclear fuel, the Fernald model of nuclear weapons production increasingly looked like a relic of the past.⁷¹

A NATIONAL STORY

In the fall of 1988, Ohio Governor Richard Celeste was increasingly preoccupied with Fernald. The plant's failures in environmental health and safety were national news, and the governor's office put together a long list of reporters writing about the plant, including Thom Shanker at the *Chicago Tribune*; Cass Peterson at the *Washington Post*; Matthew Wald, Keith Schneider, and Kenneth Noble at the *New York Times*; Robert Gillette at the *Los Angeles Times*; Ginny Carroll at *Newsweek*; and Ed Magnuson at *Time* magazine.⁷² With the Fernald controversy in widespread circulation, Celeste hoped to seize this opportunity for action and make his state safer. On October 18, he sent a letter to President Reagan requesting Fernald's immediate closure. "This facility is an environmental disaster," Celeste argued, "threatening the health and safety of thousands of Ohioans." Before restarting production, Celeste mapped out six requirements that the DOE should meet at the facility: independent health assessments for workers and neighbors, cleanup of the K-65 silos, further treatment of thorium, determining the contents of two hundred thousand containers of waste, expediting an environmental assessment of the plant, and contracting an independent board to develop recommendations for safe nuclear production at Fernald. After years of legal battles with the DOE to enforce compliance, the State of Ohio had had enough of the "insensitive and cynical treatment of our citizens" by federal officials who willfully endangered workers and public health by prioritizing production over environmental health and safety.[73]

Although Fernald's environmental movement appreciated Celeste's support, the governor's strategy was out of step with their tactics. Fernald's environmental supporters in Congress, including Senators John Glenn and Howard Metzenbaum and Representative Tom Luken, were prolabor and opposed any calls for the plant's closure. Not only would a shutdown threaten about 1,500 jobs, but Senator Glenn also believed that if Fernald was deemed no longer essential to the department's mission, the DOE would lose its sense of urgency to clean up the plant.[74] An internal memorandum written for Governor Celeste also reveals differing perspectives on environmental health and safety at Fernald between the governor's office and the state's congressional delegation. "Despite what you and [Ohio EPA] Director Rich Shank say about the immediate health risk of the facility," the memorandum stated, "these members believe the facility is safe enough to continue operation." Celeste's stepping out on his own backed the state into a corner, which had already "exhausted" its tools for unilateral action. Ohio needed "some delegation support" to "give us the club we need over" Secretary Herrington and would likely only obtain their support by softening its position on immediate closure.[75] As Fernald's movement had demonstrated, the state can be a powerful tool for environmental activism. But without congressional support, the state's hands were tied.

Celeste and Glenn took their debate to television. On October 28, they appeared as special guests for the filming of an episode of *Donahue* about Fernald, which was hosted at Hamilton High School.[76] Phil Donahue, an Ohio native who got his start at Dayton television station WLWD, pioneered the daytime talk-show genre in the late 1960s and 1970s and reached millions of viewers with thoughtful discussions of controversial subjects. *Donahue* was particularly innovative, because the host asked audience members questions. In this space, it was not only expert guests but also common people that contributed to public debate. The Fernald episode was no different, and the show set aside six hundred tickets for the public and specifically reached out to striking workers, Westinghouse managers, and area residents to attend the filming.[77]

Audience members voiced a variety of perspectives on Fernald, which should be remembered as a measure of the show's success. Many feared that radioactive and chemical contamination were making people sick. A professor of special education from nearby Miami University claimed that birth defects were shockingly high in communities surrounding the plant. "Such genetic handicaps we're expected to see one in a million," the professor stated, but "we're seeing whole neighborhoods with them."[78] Since the pollution was discovered four years before, one audience member wondered aloud, "I don't see why we should have to wait for more studies; we should just make them stop." Her statement drew applause from the crowd.[79] The wife of a Fernald worker, married for twenty-seven years, countered that "my husband is very healthy" and "I wouldn't send him into a plant to die."[80] Others were concerned with their economic future. One Fernald resident was discouraged that the home she purchased five years before had depreciated by ten thousand dollars, despite investing twenty thousand in improvements. A local real estate agent replied, however, that they had sold several hundred homes in the area without any trouble. Even in disagreement, there was one thing Glenn, Celeste, and most of the audience could agree on: the DOE was responsible for this mess.[81]

The DOE was notably absent from the show, which was part of Phil Donahue's personal decision to "keep it as simple as possible."[82] Donahue had recently watched Representative Luken and the DOE's manager of operations for Oak Ridge, Joe LaGrone, debate Fernald pollution and legal liability on PBS's *The MacNeil-Lehrer NewsHour* and found LaGrone's answers to be "so predictable."[83] The broadcast followed on the heels of a revelatory hearing of the House of Representatives' Subcommittee on Transportation, Tourism, and Hazardous Materials, which was chaired by Luken.

Luken called the hearing because the Fernald community's class-action lawsuit was rapidly progressing, and in a shocking turnaround, the DOE's legal team had submitted a memorandum and supporting affidavits to the US District Court in Cincinnati admitting responsibility for decades of environmental contamination at Fernald, as well as prior knowledge of these conditions and deploying obsolete environmental monitoring equipment.[84] The Oak Ridge Operations Office, according to the DOE's Malcolm Theisen, "did not always require that [Fernald] be in compliance with environmental standards and laws enacted by state and local governments." This "inevitably resulted in violations," Theisen continued, and "I and other Oak Ridge Operations officials instructed NLO to continue operations in the face of violations."[85] This story was featured on the front page of the *New York Times* under the headline "U.S., for Decades, Let Uranium Leak at Weapon Plant" and received earlier coverage in the *Cincinnati Enquirer*.[86] In the context of what appeared to be a multidecade conspiracy, it was difficult—if not impossible—for many PBS viewers, including Donahue, to believe a word LaGrone said.

LaGrone was candid, however, about the DOE's failures in environmental health and safety. When asked if the DOE and its contractors historically prioritized the production of nuclear materials over public health, he responded "yes," and added, "In terms of what happened at Fernald and other facilities which I am intimately familiar with, very frankly the contractors nor the federal people did their jobs."[87] This level of openness was part of an important transformation in the DOE. After Oak Ridge's mercury releases, LaGrone had recognized that the EPA and the State of Tennessee were on the verge of shutting the Y-12 plant down. The DOE, as a result, pledged to work toward environmental compliance and started acknowledging its past mistakes in the media.[88] What really angered Luken, however, was the cynical motivation behind LaGrone's openness concerning Fernald's class-action lawsuit. What LaGrone "hasn't said is that there is a contract here," Luken explained, that dictated that the "DOE is responsible if the contractor is held liable."[89] By accepting responsibility for the contamination, NLO would be exonerated of wrongdoing and the DOE's lawyers could also avoid accountability for the department by claiming sovereign immunity. In this context, LaGrone's openness entirely missed the point for Luken and demonstrated the DOE's willingness to adopt whatever strategy was necessary—even environmentalism—to protect its system of nuclear weapons production.[90] The DOE and NLO polluted Fernald's backyard, and the plant's neighbors deserved compensation for it.

The same week that the *Donahue* episode aired, Fernald's Clawson family was pictured on the cover of *Time* magazine standing against the gates of Fernald under the headline "The Nuclear Scandal."[91] Beneath the barbed wire, the subheading stated, "The Clawsons of Ohio blame the Fernald uranium plant for cancer in their family. They are not alone."[92] Marvin Clawson recalled that, for self-described "country folk," all the attention, including local, national, and even international reporters seeking interviews, was a surreal experience.[93] But for the Clawsons, as well as families with similar experiences at Hanford, Savannah River, and Rocky Flats, there was a sense of urgency to tell their stories. People's lives depended on it, so when *Time* came knocking, they answered the door.

Doris Clawson's parents, the Butterfields, had bought their home in 1940, but their families had settled the area in the early 1800s. It was over a decade before the plant's construction, a time when Fernald was known for producing agricultural commodities instead of uranium metals.[94] During the Cold War, however, these two worlds—the bucolic and the atomic—would intertwine as Fernald's uranium escaped its stacks into the air, water, soil, and bodies of its workers and neighbors. This is what Clawson feared was responsible for the cancer that spread throughout her body, resulting in a mastectomy and surgeries to remove cancerous growths from her lymph nodes and throat. Clawson's mother, Amy Butterfield, had similarly painful health issues, including six surgeries for colon and rectal cancer.[95] The Clawsons and Butterfields felt "deceived and lied to" by the federal government. "We ask for the truth," Clawson said, "but we know damned well we are not going to get it."[96]

Charles Zinser lived in a Cincinnati suburb called Greenhills, one of three towns built by the Resettlement Agency during the Great Depression as part of President Franklin D. Roosevelt's New Deal. Greenhills was a government experiment in community planning whose defining feature was its surrounding "greenbelt," which preserved open space and limited encroachment on the community's rural character.[97] From this utopian town, Zinser started renting a vegetable garden near Fernald in 1984, which quickly turned into a dystopian nightmare. He often brought his two young sons, eight-year-old Samuel and two-year-old Louis, to work in the garden. Two years later, Samuel was diagnosed with leukemia and Louis needed part of his leg amputated after also being diagnosed with cancer. Zinser had the soil tested, which revealed enriched uranium-235, and the doctor who performed Louis's procedure explained to Zinser that the amputation contained ten times more uranium than what would be expected to accumulate naturally during a lifetime. The likely pathway for this deadly concentration, the doctor explained, was breathing contaminated air.[98]

For all the suffering his family endured, all Zinser wanted from the DOE was the truth and an honest effort to make things right. "I would like to see, just like it was an individual, that they'd just admit they screwed up, that they were willing to right their wrongs," Zinser said. "There is a lot of damage they can't undo," he understood, "but if they deny responsibility, and you have a government that is not accountable to its citizens, then you do not have a republic."[99] Zinser's simple request for honesty and accountability, which really captures all nuclear weapons communities ever wanted out of the DOE, would make all the more painful the fiercely personal battles that played out in America's courtrooms in the coming years between the federal government and its citizens.

2010 REPORT

On December 11, 1988, the *Washington Post* broke a story about a forthcoming DOE document informally known as the "2010 Report," which had just been released to the National Security Council and provided a blueprint for the modernization of the nuclear weapons complex. The plan included the construction of four small reactors at Idaho National Engineering Laboratory and one large reactor at Savannah River; the relocation of plutonium projects out of the densely populated communities surrounding the Pinellas Plant near St. Petersburg, Florida, and the Lawrence Livermore National Laboratory near the San Francisco Bay Area; environmental cleanup funding for the most urgent contamination at the DOE's largest facilities; and finally, the shutdown of Fernald and Rocky Flats. Fernald's environmental movement was highly influential in the DOE's decision-making. Fernald and Rocky Flats, according to the *Post*, "have been linked to extensive environmental contamination and have become unpopular in their states."[100] The DOE also called for tens of billions more dollars in a separate report, named the "Glenn plan" after the Ohio senator, to fund long-term environmental remediation projects over the next forty years at nuclear weapons production facilities.[101]

The sudden news of Fernald's impending closure, which was also picked up by the *Cincinnati Enquirer*, infuriated Governor Celeste, who sent a scathing letter to Secretary of Energy Herrington. Celeste argued that "the almost inescapable conclusion is that the USDOE is leaking portions of the report to the press now in order to soften the impact of the full report when it is eventually released.... The most disturbing recent report, which appeared in the *Washington Post* last weekend, indicated that USDOE plans to close Fernald, perform a partial cleanup, and then move production to another site." This decision would leave "behind a contaminated and unusable 1,050 acre 'national sacrifice zone' and 1,500 unemployed workers. If this report is true, it is totally unacceptable."[102]

Governor Celeste had clearly experienced a change of heart since his call for the immediate shutdown of Fernald in October. The fear was, as Senator Glenn had warned, that if the DOE no longer had a stake in Fernald's future, then it might perform a superficial cleanup, leaving behind a "national sacrifice zone." The term, which was adopted by some US government officials and circulated widely in the press by environmental activists, described landscapes that were heavily contaminated during the Cold War through uranium mining, nuclear weapons production, and atomic testing. It was an acknowledgement that land, like a soldier's body, could be sacrificed for country. It was more complicated than that, however, because these landscapes could theoretically be reclaimed; it was just expensive and time-consuming to do so. As bureaucrats stared down the tens if not hundreds of billions of dollars necessary to clean up the Atomic Age, some reached the conclusion that the DOE should simply fence off and ban access to these areas permanently.[103] In the coming years, environmental activists in nuclear weapons communities dedicated much of their energy to ensure that this did not happen. The goal was to keep the DOE engaged and make sure that it received adequate funding for cleanup, out of fear that the nuclear weapons plants in their backyards would be boarded up, abandoned, and designated a "national sacrifice zone."

Around the same time that the 2010 report leaked, the plan for Fernald's cleanup was set in motion. The DOE and the State of Ohio signed a legally enforceable consent decree in federal court, which extended Ohio's jurisdiction over Fernald for state and federal hazardous waste laws, including mixed waste streams, and gave the state oversight of remediation under the Resource Conservation and Recovery Act (RCRA) and the Comprehensive Environmental Response, Compensation, and Liability Act (CERCLA). After the document was signed, Ohio Attorney General Anthony Celebrezze Jr. remarked, "We are making legal history today. For the first time a federal Department of Energy facility will operate under a strict court judgment requiring them to comply with all state and federal hazardous waste laws and meet proper groundwater, surface water and air pollution standards.... The state now can, and will, inspect the Fernald site and oversee cleanup."[104] Through the federal court system, the State of Ohio was hopeful that the consent decree would be the "club" it needed to wield over the DOE to clean up its radioactive backyards.

The future was looking brighter for cleanup, but the 2010 report felt like a knockout blow to Fernald's unions. Six days after the document leaked, the FATLC ended its ten-week strike against Westinghouse. Compared to 1985, when organized labor wielded significant influence because of a rising demand for Fernald's uranium products, the 1988 strike was a total failure. Although workers voted by a three-to-one margin to return to work, the decision was reached largely because "people realized that we had no more leverage to fight with."[105] Just one week before the strike was settled, 250 union workers were laid off, meaning that a skeleton crew of only 375 workers would return to Fernald, with nothing gained in their contract.[106] The future of production was now very much in doubt, which even Westinghouse president Bruce Boswell acknowledged. "I don't think there is any question," he said, "that [the 2010 Report] recommends that Fernald close.... Production levels are down, budgets are down ... it doesn't take any mental genius to read the handwriting on the wall."[107] For Westinghouse's leadership team, the shift from production to cleanup meant that the plant's business model needed a makeover. Boswell explained that "we'll spend the next year restructuring our engineering and management departments to aggressively attack environmental remediation," which would be followed by "training and reassignment for production forces."[108] Boswell hoped to get started immediately.

On December 19, union workers returned to Fernald for what some described as a day of "pep talks and propaganda." Most insulting—knowing that 250 colleagues had been laid off and that they were severely beaten at the bargaining table—was the sign that greeted their arrival at the plant entrance: "The Best Are Back."[109] From Westinghouse's perspective, the welcome was supposed to reconcile differences and reinforce safety through training sessions before restarting production, which had been shut down for the strike since October. With the 2010 report held up over a budget dispute between the DOE and the Office of Management and Budget and no official word from the DOE to cease production, Westinghouse needed to "recertify people on a lot of equipment" before restarting the plant after the holidays.[110] Despite all signs pointing toward closure, Fernald was forced to return to business as usual until Oak Ridge advised otherwise. Fernald's production workers were back but were greeted by an uncertain future.

The 2010 report, which was officially released on January 12, 1989, called for dramatic changes in the nuclear weapons complex, including the cessation of production at Hanford and the closure of Fernald, Rocky Flats, and Mound Laboratory.[111] Fernald "is severely deteriorated, and the projected workload is decreasing," the report stated, and "it would be cost-effective to transfer its remaining functions."[112] The report, which still anticipated "a relatively constant nuclear weapons program," suggests that Fernald's environmental movement and the national movement for environmental health and safety it helped build, successfully influenced DOE policy.[113] During the early 1980s, Fernald was considered an essential unit of the renewed nuclear arms race, so much so that the DOE planned to invest hundreds of millions of dollars to revitalize the aging facility and maintain its sprawling network for mass-producing nuclear weapons. After all the Fernald movement's protests, strikes, lawsuits, investigations, and media campaigns, as well as the creation of the Military Production

Network and Plutonium Challenge, the DOE recognized that its nuclear weapons production network needed to be reimagined if it was going to survive. Grassroots environmental activism had helped the DOE draft the next chapter of the Atomic Age, and it required the department to adopt modern technologies, comply with environmental laws, operate within a smaller physical footprint, and most importantly, clean up its radioactive legacy.[114]

six "America's Worst Polluter"

On February 13, 1989, US District Judge Arthur Spiegel, nominated in 1980 by President Jimmy Carter and confirmed by the Senate that same year, was seated at the bench in the Southern District Court of Ohio in Cincinnati. He was scheduled to issue an order on cross-motions for summary judgment in *Crawford v. National Lead Co.*[1] For the sixty-nine-year-old former Marine and federal judge of Jewish descent, it was another momentous decision in a lengthy career of public service, which included transformative rulings on civil rights, gay rights, prison reform, police brutality, and perhaps most famously (or infamously), sentencing Cincinnati Reds legend Pete Rose to five months in prison for tax evasion.[2] Representing the plaintiffs in Fernald's class-action lawsuit were attorneys Stanley Chesley and Louise Roselle of the Cincinnati firm Waite, Schneider, Bayless, and Chesley, and representing the defendants were the lawyers for the Department of Energy (DOE) Jake J. Chavez from Albuquerque and Russell M. Young from Washington, DC, along with Assistant US Attorney Donetta D. Wiethe from Cincinnati. The most pressing question of the day was whether Judge Spiegel would uphold the defendant's claim to sovereign immunity under the "government contractor defense."[3]

That defense—which extended the federal government's sovereign immunity to civilian contractors—was first developed in 1940, but conflicting interpretations of its application had only recently been settled. In June 1988, the Supreme Court upheld the government contractor defense in *Boyle v. United Technologies Corp.*, a case in which United States Marine helicopter pilot David A. Boyle crashed off the coast of Virginia Beach and drowned because he was unable to escape through the poorly designed and obstructed emergency escape hatch. Boyle's father sued Sikorsky, the company that designed the aircraft, under Virginia tort law, and a jury ruled in his favor. The Supreme Court, however, upheld a Court of Appeals reversal that Sikorsky was immune under the government contractor defense and clarified that federal law could preempt state law in cases of "uniquely federal interest," as well as when a "significant conflict" occurred between state and federal law. In the *Boyle* case, the conflict was the federal government's ability to procure essential equipment. "It makes little sense to insulate the Government against financial liability," Justice Antonin Scalia wrote on behalf of the court, "when the Government produces the equipment itself, but not when it contracts for the production."[4] After the Supreme Court's ruling in *Boyle*, the DOE's legal team prepared to test the government contractor defense in the booming field of "toxic torts."[5]

The plaintiffs agreed that Fernald's national security mission was of "uniquely federal interest" but argued that there was no conflict between federal law and the state tort claim because the DOE violated several federal environmental laws, including the Refuse Act of 1899, the Standards for Protection against Radiation Protection, and the As Low as Reasonably Achievable policy of the Atomic Energy Commission (AEC) for radiation emissions. "Because defendants violated pertinent environmental laws by discharging radioactive material into the environment," Judge Spiegel ruled, "there is no conflict between state tort law and the federal interests at issue here.... The government contractor defense does not apply to shield defendants from liability for those emissions, and their motion for summary judgment hereby is denied."[6] Fernald's class-action lawsuit was heading to trial.

Spiegel's ruling came at a transformative period in American history as the public's faith in the federal government was eroding during the late-twentieth century.[7] A substantial but underappreciated reason for this decline was pollution.[8] These feelings were captured in a May 3, 1990, article written by journalist Howard Kohn in *Rolling Stone*, whose title, "America's Worst Polluter," mocked the shameful environmental conditions of federal facilities. Kohn, who published the 1981 book *Who Killed Karen Silkwood?*, based on the mysterious death of the nuclear worker turned whistleblower, linked the DOE's radioactive contamination of nuclear weapons communities, including Fernald, Hanford, Rocky Flats, and Savannah River, with the extensive chemical contamination surrounding Department of Defense installations, such as the Rocky Mountain Arsenal near Denver. "How can the government in good conscience enforce the law against Exxon," asked Robert Alvarez, then a senior investigator for the Governmental Affairs Committee, chaired by Senator John Glenn of Ohio, "when it is de facto the biggest outlaw?"[9]

Alvarez's skepticism toward the federal government's environmental record was part of a larger public trend that was decades in the making. Fernald's lawsuit connected the plant's neighbors to a broader community of plaintiffs seeking redress from the federal government, including shipbuilders who breathed in deadly asbestos during World War II, Vietnam veterans who had their skin doused in the toxic defoliant Agent Orange, Navajo and Pueblo uranium miners, and "downwinders" from the AEC's nuclear weapons tests. Instead of accepting responsibility for, or even acknowledging the dangers of, radiation, asbestos, and Agent Orange, the federal government denied all liability.[10] Faced with what almost certainly felt like gaslighting by government lawyers, these contentious encounters in American courtrooms over contaminated bodies and environments represented arguably the most personal moments in the long and frustrating battles grassroots activists fought with the federal government. "The process" of fighting DOE, according to Lisa Crawford, "has made us all skeptics and cynics."[11] While congressional action was arguably the more effective venue to resolve toxic torts, legislators had historically been reluctant to settle the cases, or provided compensation that was too little and too late for victims.[12] After years of government foot-dragging at Fernald, the courts genuinely appeared to be FRESH's only option for action. "It's such a relief to go to trial," said Lisa Crawford on behalf of Fernald's neighbors. "It's like justice is being done at last. We don't have to wait for Congress to do anything; we can do it ourselves."[13] FRESH's lawsuit marked a turning point in the DOE's treatment of radiation victims, which forced the department to acknowledge past injustices and develop compensation programs.[14] Through their personal attacks in court on the communities they polluted, however, the DOE continued to alienate itself from the broader public even as it worked to clean up its operations.

A NEW MISSION

While the DOE fiercely denied that Fernald caused any resident's or worker's health problems, it was open about its responsibility for environmental contamination. On March 9, 1989, President George H. W. Bush addressed this crisis at the swearing-in ceremony for retired Admiral James D. Watkins as secretary of energy. "The most pressing challenge," President Bush told Watkins, "is to manage the modernization of America's nuclear weapons production plants. This task is critical to . . . perfecting our deterrent force, which ensures our security and, thus, a safe and stable world. But we also have a major environmental challenge: We need to clean up the pollution that's been created at these plants."[15] Fernald's environmental movement had transformed the nuclear deterrent. Not only did the United States need to maintain a strong nuclear arsenal, but it needed to do so in compliance with environmental laws.

Bush's appointment of Admiral Watkins continued the Reagan administration's legacy of filling the DOE and its nuclear weapons production plants with disciples of Hyman Rickover's nuclear navy to resolve the department's managerial failures in environmental health and safety.[16] Watkins, who was selected as an officer by Rickover, spent more than three decades in the Navy and rose through the branch's ranks from a submarine commander to its highest office, chief of naval operations.[17] "As you can glean from my own biography and the program today," Watkins said, "my training and experience began in the early days of the peaceful use of nuclear energy, where I learned the important principles of safe and reliable application of nuclear technology. . . . Nuclear power demands no less than the best from all who control it." The retired admiral, like his mentor Rickover, demanded "a commitment to excellence" from his employees. There was hope in the Bush administration, as well as the larger public, that Watkins was the right leader to raise the DOE's sinking ship.[18]

LOBBY DAYS

In early April, the Plutonium Challenge and the Military Production Network (MPN) joined forces for a mail and lobby campaign in Washington, DC, which grew into an annual tradition for the MPN known as "Lobby Days."[19] The Plutonium Challenge was campaigning for a two-year moratorium on plutonium and highly enriched uranium production in both the United States and Soviet Union, which Oregon Democrat Ron Wyden introduced in the House of Representatives as the International Plutonium Control Act.[20] To support the bill, the Plutonium Challenge drew upon the MPN for "shock troops," because they were the individuals living with the DOE's radioactive contamination in their backyards. Their stories, such as Lisa Crawford's, would make the most impact on members of Congress.[21]

During the 1980s, environmental organizations increasingly turned their attention from litigation to electoral politics.[22] After a decade spent in the courtroom, the environmental movement dramatically expanded its power and achieved sweeping legislative victories, but at the expense of demobilizing its broader base. The MPN's Lobby Days, as a result, was one of several such events intended to restore power to the grassroots.[23] If environmentalism was going to survive in a new era of antiregulatory politics, a hardworking housewife from rural Southwest Ohio like Lisa Crawford was a far more effective face for the movement than the Ivy League–educated lawyers who led the public interest movement in the 1970s.[24]

During the MPN's first two years, the organization worked through its growing pains. It surveyed its members for input on training needs and debated what the role and structure of the organization should be. In response to a survey on cross-training, Fernald Residents for Environmental Safety and Health (FRESH)'s Lisa Crawford requested to work with the Government Accountability Project and Environmental Policy Institute, which could provide political insight into Washington, DC.[25] The MPN also hosted workshops on legislation, media relations, and developing alliances with organized labor.[26] For this reason, the MPN was an excellent resource for small groups like FRESH, which could call upon national and Washington, DC–based environmental and public interest groups for political and technical expertise. MPN members agreed, however, that each group would retain its independence so "organizations can work together as they choose to, without feeling forced to subscribe to any one viewpoint or be represented by any single voice."²⁷ That way, groups with differing perspectives, experiences, budgets, and objectives could work and learn together while maintaining their autonomy.

The MPN's bottom-up structure was the vision of its cofounder, Bill Mitchell. It allowed the organization to thrive in an increasingly grassroots era of environmentalism, when local groups, and especially activists of color, clashed with national organizations over feelings of exclusion.²⁸ "The most remarkable thing about Bill Mitchell and the Military Production Network," recalled the Institute for Energy and Environmental Research's Arjun Makhijani, was that "the microphone was in the hands of the leaders and activists who were from the communities where the nuclear weapons plants were located. . . . It came naturally that Lisa Crawford, who lived near the Fernald plant was one of the people who was front and center."²⁹ Mitchell was rewarded for his vision. Crawford and FRESH, which was largely composed of working and middle-class white women, brought a blue-collar mentality to the white-collar MPN.³⁰ During one meeting, when asked about FRESH's current strategy, Crawford replied, "[We] work our asses off" and "bring experts in."³¹ This attitude undoubtedly energized the MPN, but it also represented the substantial sacrifice Crawford and her FRESH colleagues made for the movement. She did not have the luxury of being a professional activist. Her duties in FRESH and the MPN were completed *after* caring for her family and working a full-time job, so the investment of time, money, and energy was extraordinary.³²

In advance of the first Lobby Days, the MPN distributed a briefing book to Congress with materials from the MPN's national and local groups to educate politicians on the issues of nuclear weapons production and cleanup.³³ This gave the members of FRESH the opportunity to reintroduce themselves to Congress and inform them where they stood on key issues. FRESH's priorities were the health and safety of residents, the cleanup of Fernald, and the investigation of off-site contamination. FRESH's role was to educate its neighbors and serve as a watchdog for Fernald to "make sure that DOE promises are not just promises, but pledges." Even four years after its formation, FRESH never wavered from its commitment to Fernald's unions. In the briefing book, FRESH reminded members of Congress that it did "not want the Feed Materials Production Center to close or be shut down. We have always pressed for clean-up over closure. We do feel however, that production should *halt* until clean-up is completed." What FRESH needed from Congress was "a commitment for cleanup and dollars to do cleanup." Without congressional support, FRESH feared that the DOE would abandon the community and leave Fernald as a "national sacrifice zone."[34] FRESH would never bet all its chips on Congress, however. It was always fighting on two fronts: locally and nationally.

THE SETTLEMENT

On June 5, 1989, the Fernald class-action lawsuit had its first day in court, but this case would not play out like your typical toxic tort. Judge Spiegel initiated a summary trial, which is an abbreviated and nonbinding trial in which jurors issue a verdict after hearing the attorneys' opening and closing arguments and weighing key pieces of evidence. Their decision is intended to represent how a regular jury would award damages without the extensive investments of time and money required of a full trial.[35] By 1989, an explosion in high-profile toxic torts, including the Woburn, Massachusetts, community's civil suit against W. R. Grace and Beatrice Foods for their toxic waste having allegedly caused childhood leukemia, had well demonstrated that these kinds of cases were controversial, expensive, and time-consuming for all parties.[36] Through a summary trial, Spiegel hoped to expedite the process by forcing a settlement and sparing the community the exhaustion of a complete case.

It was a long time coming for Lisa and Ken Crawford. Four years had passed since they originally filed the lawsuit. The Crawfords, along with their FRESH colleagues, had persevered through years of denial and deflection by the DOE. Just to reach this point in the trial, they had sat through exhausting and hours-long depositions and undergone invasive psychological evaluations. They were asked confusing and violating questions, including "Do you put your own gas in your car?" and "How often do you have sex?" Lisa Crawford remembered the DOE-hired psychiatrist as the most "in-compassionate" doctor she had ever met.[37] Even though the DOE "tried everything in their power to wear us down," Crawford said, "it just doesn't work."[38] As environmental activists had learned over the previous two decades, the courtroom was the best place for ordinary Americans to level the playing field against the federal government and corporate polluters.[39]

In Fernald's class-action lawsuit, the plaintiffs contended that radioactive contamination from National Lead of Ohio (NLO)'s operations at Fernald diminished property values and caused significant emotional distress over fears of cancer. The defendants countered that the plaintiffs had not been harmed economically or psychologically by Fernald's pollution.[40] "Stress," according to the *Cincinnati Enquirer*, was the "key issue" on the trial's opening day. For Fernald's neighbors, this stress was triggered by living close to a uranium metals production plant, which was exacerbated the previous September when the DOE admitted "that it had known about the uranium contamination for years but did nothing to stop it."[41] FRESH's stress, however, was not a local phenomenon. It was part of a much larger story of "technological disasters," including toxic waste and radioactive contamination, destabilizing communities across the United States.[42]

During the 1980s, scholars began studying psychological patterns in communities where industrial accidents took place, such as the partial nuclear meltdown at Three Mile Island in Harrisburg, Pennsylvania, as well as places contaminated with toxic chemicals, including Love Canal in Niagara Falls, New York, and Times Beach, Missouri.[43] By banding together as FRESH, Fernald's neighbors exhibited "a way of coping common and effective among besieged groups," which tied together the experiences of grassroots activists across the country, including Fernald, Love Canal, and Woburn.[44] While community organizing can be empowering, there are also many harmful outcomes for these groups. According to environmental psychologist Michael Edelstein of Ramapo College in New Jersey and author of *Contaminated Communities: The Social and Psychological Impacts of Residential Toxic Exposure*, contamination victims no longer assume they are healthy, grow increasingly pessimistic about the future, view the environment as harmful and unpredictable, feel trapped instead of comforted at home, and lose faith in the government's willingness to protect the public.[45]

Fernald's lawsuit spoke to the growing segment of citizens whose bodies were betrayed by the federal government, including the many other nuclear weapons production communities spread across the country.[46] "What happens at Fernald is very important to us," said Kerry Cooke of the Snake River Alliance, an environmental watchdog of the DOE's Idaho National Engineering Laboratory. "It has to do, most basically," Cooke continued, "with a citizen's right to know."[47]

The largest demographic, perhaps, who could relate to the stress and feelings of betrayal experienced by Fernald's victims were veterans of the Vietnam War. For context on the trial, the *Cincinnati Enquirer* reached out to Jim Wall, a resident of Colerain Township in Hamilton County and chair of the Agent Orange Committee for the local chapter of the Vietnam Veterans of America. "There isn't a day that goes by that I don't think about it," said Wall, who sprayed Agent Orange in Vietnam and later developed a brain tumor and skin rashes, because "every day I have to cope with another problem with my body. . . . When you fight the government, it drains you to the point where you want to give up. . . . But I'll fight them till the day I die."[48]

For Fernald's victims, getting through the trial's first day was excruciating. Despite the federal government's public acknowledgement of responsibility for the plant's environmental contamination, the DOE's attorney, Henry A. Gill Jr., denied that it harmed anyone physically, psychologically, or economically. "The facts support our strongest contention," stated Gill, that "there has been no harm to the plaintiffs in this case." Homes in the area were "selling for good prices and . . . fair market value," according to Gill. Concerning the plaintiffs' health, "there is nothing off site of that plant that has caused anyone to suffer any ill-health effects," Gill asserted. "There was just no health hazard by any standard." These claims did not sit well with the plaintiffs, whose lives had been upended since the lawsuit was filed. "He's saying we're crazy," said Gerda McFarland, who lived on the western edge of Fernald's boundary with her husband Bill, who was undergoing cancer treatment. "How can he be so insensitive?" McFarland wondered.[49]

These were the kinds of moments in toxic torts that eroded the public's trust in government. For Fernald-area residents, scientific evidence and legalese were not the point. Epidemiological studies are complex, and even at their best, determining a causal link between hazardous exposures and illnesses is extremely difficult.[50] The plaintiffs also already knew that the epidemiology would not be available for the summary trial, because the DOE had derailed the research by underreporting Fernald's radioactive emissions to the Centers for Disease Control.[51] It was a violation of common sense, including decades of unregulated operations and the haphazard disposal of dangerous radioactive and chemical wastes, for the DOE's lawyers to argue otherwise. It was also a violation of right and wrong. "They're trying to hide behind what the law might stipulate," said Charles Zinser, whose children's battles with cancer were featured in *Time* magazine and an episode of *Donahue*. "That just isn't the issue."[52]

In response to the DOE's denial of harm, Chesley went on the offensive with expert depositions. To piece together the extent of Fernald's contamination and NLO's negligence, Waite, Schneider, Bayless, and Chesley had contracted the director of energy programs at the Institute for Energy and Environmental Research, Arjun Makhijani—who earned a PhD in the Department of Electrical Engineering and Computer Sciences, with a specialization in nuclear fusion, from the University of California, Berkeley—to complete a study of atmospheric uranium releases from Fernald during the years 1951 to 1985. Based on hundreds of internal documents from NLO, as well as other sources uncovered during discovery, Makhijani concluded that the company misrepresented its emissions to the DOE and the public, maintained poor records, and generally "had a complete disregard for safety" concerning the monitoring and control of radioactive materials.[53] Whereas the DOE had recently estimated that 383,000 pounds of uranium oxide had been released from the plant during this period, Makhijani cast doubt on these numbers, suggesting a much higher level: between 550,000 and 3 million pounds.[54] Based on the fragmentary evidence, it was impossible to know for certain.

Once the environmental contamination was evident, Chesley's next step was to demonstrate its impact on Fernald's neighbors. David Egilman, a medical doctor and public health specialist from Brown University, was already quite knowledgeable about Fernald by the time he provided his testimony. In his previous position with the Greater Cincinnati Occupational Health Center, Egilman helped the Fernald Atomic Trades and Labor Council (FATLC) develop its National Institute for Occupational Safety and Health (NIOSH) study. "Cancer deaths will occur," Egilman warned, "and those cancer deaths will be caused by the releases.... Safety practices by NLO show a total disregard for normal levels of care."[55] While medical testimony was important for demonstrating NLO's negligence, Chesley only needed to prove mental distress. It was psychiatrists, as a result, who provided the key evidence in the summary trial.

Speaking on behalf of the plaintiffs, Walter Stone of the Central Psychiatric Clinic at the University of Cincinnati concluded that "Fernald residents Peggy Shafer, Shirley and James Pierce, and Dorothy Lippert suffer psychological stress because of the plant's pollution." Shafer lived within sight of Fernald and viewed the plant as a "monster" that made living "hopeless to her." The Pierces lived within one mile of Fernald, but it seemed to follow them everywhere they went. Shirley came to believe that "anything she touched would contaminate her" and had grown into a "recluse," according to her husband James, who himself had contemplated suicide. These stories reflected the "anxiety, depression, lack of trust of other people, elevated agitation, and belligerence" manifested in the Fernald community, which Jacob Lindy and Bonnie Green of the Central Psychiatric Clinic called "informed of radiation contamination syndrome." These symptoms were not unique to Fernald, according to the psychiatrist and psychologist, but resembled the experiences found in Three Mile Island residents, the Beverly Hills Supper Club fire survivors, and military veterans returning from Vietnam.[56] Modern industrial hazards, including nuclear power and toxic chemicals, were causing an epidemic across the United States — not only physically but psychologically.

DOE lawyer Jake Chavez was no stranger to challenging activists in court. During the early 1980s, he worked on a major downwinder case in southern Utah in which over one thousand people sued the federal government over increased rates of cancer from nuclear weapons testing. Only ten cases were attributed to the nuclear fallout, and even those few were overturned soon after in the Tenth Circuit Court of Appeals in Denver.[57] Chavez was experienced, as a result, and planned to prove that instead of radiation exposures being traumatic events, they were in fact mundane occurrences. To help illustrate this point, Chavez transformed a Cincinnati courtroom into "Chemistry 101," according to the *Cincinnati Enquirer*.[58] "They're perfectly harmless," said Chavez, as he placed four plastic vials of uranium on the jury box. Next, Chavez set up a display of household items, including a Coleman lantern, a smoke detector, a Polaroid camera, an orange saucer, and a watch with a luminous dial. Using a Geiger counter, Chavez demonstrated that they all contained radioactive materials as the device rapidly beeped over each item. "These articles are common," said Chavez, "and have been common in the recent past."[59] If radiation exposures were routine, the jury was left to wonder, perhaps they were not so dangerous after all.

Next, the DOE's legal team waged an assault on the plaintiffs' claims to psychological distress. The federal government hired three psychiatrists of its own to conduct evaluations of residents, which "revealed no emotional problems serious enough to justify a lawsuit."[60] All the residents' ailments, according to the DOE's experts, could be traced to their personal lives. Opal Beckett had had her voice box removed from throat cancer after forty-two years of cigarette smoking. She missed her deceased husband, was losing her vision, and worried about becoming a burden to her family as she aged. Doris Clawson's fear of cancer stemmed from her personal experience with the disease, as well as watching her family suffer with the illness, not Fernald's uranium. Peggy Shafer had a multidecade history of mental health issues, which began long before Fernald's 1984 uranium leak.[61]

After airing the plaintiffs' dirty laundry, the defense turned to its psychiatrists. DOE lawyer Russell Young quoted a deposition from Jacob Lindy in which the psychiatrist acknowledged worrying about the number of serious mental health conditions that he could identify in the Fernald population. "Zero illnesses," Lindy said, "would communicate that there's nothing wrong." There was something wrong, however, so Lindy helped create the concept of "informed of radiation contamination syndrome" to capture the Fernald community's suffering. It was a difficult idea to prove. First, there were no clear-cut diagnoses Lindy could rely on in *The Diagnostic and Statistical Manual of Mental Disorders* (DSM), the foundational text for the profession. Toxic communities certainly shared characteristics with natural disaster victims or veterans of war that exhibited post-traumatic stress disorder, but the creeping and invisible threat of "slow violence" was also a very different experience than the sudden and highly visible destruction found in the wake of a bombing campaign or earthquake.[62] Psychiatrists also ran into the same challenges that epidemiologists faced in demonstrating causation. "One can't statistically state," Lindy continued, "that Fernald is the causative agent" for the plaintiffs' mental health issues.[63] Scientifically proving mental health conditions from low-level radioactive exposure—just like physical ailments—was an enormous challenge that would require, if it were even possible, significant time and resources. These kinds of studies were extremely difficult to mobilize and complete before the start of a toxic tort.

The Fernald community's lawsuit was the first major legal challenge to the DOE's power at Cold War's end. It was a "virtual dogfight," according to the *Cincinnati Post*, with "bitter attacks and counterattacks by both sides that resembled those between residents and National Lead since the suit was filed four years ago." The lawyers also presented their cases with dramatically different styles. The DOE's Henry A. Gill Jr. was calm and collected. The case was not about emotion, he said, but what the law stipulates. "We're not saying there are not people who are disturbed, angry, or have some sorts of problems," said Gill. "We're saying that under Ohio standards, to recover for emotional distress, there must be severe and debilitating problems." Stanley Chesley, arguing on behalf of the plaintiffs, was heated. With his voice turned up to capture the rage of the Fernald community, he laid into the defense. For thirty-five years, NLO "spewed and sprayed" uranium on the plant's neighbors. "They said the plant caused no harm," he continued, but "the residents have a reasonable belief there was harm," because this case was not about legalese but personal and life-altering experiences. Fernald-area residents had "every reason to feel it, to believe it, to know it," Chesley concluded.[64] After closing arguments on June 13, it was now up to the jury to decide.

Judge Spiegel issued twenty-four questions to guide the jury, which would dictate if NLO was a nuisance, was negligent, or caused harm to Fernald's neighbors. Nobody knew which direction they would lean, but one thing was certain at the time: "History is in the making," according to *Cincinnati Post* reporter Al Salvato. If the plaintiffs won, it would "signal the first success by residents against an operator of an atomic weapons plant," but if the jury sided with the defense, "it could stifle legal challenges elsewhere."[65]

After a week of deliberation, the jury ruled in favor of Fernald-area residents and recommended awarding $136 million, including $1 million for property owners, $55 million for punitive damages, and, most importantly, $80 million for the development of a medical monitoring program for the plaintiffs.[66] Despite the jury's ruling, it was still nonbinding, and the case could still potentially go to trial. Only two weeks later, however, Chesley and Gill signed a memorandum of understanding to settle the case. The DOE agreed to pay $73 million on behalf of NLO for the establishment of a medical monitoring program and claims for emotional distress and diminished property value. The settlement also left open the door for future lawsuits related to new disclosures of public health hazards; claims for cancers, physical injury, or genetic defects; and legal action from NLO's former employees.[67] "The biggest thing," said Lisa Crawford, "is that we've shown the world that the DOE is wrong, that what they did to these people is wrong." But this moral victory was only the beginning for FRESH. "The next step," she concluded, "is to get it cleaned up."[68]

The Fernald community's settlement sent a clear signal to the federal government that national security was no longer an acceptable excuse for poisoning the environment and endangering public health.[69] "Not until a 1989 ruling in favor of the residents of Fernald, Ohio," sociologist Valerie L. Kuletz argued, "did the courts begin to shift position" on atomic victims.[70] In the aftermath of the settlement, activists in nuclear weapons production communities near Hanford, Rocky Flats, Mound, and Oak Ridge filed their own lawsuits against the DOE's operating contractors.[71] In 1990, Congress passed the Radiation Exposure Compensation Act (RECA), which awarded lump-sum payments to uranium miners, on-site participants at atmospheric nuclear weapons tests, and downwinders from the Nevada Test Site who developed qualifying diseases established under the law. Although the payments awarded under RECA could not begin to account for the human suffering attributable to the Cold War nuclear arms race, it was another clear signal that the DOE's days of denial were numbered.[72]

THE POLITICS OF TIGER TEAMS

While Fernald's trial was underway, the FBI and the Environmental Protection Agency (EPA) launched an unprecedented "raid" on Rocky Flats for possible environmental crimes. This action required approval from the highest levels of the federal government, including Secretary of Energy Watkins. On the morning of June 6, the US magistrate in Denver, Hilbert Schauer, issued a search warrant for Rocky Flats, and 120 federal investigators descended on the plant. Investigators searched thirty-one buildings, seized thousands of documents, and sampled twenty waste disposal areas. The FBI's search warrant affidavit alleged a conspiracy at Rocky Flats, including the illegal burning of radioactive wastes at night to avoid detection, in a building that plant management claimed to be closed. These "dramatic accusations," according to environmental journalist Len Ackland, "made for fascinating, disturbing reading" but "would prove to be wrong, although lesser charges would be supported."[73] Despite the overblown accusations, the FBI and EPA's raid sent shock waves through the nuclear weapons complex.

At Fernald, Westinghouse was stuck between a rock and a hard place. The company was already juggling the conflicting missions of uranium metals production and radioactive waste cleanup, but after the Rocky Flats raid, operating contractors also had to worry about the possibility of criminal charges. Westinghouse undoubtedly made several missteps at Fernald, but it also inherited a neglected plant with decades of radioactive contamination piled up. In early July 1989, with the pressure mounting for cleanup, Westinghouse Materials Company of Ohio (WMCO) President Bruce Boswell took an unprecedented step of his own and halted production without DOE approval and reassigned all production workers to waste management tasks.[74] "He caught considerable grief," recalled

Public Information Officer William "Pete" Kelley, "from DOE and from lots of folks.... They were tryin' to clean up the plant and to operate the plant at the same time," but "you couldn't do that, because it was always breaking down, and you were having spills and releases.... It was too old," and the DOE "hadn't maintained it."[75] By shutting down production, Boswell made a clear statement that, at Fernald, the DOE's conflicting missions had become untenable.

Criticism of Boswell poured in, including from Fernald's environmental movement. For Senator Glenn and FRESH, the sudden shutdown threatened the position of workers in the FATLC, because they needed time to be retrained for the cleanup. Representative Tom Luken, who had called for an FBI investigation of Fernald, found the timing suspicious, because that was only about two weeks before the arrival of an investigative Tiger Team, a group of experts that Secretary of Energy Watkins had tasked with conducting environmental health and safety assessments at the DOE's thirty-five major facilities after the FBI and EPA's raid on Rocky Flats.[76] According to Boswell, however, it was about the DOE's changing mission. "I'm still seeing the mentality that production comes first," he said, "and it doesn't."[77]

From July 17 to August 4, the Tiger Team, accompanied by EPA and Ohio EPA investigators, determined unsurprisingly that Fernald was not in compliance with numerous environmental laws, including the Resource Conservation and Recovery Act (RCRA), the Comprehensive Environmental Response, Compensation, and Liability Act (CERCLA), the Superfund Amendments and Reauthorization Act (SARA), the Clean Air Act, the Clean Water Act, and DOE Order 5400.1 General Environmental Protection Program. These violations were for failures in hazardous waste storage, monitoring of atmospheric releases, and wastewater treatment, plus failing to meet the requirements of the remedial investigation and feasibility study and the National Environmental Policy Act (NEPA). Westinghouse had made strides in worker safety, the Tiger Team conceded, but it was clear that Fernald "has not kept pace with changing safety and health requirements."[78] The report also affirmed that low staffing in environmental health and safety positions, lax attitudes, and limited progress toward environmental compliance were the root causes of Fernald's problems. This was a significant failure, because Fernald's contamination was already widely viewed as a national crisis.[79] Although there was considerable emphasis on Westinghouse's technical expertise when it took over operations from NLO, the Tiger Team's report suggests that improved management could not overcome Fernald's outdated technology, as well as the challenge of balancing the DOE's counterproductive missions of production and cleanup.

Despite Fernald's regulatory violations, the Tiger Team concluded that the plant did "not currently constitute an imminent threat to public health or welfare."[80] The EPA disagreed, however, citing necessary remedial actions for contaminated groundwater, runoff from the waste pits, contaminated soil, and the K-65 silos. The Tiger Team's report stated that the differences of opinion could be explained by how the agencies defined public endangerment. The DOE's definition of "imminent threat" included "acute, near-term health effects," while the EPA utilized "endangerment to public health and welfare" under its obligations to SARA, which included potential and actual "long term, chronic health effects."[81]

Beyond the EPA, internal critics of Watkins's multiple Tiger Teams across the nuclear weapons complex began to surface. Researchers at Lawrence Livermore and Oak Ridge National Laboratories were furious to see their projects picked apart by nonscientists and their research dollars diverted.[82] Lawyers from the Natural Resources Defense Council (NRDC) also pointed out that the Tiger Team's investigations were redundant because of the baseline environmental surveys conducted under Secretary Herrington during the Reagan administration. In a two-volume follow-up report to the team's visit, Westinghouse essentially reiterated the NRDC's argument by demonstrating how all the Tiger Team's main findings had already been identified by regulatory agencies before their arrival.[83] Although Secretary Watkins hoped to show forceful action with the deployment of such teams, they were sent down well-worn paths. Practically anybody who had picked up a newspaper or turned on the television since 1984 was aware that Fernald was not compliant with environmental laws. The Tiger Team made one point, however, that was important for both Westinghouse and the DOE: Fernald needed "clear delineation" of the plant's mission to meet the department's environmental health and safety goals.[84] In other words, Fernald could produce uranium metals or cleanup its radioactive backyard. It could not do both.

THE FIVE-YEAR PLAN

On August 1, 1989, at the National Press Club in Washington, DC, Secretary Watkins announced the DOE's "Five-Year Plan" to systematically restructure the department's environmental health and safety program and clean up the Cold War's legacy of radioactive contamination within thirty years. To reflect these new priorities, Watkins established the Office of Environmental Restoration and Waste Management and appointed his special assistant Leo Duffy as its first director. The move consolidated the DOE's environmental health and safety programs under one roof to signify that after decades of being an afterthought, the environment was finally on equal footing with production. To meet the department's short-term remediation goals and reduce the most immediate threats to public health, the DOE estimated that it would need $16.5–19.5 billion over the program's first five years.[85] These projections forecast an unprecedented undertaking that would require consistent funding, in addition to bipartisan support, across multiple decades to be successful.

The five-year plan signified that the DOE was ready to move on cleanup, but it was uncertain just how efficient the department could be. Nuclear waste management was a perilous political issue. In the late 1980s, Nevada's politicians fiercely protested the designation of Yucca Mountain as the nation's high-level nuclear waste repository.[86] As Nevadans demonstrated, the states would likely contest any unilateral action by the DOE, because no governors were eager to volunteer their states to be the nation's radioactive waste dump. In light of this controversy, as well as the skyrocketing projected costs for cleanup, the DOE turned its attention to isolating radioactive materials on-site. This strategy would avoid, according to Duffy, shuffling waste "from one hole in the ground to another hole in the ground."[87] To safely encapsulate and remove radioactive materials, the DOE needed to invest in remediation technologies, including vitrification—which solidified nuclear waste into a glass-like material—and aquifer restoration, which were both underdeveloped technologies at the time but viewed as critical to the DOE's success.[88] Since political solutions to radioactive waste management appeared nearly impossible, the DOE looked toward technological ones.

But the near-term outlook for aquifer remediation looked grim. The Senate Committee on Armed Services had tasked the Office of Technology Assessment (OTA), established by Congress in 1972 to advance green technology, to investigate technological solutions for the environmental and public health crises at the DOE's nuclear weapons facilities.[89] In *Complex Cleanup: The Environmental Legacy of Nuclear Weapons Production*, the OTA projected that "it may be impossible with current technology to remove contaminants from certain groundwater plumes and deeply buried soil." The current technologies at best would be "extremely expensive or require prolonged periods of operation."[90] To advance its cleanup goals, the DOE developed a plan for applied research and development in the field to quantify, remediate, and reduce the production of future wastes.[91] After spending decades of energy focused on developing ever more powerful nuclear weapons and accurate delivery systems, the DOE now looked to innovate in the growing industry of environmental remediation.

THE SOUTH PLUME

In October 1989, the DOE hosted a public meeting to update Fernald's neighbors on the remedial investigation and feasibility study that would guide the site's cleanup. Advanced Sciences, Inc. (ASI), the DOE's contractor for the job, had been busy throughout the summer drilling wells and testing the water for uranium contamination, which was confirmed in around 115 out of 180 wells tested. Concerning levels ranged from 1,000 parts per billion under the Ore Refinery to 10,000 under the Scrap Recovery Plant. Decades of production had left pools of uranium-contaminated water underneath Fernald, and the Ohio EPA worried that further investigations would reveal that these pools were interconnected or, even worse, that the uranium had seeped beneath an underlying layer of clay into the Great Miami Aquifer.[92]

Fernald needed major resources to solve its water problems. On a national scale, there were reasons to be optimistic. In November 1989, the

EPA formally started the process to clean up "America's Worst Polluter." Out of twenty-nine sites added to the Superfund's National Priorities List (NPL) that month, twenty-six were federal facilities, including Fernald and the Idaho National Engineering Laboratory, the Brookhaven National Laboratory, Mound, Savannah River, Oak Ridge, Monticello Mill Tailings, and the Bonneville Power Administration Ross Complex.[93] The passage of SARA, which waived the federal government's sovereign immunity and extended Superfund obligations to federal facilities, was already bearing fruit for Fernald's environmental movement.[94] Locally, however, tensions were still running high as each new testing well disclosed even more uranium.

As ASI's investigation continued, computer modeling helped piece together what became known as "the south plume"—uranium contamination in the groundwater that had drifted as far as a mile south of the plant.[95] While the relatively static uranium-contaminated pools underneath Fernald's plants could be pumped, treated, and discharged in a reasonable timeframe, the south plume posed several challenges for regulators. To pump and treat the Great Miami Aquifer, it would take "10, 20, 30 years, until enough clean water has passed through," according to ASI scientist Robert M. Galbraith, and even then "the water won't return to background levels" of radiation.[96] The Ohio EPA had also discovered "hot spots" further south and further north of where regulators originally estimated the south plume's borders to be. "We don't really know yet what the dimensions of the plume area are," said the Ohio EPA's Graham Mitchell.[97] Even with its boundaries undetermined, however, one thing was clear. The south plume had seeped beyond Fernald's gates and was heading toward a residential community.

After the trauma of Lisa Crawford's contaminated well, FRESH was determined to stop the migration of the south plume and ensure that the DOE did so responsibility. On July 5, 1990, Crawford and Edwa Yocum represented FRESH at a hearing at Crosby Elementary School with the Subcommittee on Transportation and Hazardous Materials, chaired by Representative Luken. Unfortunately, the DOE already seemed to be cutting corners. Its plan was to pump the migrated plume back to Fernald and discharge it untreated through an effluent pipe, which would have released 90–250 pounds of uranium daily into the Great Miami River. FRESH refused to pass this environmental burden on to downriver communities. "Dilution is not the solution," Lisa Crawford told the subcommittee.[98] FRESH knew better than most communities, after all, that small releases of contamination over time can accumulate into an environmental disaster. Despite this knowledge, the DOE clung to the dated idea that discharged wastes would simply be rendered harmless when dissolved into larger bodies of water, which was the exact argument AEC chairman Glenn T. Seaborg had made to his academic geologist critics back in 1965.[99] Shielded from external forces by the Atomic Energy Act, the DOE remained impervious to the intellectual influences of the Age of Ecology.[100]

FRESH activist Edwa Yocum lived less than two miles south of Fernald, in Harrison, and the south plume was migrating toward her neighborhood.[101] The Yocums had moved to the area in 1970 to enjoy the outdoors, which they did through gardening and fishing in the Great Miami River, which flowed through their property. After learning about Fernald's uranium contamination, Yocum joined FRESH to protect her family and their backyard sanctuary and took the lead on health issues for the organization.[102] Early on, FRESH had realized that the burden of proof for connecting illnesses with Fernald's radioactive and toxic byproducts fell on their shoulders. The activists, as a result, "lost all trust in the credibility of the local, state, and federal health and environmental protection agencies."[103] This loss of faith in institutions and experts was common in late-twentieth-century toxic communities, who took up "popular epidemiology" to collect their own scientific data and assert ownership of their own health.[104] In 1990, Yocum created a "cancer incidence map" to identify illnesses in Fernald's neighbors and to be used as an "educational tool." Disease clusters represented in the first hundred pins placed on the map were consistent with the prevailing wind to the northeast and the southwestern flow of contaminated groundwater; these were corroborated five years later by the Centers for Disease Control's Dosimetry Reconstruction Project.[105]

The self-education required to undertake popular epidemiology empowered Yocum to speak authoritatively at the hearing, despite a lack of

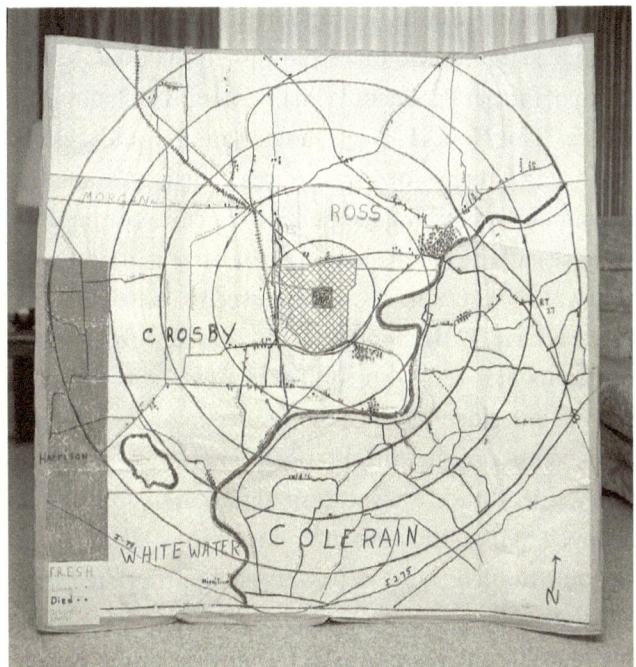

FIGURE 10. Fernald Residents for Environmental Safety and Health's cancer incidence map, April 24, 2000. Courtesy of the US Department of Energy.

professional credentials. "Uranium is a potential health risk due to its soluble compounds in the groundwater of the south plume," she began. "If ingested," uranium "can cause adverse health effects to the cardiovascular and endocrine system."[106] Yocum worked as a secretary—not a medical professional—but when threatened by hazardous materials, people challenge themselves to acquire the knowledge they need to protect themselves, their loved ones, and their neighbors.[107] Luken recognized Yocum's authenticity immediately. "You said that like you meant it," the congressman stated. "We thank you."[108]

FRESH wanted a permanent solution to the water contamination problem, so it called upon the DOE to fund a public water system in the area and pump and treat the Great Miami Aquifer indefinitely.[109] It was an idea that Crosby Township trustee Jane Harper had recently pitched to the community. She and her colleagues had surveyed 350 registered voters, and seventy-four percent enthusiastically supported the development of a public water system.¹¹⁰ Hamilton County Commissioner Robert A. Taft II, the great-grandson of former President William Howard Taft, however, had cast aside the idea. "Not Now, IF Ever," Taft declared, would a public water project be funded in Crosby Township. It was up to Representative Luken, as a result, to make something happen for the rural community. Harper reminded those gathered at the hearing that rural residents were also "VOTING, TAXPAYING CITIZENS" who deserved to "have the same services that other areas have."¹¹¹ Harper felt slighted, not only by the DOE but also local politicians like Taft who controlled Hamilton County's budget. Crosby Township residents valued their independence and open space, but not at the expense of their health or the environment. By the late twentieth century, this attitude was increasingly common in the Ohio Valley, as many believed that politicians and industry took advantage of rural residents for their limited political power and appropriated their communities to be the nation's dumping grounds.¹¹² There were many valid ways to spend Hamilton County's budget, of course, but as Harper and FRESH proclaimed, few items could be more pressing than ensuring safe drinking water.¹¹³

GREENING THE WORKFORCE

Worker morale had plummeted since production was halted. There were several explanations for the decline, according to Westinghouse senior system safety engineer Michael G. Lloyd, who wrote a guest column on the matter for the *Cincinnati Enquirer*. First, there was uncertainty surrounding future staffing levels at Fernald. By keeping the plant in limbo between production and cleanup, Fernald was "hemorrhaging" skilled workers, including the "managers, health and safety professionals, engineers and scientists" that all fled for more stable opportunities. "The seeming inability of the government to make up its collective mind as to what to do with the site," wrote Lloyd, was wreaking havoc on the possibility of cleanup. The press also deserved its share of criticism for developing what Lloyd called "Informed That You're a Good-for-Nothing Fernald Worker Syndrome." This tongue-in-cheek illness stemmed from "an almost constant barrage of negative information about your workplace, day in and day out, year after year." Its source was newspapers, television, radio, and even your own neighbors. At its best, it surfaced as a reporter accusing you of lying; at its worst, it was more menacing, such as a member of Congress calling for you or your coworkers to be thrown in jail.[114]

The "relentless Fernald-bashing," according to Lloyd, was counterproductive to anyone who wished to see the site cleaned up. The worse the morale became at the plant, the more likely technical experts — who had the essential skills to direct the cleanup as well as write compliance reports for the DOE and the EPA — were to resign. Lloyd came to Fernald after working at a "modern, state-of-the-art nuclear facility," and his initial impression was that it looked "medieval," so the engineer was far from delusional about Fernald's antiquated technologies and waste management practices. Despite these challenges, however, Lloyd, along with many colleagues, sincerely believed that with "the proper commitment of resources, the sweat of hard work, and the stamina of people filled with the desire to do good, this facility could be fixed and any damage done to the environment by its operation" could be restored. If the situation did not improve, "perhaps the Department of Energy will invite critics over for a housecleaning party."[115] After years of criticism in the media and unclear direction from the DOE, many Fernald workers were completely exhausted.

In October, Fernald was transferred to the DOE's Office of Environmental Restoration and Waste Management for cleanup. Its production days were officially over, and the time for cleanup had finally arrived.[116] To improve morale and prepare for this project, Westinghouse and Fernald's unions worked with local colleges and universities to retrain workers in environmental compliance, such as the RCRA and CERCLA. This led to the development of the seven-week DOE/Westinghouse School for Environmental Excellence. The school graduated its first class of thirty-five technical staff, including engineers and environmental scientists, on November 2, 1990.[117] In future years, the course was extended to former production workers, who took advantage of this transitional moment in Fernald's history to learn new skills.[118] It was a program that helped mend relationships between management and the unions. Former WMCO president Bill Britton recalled that the "educational courses we ran at the University of Findlay went a long way toward convincing both [us] and the union that we had common goals and could in fact work together to make this a better site."[119] Through retraining, the unions aimed to position former production workers as ideal candidates for the cleanup. Not only were they freshly schooled in environmental compliance, but through their production years they possessed intimate knowledge about Fernald's contamination.[120] The FATLC's blue-collars workers, in other words, were the perfect labor force to green Fernald's landscape.

ENVIRONMENTAL IMPACT STATEMENT

On January 14, 1991, antinuclear activists and environmentalists from across greater Cincinnati gathered in the Hilton North Hotel in Sharonville, a northern suburb of the city located off I-75 and east of Fernald along I-275, for a hearing on the Programmatic Environmental Impact Statement for the DOE's environmental restoration and waste management program.[121] It was one of twenty-three such hearings scheduled across the country, in which environmentalists and peace activists, from Hanford, Washington, to Savannah River, South Carolina, voiced their concerns about the DOE's forthcoming multibillion-dollar and multidecade cleanup program.[122] Since the passage of NEPA, federal agencies were required to issue Environmental Impact Statements in advance of development projects, which examined environmental consequences and opened federal projects to public comment.[123] As Secretary of Energy Watkins acknowledged, however, just as the DOE had bypassed other environmental laws, its NEPA program had been "haphazard."[124] Its hand was also forced, through a lawsuit by the NRDC and twenty-one other environmental organizations, which demanded public review of the DOE's cleanup plans.[125] With the hearing open from 9:00 a.m. to 9:00 p.m. to accommodate attendees' various schedules, it would be a long day for DOE officials.[126]

For those with deep roots in Cincinnati's antinuclear community, it must have felt like déjà vu to read in the newspapers about a nuclear hearing in Sharonville. In 1972, the suburb hosted one for the proposed Zimmer Nuclear Power Station east of Cincinnati.[127] This time, the hearing's focus had shifted from nuclear energy to nuclear weapons production, and how to manage a multidecade legacy of environmental contamination. As happened at the Zimmer hearing, Fernald activists voiced strong opinions on the issue. Sister Alice Gerdeman of the Sisters of Divine Providence in Melbourne, Kentucky—who was an active member of Zimmer Area Citizens, which formed after the accident at Three Mile Island—stated that "we have enough bombs—sixty thousand nuclear bombs—to kill every man, woman and child inhabiting the Earth twelve times over."[128] The executive director of Cincinnati SANE/FREEZE's Campaign for Global Security worried about the transportation of radioactive materials, arguing that the DOE needed to focus on developing technologies to contain wastes on-site, which was essentially the same position voiced by the DOE but for the reason of environmental justice instead of political feasibility.[129] Lisa Crawford represented FRESH at the hearing, and for a group that had been fighting the DOE on a daily basis for six years, it was the constant delays that were most terrifying. Every time progress on cleanup stalled, FRESH got more anxious whether the environment would be remediated or abandoned as a "national sacrifice zone."[130] Despite these criticisms, there was a growing sense of hope that cleanup could close the chapter on Fernald's production era and start a new and more sustainable one.

Ohio Senators John Glenn and Howard Metzenbaum submitted a joint statement for the hearing. They commended the DOE for the public dialogue, stating, "Today marks an important step towards openness by the Department of Energy. For the first time, the DOE is taking a generic look at its waste management and environmental restoration program with open and extensive public involvement."[131] Along with citizen input, Leo Duffy, director of the DOE's Office of Environmental Restoration and Waste Management, had hinted before the meeting how the public might envision Fernald's physical transformation, but also referred to the technological challenges that lay ahead. "One of the major areas of waste generation is going to be environmental restoration," he said. "In order to say that we're going to make Fernald green fields, we have to have some place that we will send the material."[132] For peace activists like Elizabeth Carey of the renamed Oxford Citizens for Peace and Justice, Fernald's transformation was moral as well as physical. "It is imperative that these funds go towards cleanup," Carey stated. "We ask for a new Manhattan Project—this one to cleanse ourselves of the sins of the past."[133] Carey's comment, which called for an ecological rebirth at Fernald, turned out to be more prophetic than she could have known at the time.

Like the Manhattan Project, the DOE's cleanup program in the following years would require an enormous mobilization of labor, resources, and expertise. The United States had invested $300 billion in the production of tens of thousands of nuclear weapons and the detonation of over one thousand. The industrial processes that produced this atomic arsenal left behind a legacy of twenty-four million cubic meters of waste and nine hundred million curies of radioactivity. This lake of contamination was spread across the DOE's massive nuclear weapons complex, including 2.3 million acres of land and 120 million square feet of buildings even after the Cold War's end.[134] But unlike the Manhattan Project, which invented the nuclear bomb that would eventually contaminate the earth with radioactivity through atomic testing, this green version of the Manhattan Project offered ecological salvation instead of destruction.

This form of salvation, however, could not be secured without developing a little faith in one another after a contentious decade. Ironically, the Fernald community lawsuit, which unearthed years of bad blood, was essential to this process. By securing medical monitoring and regaining at least some control over their health, an enormous burden was lifted off FRESH's shoulders, which allowed them to turn their attention to cleaning up the site.[135] With the lawsuit behind it, the DOE needed to get creative to clean up Fernald's radioactive backyard. Secrecy had created the mess during the nuclear arms race. The time had come for an honest conversation.

SEVEN FUTURESITE

On August 23, 1991, Undersecretary of Energy John Tuck spoke at the "Inauguration Day" ceremony held at Fernald.[1] Instead of a transition of political power, however, Fernald's inauguration day formally announced the site's transition from production to cleanup. "The Feed Materials Production Center is no more," said Tuck. To better reflect its new mission, the Department of Energy (DOE) rebranded the site as the Fernald Environmental Management Project. "The use of such innovations as advanced robotics and laser technology will place Fernald on the cutting edge," Tuck explained, and "the lessons learned here as a result of our cleanup efforts will have widespread application to many other facilities and communities."[2] For its role in nuclear weapons production, the aging facility was recently demonized as the "DOE's most decrepit dinosaur."[3] Those same environmental failures now presented themselves as economic opportunities in the booming environmental remediation industry.

Fernald Residents for Environmental Safety and Health (FRESH) were not impressed by the fancy new signage and boycotted the ceremony. "My feeling is you could put a piece of cardboard over the old name," scoffed Lisa Crawford. "It's still the same place. There's still contamination and, there's still a problem."[4] Under the leadership of Secretary of Energy James Watkins, the DOE was actively reorganizing to solve the department's radioactive waste crisis at its nuclear weapons production facilities, with Fernald well positioned as a major priority.[5] But the retired admiral's technological optimism, top-down approach to cleanup, and skepticism toward the environmental movement drove a wedge between the Bush administration and Fernald's activist community.[6]

In the early 1990s, both the DOE and FRESH wanted Fernald cleaned up, but they were essentially speaking different languages about the environment. One of the first challenges the DOE hoped to tackle, for example, was mitigating the approximately fifteen thousand drums of thorium stored on-site. For Leo Duffy, the DOE's assistant secretary for the Office of Environmental Restoration and Waste Management, thorium posed a technical problem with clear engineering solutions. The drums of thorium would be "overpacked" and sealed within larger containers and shipped to the Nevada Test Site, whose dry climate created a more stable environment for storing the material. While the DOE viewed nuclear cleanup through a technological lens, FRESH believed that the issue was about people, and Indigenous and rural white communities living downwind from the Nevada Test Site were already shouldering their own radioactive burden from the nuclear arms race. "I don't wish our waste on anybody else," Crawford said, especially if it would pollute somebody else's backyard.[7]

Considering the DOE's negligent record of radioactive waste disposal, FRESH was unsurprisingly skeptical of the department. But something needed to give. "We're up to our eyeballs in waste in this country," said Secretary Watkins.[8] He was hardly exaggerating. By the middle of the decade, the federal government had identified 61,155 contaminated backyards—primarily on DOE- and Department of Defense (DOD)-owned lands—that it was responsible for cleaning up with a projected price tag of $230 to $390 billion.[9] Worst of all, radioactive waste disposal politics were boiling over. In 1987, Congress designated Yucca Mountain as the nation's high-level waste repository, and the State of Nevada fought back with every tool at its disposal.[10] Since no states were rushing to accept the arms race's environmental legacy, it became clear that any cleanup program without community buy-in was destined for failure. As a result, in 1992, the Environmental Protection Agency (EPA) chartered the Federal Facilities Environmental Restoration Dialogue Committee (FFERDC) to bring together government agencies, states, tribes, local governments, and organized labor, along with Indigenous, environmental, and environmental justice activists to develop an equitable and politically feasible solution to the Cold War's legacy of contamination.[11] In many ways, this committee furthered the DOE's trajectory from secrecy to openness, but the department also concealed industry's influence on this public participation model for Superfund cleanups.

Fernald would become a technological and social "laboratory" for greening the nuclear weapons complex.[12] As part of the committee's recommendations, the DOE created citizen advisory boards, or site-specific advisory boards, to foster local inclusion in environmental decision-making.[13] The most significant and controversial decision by the Fernald Citizens Task Force (FCTF) was accepting nearly three million cubic yards of low-level radioactive soil and building debris for encapsulation in the On-Site Disposal Facility.[14] While the DOE focused much of its educational efforts on the political and economic challenges of radioactive waste disposal at Fernald, including a well-received board game called FUTURESITE, it was the influence of the environmental justice movement on members of the Task Force that transformed the conversation and broke the potential for stalemate.[15]

"You just can't be a NIMBY any more in this country," said Lisa Crawford. "It's not cool" and "it doesn't work."[16] Through discussions with citizen advisory boards in Utah and Nevada, the FCTF learned that every shovelful of Fernald's radioactive soil not disposed of on-site was going to be dumped in somebody else's backyard, posing a risk to bodies and environments hundreds of miles away and along transportation routes.[17] The Task Force agreed, as a result, that the Fernald community should bear the burden of the On-Site Disposal Facility. "This would be our little piece of the nuclear weapons age," Crawford said.[18] The Task Force's decision signaled a remarkable transformation for the environmental movement as well as the DOE. By balancing local democratic participation and technical education with a national dialogue on environmental justice, Fernald's environmental movement helped forge a pragmatic solution to one of the most complex environmental challenges of the twentieth century: the radioactive legacy of the nuclear arms race.

THE CLEANUP ECONOMY

Beginning with Fernald, the DOE planned to hire environmental restoration management contractors (ERMCs) to clean up its nuclear weapons production facilities. This strategy—hiring one company to manage the cleanup and all its subcontractors—was designed to mitigate expenses in what the DOE forecast to be a costly and multidecade program.[19] Like the Cold War years, which witnessed the construction of massive industrial facilities at Fernald, Rocky Flats, Savannah River, and other sites, the private sector was also leveraged in executing the DOE's cleanup mission.[20] Instead of building and operating nuclear weapons production plants, however, this time around, they would be tearing them down.

Going into cleanup, Fernald had a significant advantage over other nuclear weapons production facilities: its comparatively small footprint.[21] At 1,050 acres, Fernald was a speck on the map in comparison to Hanford (360,000 acres) or Savannah River (192,000 acres).[22] By testing out the ERMC program at Fernald, the DOE could more easily measure its impact before administering it across the complex.[23] Fernald's cleanup contract was also widely sought after by private companies, with more than two hundred inquiries.[24] The contract offered a potential value of $4 billion, as well as early experience with nuclear remediation technologies that would be repurposed across the DOE.[25] Whoever secured Fernald's contract would get in on the ground floor of an emerging and financially lucrative industry with plenty of opportunities—or nuclear wastelands, depending on your perspective—for growth.

Fernald's cleanup was part of a larger economic trend in post–Cold War America in which "companies that once fought environmental regulation now battle pollution for profit."[26] After the dissolution of the Soviet Union in 1991, there was a decline in demand for weapons contracts and increased pressure from environmentalists and Congress for the federal government to comply with the nation's environmental laws. The DOE and DOD, as a result, restructured their budgets increasingly around cleanup. In fiscal year 1992 alone, the federal government's two most polluting departments spent $7.1 billion "cleaning up lethal radiation, toxic waste, and a plethora of other pollutants at nuclear weapons plants and military bases."²⁷ Major corporations, including construction and engineering firms like Fluor Daniel, in addition to military contractors like Lockheed and Westinghouse, responded by redirecting their resources from weapons production to cleaning up the mess. While critics grilled the federal government for lining the pockets of companies with poor environmental records, defense and engineering contractors also possessed the technical experience and monetary resources necessary to take on daunting hazardous waste projects with high legal stakes. The government's demand for environmental cleanup, according to Sonni Efron and James M. Gomez at the *Los Angeles Times*, created a "green fever" that swept corporate America.²⁸

Fluor Daniel Inc., which built a global portfolio in energy construction projects during the twentieth century, recognized the potential of the green economy during the late 1980s. In 1989, the company founded its environmental services division and quickly filled it with hundreds of environmental engineers, toxicologists, hydrologists, and other environmental scientists. Fluor's technical staff combined proven engineering principles with state-of-the-art 3D computer modeling to gain an edge in the environmental remediation industry. Using a new program called EnviroCAD, for example, Fluor's engineers could pinpoint the source of underground pollution before breaking ground with its heavy equipment. By removing the guesswork, this technology saved the company thousands of dollars and sped up its pace by months, if not years, on remediation jobs. "It's by far the fastest-growing business," said Fluor Daniel's vice president for marketing, Thomas Merrick, about the company's environmental services division. After experiencing 30 percent growth during the 1990 recession, Merrick predicted that the 1990s would be "the decade of the environment."²⁹ By bidding on the Fernald contract, and contributing generously to Republican and Democratic political campaigns, Fluor Daniel positioned itself to reap the benefits of business's environmental decade.³⁰

Fernald's environmental movement was enormously influential in the rise of the environmental remediation industry during the late 1980s. While the early years of the Comprehensive Environmental Response, Compensation, and Liability Act (CERCLA), better known as Superfund, were highly contentious, the latter part of the decade was more cordial. After the passage of the Superfund Amendments and Reauthorization Act, thousands of contaminated federal sites were transformed into business opportunities.[31] This economic demand, which was a direct byproduct of grassroots environmental activism, unlocked billions of taxpayer dollars for cleanup. These potential contracts provided enough incentive for corporations like Fluor Daniel to restructure their business models and enter the environmental remediation industry.[32] This economic shift, which raked in tens of billions of dollars per year—including $132 billion in 1990—helped solve the nation's toxic and radioactive waste crises. It is critical to remember, however, that it was not a natural response by the market to the Cold War's end. It began during the early 1980s when grassroots environmental activists like FRESH demanded accountability from unaccountable and polluting departments like the DOE.

BLUE COLLARS IN A GREEN INDUSTRY

In January 1992, Westinghouse announced it would not bid on the Fernald remediation contract. This was a welcome relief for the DOE, because the department's critics were leery of former production contractors running the cleanup.[33] It caused more uncertainty for former production workers, however, who had supported Westinghouse's contract renewal.[34] This trust was developed through a cooperative effort between the company and Fernald's unions to develop the DOE/WESTINGHOUSE School for Environmental Excellence for managers and the School of Applied Environmental Technology for labor.[35] As part of the unions' latest contract, former production workers were given the training they needed to successfully transition from nuclear weapons production to environmental remediation jobs.[36]

In collaboration with the University of Findlay, a private university in northwest Ohio then pioneering professional environmental health and safety, Fernald's workforce attended multiweek sessions to learn to safely handle dangerous radioactive materials and toxic wastes. These courses included in-depth seminars on environmental law and toxicology, but importantly for organized labor, also went beyond book learning. At the

University of Findlay's Emergency Response Training Center, workers received hands-on training to prepare for worst-case scenarios in the field. In one simulation, Bill Daniel and Darrell Kirby put on full personal protective equipment (PPE) and proceeded to examine a leaking tank. After water and green-tinted shaving cream—which simulated hazardous contamination—splashed on them, their colleagues rushed to decontaminate them with scrub brushes and detergent while others helped them out of their PPE before oxygen supplies ran out. "When you get your vision obscured and the wind's blowing around," Kirby explained, "it gets pretty lifelike." Findlay's program was even able to tailor the class to Fernald's uniquely radioactive hazards, including how they painted and labeled waste barrels in the training center.[37]

Fernald's unions could focus on retraining because they did not have to worry about job security—or so they thought—even with Westinghouse's departure. Under pressure from Senator Glenn, the Fernald Atomic Trades and Labor Council (FATLC), and FRESH, the DOE wrote Fernald's request for proposal for a cleanup contractor in a way that guaranteed positions for current union workers and many salaried managers.[38] Although Fernald's workers were proud of their production years, the job security from what was expected to be a multidecade cleanup helped minimize some of the stress of retraining an experienced workforce. It also recognized the unions' argument that Fernald's production workers possessed intimate site knowledge that was essential to a successful cleanup.[39]

After its first two sessions in greater Cincinnati, the third DOE/Westinghouse School for Environmental Excellence was held in Richland near Hanford.[40] Despite the successful spread of this innovative program, there were still plenty of perils to the green economy.

The DOE's transition from production to cleanup at Cold War's end threatened the economic security of nuclear workers. On April 21, 1992, Senator Glenn sat down for a roundtable discussion at Fernald with representatives of FRESH and the FATLC on S. 2065, the DOE Worker Protection Bill, which Glenn had introduced three weeks earlier with his cosponsor Tim Wirth of Colorado to bridge the gap between these two eras. Through federal legislation, Glenn and Wirth hoped to expand the job security guaranteed to Fernald's production workers to the rest of the nuclear weapons complex, as well as provide additional benefits, including a medical monitoring program and medical insurance.[41] As former nuclear weapons production facilities transitioned to cleanup, union workers were concerned that by accepting cleanup jobs they might lose the generous health benefits that were secured during the production years. After decades of exposure to radiation and toxic chemicals, this possibility was daunting. From labor's perspective, production workers sacrificed their bodies to produce the nuclear weapons that transformed the United States into a global superpower and protected its citizens from communist invasion. Despite this sacrifice of health for country, Congress was slow to act, which left production workers and their families with uncertain futures.[42]

Later that day, Glenn held a press conference to speak on the moral obligation of protecting former nuclear production workers' interests as the DOE transitioned to cleanup. "With the fall of communism and the end of the Cold War," Glenn said, "the world has changed and so have our priorities.... The mission and structure of the US nuclear weapons complex is shifting from production to cleanup," and "with this shift we must ensure that as we downsize our nuclear complex, we don't downsize the rights and protections of the workers who brought us our Cold War victory."[43] Without federal intervention, Glenn worried that workers would be abandoned to an unstable job market with contaminated bodies, no medical insurance, and obsolete skills. Many of Glenn's colleagues in Congress disagreed, however, and slashed health insurance from the bill for being an "entitlement."[44]

While workers in the FATLC were guaranteed a cleanup job, it was not so simple for production workers at other sites. At Hanford, for example, the Building and Construction Trades Department of the AFL-CIO challenged production workers in the Oil, Chemical, and Atomic Workers Union and the United Steelworkers, who wanted a similar deal to Fernald. This strategy, which the Hanford Atomic Metals Council called "a thinly-veiled attempt at union busting" by the Bush administration, successfully delayed the awarding of Hanford's request for proposal and helped eliminate this protection from Glenn's bill.[45]

THE FEDERAL FACILITIES COMPLIANCE ACT

The same day as Senator Glenn's press conference, the Supreme Court ruled 6–3 that the State of Ohio could not fine the DOE for past environmental contamination of the air, soil, and water at Fernald. This decision upheld the federal government's sovereign immunity against punitive fines and overturned a 1988 ruling in favor of the state by the Sixth Circuit Court of Appeals. It was not legal for the states, as a result, to enforce consent decrees through fines under the Resource Conservation and Recovery Act (RCRA). It was "a true blow to Ohio's efforts to compel the DOE to get on with cleanup at Fernald," said US Senate Committee on Governmental Affairs researcher Robert Alvarez.[46] Although Congress was dragging its feet on supporting nuclear workers, it was on the verge of passing a largely forgotten but transformative environmental law: the Federal Facilities Compliance Act (FFCA).

In a statement on the ruling, Senator Glenn expressed his disappointment in the Supreme Court for empowering federal agencies to pollute and overturning Ohio's victory. "The Supreme Court is endorsing a double standard," Glenn said. "While financially strapped municipalities, and private industries have to pay fines brought by the federal government for environmental noncompliance, the federal government itself, as the nation's biggest polluter insists on holding itself above the law. . . . Fortunately, Congress is close to passing legislation, the Federal Facilities Compliance Act, of which I am a cosponsor, to make sure that states can have the authority, as they do under other federal environmental laws, to assure compliance through financial penalties."[47] Sponsored in the House by Ohio Democratic Representative Dennis Eckart, the FFCA was written to empower the states in their battles with America's worst polluters: the DOE and DOD.

FRESH lobbied for the FFCA, and later recalled its passage as one of its crowning achievements.[48] In supporting testimony, Lisa Crawford explained the importance of checking unrestrained federal power. "I want to encourage you to put forth the Federal Facilities Compliance Act. I want to encourage you to give the Department of Energy oversight by another agency and by states. I want to encourage you to make the DOE comply with the laws of this country. I want to encourage you to let the US EPA levy fines against the DOE for noncompliance and failing to meet their deadlines and agreements." Most importantly, she said, "I want to encourage you to remember the residents of Fernald and other nuclear weapons production facilities—residents who live in the shadows of America's bomb plants, residents who have been kept in the dark and lied to for the past forty years."[49] After years of organizing both locally and nationally, Fernald's environmental movement had finally changed as many hearts and minds in Washington, DC, as they had in Ohio.

The FFCA passed with overwhelming bipartisan support, with a 403–3 vote in favor of the legislation in the House of Representatives and unanimous approval in the Senate.[50] Together, the passage of the FFCA and the Clean Air Act amendments of 1990 demonstrate that during the George H. W. Bush administration, the bipartisan spirit of the environmental movement was still alive in Congress. President Bush, who marketed himself on the campaign trail as the "environmental president," provided strong political leadership on the Clean Air Act to control acid rain.[51] Bush pushed back against the FFCA, however, by supporting the DOE in its opposition to the bill and delaying signing it into law. The FFCA's penalties, according to Bush, complicated congressional appropriations and forced the federal government to prioritize the DOE's cleanup schedule based on which states assessed fines instead of which sites posed the greatest environmental threats.[52] The power to fine the DOE, however, is exactly what states, environmental activists, and Democratic and Republican members of Congress felt was necessary to force federal polluters into compliance.[53] It was a risky position for Bush to take in a presidential election year, and the Clinton-Gore ticket took advantage of the opportunity to connect with Ohio voters.

Arkansas Governor Bill Clinton had selected Al Gore, a senator from Tennessee and environmental leader in Congress, as his running mate. Fresh off publishing the best-selling book *Earth in the Balance: Ecology and the Human Spirit*, Gore hit the campaign trail to pitch Clinton's "ambitious environmental agenda" to the public.[54] On September 30, 1992, the vice presidential candidate spent the day in the Fernald area,

FIGURE 11. Vice presidential candidate Al Gore walking with Fernald Residents for Environmental Safety and Health's Lisa Crawford and former US Representative Tom Luken at Fernald, October 6, 1992. Courtesy of the US Department of Energy.

including a brief tour of the facility and a thirty-minute roundtable with members of FRESH, including Lisa and Ken Crawford, Don and Kathy Meyer, and former US Representative Tom Luken.[55] Gore seized the opportunity to criticize the incumbent president's opposition to the FFCA. President Bush "made a clear promise to you back in 1988. He said the federal Fernald plant should be made to obey the same laws as private industry," Gore explained. "But he has done nothing."[56] Gore promised that, if elected, Clinton would sign the FFCA using "a ballpoint pen with the FRESH logo on it."[57] Crosby and Ross Townships are a little off the beaten path in Southwest Ohio. Although only about twenty miles from Cincinnati, it still takes effort to get there. That Gore took the time to meet with area residents was meaningful for these rural communities.[58]

Clinton never got the chance to use that FRESH-branded pen because on October 6, President Bush signed the FFCA into law. After nearly eight years of activism, FRESH and the State of Ohio had finally obtained the legal leverage they needed to force the DOE's hand on cleanup. The FFCA required federal agencies to comply with federal, state, and local hazardous waste regulations, including those more strict than federal laws. After the FFCA waived federal sovereign immunity, states and local governments could administer fines and penalties for noncompliance. Federal agencies were also made vulnerable to lawsuits from states, citizens, and environmental organizations. Congress established strict deadlines through the FFCA, which required federal agencies to develop plans for managing mixed wastes, as well as submitting inventories, cleanup schedules, and progress reports to the EPA and state agencies.[59] By curbing federal power, the nation was better prepared to take on the enormous challenge of cleaning up the Cold War's radioactive and toxic legacy. At Fernald, the community would come together to accomplish this unprecedented task.

THE FERNALD CITIZENS TASK FORCE

In the fall of 1992, the Department of Energy selected Fluor Daniel Environmental Restoration Management Corporation (FERMCO), a subsidiary of Fluor Daniel, as Fernald's cleanup contractor. It was the first such contract awarded in the nuclear weapons complex and a "milestone" in the DOE's cleanup program, according to Secretary Watkins.[60] The five-year contract, valued at $2.2 billion, also included a three-year option for an additional $1.8 billion. Fluor Daniel would manage all the project's subcontractors, including Jacobs Engineering Group Inc., the Haliburton NUS Environmental Corporation, and Nuclear Fuel Services.[61] While the Irving, California–based Fluor Daniel controlled the purse, the greater Cincinnati business community was hopeful that construction subcontracts would be liberally distributed throughout the local economy.[62]

After Clinton's election in November, the incoming administration worked to keep Vice President Gore's promise to FRESH to expedite Fernald's cleanup.[63] With a contractor in place, it all suddenly seemed possible. But Fernald's environmental movement was not going anywhere. "We want them to know who we are, that we've been here a long time, that we're staying, and we expect them to do an A-1 job," said Lisa Crawford. Fernald's labor unions were even more leery, particularly after having developed a positive working relationship with Westinghouse. Fluor "shouldn't come in, pretend they know everything, and not listen to anyone," said the FATLC's Gene Branham. The *Cincinnati Enquirer* also observed that after transforming "a secretive and unresponsive Energy Department into an agency that strives to keep Fernald residents happy," FRESH and the FATLC wanted to lead—not follow—the cleanup process.[64]

Keeping Fernald and communities across the nuclear weapons complex happy was a significant undertaking for the Clinton administration. To accomplish this goal, the DOE—under the leadership of Secretary of Energy Hazel O'Leary—promised significant reform through "stakeholder" participation in the department's decision-making process. O'Leary, an African American woman with experience in public and private energy affairs, including the Federal Energy Administration and Northern States Power Company, was confirmed with little opposition from Congress or industry and provided a step in the right direction for the Clinton administration's goal of building an inclusive cabinet.[65] O'Leary's biggest critics at the time were actually activists in the Military Production Network, who called out the secretary's "lack of knowledge about nuclear-weapons production and cleanup issues."[66] By taking citizen participation seriously and pulling back the curtain on the Cold War's shocking secrets about human radiation experiments, she would quiet many of her progressive doubters.[67]

O'Leary was also a trustee of the Keystone Center, an industry-backed nonprofit organization located in Keystone, Colorado, that focused on environmental conflict. During the early 1990s, its board included representatives of Dow Chemical, Amoco, and Monsanto, which demonstrated a corporate willingness to engage environmentalists, an interest in greening public images for historically polluting industries, and the development of increasingly subtle venues for influencing environmental policy.[68] In 1990, the EPA tasked the Keystone Center with convening "a national policy dialogue on federal facility environmental restoration priority-setting," an idea that had been gaining steam since the late

1980s.[69] These conversations led to the development of the FFERDC, also known as the Keystone Committee, which brought together employees of federal agencies, environmental activists, labor unions, state representatives, local communities, and tribal leadership to develop a constructive dialogue between citizens and federal agencies in order to clean up the enormous environmental legacies of the Cold War.[70]

This challenge was complicated by "a long history of deep-seated mutual distrust," the Keystone Committee wrote.[71] At the time, communities living in the shadow of nuclear weapons production facilities or military bases, for example, understandably had little faith that the federal agencies that contaminated their bodies and environments worked in their interest. Government technical experts were frustrated that their knowledge and experience were no longer valued in a society increasingly skeptical of big government.[72] To bridge this gap in trust, the Keystone Committee recommended that the federal government rethink how it communicated with its citizens. The "decide, announce, defend" model, in which government agents make decisions behind closed doors, announce them to the public, and later defend their predetermined decisions, had eroded the public's confidence.[73] Something more meaningful and democratic needed to be built in its place.

The Keystone Committee's interim report, released in February 1993, recommended the creation of citizen advisory boards, or site-specific advisory boards, at the DOE's contaminated sites. Citizen advisory boards were not a new idea. Their roots can be traced to President Lyndon Johnson's Great Society programs on race relations and urban development, which were established to give a voice to—or better control, depending on your perspective—civil rights activists. By bringing together a diverse group of "stakeholders" for regular meetings, the Keystone Committee argued that citizen advisory boards would nurture trust building through face-to-face communication, provide adequate time for a meaningful citizen review of cleanup projects, and allow space for local values to work their way into government planning.[74]

The first step in developing the Fernald Citizens Task Force was finding a convener. In May 1993, the DOE, EPA, and Ohio EPA, working through the Alliance of Ohio Universities, hired University of Cincinnati professor of environmental health Eula Bingham.[75] Bingham possessed stellar credentials in environmental health and safety as both a scientist and public servant. At the University of Cincinnati, she directed the Ohio Hazardous Substances Research, Education, and Management Institute. Bingham also served as the assistant secretary of labor for the Occupational Safety and Health Administration (OSHA) during the Carter presidency. At OSHA, Bingham is credited with dismantling tedious regulations that handcuffed the agency in favor of enforcement powers that protected workers against some of industry's most dangerous threats, including lead, benzene, and arsenic. Bingham also fought for environmental justice by regulating cotton dust for Southern textile workers, an industry largely built on the labor of poor women of color. Through her workplace advocacy, Bingham earned the respect of labor unions, and she was a sought-after expert witness and consultant.[76] These experiences gave her "credibility with the public," according to Assistant Secretary for Environmental Management Thomas Grumbly, and her independence ensured that critics could not say that the DOE had "tarnished" the FCTF "with our dirty hands."[77]

Bingham's primary task was recommending members for the Task Force that she recruited through her academic network, public meetings and mailers, and personal recommendations from local organizations. For its chair position, Bingham selected University of Cincinnati law professor John Applegate. As an environmental legal scholar, he brought the necessary experience to help the board navigate the complex regulations governing nuclear cleanup.[78] Applegate credited Bingham with bringing together a broad group of "stakeholders" to the Task Force, including Fernald residents, local officials, schoolteachers, labor leaders, scientists, professors, and community activists. Each member also lived in greater Cincinnati, so all parties had a personal, or at least professional, interest in the success of Fernald's cleanup. In August, the DOE recognized the Fernald Citizens Task Force as the official voice of the community.[79]

CLEAN SITES INC.

In January 1994, Grumbly traveled to Fernald on a two-day site visit to speak with FRESH and the FATLC about cleanup. His presence was meant to convey that the top-down and union-busting approach of the previous administration was over. The next chapter of the DOE's history, including its transition to environmental remediation and stewardship, was going to come from the bottom up. "There's a whole new attitude on the part of management that we have an obligation to those who worked here during the Cold War," Grumbly said.[80] Fluor's first year on the job had gone poorly, including a conflict with labor over layoffs and collective bargaining. It turned out that despite the DOE's guarantee of cleanup jobs for former production workers, FERMCO's intent was to let most of them go in favor of subcontractors. But after a heated congressional hearing and the firing of FERMCO's president, Nick Kaufman, Grumbly acknowledged that Fluor was "on the way to a passing grade."[81] The DOE's two biggest critics at Fernald, FRESH's Lisa Crawford and the FATLC's Gene Branham, were both on board. Grumbly "has an awareness and, surprisingly, a site-specific knowledge that others in his job before didn't have," Branham said. "I think there will be change," Crawford added, but "we need to pull more people out of their four-walled offices and get them out in the field."[82] While Secretary Watkins largely shut out grassroots activists during the Bush administration, Grumbly made it clear that they now had a seat at the table. This spirit of cooperation inspired the Fernald Citizens Task Force to work together and get Fernald cleaned up.

After eight years of juggling work, family, and activism, including countless late nights and no vacations, Crawford was getting burnt out.[83] The FCTF came at a perfect time to help carry this seemingly impossible load and transition FRESH from anger and cynicism and toward a collaborative future. "When you do this work for as long as we've done it," Crawford said, "you begin to get some blinders on your eyes, and you only see what you want to see."[84] FRESH, represented by Crawford and Pam Dunn, and the FATLC, represented by Bob Tabor, deserve a lot of credit for relinquishing control to the Task Force, particularly since their bodies were most impacted by Fernald's radioactive waste. This transition was due, in part, to the near-universal respect that Applegate earned as chair of the FCTF.[85]

From its first meeting in September 1993, the Task Force was playing catchup with the complex Superfund process. The EPA and the DOE had divided Fernald into five "operable units," or cleanup projects: waste pits; fly ash piles, sludge ponds, and landfills; production areas; silos; and groundwater and surface water. After every operable unit was thoroughly investigated, the EPA developed cleanup recommendations for each project. The FCTF's role, as a representative body of the Fernald community, was to offer guidance on the future use of the site, final remediation levels and acceptable cancer risks, and locations for waste disposal, and to prioritize remedial projects.[86]

These questions were formidable, and the Task Force struggled to work through the issues during the first few months. Applegate realized, as a result, that the Task Force could use some external help. He stumbled across an article by Doug Sarno, a civil engineer by training and former EPA employee who worked for the Alexandria, Virginia–based nonprofit Clean Sites Inc.[87] "Remedy selection," Sarno wrote, "is the linchpin of the Superfund program. It is what determines the level of protection for citizens living near a site, the level of restoration of the land," and finally, "the cost to either the responsible parties or the Superfund trust fund."[88] Clean Sites Inc., it appeared, had developed a language for discussing the complexities of the Superfund. Applegate was impressed with Sarno's work and invited him to apply for a soon-to-be-announced facilitator position at Fernald, which would be tasked with serving as the group's technical advisor and mediator with the DOE. Sarno applied, and at the December 9, 1993, FCTF meeting, Applegate welcomed him to the Task Force.[89]

Sarno brought much-needed experience with the Superfund process, both as a private hazardous waste consultant and EPA employee, which significantly helped the Task Force with interpreting technical information.[90] During the 1980s, he witnessed just how contentious hazardous waste issues became between environmentalists, the EPA, and industry. From a waste management perspective, it was frustrating, because, he said, "technically we could solve these problems," but "we could never get them implemented because of policy reasons or reasons of public participation." Inside the EPA, Sarno found it disingenuous that it was assumed that every Superfund site was going to be cleaned up for unrestricted land use, because, in practice, very few cleanups achieved this standard of remediation.[91] The solution to this problem, he believed, was public participation.

He was not the only one. Established in 1984, Clean Sites Inc. was the brainchild of Dr. Louis Fernandez, outgoing chairman of the Chemical Manufacturers Association and chairman of the Monsanto Corporation at the time, and Douglas M. Costle, former administrator of the EPA during the Carter administration.[92] It was modeled after the Health Effects Institute (HEI), a nonprofit organization that Costle developed to produce an "independent, third-party source of facts" on air pollution to support the next reauthorization of the Clean Air Act. By splitting its funding between the federal government and the auto industry, the Health Effects Institute forged a middle ground between "defensive" corporate research and the attacks of "Nader's Raiders" on industry and government.[93] Clean Sites Inc.'s board represented powerful corporations, including Fernandez at Monsanto and Edwin A. Gee, CEO of the International Paper Company; leaders in higher education, including Stanford University president Donald Kennedy and Rockefeller University president Joshua Lederberg; and conservative-leaning environmentalists, including World Wildlife Fund president and former EPA administrator Russell E. Train and the Conservation Foundation's president William K. Reilly, who would go on to serve as the EPA administrator during the George H. W. Bush administration. During its development, Clean Sites Inc. received funding from over a hundred companies, including members of the electrical, chemical, steel, petroleum, and paper industries. In 1985, its policies were entrenched in the regulatory state when it was indemnified by the EPA for managing toxic waste cleanups. It created a "constructive dialogue between the chemical industry and people in the environmental movement," according to Fernandez, "who have a sincere desire to accommodate some of the differences that unfortunately were all too prevalent in our historical relationship."[94] Its goal was to incentivize voluntarily compliance with CERCLA, and its primary role was to serve as an intermediary between the EPA and corporate polluters and expedite cleanup through settlements, cost reduction, and ensuring compliance with environmental laws.[95] What emerged from the formation of Clean Sites was a pragmatic brand of environmentalism that was intellectually grounded in engineering and political economy, and unapologetic about its dialogue with corporate polluters and toxic communities to break Superfund's paralysis during the 1980s.

After the idea for Clean Sites was conceived, it was briefly tabled during the early Reagan years. But this antiregulatory honeymoon was short-lived. Reagan's EPA was plagued by scandal, including its administrator, Ann Gorsuch, and top hazardous waste official Rita Lavelle being forced out of office. These political controversies and high-profile toxic torts generated plenty of bad publicity for the chemical industry, so in 1983, chemical executives went back to the drawing board. Superfund was here to stay, it was decided, and the time had come to control the damages instead of avoiding them all together. Clean Sites Inc. was born.[96] The best way to mitigate costs, it discovered, was imagining the future use of Superfund sites in advance of remediation. A park with higher levels of contamination and a residential development with lower levels of contamination, for example, can provide the same levels of cancer risk, because people spend less time at parks than they do in their homes. "In the first case," Sarno wrote, "residual risk is controlled by limiting exposure while, in the second case, residual risk is controlled by reducing contaminant concentrations."[97] Sarno's argument was part of a larger conversation during the 1980s in which technical experts from the hazardous waste industry worked to carve out a middle ground for the Superfund that balanced protecting public health, reducing costs for industry, and managing the limitations and public expectations of remediation technologies at heavily polluted sites.[98]

Through public participation, Clean Sites Inc.'s strategy gave communities a voice in their regulatory future and direct access to environmental health and safety data and technical experts. This concept was innovative, primarily because it addressed a key concern of the hazardous waste industry. Without community involvement, a site is more likely to wind up like Love Canal, which experienced renewed controversy decades after Superfund's passage when another pocket of contamination was discovered during road construction in 2011; subsequently, multiple lawsuits were filed on behalf of nearby residents.[99] By educating impacted communities on the cleanup process, including the extensive but not exhaustive field surveys completed by scientists and engineers, as well as the implementation of technologically—and cost-effective—solutions to cleanup, citizens can better appreciate the value of environmental remediation and the political, technological, and economic limitations placed on the industry.[100]

This was a risk-based brand of environmentalism that maximized efficiency and balanced public health with industry's bottom line. By making cleanup profitable for the hazardous waste industry and less litigious for corporate polluters, known as potentially responsible parties in the Superfund process, Clean Sites Inc. helped incentivize the multibillion-dollar environmental remediation industry, which provided green jobs and helped clean up the Cold War's toxic and radioactive legacies. It was a bipartisan project, including moderate and environmentally conscious Republicans like Train and Reilly, as well as Democrats like Costle from the Carter administration who favored market-based solutions to environmental problems. This was the intellectual foundation on which the DOE's cleanup program was built.[101] Secretary of Energy Hazel O'Leary worked in the Federal Energy Administration during the Carter years and joined the board of the Keystone Center as an energy consultant.[102] Assistant Secretary for Environmental Management Thomas Grumbly was a regulator in Carter's Food and Drug Administration and served as president of Clean Sites Inc.[103] FCTF convener Dr. Eula Bingham directed OSHA during the Carter administration and was selected to assemble the FCTF, which hired Sarno under the direction of the DOE at Fernald.[104] For many moderate environmentalists, the efficiency and pragmatism of Clean Sites were commendable. "More power to them," said Wisconsin Senator and Earth Day architect Gaylord Nelson, because "the chemical industry fought the law for years, but they now recognize the public is not going to stand for hazardous waste dumps."[105] For Nelson, the more toxic waste and the faster it was cleaned up, the better, regardless of who benefited.

It is dishonest, however, to suggest that Clean Sites Inc. and the Keystone Center were impartial nonprofit organizations. Funded by polluting industries and indemnified by the EPA, Clean Sites was granted unprecedented access to influence the Superfund program. Its ideas also heavily favored industry's bottom line, most importantly the future-use concept but also "stakeholder" inclusion. According to Sarno, "the views of responsible parties," or the polluters that the Superfund was originally designed to punish, and "the views of directly affected citizens," or the people whose bodies and environments were contaminated, were all given consideration in developing "site-specific objectives" for cleanup.[106] This arrangement tipped the already unequal scales further in the favor of corporate polluters. It was like "sending the criminals out to clean up the evidence," according to Love Canal activist Lois Gibbs.[107] For her, those who created the mess deserved to pay with their wallets and their reputations for poisoning communities.

One critic charged that besides FRESH, there were no environmental organizations, such as local chapters of the Sierra Club or Greenpeace, represented on the FCTF.[108] Bingham understood, however, that the Fernald area was a politically conservative community that wanted local control over cleanup. Would it be truly representative, as a result, to include progressive environmentalists on the FCTF? This decision also aligns with Clean Sites Inc.'s recommendation that only "the views of directly affected citizens" be included in developing site-specific objectives.[109] Through her connections with the Military Production Network, Lisa Crawford had grappled with this very issue of local versus national control. In one conversation, a Greenpeace representative suggested that FRESH step aside so the national environmental organizations could take over at Fernald. Crawford, whose family had literally drunk Fernald's uranium, politely declined Greenpeace's overstep. It was nothing personal. FRESH had worked closely with progressive activists, and Crawford considered many of them her friends.[110] But Fernald was first and foremost a local issue for FRESH, despite its success in elevating it to a national audience. "Do not allow a national group's agenda," FRESH later advised local grassroots movements, "to overshadow your goals."[111] While assembling the FCTF, Bingham agreed, and local voices were empowered at the expense of external critics.[112] By mitigating potential conflict early on, Fernald's cleanup was able to proceed quickly, which after years of fighting the DOE and dreading being abandoned as a "national sacrifice zone," was a welcome outcome for the community.[113]

BOARD GAMES AND RADIOACTIVE WASTE MANAGEMENT

To help the Task Force visualize the challenges of Fernald's cleanup, John Applegate, Doug Sarno, and two consultant colleagues, Nolan Curtis and Sarah Synder, developed a board game called FUTURESITE, which built upon an earlier concept created by the DOE called "Cleanupoly." Its goal was to "decide on a desirable future use or uses of the Fernald site while keeping the overall need for excavation and disposal of uranium contamination and their associated costs within environmentally, fiscally, and politically manageable limits."[114] FUTURESITE's board was a map of Fernald divided into a grid, with each square, representing one thousand feet on each side, covered in poker chips, which, based on computer modeling, indicated the quantities of contaminated soil in that location. Since Applegate and Sarno's goal was to get FUTURESITE's players thinking about future use, the chips were colored to represent different land use alternatives and their accompanying levels of acceptable risk, including red for restricted access, yellow for undeveloped green space, green for a developed park, blue for commercial or industrial use, and white for agricultural or residential land, and there was also an aquifer card, which represented the remediation level necessary to prevent uranium from seeping into the aquifer. By removing the poker chips (the contaminated soil), the players excavated Fernald's earth down toward naturally occurring levels of radiation. Players then placed them in one of two bins representing an on-site waste disposal facility or off-site waste disposal facility in the American West.[115]

Players were also asked to consider the economics, transportation risks, environmental damages, community needs, and political restraints of waste disposal, which limited offsite removal to one million cubic yards of material, including the site's most hazardous wastes, which were rep-

FIGURE 12. Community residents, Department of Energy employees and contractors, and members of the Fernald Citizens Task Force play FUTURESITE, June 23, 1994. Courtesy of the US Department of Energy.

resented by black chips and were required to be shipped off-site. After completing the simulation, groups calculated volume of excavated soil, costs of remediation, transportation needs (including trucks and trains to haul away waste), and the space required for on-site disposal. Different groups of players revealed different values in their simulated cleanups. The DOE's technical experts, for example, focused on reducing the highest levels of contamination first, while Fernald residents removed the lesser hazards on the site's outskirts to establish a buffer between the plant and their community. Such varying results, according to the game's developers, "became the basis for a discussion of values, goals, and trade-offs that led to consensus on the actual decision."[116] At a time when the public's faith in the DOE was rock bottom, the Task Force's recommendations—which were informed by playing FUTURESITE—provided the DOE with the community support it needed to cleanup Fernald.

FUTURESITE's developers focused on future use to expose the technical limitations and high costs of nuclear cleanup, which they hoped would influence the Task Force to accept higher cancer risk levels, restricted land use, and the on-site disposal of low-level radioactive waste.[117] The FCTF accepted these principles, knowing that the taxpayer—not Fernald's original operating contractor, National Lead of Ohio—would be footing the bill.[118] But even more influential to the Task Force's decision than economics was environmental justice. The more they learned about nuclear waste disposal, the more they worried about poisoning others with Fernald's uranium.[119] By shipping 2.4 million cubic yards of Fernald's low-level contaminated soil out west, for example, a risk assessment determined that six deaths would occur in the public along the transportation route. On-site disposal, however, resulted in a minimal increase in risk to the public or workers.[120] The FCTF also collaborated with DOE site-specific advisory boards in Utah and Nevada, who encouraged Fernald to bury its low-level waste on-site.[121] At Fernald, the DOE's uranium had already done its damage, but by building the On-Site Disposal Facility, the Task Force could minimize the harm that Fernald's waste would inflict on others.

The FCTF's first decisions appeared in a November 1994 interim report. The Task Force recommended restricting land use at Fernald, preventing agricultural and residential development, and remediating uranium levels to a one-in-ten-thousand excess risk of contracting cancer from exposure to the site's contaminants, which is the highest level of risk allowed under Superfund law.[122] In July 1995, the FCTF released its final report, which in agreement with the DOE's technical experts, called for a "balanced approach" to Fernald's nuclear waste, including the off-site disposal of high-level nuclear waste and the on-site disposal of low-level nuclear waste. Importantly for the community, there were some guardrails placed on the DOE. This facility, according to the Task Force, could not accept any wastes from other sites, would be constructed with the best available technologies, and must be developed with a buffer zone to protect public health. The federal government was required to accept permanent ownership of the On-Site Disposal Facility, including the continuous monitoring of the wastes and the responsibility to release environmental monitoring data to the community, and to mitigate any future threats from the waste that could impact the environment or public health.[123]

During the Clinton administration, the DOE created a space through citizen advisory boards where nuclear weapons production communities could be educated on the technical, political, and economic limitations of Superfund, as well as network and learn from each other. This political strategy balanced the risk-based and technically minded environmental solutions of the hazardous waste industry, which were originally conceptualized in Clean Sites Inc., with growing calls for environmental justice, which the DOE adopted in its 1995 Environmental Justice Strategy in response to President Clinton's Executive Order 12898 (Federal Actions to Address Environmental Justice in Minority Populations and Low-Income Populations).[124] The DOE's remediation program, in other words, worked toward a middle ground between efficiently cleaning up the nuclear arms race and protecting public health.

This concept worked for Fernald's environmental movement. As a predominantly white and blue-collar community, it was easier to be pragmatic, despite their general distaste for those they considered to be elitist bureaucrats staffing the DOE. FRESH had the advantage of fighting to improve a system through class- and environmental health and safety-based arguments instead of dismantling a system. Although class and environmental interests had long played second fiddle to production, the DOE at least recognized these arguments as valid—if not often exaggerated claims—because they emerged from the same Western culture.

For many Indigenous peoples in the American West, however, it was not so simple. Their primary critiques of the nuclear weapons production complex were rooted in cultural and spiritual displacement from traditional spaces that were not even recognized on maps that validated colonialism and privileged private property.[125] Indigenous activists, as a result, faced an even steeper uphill battle against the DOE than FRESH.

Overlapping ideals, interests, and experiences surrounding radioactive contamination, however, have opened the door for cross-cultural alliances between white activists and Indigenous peoples.[126] Environmental and antinuclear activists in the Military Production Network, for example, called upon the DOE to "stabilize and isolate nuclear waste at the point of origin for the interim" because Yucca Mountain "was not selected through an objective, scientific process and . . . is strongly opposed by Nevadans and Indian Tribes."[127] The Task Force also refused to dump all their waste in another nuclear weapons production community. "It wasn't an easy decision," Lisa Crawford said, but "it was the right decision."[128] Fernald produced this waste and was now committed to its long-term care. By cleaning up its own backyard, FRESH cleaned up everyone's.

EIGHT Grassroots Cleanup

On the morning of September 10, 1994, dozens of spectators, including Fernald Residents for Environmental Safety and Health's (FRESH) Lisa Crawford, Fernald Citizens Task Force chairman John Applegate, Ohio Democratic Representative David Mann, and Ohio Republican Representative Rob Portman, gathered at Fernald for the planned demolition of Plant 7, or the Hexafluoride Reduction Plant, which was built to convert uranium hexafluoride to green salt.[1] Standing seven stories tall, Plant 7 was the most visible feature of Fernald's skyline and the first former production facility slated for destruction, although it was heavily underutilized during the Cold War. While operations began in 1954, the Atomic Energy Commission (AEC) shut down the facility only eighteen months later, because its processes were replicated at the Paducah Gaseous Diffusion Plant in Kentucky, so the plant primarily served as a warehouse for green salt. Its demolition had been a year in the making. Fernald's workforce began the project by removing 3,400 linear feet of asbestos insulation from the HVAC system and 400 square feet of asbestos-containing floor tiles. Next, ten thousand gallons of water were sprayed in the plant's interior to decontaminate the radioactive structure. Finally, seven hundred gallons of latex acrylic paint were applied to encapsulate any remaining uranium or asbestos fibers.[2]

After stripping the building, all that remained of Plant 7 was its steel skeleton. Twenty-five pounds of explosives were placed on the first and third floors. At 10:15 a.m., fifty explosive devices echoed across Fernald's landscape. Plant 7 fell, but only 45 of its 110 feet. The structure tilted fifteen degrees toward the northwest and froze. "Just a moment," said Phil Hamric of the Department of Energy (DOE), as the demolition team huddled to figure out what went wrong. The following day, subcontractors strapped cables to the structure and tried to pull it down with bulldozers. Plant 7's bones did not budge. "It's disappointing. We really had our hopes up for this," said Crawford.[3] Amid the excitement surrounding the cleanup, Plant 7's failed demolition was a sobering reminder that after decades of operations, Fernald's radioactive legacy was deeply entrenched in the soil.

The following week, about a hundred spectators returned to Fernald for another attempt at bringing down Plant 7. Subcontractors placed 270 explosives throughout the partially fallen structure, a job made increasingly dangerous by its poor structural integrity.[4] Fernald's cleanup team would not be denied again. Loud pops and bright red flashes illuminated the sky like fireworks as Plant 7 crumbled into a forty-foot pile of rubble. The audience applauded as the DOE and its contractors breathed a sigh of relief. "We pulled together to come up with a new plan. There were a lot of long hours from a lot of dedicated people," said Hamric. Over the

FIGURE 13. The successful demolition of Plant 7, September 17, 1994. Courtesy of the US Department of Energy.

following week, the steel was cut into pieces using hydraulic sheers and hauled away for recycling.[5] One down, 254 production-era buildings to go.[6]

Fernald's environmental movement had built a resilience that was even stronger than Plant 7's steel. From the highest levels of the DOE down to the former production workers dismantling Fernald, the cleanup of the nuclear arms race began with an enthusiasm and mass deployment of resources similar to the Cold War four decades earlier. "The United States built the world's first atomic bomb to help win World War II and developed a nuclear arsenal to fight the Cold War," wrote Secretary of Energy Hazel O'Leary. "It is a story of extraordinary challenges brilliantly met, a story of genius, teamwork, industry, and courage. We are now embarked on another great challenge and a new national priority: refocusing the commitment that built the most powerful weapons on Earth towards the widespread environmental and safety problems at thousands of contaminated sites across the land."[7] At former nuclear weapons production sites across the nation, Americans came together to clean up the radioactive legacy of the nuclear arms race. Fernald's environmental movement accomplished this unprecedented project by balancing local grassroots participation with federal power and corporate resources and demonstrated on a national scale the power of cleaning up your own backyard.

ACCELERATING CLEANUP

Fernald's cleanup felt under threat almost as soon as it began. In the 1994 midterm elections, Republicans, rallying behind Georgia Representative Newt Gingrich's Contract with America platform, took control of the House of Representatives and Senate for the first time since 1955. The Republican campaign put federal regulations and government spending, among other issues, in their crosshairs.[8] Critical Fernald allies, including Ohio Senator John Glenn and Michigan Representative John Dingell, were also forced out of key leadership positions on the Senate Committee on Governmental Affairs and the House Energy and Commerce Committee, respectively.[9] The DOE slashed its projected cleanup budget in half. "We simply cannot afford the $500 billion bill," said Assistant Secretary for Environmental Management Thomas Grumbly, "to clean up these sites the way they were prior to World War II."[10] With the political tides turning and the enormity of the issue coming into focus, the Fernald Citizens Task Force approached cleanup from an increasingly pragmatic perspective.[11]

This was not particularly difficult for the Task Force. Since its founding, FRESH took a pragmatic approach to nuclear activism by identifying as environmentally conscious mothers fighting to clean up but never close Fernald.[12] "It is not going to make everybody happy," said Lisa Crawford, but it will put Fernald "in a better form and a better configuration than it is now."[13] This flexibility secured the Task Force a new ally in the Ohio Second Congressional District's Republican representative, Rob Portman, who actively supported the cleanup during his years in the House.[14] Fiscal conservatives had a point. The DOE was stuck between two eras: nuclear weapons production and environmental remediation, and it was costing a lot of money to manage both. Accounting for seventeen million pounds of usable nuclear materials and 82,000 drums of radioactive and mixed chemical wastes that needed to be shipped out West, as well as providing security for former production buildings and maintaining infrastructure that was scheduled for demolition, tied up a lot of funds that the Task Force would rather see spent on cleanup.[15]

Faced with budget cuts, the Task Force recommended "implementing an accelerated remediation." If the DOE invested its resources up front — instead of sporadically over the long haul — the site could be remediated in seven to ten years instead of twenty-five, which would save taxpayers several billion dollars and also prioritize the Task Force's most pressing concern of removing the most dangerous wastes as soon as possible to protect environmental health and safety.[16] The Task Force, the Environmental Protection Agency (EPA), and the Ohio EPA also supported granting the DOE regulatory flexibility in Fernald's cleanup. The DOE's regulations, which were developed for managing and not remediating radioactive materials, along with redundancies between the Resource Conservation and Recovery Act and the Comprehensive Environmental Response, Compensation, and Liability Act, were streamlined to expedite the process.[17] "Given the tools and the reforms," the Task Force wrote, "Fernald can lead the way" in cleaning up the nuclear arms race.[18]

Fernald's citizen advisory board worked quickly, which placed the site on the forefront of the DOE's cleanup program. "Fernald holds a unique position among DOE's major remediation sites," the Task Force wrote. "Its decision making is nearly complete, needed technologies are in place, and its size is manageable."[19] Despite these advantages, few regulators or DOE managers believed early on that it was possible to clean up Fernald in ten years.[20] That did not matter. On June 20, 1996, Assistant Secretary for Environmental Management Alvin Alm, who previously served as the first staff director of the Council on Environmental Quality and deputy administrator of the EPA, announced that "a 10-year plan will be developed for the entire EM program" and that "the process needs to begin immediately."[21] DOE headquarters called for Fernald, Mound Laboratory, Rocky Flats, Los Alamos National Laboratory, and seven other major nuclear weapons sites to be cleaned up by 2006.[22] Alm knew ten years was a "stretch goal," but his plan was intended to pressure as well as inspire; it was modeled after President John F. Kennedy's call to land a man on the moon "before this decade is out."[23] This was a fiscally conservative and goal-oriented environmental policy. By closing the door on the production era quickly, Alm hoped to redirect the DOE's shrinking resources to the nuclear weapons complex's worst environmental hazards and prevent even more waste from piling up.[24]

This was no easy task for the DOE's third largest radioactive waste dump, but organized labor, regulators, the Task Force, Fluor, and the DOE worked together to make Fernald's cleanup possible.[25] The first order of business was labor relations. An accelerated cleanup meant an increased role for the private sector, which clashed with Fernald's commitment to former production workers. By hiring John Bradburne as the Fluor Daniel Environmental Restoration Management Corporation's president, however, Fluor was able to resolve this conflict. Bradburne, who served as the director of congressional affairs for the Nuclear Regulatory Commission during the late 1980s, "truly understands labor relations," according to longtime Fernald Atomic Trades and Labor Council (FATLC) leader Gene Branham, who personally recruited Bradburne to join the Fernald project.[26] Through careful planning and a commitment to environmental health and safety, Bradburne and FATLC president Bob Schwab were able to meet the DOE's call for economy in Fernald's cleanup while respecting the rights of unionized workers.[27]

The next challenge was securing consistent funding. If Fluor was going to clean up Fernald, the company needed a long-term commitment from Congress. "Fluor approached the DOE with a bold and innovative proposal," according to Brinley Varchol and Dennis Carr, to "establish a set funding level that permits the efficient execution of the cleanup scope.... This proposal became the foundation of the DOE's accelerated cleanup program," which "was adopted as a congressional mandate."[28] This was a major coup for Fluor. Not only had the company secured the DOE's first major cleanup contract, but it also influenced the direction of the program for the next decade.[29] With funding in place and a positive working relationship developed between management and labor, Fluor was prepared to clean up Fernald's radioactive backyard and beyond.

CLEANUP PROJECTS

Operable Unit 1, or the Waste Pit Area, was the first of five major remediation projects at Fernald. Covering thirty-seven acres, it contained six waste pits, a burn pit, and a settling pond for wastewater called the Clearwell, with surface areas ranging from half an acre to five acres and depths ranging from twelve to forty-two feet. These pits contained an estimated six hundred thousand cubic yards of waste, including uranium, thorium, radium, and toxic metals, which needed to be excavated, sampled, treated, and shipped off-site for disposal. The logistics were complex. In 1994, the DOE granted the project an exemption, which permitted Fernald to ship its wastes to a commercial facility instead of a government-owned radioactive waste dump.[30] Four years later, the DOE awarded a $66 million contract to the Utah-based company Envirocare for the permanent disposal of low-level radioactive wastes from Fernald, which would be transported along the CSX and the Union Pacific Railroads to Envirocare's disposal facility in Clive, about seventy-five miles west of Salt Lake City.[31] Whether producing nuclear weapons or cleaning up the arms race, the DOE relied on railroads to transport dangerous radioactive materials across the country.

In environmental remediation, there is ironically as much construction as there is demolition. To prepare for increased traffic, workers cleared and graded the land, built a stormwater management system, and developed new rail lines.[32] In 1997, Fluor awarded a $122 million subcontract to the IT Corporation for the construction and management of the Waste Pit Area's remediation facility.[33] This process included sorting, blending, thermally drying, and storing contaminated materials before they were loaded onto train containers, which were lined in plastic and sealed with fiberglass tops.[34] On April 29, 1999, the Waste Pit Area's first shipment departed Fernald for Envirocare. Over the next six years, 154 trains made this journey and transported a total of 975,100 tons of Fernald's low-level radioactive waste. During this period, the DOE's fleet expanded from 170 to 250 railcars. As deadlines approached, the remediation facility shifted from twenty-four hours, five days a week to 24/7 operations. On June 15, 2005, the Waste Pit Area's final train shipment left Fernald.[35] After decades of being filled with radioactive sludge, the waste pits were empty. Like the booming production days, Fernald's workforce kept the site buzzing with activity during cleanup to complete its mission while the rest of the community slept.

Operable Unit 2 contained six waste units scattered across the western half of the site: the Solid Waste Landfill, which accepted cafeteria waste, garbage, and construction debris; the north and south Lime Sludge Ponds, which contained sludge from the water treatment plant, the boiler plant, and coal pile stormwater runoff; the Inactive Flyash Pile, which received boiler plant ash and construction debris; the Active Flyash Pile, which received boiler plant coal ash; and the South Field, which was a catchall burial site for fly ash, construction debris, contaminated soils, laboratory waste, old drums, uranium products, and lead bullets buried in the earth from the security force's firing range. The bulk of this waste was scheduled for disposition in the On-Site Disposal Facility, which was built along the site's eastern boundary. To transport the waste, Fernald needed new roads. Beginning in August 1997, Kelchner Environmental prepared the landscape and Barrett Paving finished what became known as Waste Haul Road. During Fernald's cleanup, nearly half a million banked cubic yards of material were removed from Operable Unit 2 and traveled down

Waste Haul Road for encapsulation in the On-Site Disposal Facility.[36] In Cold War history, scientists and advanced technologies attract a lot of the attention, but construction firms also played critical roles both in raising and dismantling the nuclear weapons complex.

Operable Unit 3 contained Fernald's former Production Area, including 255 production-era structures, 31 million pounds of uranium products, 35,600 cubic yards of containerized waste, and 1,000 cubic yards of containerized thorium. Fernald's sudden shutdown in 1989 also created a unique challenge for Fluor. Radioactive materials were never cycled through or removed from the system, so process lines, tanks, drumming stations, and other areas of the plant were still filled with uranium and toxic chemicals. The DOE, Fluor, and regulators, as a result, were essentially dealing with a plant frozen in the Cold War that was unsafe for demolition. This led to the development of a project called "Safe Shutdown," which required removing hazardous materials, decontaminating surfaces, disconnecting utilities, and salvaging equipment from Fernald's former production facilities.[37] On March 22, 1999, Secretary of Energy Bill Richardson toured Fernald's cleanup to celebrate the first major facility to complete a "Safe Shutdown" and honor the dedication of former production workers to fighting the Cold War and then cleaning up the mess. "You've set the pace for the safe, efficient cleanup of one of America's nuclear weapons facilities," Richardson said, "the mission the United States entrusted the DOE to carry out."[38] It was dangerous and tedious work, but as the FATLC stated years earlier, nobody was better equipped to cleanup Fernald's radioactive legacy than former production workers.

Dismantling the Production Area required an enormous disposition of waste, including shipping 6.6 million cubic feet of low-level radioactive waste to the Nevada Test Site, redistributing 31 million pounds of usable nuclear materials throughout the DOE and the private sector, transferring 174,912 gallons of mixed waste off-site for incineration, and shipping 59,147 cubic feet of low-level mixed waste off-site for treatment. Demolishing hundreds of structures also created an additional 523,455 cubic yards of waste, which was buried in the On-Site Disposal Facility.[39] As each building fell, however, it was a reminder that while the Cold War was waged as an indefinite undertaking, Fernald's cleanup was finite.

In the wake of remediation, Fernald's economic contributions to the community were expected to decline from $735 million and 4,394 jobs in 1997 to $136 million and 1,629 jobs by 2008. During this transition from uranium metals production to environmental stewardship, the DOE funded the Community Reuse Organization to plan for a future in which Fernald's primary contribution shifted from employment to recreation and education.[40]

Operable Unit 4, or Silos 1, 2, 3, and the empty Silo 4, contained the most dangerous materials on-site and proved to be the most controversial cleanup project. Silos 1 and 2, better known as the K-65 silos, were filled with 8,900 cubic yards of radioactive residues leftover from uranium processing during the Manhattan Project. Silo 3 contained 5,100 cubic yards of metal oxides.[41] Together, according to the DOE and Fluor, these concrete vaults, which stood only a thousand feet from Fernald's closest neighbor—were the largest point source of radon gas in the world.[42] Initially, they were the DOE's proving ground for vitrification technology, which was designed to heat the silos' radioactive contents into a glass-like material for safer and more stable disposal. In December 1996, during a test with surrogate K-65 material, however, hardware failed in the vitrification pilot plant. Testing was brought to a halt, which raised costs and set back the project at the same time Fernald's cleanup was under intense scrutiny by the *Cincinnati Enquirer*, although a follow-up General Accounting Office (GAO) investigation found the newspaper's more serious claims unsubstantiated.[43] Either way, the DOE and EPA agreed it was best to abandon vitrification for the chemical stabilization of Fernald's silos.[44]

Beginning on March 23, 2005, Silo 3's contents were vacuumed and mechanically removed using remote controlled excavation equipment, mixed with chemicals to bind the materials together, and double packaged for shipment. Filling nearly 2,300 containers, Silo 3's wastes were sent to Envirocare in Utah for disposal. Silos 1 and 2 were highly radioactive, which required additional environmental health and safety measures. Between July 2002 and February 2005, a reinforced remediation facility was constructed to protect workers during processing. A silo retrieval system pumped 2.2 million gallons of K-65 slurry, as well as 400,000 gallons of water, through double contained piping into four 750,000-gallon steel tanks housed in concrete to reduce radioactive exposures. An identical pumping system then transferred the wastes to the remediation facility, where they were mixed with cement and fly ash and prepared for shipment.[45]

Fernald's failed vitrification project reveals that trial and error was a part of developing environmental remediation technologies in the field. This uncertainty, however, proved incompatible with the budgetary constraints placed on Fernald's accelerated cleanup. Fernald's cleanup team admirably transitioned to chemical stabilization to stay on schedule, but this political pressure also complicated the waste disposal process. In total, 3,776 containers of K-65 wastes were shipped to Waste Control Specialists (WCS) in Andrews, Texas, because the material was too radioactive for Envirocare to accept, and the State of Nevada protested its disposal at the Nevada Test Site. When the K-65 transfer was completed in 2006, WCS only possessed a license for the interim storage of the waste, which meant it might be dumped in yet another community. On May 29, 2008, however, WCS was finally approved for the permanent disposal of the K-65 residues. It was a long journey from their production at Mallinckrodt Chemical Works in St. Louis during the Manhattan Project, to temporary storage at Fernald during the Cold War, and finally, their shallow burial in Texas.[46] It was not an ideal solution. The K-65 wastes "should be disposed of in a deep geologic repository," warned antinuclear activists Annie and Arjun Makhijani, for their shared radioactive characteristics with transuranic wastes.[47] Even fifteen years after the Cold War's end, American politics continued to complicate the implementation of scientifically sound and socially equitable solutions to radioactive waste disposal.

Operable Unit 5 included three major projects: building the On-Site Disposal Facility, removing soils to reduce on-site radioactivity, and aquifer restoration. Constructing the On-Site Disposal Facility was a complex, multiyear undertaking. While Fernald's position above the Great Miami Aquifer was attractive for siting the plant during the Cold War, it was technically illegal to place a radioactive waste dump at Fernald because of its location above the sole-source aquifer for Southwest Ohio, although the site basically served as one for decades. After receiving a waiver from the State of Ohio, the disposal facility was placed along the plant's eastern

FIGURE 14. The On-Site Disposal Facility was divided into eight individual cells that were completed between December 2001 and October 2006. In this photograph, remediation workers and heavy equipment construct the cover system on cell 2, August 2003. The three-foot layer of rock prevents the intrusion of vegetation and burrowing animals. Courtesy of the US Department of Energy.

boundary, which featured the most favorable soil conditions to prevent the waste from seeping into the groundwater. The facility was designed by the engineering consulting firm Geosyntec and constructed by Fluor. It featured eight disposal cells, a five-foot-thick and double composite liner system with leachate collection and detection technologies beneath the waste, and a nearly nine-foot-thick and multilayer composite cover system. In the fall of 2006, the last shovels of soil were placed and the capping system was completed. In total, the On-Site Disposal Facility stands 3,700 feet long, 800 feet wide, and 65 feet tall; contains almost three million cubic yards of radionuclide- and chemical-contaminated soil and building debris; and was designed to last from two hundred to one thousand years.[48]

Fernald's remedial investigation determined that the site was widely contaminated with radioactive uranium, radium-226, thorium, and technetium-99. Uranium contamination in the soil generally ranged from more than double to twenty-three times what is considered "background," or naturally occurring, levels. Beneath Fernald's former production area, above-background levels were discovered at depths greater than twenty feet. Other toxic byproducts of Fernald's industrial operations, including cadmium, beryllium, arsenic, volatile organic compounds, and polychlorinated biphenyls were also common. The site was divided into nine areas and three excavation phases to coordinate between all operable units. Regulators approved Fluor's use of in situ gamma spectrometry, which allowed the company to take real-time measurements of radioactive contamination in the field and plot the data using geographic information systems. Radioactivity could literally be measured with each scoop of Fernald's earth to determine its appropriate disposal method, as well as when soils were ready for final certification. This massive earth-moving project, which relied on heavy equipment like backhoes and dump trucks, reveals the collaborative nature between green engineering and blue-collar labor in the environmental remediation industry.[49]

When Lisa and Ken Crawford learned in early 1985 that Fernald's uranium had polluted their well, there was little regulatory guidance on the issue. Water pollution standards, however, underwent rapid change during this period. By the late 1980s, as historian Teresa Sabol Spezio observed, detection technologies allowed regulators to measure contaminants at the parts per billion instead of parts per million level.[50] This increased sensitivity transformed scientists' knowledge of water pollution and permitted stricter enforcement. The Safe Drinking Water Act Amendments of 1986, for example, required the EPA to develop its first maximum contaminant level (MCL) for uranium, which during the early 1990s was proposed at twenty parts per billion. This tentative standard, which was endorsed by the Fernald Citizens Task Force, guided the early restoration of the Great Miami Aquifer until it was raised to thirty parts per billion in 2001 to match the EPA's finalized MCL.[51]

Fernald's cleanup team developed a sophisticated network of water treatment infrastructure to remediate pollution during the cleanup and protect public health. These projects included the completion of a public water system for the area, the development of a storm water retention basin, biosurge lagoon, slurry dewatering facility, and advanced wastewater treatment facilities, as well as a series of well fields to pump and treat groundwater on-site and halt the migration of the South Plume. These methods have successfully stopped the migration of contamination, reduced the quantities of uranium in the aquifer, and drastically improved compliance with uranium discharges into the Great Miami River. Despite technological advancements, however, aquifer restoration remains a costly and challenging project. The DOE understood that even after the completion of accelerated cleanup, groundwater monitoring would continue decades into the future.[52]

HEALTH AND STEWARDSHIP

On October 30, 2006, Fluor announced that Fernald's cleanup was complete. It was a massive ten-year undertaking at the cost of $4.4 billion.[53] "I never thought I'd live to see this day," the DOE's director of the Fernald Closure Project, Johnny Reising, told the *New York Times*.[54] The courageous efforts of Fluor's workforce and subcontractors, who solved complex environmental problems at risk to their own personal safety, should be commended. The collaborative efforts between the DOE, EPA, Ohio EPA, and Fernald Citizens Task Force—which changed its name during cleanup to the Fernald Citizens Advisory Board (FCAB)—also stands as a powerful example of government reform, which, as Jennifer Duffield Hamilton argued, created space for conflict and compromise in the fiercely partisan realm of environmental politics in the 1990s and 2000s.[55] But the compromise of accelerated cleanup also created another challenge for the DOE. Since Fernald and other former nuclear weapons production facilities were not remediated to "unrestricted use," the DOE was going to have to monitor or provide stewardship over these sites forever.[56]

The DOE defined stewardship as "all activities required to protect human health and the environment from hazards remaining at DOE sites after cleanup is complete."[57] On December 15, 2003, the DOE established the Office of Legacy Management to oversee this mission.[58] At Fernald, stewardship activities included aquifer restoration, maintaining the On-Site Disposal Facility, ecological restoration, environmental monitoring, and providing public access.[59] The DOE's commitment to environmental stewardship will ensure that Fernald's radioactive legacy has minimal impact on future generations. It is important to remember, however, that this profound institutional change was not inevitable. In its report *From Cleanup to Stewardship*, the DOE claimed that from the passage of the Atomic Energy Act of 1954 to the Cold War's end, "one thing has remained constant—the Federal Government's obligation to protect human health and the environment."[60] This interpretation, however, ignored the most conflicted years of Fernald's environmental movement, when FRESH and the FATLC helped dismantle the DOE's iron grip on atomic knowledge. Only then was the door opened to a more transparent form of long-term stewardship.

Critical to this process was inserting alternative perspectives into atomic medicine. Nobody represents this controversy better, perhaps, than University of Cincinnati radiologist Eugene Saenger. From 1960 to 1971, he received funding from the Department of Defense to "find a biological dosimeter" for radiation in the human body, such as found in urine or amino acids. As part of this study, eighty-two terminally ill cancer patients were given total-body irradiation, or at least partial-body irradiation, with questionable levels of consent or benefits to patient care and quality of life. These studies raised ethical concerns internally in the University of Cincinnati's College of Medicine during the 1960s, including a denied funding request on "ethical grounds" from the National Institutes of Health, before receiving widespread criticism in the early 1970s. As part of Secretary of Energy Hazel O'Leary's Openness Initiative, the case was reexamined after the Cold War's end.[61] This gave FRESH's Lisa Crawford the opportunity to "tie two very disturbing issues together" at the outreach panel meeting for the Advisory Committee on Human Radiation Experiments in Cincinnati. Not only did Saenger conduct these ethically questionable total-body-irradiation experiments for the military, but he was also a hired expert witness for the DOE in the Fernald community and worker class-action lawsuits and worker compensation cases. In depositions and testimony, Saenger consistently argued on behalf of the DOE that chronic exposures to low levels of radiation were perfectly harmless. He even went so far as to claim, according to Crawford, that "no one is in any greater risk from having lived near Fernald than they would have been had Fernald not been there."[62] As Crawford demonstrated, Cold War science was conducted to protect the interests of the military and nuclear industry, not workers, the public, or patients.

Through class-action lawsuits, Fernald's environmental movement created a large body of data that challenged the DOE's Cold War claims that exposure to Fernald's uranium was harmless. Following the community's settlement, the University of Cincinnati was selected to design a medical monitoring program for the population who lived within five miles of Fernald between January 1, 1952, and December 18, 1984 — dates which were determined to be the plant's secretive production years. Nine thousand seven hundred and seventy-five Fernald-area residents participated in this eighteen-year program, which physicians believed to be the largest medical monitoring program of its kind. Unlike Saenger's study, which was designed to benefit the Department of Defense, the Fernald Medical Monitoring Program (FMMP) was designed to benefit patients. Since there were few options for doctors to improve outcomes from past uranium and toxic exposures, the FMMP conducted comprehensive examinations to mitigate common causes of death, such as heart disease, prevalent cancers, and stroke.[63] Despite finding that the Fernald community was at greater risk for urinary cancer, nonmalignant kidney disease, nonmalignant bladder disease, and lupus, participation in the FMMP improved mortality and common risk factors for participants, such as cholesterol and high blood pressure.[64] "Such monitoring," said the FMMP's physicians, "can be a very effective legal remedy by providing general health benefits to balance potential harms that could result from environmental contaminants."[65] Fernald's radioactive legacy created a lot of despair. The FMMP offered the community hope.

On July 26, 1994, Fernald workers settled their own class-action lawsuit against former plant operator National Lead of Ohio, which secured them lifetime medical monitoring. In 2013, the National Institute for Occupational Safety and Health (NIOSH) published a study, which found 15 percent more cancer-related deaths and 25 percent more lung cancer deaths in Fernald's male blue-collar workers, 52 percent more lymph and blood cancers in Fernald's male white-collar workers, four times higher-than-expected rates of bladder and kidney cancer in female white-collar workers, and a dose response between internal radiation and intestinal cancer in male workers.[66] During the Cold War, the DOE and its predecessor agencies insisted that Fernald's uranium was harmless. These grassroots lawsuits, however, produced medical monitoring data that strongly suggested otherwise and were influential precursors for the Energy Employees Occupational Illness Compensation Program Act, which was enacted in 2000 and provides cash payments and medical benefits to former nuclear weapons production workers and surviving family members.[67] This transformation of atomic knowledge made it nearly impossible for the DOE to approach its stewardship program from its formerly cynical perspective on environmental health and safety. Pumping and treating groundwater for uranium, along with maintaining Fernald's On-Site Disposal Facility, was prioritized, because chronic low-level radiation exposures were finally treated as an ongoing threat to public health.

None of this would have been possible without the Clinton administration bringing new leadership into the DOE, including Alvin Alm, Thomas Grumbly, and Hazel O'Leary, that prioritized environmental health and safety over production and demonstrated a willingness to work with grassroots activists in nuclear weapons production communities. "I do not think that [hazardous waste issues] are fundamentally technical decisions," said Grumbly. "I think they are fundamentally social decisions."[68] Highly technical problems, like the study, stabilization, and disposal of nuclear waste, however, also required the perspectives of highly technical people. James Werner's career, for example, illustrates the importance of environmental engineers in greening the DOE both inside and outside of government during the 1980s and 1990s. As a senior environmental engineer at ICF Technology, Inc., Werner was hired as a consultant to the DOE during the Reagan administration, performing hazardous waste field investigations across the nuclear weapons complex, including Fernald. Afterward, he worked as a senior engineer for the Natural Resources

Defense Council, providing policy and budget analyses for environmental health and safety issues at DOE nuclear weapons production facilities. Finally, President Clinton appointed Werner as policy director for the DOE's Office of Environmental Management, where he oversaw the production of two influential government reports, including *Closing the Circle on the Splitting of the Atom* and *Linking Legacies*, which detailed the nuclear weapons production life cycle and quantified its environmental impact on society.[69] While environmental historians are more familiar with social activists, environmental activist-engineers, such as Arjun Makhijani and James Werner, also played critical roles in cleaning up the nuclear weapons complex. Their knowledge was essential for a problem that not only required institutional and policy reform but also the reimagining of a technological system.

HISTORY AND RESTORATION

As part of the State of Ohio's 1986 lawsuit, the DOE was potentially on the hook for $206 million in natural resource damages from uranium production. In the following years, this looming claim ensured that ecological restoration took place alongside Fernald's cleanup.[70] The Society for Ecological Restoration defines this process as "assisting the recovery of an ecosystem that has been degraded, damaged, or destroyed." The key word here, according to historian Laura J. Martin, is "assist," since restorationists "attempt to co-design nature with nonhuman collaborators."[71] Based on Ohio's natural resource damages claim, the restricted access required by ongoing contamination at the site, and the interest of the community, the DOE determined that Fernald's future use would be as a park.[72] It was a remarkable turnaround for the site. Its history was rooted in humanity's most sophisticated attempt at mastering nature—the production of nuclear weapons—but despite Fernald's industrial might, its radioactive backyard proved the shortsightedness of this one-sided project. Through the promise of green industry, including environmental remediation and ecological restoration, the next phase of Fernald's history would balance technological ingenuity with the environment.

No matter how beautiful Fernald's restoration is, however, the Fernald

Citizens Advisory Board understood that sharing the site's history was essential to both future success and public health, because the site is still contaminated. "Cleanup is a misnomer," wrote the Advisory Board, since the DOE's strategy "relies heavily on the on-site management of hazardous materials, rather than on their removal." There were ongoing hazards, as a result, that needed to be monitored and communicated to the public, perhaps for tens of thousands of years. These "controls," such as physical barriers and restricted access to the On-Site Disposal Facility, were useless if people were not made aware of them. The Advisory Board also recognized the importance of storytelling, identifying four critical chapters in the site's history to share with the public: the Cold War and Fernald's role in nuclear weapons production, the impact of production and cleanup on workers and communities, the power of grassroots environmental activism, and the past and present experiences of Indigenous peoples.[73] As part of greening the DOE, the Advisory Board demanded room for diverse voices in Fernald's history, which had been shut out during the Cold War to ensure that production proceeded uninterrupted.

Led by Professor of Communication Stephen Depoe, the University of Cincinnati's Center for Environmental Communication Studies launched the Fernald Living History Project in 1997 to collect oral history interviews with the workers, activists, politicians, regulators, government officials, and area residents that shaped, and in turn were shaped by, Fernald's radioactive legacy. This project created an invaluable archive of over one hundred interviews that documented the DOE's dramatic transformation from Cold War nuclear weapons production to environmental remediation and stewardship.[74] The Fernald Citizens Advisory Board also called for public space to share this history. Through the sustained activism of FRESH, the Fernald Living History Project, and the Advisory Board, the DOE eventually agreed to develop a visitor center to protect public safety, sustain community dialogue, and interpret the site's history.[75] Fernald's cleanup, as a result, would not simply conceal the scars on the land. They would be discussed, so, in the words of FRESH's Lisa Crawford, future generations do not "make this mistake again."[76]

THE FERNALD PRESERVE

Historians of the Atomic Age have documented the enormous human, ecological, and economic costs of the Cold War nuclear arms race.[77] Fernald's On-Site Disposal Facility, as well as others like it across the former production complex, stand as "unofficial monuments," in the words of historian Jason Krupar, to the toll the United States government paid on the home front for political and military dominance abroad.[78] Fernald's landscape, however, is more than a tomb for radioactive waste. It is a living laboratory for the promise of environmental remediation and ecological restoration. Its cleanup demonstrated the potential for rapid institutional change. Only five years after the Cold War's end, the DOE was funding an estimated 20 percent of the global environmental remediation market, which represents a significant refocus in its mission.[79] After building its portfolio in mining and fossil fuels, Fluor's entrance into the green economy is also a reminder that corporate power can be incentivized for environmental change.[80] Although environmental activism was heavily influenced by the antimodern appropriate technologies movement of the 1970s, this small-scale framework is nearly impossible to apply to megaprojects like Fernald, which relied on big expertise, big resources, and close collaboration with the federal government.[81] Fernald's cleanup, however, was not a top-down story. Through grassroots environmental activism, this megaproject's commitment to the community, blue-collar workers, and principles of environmental justice remedied relationships poisoned by Fernald's uranium during the Cold War.

The creation of the Fernald Preserve healed the land and people. On January 19, 2007, more than seven hundred people gathered at the Fernald Preserve to celebrate the site's transformation from nuclear weapons production plant to park and honor the workers who both waged the Cold War and cleaned up Fernald.[82] "I'm speechless," Lisa Crawford began. "I thought many times that we would never see it turned into something useable and safe for residents.... It's been a long road, but we finally got there."[83]

The long road that FRESH and the FATLC marched from nuclear wasteland to the Fernald Preserve speaks to the power of local environmental activism. By cleaning up their own backyard, Fernald's environmental movement transformed the nuclear weapons production complex. During the increasingly partisan 1980s and 1990s, however, this transformation required patience. Over three frustration-filled decades, Fernald's environmental movement combined local organizing, statewide networking, and lobbying in Washington, DC, to green the DOE. This daily-grind approach, which reflects the community's blue-collar mentality, is perhaps the most inspiring part of Fernald's story. At the time of this writing, the Fernald Community Alliance continues to provide citizen oversight for ongoing environmental monitoring and groundwater restoration and promotes the site's history and environmental transformation.[84] This local engagement has helped ensure that the DOE upholds its commitments to the community, which is not guaranteed. As geographer David G. Havlick observed at military-to-wildlife (M2W) refuges, military branches have been quick to distance themselves from unexploded ordinance and lingering environmental contamination at closed military bases now under ownership of the US Fish and Wildlife Service.[85] Sustained federal commitment to environmental remediation, combined with grassroots oversight at DOE and M2W parks, perhaps, is what separates the Superfund success stories from the national sacrifice zones.

Across the Fernald Preserve, visitors can walk seven miles of hiking trails through wetlands, forest, and fields, which, following ecological restoration, are alive with wildlife.[86] The National Audubon Society has recognized Fernald as a birding "hot spot" in Southwest Ohio, with over 250 species identified and over 100 nesting at the site.[87] At the visitor center, exhibits educate the public on Fernald's role in the Cold War, the resulting environmental contamination, and the collaborative efforts between the community, workers, and government to clean up the nuclear weapons complex.

In 2008, the DOE and the State of Ohio settled the natural resource damages claim for $13.75 million. Along with $14 million that the DOE invested in Fernald's restoration, these funds have stretched the site's environmental impact beyond the preserve's boundaries. Through a partnership with the Three Valley Conservation Trust, a land trust located in nearby Oxford, Ohio, the Fernald Natural Resource Trustees—the DOE,

FIGURE 15. Aerial view of the Fernald Preserve, formerly the Feed Materials Production Center, July 21, 2007. Courtesy of the US Department of Energy.

Ohio EPA, and US Fish and Wildlife Service—have preserved thousands of acres along Paddy's Run to protect the watershed for future generations.[88]

The Fernald Preserve's beauty is subtle in a uniquely Midwestern way. There are no towering mountains or boundless oceans, but its golden fields and pockets of trees blend into the surrounding farmlands and create a sense of continuity between people and nature.[89] With the "slow violence" of uranium metals production in the rearview mirror, visitors can now find the pieces of an ecotechnological landscape designed to solve environmental problems instead of create them, including the visitor center, which was the first LEED-platinum-certified building in the State of Ohio; the On-Site Disposal Facility; and groundwater protection infrastructure.[90] These structures, along with Fernald's restored landscape, offer hope that the same human ingenuity and industrial might that mass-produced nuclear weapons can be repurposed toward building a safe and sustainable future when informed by environmental activism instead of Cold War fear.[91] This will require a recalibration, however, of

Americans' understanding of national security that better recognizes the social and environmental costs of military dominance. While the AEC trumpeted the economic and national security benefits of Fernald, these were short-term gains. Fernald's environmental history teaches us that the bomb's primary legacy in Southwest Ohio is long-term insecurity, which eroded a sense of place, economic possibilities for the land, and trust in government and experts through nuclear secrecy and environmental contamination.[92] It has taken decades of actions by the DOE and its contractors in environmental protection, in addition to local community engagement since the Cold War's end, to mend these relationships. This kind of work, including nuclear downsizing, environmental monitoring and remediation, ecological restoration, and local democratic participation, has a proven track record of restoring public trust at Fernald by prioritizing environmental health and safety over production and must continue across the current and former nuclear weapons complex. The emerging threat of another and even more complex nuclear arms race threatens to unravel it all.[93]

Despite Fernald's ecological restoration, however, its soils remain toxic and radioactive and will require our attention and resources for thousands of years.[94] Perhaps the most sobering part of its monumental cleanup is that despite the mass mobilization of federal, state, corporate, and local resources and technical expertise, the bomb's environmental legacy cannot be undone; it can only be made safer. The nuclear arms race has forced humanity to confront two problems that continue to challenge the boundaries of human logic. The first is global. Even after the post–Cold War downsizing of nuclear arsenals, human beings still possess about 13,080 nuclear warheads—with 90 percent belonging to the United States and Russia—which is still enough firepower to destroy much of human civilization.[95] The second is local. Through the production of nuclear weapons, landscapes across the nation are so contaminated that we must plan for their safe management thousands of years into the future.[96] There are no simple answers to these questions, but they will require an educated and engaged public on nuclear issues and accountable government agencies. Finding the nuclear weapons production facility in your own backyard is the best place to start.

Conclusion

In March 1993, Oxford Citizens for Peace and Justice (OCPJ) president Linda Musmeci Kimball received a telephone call from her son Daryl. After graduating with a degree in political science from Miami University of Ohio, where his father Jeffrey taught in the history department and wrote about the Vietnam War, Daryl accepted a position with Physicians for Social Responsibility in Washington, DC, an antinuclear organization founded in 1961 by cardiologist and Harvard School of Public Health professor Bernard Lown.[1] Daryl's assignment was to scour recently declassified documents on Cold War nuclear weapons production for "clandestine facilities that had fallen off the radar." He informed his mother that Alba Craft Inc., one of these small and largely forgotten nuclear contractors, had operated in their hometown of Oxford, just a few blocks from their house.[2] At the same time that the Department of Energy (DOE) started to dismantle its aging nuclear weapons production complex, the public's knowledge of its unparalleled environmental legacy continued to grow.

Musmeci Kimball was stunned. As president of the OCPJ, she had educated the public on the dangers of nuclear weapons for nearly fifteen years. Ten years after helping organize the Trinity Day protest at Fernald, however, she learned that the Atomic Energy Commission's tangled web of uranium metals production had operated in her own neighborhood. She got in her car and made the short drive to the address at 10–14 West Rose Avenue, located in a residential area near Stewart Junior High, where Daryl had gone to school. The L-shaped concrete-block building that formerly housed Alba Craft was still standing. It needed a fresh coat of paint but was otherwise in stable condition. In 1988, Miami University chemistry professor Gilbert Pacey and his wife bought the property and converted it into a collegiate embroidery company. They also rented workspace to a food warehouse and laboratory business. When the Paceys bought the former Alba Craft building, however, they had no knowledge of its nuclear past.[3]

During the 1950s, Alba Craft Inc. subcontracted with National Lead of Ohio (NLO), Fernald's operating contractor, to manufacture uranium slugs to meet the Atomic Energy Commission (AEC)'s booming demand for feed materials during the Cold War nuclear arms race. About forty workers shaped the radioactive material with lathes, drill presses, milling machines, grinders, filers, and saws, which were operated around the clock. Workers were exposed to many of the same hazards as those at Fernald, including uranium dust and toxic chemicals. By the early 1990s, the DOE's major nuclear weapons production facilities were well known to the public and on the path to remediation under the Superfund program. As the rediscovery of Alba Craft demonstrates, however, there were many layers to the nuclear weapons production network.[4] Fernald received uranium ores from mining operations in the western United States, Canada, Belgian Congo (as it was known at the time), South Africa, Australia, and Portugal.[5] NLO worked with smaller companies, such as Alba Craft and Reactive Metals Inc. in Ashtabula, Ohio, to assist in the manufacturing process.[6] Finally, its uranium metal products were shipped to major nuclear weapons production facilities, including Hanford, Savannah River, Oak Ridge, and Rocky Flats.[7] Fernald's local operations were part of a uranium metals production system that left behind radioactive and chemical contamination across the globe.

Oxford's rediscovery of Alba Craft had disturbing parallels to Fernald. In 1992, the DOE listed the property for potential cleanup under the Formerly Utilized Sites Remedial Action Program (FUSRAP), which Congress established in 1974 to identify and remediate early nuclear weapons production sites. Later that year, the DOE dispatched investigators to measure lingering radiation levels at the former Alba Craft property, which detected radioactivity ten to one hundred times above background levels but also determined that the site posed no health risks. Although not a present danger, the site was contaminated enough to qualify for cleanup under FUSRAP. Like Fernald, the DOE shared this information on a need-to-know basis with the property owner, city officials, and the owner of a neighboring apartment complex. Not surprisingly, the DOE's failure to quickly inform the larger community about the radiological investigation sewed distrust in neighbors, who started to wonder if their own ailments were connected to uranium metals production. Musmeci Kimball and OCPJ drafted a document on the issue, which was read at the next city council meeting. This action set in motion a multiyear campaign to clean up Alba Craft.[8]

While the DOE's decisions were based on contemporary radiation data, which suggested that the property posed little to no public health threat, the community's concerns were rooted much deeper in the local environment. The Robinson sisters—Terry, Gail, Carol, Kelley, Peggy, and Amy—for example, grew up on South Main Street during the first two decades of the Cold War. They recalled splashing in pools of water, making mud pies, and building a secret hideout near the site. Five out of the six sisters developed thyroid conditions, including colloid cysts, goiters, and malignant growths, among other afflictions. This story of suffering human bodies serves as a powerful reminder that the legacy of the atomic bomb cannot be understood outside of its production network and the environments it poisoned.[9] Atomic environments were never restricted to distant laboratories or proving grounds; they are everywhere. As Musmeci Kimball discovered, they were even in your own backyard.

The DOE and US Army Corps of Engineers' work continues to clean up the radioactive legacy of the Cold War nuclear weapons complex, including major and retired DOE production facilities like Hanford and the Portsmouth Gaseous Diffusion Plant, active nuclear weapons production facilities like Oak Ridge and Los Alamos National Laboratory, and smaller sites being remediated under FUSRAP, such as the lingering uranium production contamination from the Mallinckrodt Chemical Works that remains scattered across greater St. Louis.[10] The DOE alone is responsible for an estimated $520 billion, or 83 percent, of the federal government's future environmental liabilities. These cleanup efforts are projected to last decades into the future.[11] Both kinds of knowledge—the scientific and technical expertise of government agencies and the personal experiences and family histories of plant neighbors—will be essential to restoring environments and trust in these contaminated communities.[12] As a pilot project, Fernald's decade-long cleanup demonstrated that this type of work, which balanced technical problem-solving with community dialogue, was a meaningful use of federal resources.

REMEMBERING THE NUCLEAR ARMS RACE

During the early 1980s, photographer Robert Del Tredici came to the realization that he had "never seen an H-bomb factory. I knew that nuclear weapons didn't grow on trees, but I couldn't tell you how they did grow."[13] Public ignorance surrounding the nuclear weapons production process was the result of a carefully coordinated national security program, but Del Tredici set out to change that.[14] Instead of highlighting the familiar and well-worn symbols of a "distant mushroom cloud, a city turned to ash," or "rockets in the atmosphere," the photographer trekked across the country to document the industrial spaces, workers' bodies, and technologies that made the bomb a reality.[15] His photographic record in *At Work in the Fields of the Bomb* represents how peace and environmental activists transformed the public's understanding of the nuclear bomb in the final decade of the Cold War. Nuclear physics and explosive yields were theoretical and intangible calculations. Factories and human bodies, on the other hand, were physical spaces that the public could engage. For many Americans, these spaces were in their own communities.

This material knowledge is essential for a safe and transparent nuclear future. During the Cold War, nuclear weapons production was shielded from the public. Without democratic participation, this self-regulating system became stagnant, slowly spiraled out of control, and left behind an environmental legacy that is still being remediated at places like Hanford, where former Fernald activist and whistleblowers' attorney Tom Carpenter started the watchdog organization Hanford Challenge in 2007.[16] While the major cleanup work is complete at Fernald and Alba Craft, "there is so much more to be done," said Musmeci Kimball. "We must make people aware of what happened here and in too many other communities. We must teach the history of the nuclear arms race and the risks we took and still take with Americans' health and safety in our country's pursuit of security through superior military power.... What I would like to see is nuclear age education for everybody everywhere, so that none of these lessons are lost."[17]

The peace movement has built an influential network of nongovernmental organizations, such as the Union of Concerned Scientists and the Arms Control Association, that carefully track America's nuclear arsenal and advocate for diplomatic solutions to nuclear weapons issues.[18] In light of this sobering work, it is also important to remember Fernald's environmental history, which demonstrates that the bomb is more than a number. It is a physical object that is a product of human labor, natural resources, and industrial systems. Its byproducts are deeply engrained in our bodies, neighborhoods, and global environment, and will remain so for thousands of years. For this reason, nuclear fallout has increasingly been recognized by scientists for its reliability in detecting geological strata from the Anthropocene—the era in which human beings are the primary driver of global environmental change—because it is widely deposited in the earth's crust from nuclear weapons testing.[19] To solve the greatest environmental threat facing their generation—the nuclear arms race—peace and environmental activists during the late 1970s and 1980s mapped the intricacies of the nuclear weapons production complex and protested the bomb plants in their own backyard. This was a local view of a global environmental problem, which transformed the highly technical and intangible issue of nuclear war into something accessible and tangible through physical landscapes. It was a powerful idea that forced the DOE to develop a greener model for nuclear weapons production.

Del Tredici's photographs also illustrated the DOE's report *Closing the Circle on the Splitting of the Atom*, which described "environmental, safety, and health problems throughout the nuclear weapons complex and what the DOE is doing to address them" to lay "the groundwork for informed debate on these difficult issues." In coordination with this report's release, several of Del Tredici's photographs from the late Cold War were on display in the Russell Rotunda of the Senate Office Building from March 27 to March 31, 1995. "We encourage you, your staff, and any constituents who may visit your office to walk through the exhibit," wrote Senators John Glenn of Ohio and Dirk Kempthorne of Idaho.[20] Only a decade earlier, Senator Glenn had first introduced Fernald's uranium leak and the corresponding environmental crisis across the nuclear weapons complex to his colleagues at a Committee on Governmental Affairs hearing in Cincinnati. Through Del Tredici's photograph exhibit, this pivotal moment—which brought together Fernald's environmental movement for the first time to challenge the DOE's culture of production—was suddenly transformed into history. Fernald's environmental movement serves as a powerful reminder that rapid institutional change for the sake of environmental protection is possible even in a polarized political environment. Few would have thought in the early 1980s, when President Ronald Reagan ramped up production at Fernald, that the same administration would be calling for its closure in 1989.[21]

A FRESH APPROACH TO GRASSROOTS ACTIVISM

Unlike the bipartisan 1960s and 1970s, Fernald Residents for Environmental Safety and Health (FRESH) was born into a tumultuous decade for environmental politics. This antagonism was both internal and external. Beginning with the Reagan administration, the rise of conservatism in the Republican Party slowly normalized attacks on the regulatory state and science, which weakened federal enforcement and stunted Congress's ability to pass environmental laws.[22]

At the same time, the environmental movement experienced its own growing pains as women and activists of color formally confronted its history of exclusion based on race, class, and gender so as to dismantle the old model and build a more inclusive version in its place. At the first National People of Color Environmental Leadership Summit in 1991, the Panos Institute's Dana Alston gave what is perhaps the defining speech of this era on behalf of the three hundred participants of African, Latino, Indigenous, and Asian ancestry: "We have come here to define for ourselves the issues of the ecology and the environment. . . . To speak these truths that we know from our lives to those participants and observers who we have invited here to join us."[23]

In this moment of great change and great distrust, it is worth reflecting on how FRESH—a grassroots organization led by white, nonprofessional, working- and middle-class housewives from a rural corner of Southwest Ohio—was able to clean up the nuclear weapons production complex.

Its determination to clean up Fernald was unparalleled, but the enormity of nuclear contamination also called for something far larger than any grassroots organization like FRESH could manage alone. FRESH recognized this early on, which makes Fernald an important case study for a movement that often ran counter to what historian James Morton Turner called the "currents of antimodernism" in environmentalism.[24] While many not-in-my-backyard movements were widely praised but also criticized for halting the placement of hazardous waste incinerators and commercial nuclear power plants in their neighborhoods, these tactics of slowing and stalling projects into bankruptcy are less useful for contaminated communities, like Fernald, that demand urgent action.[25] Instead, Fernald's successful environmental remediation relied upon responsive government agencies, corporate technical expertise, union participation, and community oversight to clean up the mess in a technically sound and equitable fashion. FRESH's brand of environmentalism learned not only how to stop something but how to build something new.

The challenge of building things has long plagued environmentalism. Stewart Brand recognized this back in the late 1960s, when he conceived of the *Whole Earth Catalog*.[26] "Communes were trying to reinvent civilization, which is bold and admirable," Brand recalled, but were "doing it poorly because they were all liberal arts majors who had dropped out and had no idea how to do anything. . . . My perspective was to try to bring a kind of respect for science, technology, engineering, and making things to that movement."[27] By designing its movement around the interests of working people, FRESH was more open, perhaps, than most environmentalists to collaborate with the DOE, union workers, and corporate contractors on Fernald's cleanup. This was important for developing alliances with two overlooked populations in environmental history that were essential to cleaning up Fernald's radioactive backyard: blue-collars workers and environmental engineers.[28] Through the lens of these groups, the "currents of antimodernism" that often make environmentalists uncomfortable, including "suspicion of synthetic materials" and "discomfort with scale," according to Turner, appear more ordinary than overwhelming.[29] Union workers and environmental engineers are frequently exposed to hazardous materials in the field and seek to reduce exposures to human bodies and the environment, but not necessarily eliminate them from society entirely. Similarly, workers and engineers also view corporations as employers or clients, respectively, instead of a nefarious enemy. There is a built-in belief, as a result, that the work they do can be for good as well as ill. By serving on the Fernald Citizens Task Force, Lisa Crawford learned to see Fernald not only as a grassroots activist but as a union worker, a regulator, and an engineer.[30] This is how the Task Force came to perceive Fernald's risk-based cleanup as a Superfund success story instead of a government cover-up.[31] It was all a matter of perspective.

At the same time, FRESH worked closely with peace activists and progressive environmentalists on several fronts, who were extremely skeptical of the DOE and corporate influence on nuclear policy. Biologist Dave Fankhauser and engineer Arjun Makhijani, for example, served as vital countermeasures to the more extreme and outdated interpretations of radiation safety that lingered in the DOE and nuclear industry, which were prevalent at Fernald, particularly in the 1980s.[32] The antinuclear movement in the United States was originally driven by the same nuclear scientists that developed the atomic bomb, so peace activists have much closer historical ties to technical experts than many in the environmental movement.[33] After joining the Military Production Network (MPN) in 1987, FRESH was able to learn from activists who had dedicated their lives to nuclear issues and were also experienced with Washington politics.[34] This was the primary allure of going national.

As part of the MPN, FRESH was on the cutting edge of environmental activism. The organization's structure was designed to respect grassroots autonomy while at the same time building a broad coalition to "act locally and nationally."[35] At a time when the environmental justice movement was also gaining steam, the MPN paid close attention; its meeting minutes reflect a predominantly white but gradually diversifying organization that was sensitive to issues of race and class and actively worked to transform itself into a truly representative coalition through educational workshops and membership recruitment.[36] Good intentions, however, could not insulate the MPN from the broader challenges facing many activists of color, who were offered equality in the MPN, but who actually needed equity to participate in a meaningful way. At the MPN's 1993 lobbying event in Washington, DC, Teresa Juarez and Makini McClain of the Rural Alliance for Military Accountability (RAMA) accused the MPN of being a racist organization. These accusations, which stemmed from frustrations with resources, access, and representation in the MPN, were allegedly voiced before government officials and potential donors, and were reiterated by additional members of the MPN's Unity/Diversity Council, including Juan Montes and Reyna Juarez.[37] For the MPN, the timing was terrible. With nuclear cleanup just getting underway, the MPN's ability to influence Congress was thrust into jeopardy at a time when nuclear communities needed them the most. Charges of racism were also taken seriously within the broader environmental movement. RAMA's accusations led to a canceled joint meeting with the Military Toxics Project that was two years in the making and a boycott of MPN membership by numerous environmental justice groups in a show of solidarity with RAMA. After multiple failed attempts to formally mediate the conflict, the MPN's board of directors—Sharon Cowdrey of Miamisburg Environmental Health and Safety, Pam Dunn of FRESH, Ralph Hutchinson of the Oak Ridge Environmental Peace Alliance, Pamela Kingfisher of Native Americans for a Clean Environment, and Arjun Makhijani of the Institute for Energy and Environmental Research—voted on September 16, 1995, to remove Teresa Juarez from the membership board.[38] It was deemed a difficult but necessary decision for the MPN's survival.

RAMA's accusations represented the material inequalities of the environmental movement at the time rather than overt racism by the MPN's members. Environmental activism—even in a comparatively small, highly democratic, and progressive organization like the MPN with diversity on its board of directors—still mirrored the racial disparities of American society. "It was not just yesterday that we have raised specific problems within the MPN institutional culture," RAMA's executive director, Maria

Painter, wrote. "These problems are not about individual bigotry," because "there are no bigots in the MPN." Instead, "it is about institutional racism" and the "subtle and complicated ways in which racism continued to haunt the Network."[39] For RAMA and other boycotting organizations, such dissent was viewed as part of a healthy dialogue to build an inclusive environmental movement, and the MPN's defensive posture signaled a hollowness in its diversity efforts.[40] Racism's subtleties, however, were difficult to see for an organization that had spent considerable energy on issues of race, class, and gender to diversify the MPN and was disturbed by accusations that struck each member personally and threatened to sink the organization.[41] At times, there was also a general confusion about the levels of resources, both personally and professionally, that members of the MPN's board actually had at their disposal.[42] Ultimately, it was a conflict that nobody won. RAMA lost access to technical expertise and a network of powerful allies, and the MPN suffered public humiliation and missed out on several valuable and diverse member organizations.

This was the fallout of going national. On its own, FRESH was a nimble and highly respected grassroots group that possessed credibility with environmental justice activists and national organizations. As a member of the MPN, however, FRESH was part of a bureaucracy and all the trappings of power that came with it. The MPN's boycott demonstrates that by the mid-1990s, white and environmental activists of color, as well as grassroots and national organizations, shared a common understanding of diversity but had not yet developed a shared vocabulary for productively discussing equity in environmental activism. While racial disparities were easily overlooked when class leveled the playing field between underfunded grassroots organizations, they were impossible to ignore on the national stage, where the differences between the haves and the have-nots, and the insiders and the outsiders, are amplified.[43] The end result was hurt feelings, missed opportunities, and an irresolvable conflict for both sides. By prioritizing equity in the environmental movement, activists can ensure that everyone, regardless of race, class, gender, ability, and education, is given equal access to Washington's halls of power.

ATOMIC NATURE PRESERVES

On October 29, 2016, nearly four hundred people, including former workers, community residents, activists, regulators, and contractors, gathered at the Fernald Preserve for "Weapons to Wetlands: A Decade of Difference," a celebration in honor of the ten-year anniversary of Fernald's cleanup. The megaproject's achievements were formidable: eliminating the world's largest point source of radon gas in the K-65 silos, dismantling 323 buildings, excavating and shipping one million tons of toxic and radioactive sludge from the waste pits, constructing and disposing of three million cubic yards of contaminated soil and building debris in the On-Site Disposal Facility, pumping and treating a 225-acre plume of uranium in the Great Miami Aquifer, shipping more than one hundred thousand barrels and thirty-one million pounds of uranium product off-site, and designing, constructing, operating, and demolishing $300 million in environmental remediation infrastructure. At the time, it was one of the largest cleanups in American history.[44]

"The Fernald Preserve is an amazing place," said FRESH's Lisa Crawford. "I see how this site has grown, changed, and healed itself, and we did it all together."[45] As Crawford recognized, making the community—and the nation—less radioactive took collaboration. Perhaps this was FRESH's greatest insight: accepting that a grassroots movement needed support from all kinds of people, including nuclear workers, peace activists, local communities, academics, scientists, government regulators, corporate engineers, and even the target of their environmental movement, the DOE, to accomplish something as large, complex, and unprecedented as remediating nuclear wastelands. If the DOE's culture of production helped destroy the public's faith in experts and institutions during the Cold War, Fernald's decade-long cleanup proved that these same forces could be repurposed to protect people and the environment.

Crawford also understood, however, that Fernald's cleanup was making the best of a terrible situation. Many scholars and activists agree—and rightfully worry—that ecological restoration at atomic nature preserves, such as Fernald or Rocky Flats, creates a superficial beauty that shields the public from learning about these sites' more dangerous and complicated histories.⁴⁶ In the short term, environmental activists in FRESH and the Fernald Citizens Advisory Board worked hard to ensure that did not happen. After walking through the Fernald Preserve exhibit gallery or reading the site's interpretive signage, visitors are introduced to many of Fernald's stories, including Indigenous peoples, the agricultural-to-industrial transformation, the beginnings of the Cold War, environmental contamination, and the DOE's environmental remediation program. It is not the whole story, and Fernald's grassroots environmental movement deserves considerably more attention, but overall, it is commendable work that draws upon diverse perspectives and does not sugarcoat the permanence of Fernald's radioactive legacy.⁴⁷

The most important thing, however, is that the community played an active role in telling Fernald's story, and their intention was that visitors should walk away with an understanding of why an untethered nuclear arms race should "never happen again."⁴⁸ The real challenge actually lies with the next generation. In the year of this book's publication, Fernald's uranium leak will turn forty years old, and these stories must continue to be passed down for local environmental health and safety, as well as global national security. After the downsizing of the Cold War nuclear weapons production complex—for better or worse—there are fewer bomb plants in our backyards. Nuclear weapons, as a result, are perhaps more invisible to the American public than they have been since the Manhattan Project.

A FABLE FOR FERNALD

On April 30, 2011, two bird watchers spotted something unusual at the Fernald Preserve. It was a garganey duck—a waterfowl native to Europe and Asia with a black and white cap above its eyes—that had flown off course during its long-distance migration and stumbled upon Southwest Ohio. Once reported, its presence inspired bird watchers from across the country to drive to the atomic nature preserve to get a glimpse of a species rarely seen in North America.⁴⁹

The nuclear arms race also steered America off course. The DOE's culture of production, insulation from broader society, and amplification of an external communist threat, blinded the department from the damage it was causing to people and the environment. Now we are left to clean up and manage the Cold War's environmental legacy indefinitely. Like the bird watchers, however, we must bear witness to what occurred at Fernald, because it offers important lessons for a secure and sustainable future.

Beginning in 2007, the *Bulletin of the Atomic Scientists* started factoring in climate change along with nuclear weapons when setting the time on its Doomsday Clock.[50] Despite the DOE's institutional changes in the wake of the Cold War, the department's primary mission remains the development and maintenance of nuclear weapons. As military competition grows between the United States, Russia, and China on the global stage, the pressure to fund increasingly sophisticated nuclear weapons and delivery systems will follow.[51] If history serves as a guide, environmental arguments—which helped ban atmospheric nuclear weapons testing in 1963 and downsize and clean up the American nuclear weapons complex after the Cold War—will remain instrumental in reducing the nuclear threat and protecting public and environmental health from another arms race. Even if environmental arguments are incapable of banning the bomb entirely, it is essential that we remember its environmental impact from mining, production, testing, and accidents to keep nuclear diplomacy grounded in the material world.[52] For both domestic and international politics, the environment can provide common ground for rational dialogue at times when resurgent Cold War paranoia threatens to take over. In both nuclear diplomacy and long-distance migration, sometimes you need a temporary refuge.

Unfortunately, the seemingly rare sight of a Eurasian duck swimming across a man-made pond at a Midwestern nature preserve where a uranium processing plant once stood is not so unusual in the Anthropocene. The earth's natural systems are under increasing strain from climate change, which is worsening droughts, heat waves, heavy precipitation, sea level rise, and biodiversity loss.[53] From the perspective of the Anthropocene, including its global nuclear and chemical contamination, an atomic nature preserve like Fernald appears quite ordinary.[54] Its contaminated version of nature, perhaps, better represents the state of the American environment in the twenty-first century than any seemingly pristine and iconic wilderness, such as Yellowstone.[55] While daunting, this provides a more realistic and productive view of our world. The Fernald Preserve's landscape requires environmental remediation, ecological restoration, and ongoing monitoring to protect human and environmental health. So does the earth. Scientists are discovering that the active management of natural areas improves conservation outcomes.[56] Setting aside land will not be enough. Human intervention is key to a healthier natural world in the Anthropocene.

Fernald's environmental history teaches us that humanity's global industrial imprint on the environment cannot be undone, but it can be improved. Like Fernald's cleanup, this process will require large-scale human intervention that delicately balances the material needs of a renewable energy transition with labor interests and environmental justice.[57] "A hundred years from now, I really hope people will come back and say, 'Gosh, look what happened here, but they fixed it,'" said Lisa Crawford. "Maybe not a hundred percent, but they did what they could at that point and time, and that will be our legacy. That will be our defining moment."[58] Like the garganey, FRESH made the best of an imperfect situation at Fernald. Now it is up to the next generation to turn back the hands of the Doomsday Clock.

NOTES

INTRODUCTION

1. Oak Ridge Incident Investigation Board, *Investigation*, 10–13, 16; Fernald Preserve Visitors Center Reading Room, Hamilton, Ohio.

2. Oak Ridge Incident Investigation Board, *Investigation*, 9–10, 16; Michael Joshua Silverman, "No Immediate Risk: Environmental Safety in Nuclear Weapons Production, 1942–1985" (PhD diss., Carnegie Mellon University, 2000), 266; Del Tredici, *At Work*, plates 19–24; Carlisle, *Supplying the Nuclear Arsenal*, 107–30; Makhijani, Hu, and Yih, *Nuclear Wastelands*, 207; *First Link: The Story of Fernald*, directed by Joyce Bentle, Fernald, OH: Fluor and Department of Energy, 2001.

3. Silverman, "No Immediate Risk," 356–60.

4. Plokhy, *Atoms and Ashes*; Brown, *Manual for Survival*; Walker, *Three Mile Island*; Hacker, *Elements of Controversy*, 131–55.

5. Plokhy, *Atoms and Ashes*, xvii.

6. Quote from Nixon, *Slow Violence*, 2–3.

7. Radioactive Waste Campaign, *Deadly Defense*, 117; General Accounting Office, *Department of Energy*, 11.

8. Silverman, "No Immediate Risk," 364–70; Oak Ridge Incident Investigation Board, *Investigation*, 29; Westad, *Cold War*.

9. Makhijani, Hu, and Yih, *Nuclear Wastelands*, 35.

10. Oak Ridge Incident Investigation Board, *Investigation*, 21, 40.

11. Silverman, "No Immediate Risk," 358–64; Oak Ridge Incident Investigation Board, *Investigation*, 6; Ben Kaufman, "NLO Checking Possible Uranium Leak," *Cincinnati Enquirer*, December 11, 1984, 1; Rainey, *One Hundred Miles from Home*, 95–125.

12. Lisa Crawford, interview with Fernald Living History Project, 8.

13. White, "Are You an Environmentalist?," 171–85.

14. Lisa Crawford, interview with Fernald Living History Project, 11; "Fernald Residents for Environmental Safety and Health," Briefing Book, DG 250, Alliance for Nuclear Accountability, Acc. 2017-074, Box 36, Swarthmore College Peace Collection.

15. US Congress. Senate, Committee on Governmental Affairs, *Management and Operation*, hearing held in Cincinnati, Ohio.

16. Turner and Isenberg, *Republican Reversal*, 5–8.

17. Halvorson, *Valuing Clean Air*, 132–33, 160–62; Shabecoff, *Fierce Green Fire*, 210–13.

18. Donaghy, *Second Cold War*, 2; Knoblauch, *Nuclear Freeze*, 4–5.

19. Oak Ridge Incident Investigation Board, 8; Westad, *Cold War*, 381–82, 417–19.

20. Oak Ridge Incident Investigation Board, *Investigation*, 8, 32–33; Silverman, "No Immediate Risk," 362–63; Westad, *Cold War*, 381–82, 417–19.

21. Hamilton, "Convergence and Divergence," 58; Gosling and Fehner, *Closing the Circle*, 34–35; Silverman, "No Immediate Risk," 342–47, 368.

22. Shabecoff, *Fierce Green Fire*; Hays, *Beauty, Health, and Permanence*; Gottlieb, *Forcing the Spring*; Rothman, *Saving the Planet*; Spears, *Rethinking*.

23. Gosling and Fehner, *Closing the Circle*, 51–52; Kohn, "America's Worst Polluter," 37–50.

24. Quote from Spears, *Rethinking*, 90. See also 89–123.

25. Turner and Isenberg, *Republican Reversal*, 15–18.

26. Newman, *Love Canal*, 211–21.

27. McGurty, *Transforming Environmentalism*, 81–110, 113–18.

28. Spears, *Rethinking*; Gottlieb, *Forcing the Spring*; Lisa Crawford, interview with Fernald Living History Project, 8–10, 20.

29. Melosi, "Environmental Justice," 51.

30. McGurty, *Transforming Environmentalism*, 81–110.

31. Cahn, ed., *Environmental Agenda*, 4.

32. Ackland, *Making a Real Killing*, 181–94.

33. Wittner, *Toward Nuclear Abolition*, 75–76; Winkler, *Life under a Cloud*, 201–2; Knoblauch, *Nuclear Freeze*, 6–7.

34. Oak Ridge Incident Investigation Board, *Investigation*, 6–12, 14–18, 32, 40.

35. Decker, "Ecological Restoration of Native Plant Communities at the Fernald Preserve" (MA thesis, Miami University, 2013), 1.

36. Werner, interview; Advisory Committee on Human Radiation Experiments, *Human Radiation Experiments*, xxi–xxxii; Turner and Isenberg, *Republican Reversal*, 134–35.

37. "LM Sites," US Department of Energy Office of Legacy Management, accessed May 6, 2023, https://www.energy.gov/lm/lm-sites.

38. Turner, *Charged*, 170–71.

39. "Cleanup Sites," Department of Energy Office of Environmental Management, accessed December 19, 2023, https://www.energy.gov/em/cleanup-sites#:~:text=As%20the%20largest%20environmental%20cleanup,of%20Rhode%20Island%20and%20Delaware.

40. "Celebrating the 10th Anniversary," Department of Energy Office of Legacy Management, October 31, 2016, https://www.energy.gov/management/articles/celebrating-10th-anniversary-successful-em-cleanup.

41. Turner, *Charged*, 170–72; Kirk, *Counterculture Green*, 28–31.

42. "Fernald Preserve Fact Sheet," US Department of Energy Office of Legacy Management, accessed May 6, 2023, https://www.energy.gov/sites/default/files/2022-09/FernaldPreserveFactSheet.pdf.

43. "On-Site Disposal Facility," US Department of Energy Office of Legacy Management, accessed May 6, 2023, https://www.energy.gov/sites/prod/files/2020/04/f74/Fernald%20Preserve%2C%20Ohio%20On-Site%20Disposal%20Facility.pdf.

44. "Fernald Residents for Environmental Safety and Health," Briefing Book, DG 250, Alliance for Nuclear Accountability, Acc. 2017-074, Box 36, Swarthmore College Peace Collection; Hamilton, "Convergence and Divergence," 41–72.

45. Fernald Citizens Advisory Board and the Perspectives Group, Inc., *Telling the Story of Fernald*, 7–8.

46. Lisa Crawford, interview with Fernald Living History Project, 23.

47. Rothman, *Saving the Planet*, 156–57, 205; Rabe, *Beyond NIMBY*, 1–3; Shabecoff, *Fierce Green Fire*, 236–38; Gottlieb, *Forcing the Spring*, 166.

48. Gordin, *Red Cloud at Dawn*, 12–13.

49. Hamilton, "Convergence and Divergence," 41–72; Williams, *Determining Our Environments*.

50. Applegate and Sarno, "FUTURESITE," 13–27.

ONE. ATOMIC FARMLANDS

1. Ellen Reidy, "The First Days of Construction," *The Atomizer* (June–July 1961): 6; Silverman, "No Immediate Risk," 291–93; James Ray Wilson, "The Fernald Project of the Atomic Energy Commission: An Agricultural-Industrial Transformation" (MA thesis, The Ohio State University, 1956), 1, 22–32.

2. "Uranium Plant Land Turned Over to US," *Cincinnati Post*, April 24, 1951, 26; Wilson, "Fernald Project," 20–32.

3. "Uranium Plant Land," 26.

4. "Bulldozers Push Aside Wheat, Alfalfa as Work Starts on Fernald Station Plant," *Cincinnati Post*, June 14, 1951, 2; Wilson, "Fernald Project," 15–21.

5. Balogh, *Chain Reaction*, 29–32; May, *Homeward Bound*, 26–28.

6. Balogh, *Chain Reaction*, 29.

7. Silverman, "No Immediate Risk," 4–5, 22–23; Balogh, *Chain Reaction*, 90.

8. Balogh, *Chain Reaction*, 60–94; Silverman, "No Immediate Risk," 264–66; Wellerstein, *Restricted Data*.

9. Hewlett and Duncan, *Atomic Shield*, 2:96.

10. Balogh, *Chain Reaction*, 86; Silverman, "No Immediate Risk," 4–5.

11. Egan, *Barry Commoner*, 66–72; Carson, *Silent Spring*; Lear, *Rachel Carson*.

12. Spears, *Rethinking*, 89–123.

13. Sabin, *Public Citizens*, 17–23.

14. US Congress. Senate. Committee on Governmental Affairs, *Management and Operation*, hearing held in Cincinnati, Ohio.

15. Silverman, "No Immediate Risk," 342–47; Gosling and Fehner, *Closing the Circle*, 34–35.

16. Hartsock, *Geologic Considerations*, 19.

17. "Bulldozers Push Aside," 2.

18. Quote from Silverman, "No Immediate Risk," 292.

19. Brown, *Plutopia*, 18; Freeman, *Longing for the Bomb*, 16–17.

20. Robey, *Atomic Americans*, 14–18.

21. Gordin, *Red Cloud at Dawn*, 12–13.

22. Feldman, ed., *Nuclear Reactions*, 59–64.

23. Hewlett and Duncan, *Atomic Shield*, 586–87.

24. Hewlett and Duncan, *Atomic Shield*, 586–87; Westad, *Cold War*, 224–25; Rhodes, *Arsenals of Folly*.

25. Robey, *Atomic Americans*, 18.

26. Spears, *Rethinking*, 89–123.

27. Hamilton, "Convergence and Divergence," 58; Silverman, "No Immediate Risk," 307, 342–47, 368; Olwell, *At Work in the Atomic City*, 128–30.

28. Reidy, "First Days," 6.

29. Williams, *Determining Our Environments*, 44; Wilson, "Fernald Project," 62.

30. Krupar, "Burying Atomic History," 40; History Associates, Inc., *History of the Production Complex*, 60–63; Wilson, "Fernald Project," 5, 46, 69–70.

31. Reidy, "First Days," 6.

32. Silverman, "No Immediate Risk," 298; Wilson, "Fernald Project," 35.

33. Reidy, "First Days," 6–7; Wilson, "Fernald Project," 59–61, 66.

34. Silverman, "No Immediate Risk," 283, 297.

35. Silverman, "No Immediate Risk," 399–403; US Department of Energy, *Closer Look*, 6–10.

36. Silverman, "No Immediate Risk," 403–6; US Department of Energy, *Closer Look*, 12–20.

37. Silverman, "No Immediate Risk," 316–17, 367–68.

38. Balogh, *Chain Reaction*, 80–81.

39. Silverman, "No Immediate Risk," 323.

40. Kasparek, interview 5.

41. "Fact Sheet: Feed Materials Production Center," *The Atomizer* (June–July 1961), 12–14; Fluor Corporation, *Fernald at 50*, 8–9; Wilson, "Fernald Project," 46–52.

42. Pinney et al., "Health Effects," 145.

43. Oak Ridge Incident Investigation Board, *Investigation*, 8, Fernald Preserve Visitors Center Reading Room; US Census Bureau, *Number of Inhabitants: Ohio*.

44. Fluor Corporation, *Closing the Circle of History*, 32.

45. Wilson, "Fernald Project," 61.

46. Wilson, "Fernald Project," 68; Stradling and Stradling, *Where the River Burned*; Rome, *Bulldozer in the Countryside*.

47. Weart, *Nuclear Fear*, 155–69.

48. Fluor Corporation, *Closing the Circle of History*, 32.

49. Branham, interview 1.

50. Branham, interview, 2; Fluor Corporation, *Closing the Circle of History*, 32.

51. Fluor Corporation, *Closing the Circle of History*, 32.

52. Sneed, interview, 1–9.

53. Silverman, "No Immediate Risk," 305–6; "Weapons Seized to Prevent Violence at Fernald," *Cincinnati Post*, May 22, 1952, 1.

54. Sneed, interview, 1–9; Weart, *Nuclear Fear*, 333–35.

55. Sneed, interview, 4.

56. Carlisle, *Supplying the Nuclear Arsenal*, 201–4.

57. Seaborg, *Journal*, 4:427–28.

58. Darleane Christian Hoffman, "Glenn T. Seaborg," *American National Biography*, October 2001; Rhodes, *Making of the Atomic Bomb*.

59. Seaborg, *Journal*, 4:427.

60. "Atomic Energy Holds Key to Space Probes," *Cincinnati Enquirer*, November 10, 1962, 2.

61. Quotes from Hamblin, *Poison in the Well*, 224–28.

62. "Work on AEC Feeder Plant in High Gear; Project Commitments Reach 3.5 Million," *Cincinnati Enquirer*, August 17, 1951, 19; Silverman, "No Immediate Risk," 299–303.

63. Fluor Corporation, *Closing the Circle of History*, 36, 59; US Department of Energy, *Final Remedial Action Report for Operable Unit 1*, 14.

64. Varchol, Brinley and Dennis Carr, "The Fernald Closure Project—from Weapons to Wetlands" (paper presented at PMI Global Congress, Atlanta, GA, May 14–16, 2007); US Department of Energy, "Celebrating the 10th Anniversary."

65. US Congress. Senate. Committee on Governmental Affairs, *Management and Operation*, 144–45; "Atomic Material Coming," *Cincinnati Post*, August 11, 1979, 3.

66. Walker, *Road to Yucca Mountain*; Kuletz, *Tainted Desert*.

67. Makhijani, Hu, and Yih, *Nuclear Wastelands*, 212–15, 229–33, 249–53.

68. Wellerstein, *Restricted Data*, 32.

69. Silverman, "No Immediate Risk," 22–23.

70. Fluor Corporation, *Closing the Circle of History*, 40–42; Wellerstein, *Restricted Data*, 193, 255–56.

71. Davies, interview, 2; "In Memoriam," *The Atomizer* (July–August, 1966).

72. Hales, *Atomic Spaces*, 37, 118–19; Fluor Corporation, *Closing the Circle of History*, 40–42.

73. Silverman, "No Immediate Risk," 307.

74. Harper, interview, 3.

75. Silverman, "No Immediate Risk," 299–300; Hacker, *Elements of Controversy*, 278; Carr Childers, *Size of the Risk*, 69–102.

76. Wellerstein, *Restricted Data*, 106–7, 118–21; Kiernan, *Atomic Bill*.

77. First quote from Silverman, "No Immediate Risk," 301, 348–49; second quote from Chace, "'A-Bomb Plant' Sheds Aura of Hidden Horror," *Cincinnati Enquirer*, November 28, 1974, 4B.

78. Dick Perry, "Rumors Familiar Part of Controversial Plant," *Cincinnati Post*, October 27, 1981, 4.

79. *Oxford English Dictionary Online*, s.v., "Détente," accessed November 7, 2022; Westad, *Cold War*, 381–82, 417–19.

80. Westad, *Cold War*, 381–82.

81. Carlisle, *Supplying the Nuclear Arsenal*, 135, 148–49, 153–54, 156–60.

82. Oak Ridge Incident Investigation Board, *Investigation*, 8; Fluor Corporation, *Closing the Circle of History*, 74; "Firm Gets Army Bullet Contract," *Cincinnati Post*, April 21, 1977, 5; Wayne Buckhout, "American Tool Aims at Antitank Contract," *Cincinnati Enquirer*, August 25, 1978, 20; David Flick, "GAO Report Blow to Fernald Hopes for Big Contract," *Cincinnati Post*, March 31, 1977, 14.

83. Silverman, "No Immediate Risk," 362–63; Fluor Corporation, *Closing the Circle of History*, 59; US House of Representatives, Committee on Appropriations, Pubic Works for Water and Power Development and Atomic Energy Commission Appropriation Bill, 92nd Cong. (1972), 57.

84. Lisa Crawford, interview with Fernald Living History Project, 3; US Department of Commerce, *Population and Housing Unit Counts: Ohio*, 27; US Census Bureau, *Number of Inhabitants: Ohio*; Stradling, *Cincinnati*; Fluor Corporation, *Closing the Circle of History*, 59.

85. "Atomic Material Coming," *Cincinnati Post*, August 11, 1979, 3.

86. Dillhoff, interview, 2.

87. Sellet, interview, 1–2.

88. Yocum, interview, 1; Warren, *Brush with Death*.

89. Morgan and Stegner, "How Clean Is Clean?," 66.

90. May, *Homeward Bound*, 26–28; Krupar, "Burying Atomic History," 40; Balogh, *Chain Reaction*, 28–32.

91. Sabin, *Public Citizens*, 17–23.

92. Higuchi, *Political Fallout*, 2–3.

93. Plokhy, *Atoms and Ashes*, 1–42; Hacker, *Elements of Controversy*, 278; Carr Childers, *Size of the Risk*, 69–102.

94. Egan, *Barry Commoner*, 66–72.

95. Lear, *Rachel Carson*, 375–453.

96. Lear, *Rachel Carson*, 374–375; Winkler, *Life under a Cloud*, 102; Rome, *Genius of Earth Day*, 31.

97. Rome, *Genius of Earth Day*, 10; Stradling and Stradling, *Where the River Burned*; Spezio, *Slick Policy*.

98. Spears, *Rethinking*, 89–123.

99. Sabin, *Public Citizens*, xi–xviii, 120, 162–83, 182–83; Turner and Isenberg, *Republican Reversal*, 54–56.

100. Turner and Isenberg, *Republican Reversal*, 54–56; Halvorson, *Valuing Clean Air*, 132–34, 141–51; Shabecoff, *Fierce Green Fire*, 203–30.

101. Donaghy, *Second Cold War*, 2; Knoblauch, *Nuclear Freeze*, 4–5.

102. Donaghy, *Second Cold War*, 2; Knoblauch, *Nuclear Freeze*, 4–5.

103. US Congress. Senate. Committee on Governmental Affairs, *Management and Operation*, 16.

104. Worster, *Nature's Economy*, 342–47; Zaretsky, *Radiation Nation*, 1–6; Spears, *Rethinking*, 70–76.

105. *First Link: The Story of Fernald*, directed by Joyce Bentle.

106. Finfrock, interview, 11.

TWO. TRINITY DAY

1. "Anti-nuke Demonstrators Stage Protest at NLO," *Journal-News* (Hamilton, Ohio), July 17, 1983; Howard Wilkinson, "Anti-nuke Rally Ends with Arrest of Six Protesters," *Cincinnati Enquirer*, July 17, 1983, 1.

2. Rhodes, *Making of the Atomic Bomb*, 670–76.

3. Flyer, "Ohio Nuclear Weapons Awareness Day," July 16, 1983, personal papers of Linda Musmeci Kimball, Oxford, Ohio; "Anti-nuke Demonstrators"; "Anti-nukes Target Fernald Plant," *Journal-News* (Hamilton, Ohio), July 15, 1983.

4. Press Release for Ohio Nuclear Weapons Day, July 16, 1983, personal papers of Linda Musmeci Kimball.

5. Wilkinson, "Anti-nuke Rally," A-1.

6. Wilkinson, "Anti-nuke Rally"; Aaron Javsicas, "Polly Brokaw: The Life and Death

of an Activist," *Friends Journal*, July 1998, 21; Mary McCarty, "Freedom Fighters," *Cincinnati Magazine*, June 1987, 60–61; Alyssa S. McClanahan, "The Case for Safe and Affordable Energy: The Popular Movement against the William H. Zimmer Nuclear Power Station" (unpublished manuscript, 2020), 71.

7. Hamm, *Quakers in America*, 12.

8. Wilkinson, "Anti-nuke Rally," A-1.

9. Wilkinson, "Anti-nuke Rally," A-1; Rhodes, *Making of the Atomic Bomb*, 413–15.

10. Wilkinson, "Anti-nuke Rally," A-1; Amundson, *Yellowcake Towns*; Voyles, *Wastelanding*.

11. Wilkinson, "Anti-nuke Rally," A-1.

12. Hacker, *Elements of Controversy*, 278; Walker, *Road to Yucca Mountain*, 45–46; Hamblin, *Poison in the Well*, 53; Silverman, "No Immediate Risk," 350–51, 354–55, 359; Carr Childers, *Size of the Risk*, 69–102.

13. Wilkinson, "Anti-nuke Rally," A-18.

14. "Nuclear Protester Released," *Cincinnati Post*, July 29, 1983, 11C.

15. "Activists Support Colleague," *Cincinnati Post*, July 23, 1983, 7A.

16. "Protests Mark Atomic Test Anniversary," *Dayton Daily News*, July 17, 1983, 10-A; Wilkinson, "Anti-nuke Rally," A-1; "Anti-nuke Demonstrators"; Virginia Wiegand, "Nuclear Weapons Foes Hold Rally against Local Firms in Arms Race," *Beacon Journal (Akron, Ohio)*, July 17, 1983, F8; "Protests Mark Anniversary," *Columbus Dispatch*, July 18, 1983, B-6.

17. Elmore, *Seed Money*, 66–67.

18. Hewlett and Duncan, *Atomic Shield*, 586–587.

19. "Protests Mark Anniversary," B-6.

20. Quotes from Harvey, *American Anti-Nuclear Activism*, 48; Shabecoff, *Fierce Green Fire*, 236–38.

21. Silverman, "No Immediate Risk," 349; Jeffrey Kim Stine, "Environmental Politics and Water Resources Development: The Case of the Army Corps of Engineers During the 1970s" (PhD diss., University of California Santa Barbara, 1984); Gordin, *Red Cloud at Dawn*; Stern, *Cuban Missile Crisis*.

22. US Congress. Senate. Committee on Governmental Affairs, *Management and Operation*, 361–66.

23. McClanahan, "Case for Safe and Affordable Energy," 70–71; Carpenter, interview; Rachel Carson, *Silent Spring*; Lear, *Rachel Carson*.

24. Jundt, *Greening the Red, White, and Blue*.

25. Carpenter, interview; McClanahan, "Case for Safe and Affordable Energy," 70–71.

26. Carpenter, interview; McClanahan, "Case for Safe and Affordable Energy," 70–71.

27. Hamblin, *Wretched Atom*, 38.

28. Caldicott, "Nuclear Madness," 200–203; Abalone Alliance, "Declaration of Nuclear Resistance," 204–6.

29. Michael Aron, "The Clamshell Alliance Holds Nukes at Bay," *Rolling Stone*, July 28, 1977.

30. Shabecoff, *Fierce Green Fire*, 121.

31. Carpenter, interview; McClanahan, "Case for Safe and Affordable Energy," 70–71.

32. Ackland, *Making a Real Killing*, 1–6, 152–59.

33. Quote from Ackland, *Making a Real Killing*, 169. See also 161–64.

34. Ackland, *Making a Real Killing*, 185–86; "S. Carolina Atom Plant Protested," *New York Times*, May 1, 1978, 14.

35. Ackland, *Making a Real Killing*, 186–87; Carpenter, interview; McClanahan, "Case for Safe and Affordable Energy," 71; Joseph Daniel, "Police Moving in to Arrest Rocky Flats Demonstrators," Daniel Ellsberg Papers, May 8, 1979, Special Collections and University Archives, University of Massachusetts Amherst Libraries, https://credo.library.umass.edu/view/full/mums1093-s10a-i213.

36. McClanahan, "Case for Safe and Affordable Energy," 71–72.

37. Carpenter, interview.

38. McClanahan, "Case for Safe and Affordable Energy," 71–72.

39. Quote from McClanahan, "Case for Safe and Affordable Energy," 52.

40. McClanahan, "Case for Safe and Affordable Energy," 52.

41. Wellock, *Critical Masses*, 46, 66.

42. Walker, *Three Mile Island*, 242–43.

43. Carpenter, interview.

44. Rainey, *One Hundred Miles from Home*, 101; Carlisle, *Supplying the Nuclear Arsenal*, 146–48, 165.

45. Rainey, *One Hundred Miles from Home*, 105; "Anti-Nuke Group Says EPA Ignoring Radiation in Creek," *Cincinnati Enquirer*, January 13, 1980; "Amos and Polly Brokaw," *Community Companion (Cincinnati, Ohio)* 18, no. 2 (February 2012): 6; Carpenter, interview.

46. "Anti-Nuke Group."

47. Rainey, *One Hundred Miles from Home*, 105

48. Rome, *Genius of Earth Day*, 67–70.

49. "Anti-Nuke Group."

50. Zaretsky, *Radiation Nation*, 101–43.

51. Stradling and Stradling, *Where the River Burned*, 147–52; Knepper, *Ohio and Its People*, 414–16.

52. Rome, *Genius of Earth Day*, 229–34.

53. "Ecology Lab in a Nike Site," *Dayton Daily News*, January 6, 1972, 25.

54. Mitchell, interview, 1; Graham Mitchell, LinkedIn profile, accessed March 19, 2021, https://www.linkedin.com/in/graham-e-mitchell-6a96b312.

55. Silverman, "No Immediate Risk," 350; "No Radioactivity Found near Plant," *Cincinnati Post*, January 17, 1980, 38:1.

56. Silverman, "No Immediate Risk," 330.

57. Silverman, "No Immediate Risk," 338.

58. "No Radioactivity Found near Plant," 38:1.

59. Carpenter, interview; "Uncle Sam's Hot Spot," *Washington Post*, July 28, 1985; Tom Carpenter, "An Open Letter to the Peace Movement," [1983], the Personal Papers of Linda Musmeci Kimball.

60. Titus, *Bombs in the Backyard*, 107–10; Walker, *Permissible Dose*, 92.

61. Carpenter, interview.

62. CARE Press Release, "Feed Materials Production Center, Fernald, Ohio," June 15, 1980, Personal Papers of Linda Musmeci Kimball.

63. CARE Press Release, "Feed Materials Production Center."

64. CARE Press Release, "Feed Materials Production Center."

65. Silverman, "No Immediate Risk," 357–58.

66. CARE Press Release, "Feed Materials Production Center."

67. CARE Press Release, "Feed Materials Production Center."

68. Nixon, *Slow Violence*, 2–3.

69. McClanahan, "Case for Safe and Affordable Energy," 94.

70. McClanahan, "Case for Safe and Affordable Energy," 94.

71. Quotes from McClanahan, "Case for Safe and Affordable Energy," 94.

72. McClanahan, "Case for Safe and Affordable Energy," 94.

73. McClanahan, "Case for Safe and Affordable Energy," 95; Carpenter, interview.

74. McClanahan, "Case for Safe and Affordable Energy," 95; Carpenter, interview; Halvorson, *Valuing Clean Air*, 84–85.

75. McClanahan, "Case for Safe and Affordable Energy," 95.

76. Carpenter, interview; McClanahan, "Case for Safe and Affordable Energy," 95.

77. McClanahan, "Case for Safe and Affordable Energy," 94–100.

78. McClanahan, "Case for Safe and Affordable Energy,", 70; Spears, *Rethinking*, 107–10.

79. McClanahan, "Case for Safe and Affordable Energy," 104, 117.

80. Wittner, *Toward Nuclear Abolition*, 73–76; Winkler, *Life under a Cloud*, 105–6, 195–99; Knoblauch, *Nuclear Freeze in a Cold War*, 2–6.

81. Winkler, *Life under a Cloud*, 201–2; Knoblauch, *Nuclear Freeze in a Cold War*, 6–7; Wittner, *Toward Nuclear Abolition*, 75–76.

82. Wittner, *Toward Nuclear Abolition*, 76.

83. Winkler, *Life under a Cloud*, 202–3.

84. Winkler, *Life under a Cloud*, 202; Wittner, *Toward Nuclear Abolition*, 176; Knoblauch, *Nuclear Freeze in a Cold War*, 7, 23–24.

85. Knoblauch, *Nuclear Freeze in a Cold War*, 7, 8, 41, 43; "Yes, 'The Day After' Really Was the Profound TV Moment 'The Americans' Makes It Out to Be," *Washington Post*, May 11, 2016.

86. Knoblauch, *Nuclear Freeze in a Cold War*, 6–7, 23; Harvey, *American Anti-Nuclear Activism*, 29–30.

87. Sara Kirschebaum, Pamphlet, "Answer One Question to Find Out If You Support the Nuclear Freeze," Ohio Nuclear Weapons Freeze Campaign, Personal Papers of Linda Musmeci Kimball, Oxford, Ohio.

88. Knoblauch, *Nuclear Freeze in a Cold War*, 23–24.

89. *Grassroots Peace Directory: A Guide to Peace Groups and Resources: Ohio* (Pomfret, CT: Topsfield Foundation, 1984), 1–3, MSS 869 Reverse the Arms Race Federation [Freeze], Box 1, File 16, Ohio History Connection, Columbus, Ohio.

90. Scott Mason, "Peace and Justice in Oxford," Oxford Project, Miami University, accessed March 17, 2021, https://www.orgs.miamioh.edu/projectoxford/masons3.htm; Linda Musmeci Kimball, email to author, October 8, 2017; "Civil-Rights Activist Kimball Prioritizes People, Peace," *Journal-News* (Hamilton, Ohio), December 21, 1992.

91. Linda Musmeci Kimball, email to author, October 8, 2017.

92. "Public Endorsers from the Oxford Area," Oxford Citizens for Peace, July 1982–March 1983, Personal Papers of Linda Musmeci Kimball; Mason, "Peace and Justice in Oxford."

93. Spears, *Rethinking*.

94. Egan, *Barry Commoner*, 47.

95. Higuchi, *Political Fallout*, 3–4.

96. Map, "Man-Made Radiation Hazards," [n.d.], Women Strike for Peace; Map, "Nuclear America," June 1979, War Resisters League; Personal Papers of Linda Musmeci Kimball.

97. Harvey, *American Anti-Nuclear Activism*, 18.

98. "Nuclear Wastes Fact Sheet," SANE, [n.d.]; Personal Papers of Linda Musmeci Kimball.

99. Tom Carpenter, "Fernald Fact Sheet," [1983?], Personal Papers of Linda Musmeci Kimball.

100. Flyer, "Trinity Day Commemoration," July 16, 1983; Flyer, "Ohio Nuclear Weapons Awareness Day, July 16, 1983; "Stop the Drift Towards Death," July 16, [1983], Personal Papers of Linda Musmeci Kimball; Flyer, "The Days after Trinity," July 16, 1983, and Flyer, "Rally for Peace," July 16, 1983, MSS 869 Reverse the Arms Race Federation [Freeze], Box 1, File 46, Ohio History Connection, Columbus, Ohio.

101. Carpenter, "Open Letter."

102. Walker, *Permissible Dose*, 92–93.

103. US Congress. Senate. Committee on Governmental Affairs, *Management and Operation*, 361–66.

104. Carpenter, "Open Letter."

105. US Congress. Senate. Committee on Governmental Affairs, *Management and Operation*, 361–66. For quote, see 361.

106. US Congress. Senate. Committee on Governmental Affairs, *Management and Operation*, 361–66.

107. "Anti-nuke Demonstrators"; "Area Plant Part of Protest," *Journal-News* (Hamilton, Ohio), July 17, 1983; "Oldest Protester," *Cincinnati Enquirer*, July 17, 1983; "Protests Mark Anniversary," B-6; Clipping, American Friends Service Committee Peace and Justice Calendar, [1983], the Personal Papers of Linda Musmeci Kimball.

108. Clipping, American Friends Service Committee Peace and Justice Calendar, [1983], the Personal Papers of Linda Musmeci Kimball.

109. Carpenter, "Open Letter."

110. Carpenter, interview; Tom Carpenter, LinkedIn profile, accessed March 13, 2021, https://www.linkedin.com/in/tom-carpenter-16748a55; McClanahan, "Case for Safe and Affordable Energy," 95; "Antioch's Reach like an Octopus," *Dayton Daily News*, October 29, 1972, 4-B.

111. "Antioch School of Law Offers New Concept in Legal Education," *Asbury Park Press* (New Jersey), September 10, 1972, E21; "Antioch's Reach," 4-B.

112. McClanahan, "Case for Safe and Affordable Energy," 67, 151; Carpenter, interview; Tom Carpenter, LinkedIn profile.

113. Hamblin, *Poison in the Well*, 224–28; Walker, *Road to Yucca Mountain*, 2–3, 29.

114. Hartsock, *Geologic Considerations*, 19.

115. Silverman, "No Immediate Risk," 351–53; Sedam, *Occurrence of Uranium*, 5, 9; US Congress. Senate. Committee on Governmental Affairs, *Management and Operation*, 246.

116. Silverman, "No Immediate Risk," 353; "Background on EPA's 2000 Drinking Water Regulations for Radionuclides," US Nuclear Regulatory Commission, accessed April 1, 2021, https://www.nrc.gov/docs/ML0601/ML060130112.pdf.

117. Silverman, "No Immediate Risk," 353–54; Adams, interview, 32–36.

118. "Uncle Sam's Hot Spot," *Washington Post*, July 28, 1985.

119. Knollman, interview, 6–7.

120. Silverman, "No Immediate Risk," 353–54.

121. Adams, interview, 35.

122. Silverman, "No Immediate Risk," 354.

123. Silverman, "No Immediate Risk," 354; Makhijani, Hu, and Yih, *Nuclear Waste-*

lands, 214; "Radiation Exceeds Normal: Soil Contamination Found near Tanks," *Cincinnati Enquirer*, August 30, 1983, A-8; Makhijani and Makhijani, *Shifting Radioactivity Risks*, 7; D. S. Janke, "Results of Vitrifying Fernald K-65 Residue," in US Department of Energy, *Environmental Remediation '91*, 703.

124. Makhijani, Hu, and Yih, *Nuclear Wastelands*, 214; Adams, interview, 11.

125. "Radiation Exceeds Normal," A-8.

126. Silverman, "No Immediate Risk," 354.

127. "Draft: NLO, Inc. K-65 Silos Study and Evaluation, Fernald, Ohio," Camargo Associates, [n.d.], Personal Papers of Dave Fankhauser, Cincinnati, Ohio.

128. Adams, interview, 11-12.

129. Quote from Silverman, "No Immediate Risk," 355; Rainey, *One Hundred Miles from Home*, 105.

130. Peyton, "Kentucky's 'Atomic Graveyard,'" 227-28.

131. Silverman, "No Immediate Risk," 355.

THREE. FRESH ACTIVISM

1. Quotes from Silverman, "No Immediate Risk," 358-59. See also 299-301, 248-49; Rainey, *One Hundred Miles from Home*, 101; Ben Kaufman, "NLO Checking Possible Uranium Leak," *Cincinnati Enquirer*, December 11, 1984; Oreskes and Conway, *Merchants of Doubt*; Markowitz and Rosner, *Deceit and Denial*.

2. Silverman, "No Immediate Risk," 358-60; Kaufman, "NLO Checking Possible Uranium Leak"; Gosling and Fehner, *Closing the Circle*, 34-36; Smothers, "Discovery of Mercury Contamination Prompts Dispute in Oak Ridge, Tenn.," *New York Times*, May 26, 1983, A-14.

3. "Uranium Leak Called 'a Probability,'" *Cincinnati Post*, December 12, 1984, 1.

4. Brown, *Manual for Survival*, 256.

5. Silverman, "No Immediate Risk," 358-61; Rainey, *One Hundred Miles from Home*, 106; Kaufman, "NLO Checking Possible Uranium Leak"; "Uranium Leak Called 'a Probability,'" 1.

6. Silverman, "No Immediate Risk," 358-61; Rainey, *One Hundred Miles from Home*, 106; Kaufman, "NLO Checking Possible Uranium Leak"; Meyer, interview.

7. Charles Halvorson, *Valuing Clean Air*, 132-43, 160-62; Shabecoff, *Fierce Green Fire*, 203-30; Turner and Isenberg, *Republican Reversal*.

8. Donaghy, *Second Cold War*, 2; Knoblauch, *Nuclear Freeze in a Cold War*, 4-5.

9. Oak Ridge Incident Investigation Board, *Investigation*, 11-13.

10. Oak Ridge Incident Investigation Board, *Investigation*, 14-15.

11. Oak Ridge Incident Investigation Board, *Investigation*, 16.

12. Oak Ridge Incident Investigation Board, *Investigation*, 17-19.

13. Silverman, "No Immediate Risk," 357–58, 373; Weidner, interview, 2–3.

14. Dunaway, interview, 14.

15. "FDR's 'Day of Infamy' Speech: Crafting a Call to Arms," *Prologue 33*, no. 4 (Winter 2001), https://www.archives.gov/publications/prologue/2001/winter/crafting-day-of-infamy-speech.html.

16. Stine, "Environmental Politics," 33–36.

17. Gosling and Fehner, *Closing the Circle*, 35; Wellerstein, *Restricted Data*.

18. Fehner and Gosling, "Coming in from the Cold," 14–15.

19. Silverman, "No Immediate Risk," 25, 344; Fehner and Gosling, "Coming in from the Cold," 16–17; Gosling and Fehner, *Closing the Circle*, 34–36; Power, *America's Nuclear Wastelands*, 38.

20. Oak Ridge Incident Investigation Board, *Investigation*, 19.

21. "Appointments at National Lead," *Journal-News* (Hamilton, Ohio), March 5, 1976, 19.

22. Adams, interview, 3.

23. Silverman, "No Immediate Risk," 364–70.

24. Oak Ridge Incident Investigation Board, *Investigation*, 29.

25. Oak Ridge Incident Investigation Board, *Investigation*, 28.

26. Rome, *Genius of Earth Day*, 229–234.

27. Silverman, "No Immediate Risk," 22–23; Hamblin, *Poison in the Well*, 224–30; Martin, *Wild by Design*, 93–112.

28. Silverman, "No Immediate Risk," 348; Hamblin, *Poison in the Well*, 224–30.

29. US Congress. Senate. Committee on Governmental Affairs, *Management and Operation*, 253.

30. "Anger Vented," *Cincinnati Post*, December 14, 1984, 12B.

31. Quote from Donald M. Rothberg, "Radiation Limits Debated by Scientists, AEC," *Spokane Chronicle*, July 22, 1970, 22; "AEC Denies Infant Toll of Fallout," *Courier-Post* (Camden, New Jersey), August 6, 1969, 33; "Keeps Its Cool while Shedding Light on Power Plant," *Independent Coast Observer* (Gualala, California), September 1, 1971, 5.

32. Silverman, "No Immediate Risk," 360.

33. Silverman, "No Immediate Risk,", 361.

34. Adams, interview, 31–32.

35. Walker, *Permissible Dose*, 91–156.

36. Brown, *Manual for Survival*, 246–47.

37. "Anger Vented," *Cincinnati Post*, December 14, 1984, 12B.

38. "Anger Vented," *Cincinnati Post*, December 14, 1984, 12B; Rainey, *One Hundred Miles from Home,* 106; Silverman, "No Immediate Risk," 361; Meyer, interview.

39. Adams, interview, 27, 32; Meyer, interview.

40. "Anger Vented," *Cincinnati Post*, December 14, 1984, 12B; Silverman, "No Immediate Risk," 376.

41. Walker, *Three Mile Island*.

42. Silverman, "No Immediate Risk," 263–378; Walker, *Permissible Dose*; Hacker, *Elements of Controversy*; Caufield, *Multiple Exposures*, 220–21.

43. Adams, interview, 31–32; Clawson, interview, 17.

44. "Anger Vented," *Cincinnati Post*, December 14, 1984, 12B.

45. US Congress. Senate. Committee on Governmental Affairs *Management and Operation*, 362.

46. "Health Risks Found at Uranium Plant," *Cincinnati Post*, December 14, 1984, 1A, 6A.

47. "Health Risks Found," 1A, 6A.

48. Olwell, *At Work in the Atomic City*, 129–30, 153–54n.

49. Jerome Wilson, "An Epidemiologic Investigation of Non-Malignant Respiratory Disease among Workers at a Uranium Mill" (PhD diss., University of North Carolina, 1983), iii–iv, viii, 128; "Health Risks Found," 1A, 6A; Griffis, "Oral History," 1.

50. Wilson, "Epidemiologic Investigation," viii.

51. "Health Risks Found," 1A, 6A.

52. Olwell, *At Work in the Atomic City*, 49–50; Advisory Committee on Human Radiation Experiments, *Human Radiation Experiments*, 144–45.

53. Brown, *Manual for Survival*, 151.

54. Olwell, *At Work in the Atomic City*, 49–50; Brown, *Manual for Survival*, 152; Advisory Committee on Human Radiation Experiments, *Human Radiation Experiments*.

55. Quotes from Brown, *Manual for Survival*, 150.

56. Brown, *Plutopia*, 334–35.

57. Wilson, "Epidemiologic Investigation," 1, 46–48; Olwell, *At Work in the Atomic City*, 127–30.

58. Brown, *Dispatches from Dystopia*, 75.

59. "Health Risks Found," 1A, 6A.

60. "Health Risks Found," 1A, 6A.

61. Hamblin, *Arming Mother Nature*, 32–36; Olwell, *At Work in the Atomic City*, 127–30; Higuchi, *Political Fallout*; Hacker, *Elements of Controversy*; Titus, *Bombs in the Backyard*.

62. Silverman, "No Immediate Risk," 362–63; Oak Ridge Incident Investigation Board, *Investigation*, 29.

63. "Arms Race Saved Fernald Plant, Ex-Aide Says," *Cleveland Plain Dealer*, March 8, 1986, 16E.

64. Silverman, "No Immediate Risk," 377.

65. Carlisle, *Supplying the Nuclear Arsenal*, 201–4.

66. US Congress. Senate. Committee on Governmental Affairs, *Management and Operation*, 257.

67. Silverman "No Immediate Risk," 265; Fehner and Gosling, "Coming in from the Cold," 17; Westad, *Cold War*, 224–25; Feldman, *Nuclear Reactions*, 57; Gordin, *Red Cloud at Dawn*.

68. "Uranium Leaks Probed," *Palladium-Item* (Richmond, Indiana), December 20, 1984, A14; "Ohio Will Sue U.S. over Fernald Leaks," *Cincinnati Enquirer*, December 21, 1984; Meyer, interview.

69. Lisa Crawford, interview with Fernald Living History Project, 3.

70. Lisa Crawford, interview with Fernald Living History Project, 3; Ken Crawford, interview, 5–7; Lisa Crawford, interview with the author; Glazer and Glazer, *Environmental Crusaders*, 6; Knollman, interview, 6–7.

71. Silverman, "No Immediate Risk," 353–54, n14; Glazer and Glazer, *Environmental Crusaders*, 6–7; US Congress. Senate. Committee on Governmental Affairs, *Management and Operation*, 266; Lisa Crawford, interview with Fernald Living History Project, 3; Ken Crawford, interview, 5–7.

72. Clawson, interview, 21–22; Flour Corporation, *Closing the Circle of History*, 56.

73. Clawson, interview, 21–22.

74. Lisa Crawford, interview with Fernald Living History Project, 7; Meyer, interview.

75. Lisa Crawford, interview with Fernald Living History Project, 10–11; Emily Lewis, "Exploring Models of Community Organizing for Environmental Justice: The Cases of Fernald and the ELDA Landfill in Cincinnati, Ohio" (MA thesis, University of Cincinnati, 2011), 32–33.

76. Glazer and Glazer, *Environmental Crusaders*, 9.

77. "NLO Probe Quantifies Dust Leaks," *Cincinnati Enquirer*, January 13, 1985, A1, A16; "Uncle Sam's Hot Spot," *Washington Post*, July 28, 1985.

78. Lisa Crawford, interview with Fernald Living History Project, 4.

79. Silverman, "No Immediate Risk," 316–17, 323–24, 367.

80. Glazer and Glazer, *Environmental Crusaders*, 7.

81. Longhurst, *Citizen Environmentalists*, 108–11.

82. Winkler, *Life under a Cloud*, 102, 106–8; Higuchi, *Political Fallout*, 3–4.

83. Stradling, *Nature of New York*, 211–15; Gibbs, *Love Canal*; Blum, *Love Canal Revisited*; Newman, *Love Canal*.

84. Newman, *Love Canal*, 212–18.

85. Shabecoff, *Fierce Green Fire*, 237.

86. Newman, *Love Canal*, 221.

87. Rabe, *Beyond NIMBY*, 2.

88. Rabe, *Beyond NIMBY*, 2; Shabecoff, *Fierce Green Fire*, 237.

89. Quote from Shabecoff, *Fierce Green Fire*, 237.

90. White, "Are You an Environmentalist?," 171–73.

91. Lisa Crawford, interview with Fernald Living History Project, 7.

92. Ken Crawford, interview, 8–9; Meyer, interview; Brown and Mikkelsen, *No Safe Place*, 54.

93. Lisa Crawford, interview with the author.

94. Lisa Crawford, interview with Fernald Living History Project, 10; Ken Crawford, interview, 8–10; Brown and Mikkelsen, *No Safe Place*, 81–91.

95. Lisa Crawford, interview with Fernald Living History Project, 9.

96. Ken Crawford, interview, 8.

97. Clawson, interview, 7.

98. Clawson, interview, 7; Ken Crawford, interview 8.

99. "'Prince of Torts,'" Stanley Chesley, interview with John Bach, *UC Magazine* (Cincinnati, Ohio) (August 2010), https://magazine.uc.edu/issues/0810.html; Deirdre Fanning, "Master of Disaster," *Forbes*, February 22, 1988, 48.

100. Alexander, *Place of Recourse*, 189–90; "'Prince of Torts.'"

101. "Bhopal Settlement Challenged," *Washington Post*, March 24, 1986; "Fernald Residents Sue NLO for $300 Million over Leaks," *Cincinnati Enquirer*, January 24, 1985, D1; Lakshmi and Sharma, "Building a Safe Space," 136.

102. Ken Crawford, interview, 8.

103. "Fernald Residents Sue NLO," D1.

104. "Fernald Residents Sue NLO," D1; Rainey, *One Hundred Miles from Home*, 107.

105. "Fernald Residents Sue NLO," D1.

106. Brown and Mikkelsen, *No Safe Place*, 8, 21.

107. Brown and Mikkelsen, *No Safe Place*, 198.

108. Lisa Crawford, interview with Fernald Living History Project, 4, 6; Lisa Crawford, interview with the author.

109. Lisa Crawford, interview with Fernald Living History Project, 6.

110. Donald S. Marshall to Robert M. Spenceley, March 26, 1984, Ohio EPA Southwest District Office, obtained through an Ohio Public Records Request in June 2022.

111. Glenn and Taylor, *John Glenn*, 351–52.

112. Glenn and Taylor, *John Glenn*, 351–52.

113. Lisa Crawford, interview with Fernald Living History Project, 11.

114. Senator John Glenn to President Jimmy Carter, April 21, 1977, Box 60, Folder 38, John H. Glenn Archives, Senate Papers, Ohio State University.

115. "Ohio Politicians Step Up Effort to Locate SDI Plant at Piketon," *Beacon Journal* (Akron, Ohio), January 13, 1987, C3; "Feds Playing Game with 'Star Wars,'" *Chillicothe Gazette*, March 7, 1987, 1;. Wittner, *Toward Nuclear Abolition*, 341–42.

116. *Columbus Dispatch*, July 21, 1980; Mike Woods, "Radiation Protection Plan Lacking," *Daily Register* (Red Bank, New Jersey), December 12, 1979; "Opening Statement by Senator John Glenn at Hearings on Health and Safety Practices at Uranium Enrichment Plants, July 21, 1980" and Clipping [n.d.], "Atomic Plant: Dispute Blamed

for Health Probe Delay," [*Chillicothe Gazette?*], Box 518, Folder 12, John H. Glenn Archives, Senate Papers, Ohio State University.

117. Mitchell, interview, 2; Chesley, interview, 1–2; Craig, interview, 2.

118. "Glenn Wants Power Shift at NLO," *Cincinnati Enquirer*, March 2, 1985, 1.

119. "Glenn Wants Power Shift at NLO," 1; Fernald Tour, 1986, Personal Papers of Dave Fankhauser, Cincinnati, Ohio.

120. "Glenn Wants Power Shift at NLO," 1.

121. US Congress. Senate. Committee on Governmental Affairs, *Management and Operation*, 2–3.

122. US Congress. Senate. Committee on Governmental Affairs, *Management and Operation*, 255–56.

123. US Congress. Senate. Committee on Governmental Affairs, *Management and Operation*, 256–58.

124. US Congress. Senate. Committee on Governmental Affairs, *Management and Operation*, 341.

125. US Congress. Senate. Committee on Governmental Affairs, *Management and Operation*, 341–42.

126. "Leaks of Uranium Dust an Ohio Issue," *New York Times*, January 2, 1985, B11; "Uncle Sam's Hot Spot."

127. "Leaks of Uranium Dust an Ohio Issue," B11.

128. Kelley, interview, 4–10.

129. Quote from Fehner and Gosling, "Coming in from the Cold," 17; US Congress. House of Representatives. Committee on Energy and Commerce, *DOE Regulation of Mixed Waste*, 2.

130. Gosling and Fehner, *Closing the Circle*, 44.

131. Gosling and Fehner, *Closing the Circle*, 43–44.

132. Bob Alvarez to John Glenn, April 15, 1992, Box 29, Folder 15, John H. Glenn Archives, Senate Papers, Ohio State University.

133. Quote from Fehner and Gosling, "Coming in from the Cold," 17.

FOUR. THE STRIKE

1. James F. McCarty, "Fernald Workers Strike, Union Seeking New Safety Rules," *Cincinnati Enquirer*, October 5, 1985, 1; Fluor Corporation, *Closing the Circle of History*, 54–55.

2. McCarty, "Fernald Workers Strike," 1.

3. McCarty, "Fernald Workers Strike," 1; "Wildcat Strike Hits Fernald," *Cincinnati Post*, May 22, 1969, 44; Bill Keller, "Reagan to Bypass Union Leaders in his Quest for Members' Votes," *New York Times*, July 2, 1984, 1.

4. Branham, interview, 14–15; "Vote May Bring Strike at Fernald," *Cincinnati Enquirer*, October 2, 1985, F-1.

5. McCarty, "Fernald Workers Strike," 1, 8; "Vote May Bring Strike at Fernald," F-1; "Metal Production, Metric Tons Uranium Weight," Fernald Preserve Visitors Center Reading Room, Hamilton, Ohio; Fehner and Gosling, "Coming in from the Cold," 16–22.

6. "Uncle Sam's Hot Spot"; Fluor Corporation, *Fernald at 50*, 11.

7. US Congress. Senate. Committee on Governmental Affairs, *Management and Operation*, 259–60; Clawson, interview, 17.

8. US Congress. Senate. Committee on Governmental Affairs, *Management and Operation*, 259–60; Clawson, interview, 17; US Congress. House of Representatives. Committee on Energy and Commerce, *DOE Nuclear Facility at Fernald, Ohio*, 142.

9. "Task Force Calls NLO Deficient in Worker Safety," *Cincinnati Post*, October 26, 1985, 9; *First Link: The Story of Fernald*, directed by Joyce Bentle; See also the Fernald Living History Project, https://www.fernaldcommunityalliance.org/interviews.html.

10. "Strikers at Fernald to Have Unity Rally," *Cincinnati Enquirer*, October 7, 1985, D2; "NLO Wants Court to Limit Picketing," *Cincinnati Post*, October 8, 1985, 3B; McCarty, "Fernald Workers Strike," 1.

11. Branham, interview, 15.

12. "Strikers at Fernald to Have Unity Rally," D2.

13. Lisa Crawford, interview with the author; Meyer, interview; Carah Lynn Ong Whaley, "Reaching Critical Mass: The Rise of Grassroots Groups and the Politics of Nuclear Accountability" (PhD diss., University of Virginia, 2015), 84.

14. "Sierra Clubbers Join NLO Pickets," *Cincinnati Enquirer*, October 13, 1985, B-2; US Congress. Senate. Committee on Governmental Affairs, *Management and Operation*, 431–35.

15. "Boost at Fernald Uranium Plant Questioned," *Beacon Journal* (Akron, Ohio), October 17, 1984, D4.

16. Branham, interview, 15; "Fernald Talks on Pensions after Progress on Safety," *Cincinnati Enquirer*, October 18, 1985, C-5.

17. US Congress. House of Representatives. Committee on Energy and Commerce, *DOE Nuclear Facility at Fernald, Ohio*, 140; "NLO Plant Strikers Approve Contract," *Cincinnati Enquirer*, October 24, 1985, 65; "New Blackout Ordered," *Cincinnati Enquirer*, October 17, 1985, B-8; Olwell, *At Work in the Atomic City*, 108.

18. US Congress. House of Representatives. Committee on Energy and Commerce, *DOE Nuclear Facility at Fernald, Ohio*, 140, 142; "NLO Plant Strikers Approve Contract," 65.

19. "NLO Plant Strikers Approve Contract," 65.

20. Montrie, *Myth of Silent Spring*, 141–43; Spears, *Rethinking*, 151–53.

21. Shabecoff, *Fierce Green Fire*, 236–38; Newman, *Love Canal*, 212–18, 220.

22. James F. McCarty, "Fernald Worker Says Unknown Is Worst Fear," *Cincinnati Enquirer*, October 6, 1985, B1–B2.

23. Spears, *Rethinking*, 135.

24. Spears, *Rethinking*, 136.

25. Cahn, ed., *Environmental Agenda*, 4.

26. Cahn, *Environmental Agenda*, 28.

27. Ackland, *Making a Real Killing*, 185–88; Nixon, *Slow Violence*, 2–3.

28. Cahn, ed., *Environmental Agenda*, 31.

29. General Accounting Office, *Environment and Workers*, 1–3.

30. Makhijani, Hu, and Yih, *Nuclear Wastelands*, xxi–xxii.

31. General Accounting Office, *Environment and Workers*, 20–22, 24.

32. General Accounting Office, *Environment and Workers*, 21.

33. General Accounting Office, *Environment and Workers*, 4, 21

34. US Congress. Senate. Committee on Governmental Affairs, *Management and Operation*, 269.

35. General Accounting Office, *Environment and Workers*, 40–41.

36. General Accounting Office, *Environment and Workers*, 5.

37. "Fernald's Changeover Is Official," *Cincinnati Post*, December 28, 1985, 9.

38. Carlisle, *Supplying the Nuclear Arsenal*, 111.

39. "For New Atomic Plant Contractor, a Daunting Task," *New York Times*, November 13, 1988, 38.

40. "Fernald's Changeover Is Official," 9.

41. Williams, *Determining Our Environments*, 45; US Congress. House of Representatives. Committee on Energy and Commerce, *DOE Nuclear Facility at Fernald, Ohio*, 200.

42. *Cincinnati Enquirer*, January 19, 1986, 119; *Courier-Journal* (Louisville, Kentucky), January 19, 1986, 92.

43. US Congress. House of Representatives. Committee on Energy and Commerce, *DOE Nuclear Facility at Fernald, Ohio*, 141; Lisa Crawford, interview with Fernald Living History Project, 10.

44. Britton, interview 1.

45. Plokhy, *Atoms and Ashes*, 140–41. Quote from 164.

46. Britton, interview 1.

47. "Arms Race Saved Fernald Plant, Ex-Aide Says," *Cleveland Plain Dealer*, March 8, 1986, 16E.

48. Britton, interview 2.

49. Lisa Crawford, interview with Fernald Living History Project, 14.

50. Britton, interview 3; Dunaway, *Seeing Green*, 64–72.

51. Britton, interview 3; Dunaway, *Seeing Green*, 64–72.

52. *First Link: The Story of Fernald*, directed by Joyce Bentle. See also Fernald Living History Project, https://www.fernaldcommunityalliance.org/interviews.html.

53. Rathgens, interview 1–3, quote from 11.

54. US Congress. House of Representatives. Committee on Energy and Commerce, *DOE Nuclear Facility at Fernald, Ohio,* 55–59. Quote from 59.

55. US Congress. House of Representatives. Committee on Energy and Commerce, *DOE Nuclear Facility at Fernald, Ohio,* 66–73; Rocco Arcieri, "Kindness into Big Building Block Process," *Lancaster Eagle-Gazette* (Lancaster, Ohio), January 2, 1986, 3.

56. Richard Gibeau, "Fernald Tried Coverup, Probers Say," *Cincinnati Post*, October 10, 1986, 1B.

57. Rainey, *One Hundred Miles from Home*, 107.

58. Gibeau, "Fernald Tried Coverup," 2B.

59. Lisa Crawford, interview with Fernald Living History Project, 9–10; Lewis, "Exploring Models of Community Organizing," 32–33.

60. Glazer and Glazer, *Environmental Crusaders*, 8; Lisa Crawford, interview with Fernald Living History Project, 11.

61. Gosling and Fehner, *Closing the Circle*, 37; US Congress. House of Representatives. Committee on Energy and Commerce, *DOE Regulation of Mixed Waste*, 28–29.

62. US Congress. House of Representatives. Committee on Energy and Commerce, *DOE Regulation of Mixed Waste*, 25–33, 127–35.

63. US Congress. House of Representatives. Committee on Energy and Commerce, *DOE Regulation of Mixed Waste*, 28.

64. Werner, interview.

65. US Congress. House of Representatives. Committee on Energy and Commerce, *DOE Regulation of Mixed Waste*, 137.

66. Walker, *Three Mile Island*, 237–41; Plokhy, *Atoms and Ashes*, 223–24.

67. "Silo for Hazardous Materials Worries Fernald Neighbors," *Cincinnati Enquirer*, June 22, 1986, B5; "Fernald Storage Defective," *Cincinnati Enquirer*, June 21, 1986, 1.

68. US Congress. House of Representatives. Committee on Energy and Commerce, *DOE Regulation of Mixed Waste*, 204–5; "Leak: Can Fernald Handle Plutonium with Care?," *Cincinnati Enquirer*, March 30, 1986, 1.

69. "Silo for Hazardous Materials Worries Fernald Neighbors," B5.

70. "Silo for Hazardous Materials Worries Fernald Neighbors," B5.

71. Fankhauser, interview, 1.

72. McClanahan, "Case for Safe and Affordable Energy," 30–31, 49.

73. Advisory Committee on Human Radiation Experiments, *Human Radiation Experiments*, 239–48.

74. Fankhauser, interview, 1.

75. Fankhauser, interview, 1–2; "Radiological Survey of FMPC, Fernald, Ohio," 6, Personal Papers of Dave Fankhauser, Cincinnati, Ohio.

76. "Radiological Survey of FMPC, Fernald, Ohio," 6, Personal Papers of Dave Fankhauser, Cincinnati, Ohio.

77. "Radiological Survey of FMPC, Fernald, Ohio," 6, Personal Papers of Dave Fankhauser, Cincinnati, Ohio; *Wasting Away: A Special Report on Governmental Neglect of the "K-65" Radioactive Waste at Fernald* (Washington, DC: Government Accountability Project, 1987), Personal Papers of Dave Fankhauser.

78. Fankhauser, interview, 2–3.

79. Fankhauser, interview, 3; Lisa Crawford, interview with Fernald Living History Project, 12–13.

80. Lisa Crawford, interview with Fernald Living History Project, 13.

81. Fluor Corporation, *Fernald at 50*, 11–12; Also see Plate 16, "Walking the Derby," in Del Tredici, *At Work in the Fields of the Bomb*.

82. Fankhauser, interview, 3–4; "17. Uranium Derbies," Personal Papers of Dave Fankhauser, Cincinnati, Ohio.

83. Fankhauser, interview, 7.

84. "10. Radioactive UF4 Dust" and "11. Bare-Armed UF4 Packager," Personal Papers of Dave Fankhauser, Cincinnati, Ohio.

85. "19. Uranium Ingots Stored on Street," Personal Papers of Dave Fankhauser, Cincinnati, Ohio.

86. "3. Barrels of Uranium," Personal Papers of Dave Fankhauser, Cincinnati, Ohio.

87. "4. Above Ground RadWaste," Personal Papers of Dave Fankhauser, Cincinnati, Ohio; "Cleanup Plan Includes Plant Here," *Cincinnati Post*, February 26, 1986, 14.

88. "Troubles Infest System for Making Plutonium," *New York Times*, December 14, 1986, 1; "Metal Production, Metric Tons Uranium Weight," Fernald Preserve Visitors Center Reading Room, Hamilton, Ohio.

89. "The Bomb Factories: Contamination Abounds at DOE's Ohio Uranium Mill," *Seattle Times*, December 15, 1986. For Fernald's ranking in volume of nuclear waste, see Radioactive Waste Campaign, *Deadly Defense*, 117.

90. "Bomb Factories."

91. Fluor Corporation, *Fernald at 50*, 20–21; Hamilton, "Convergence and Divergence," 50; US Environmental Protection Agency and Department of Energy, *Federal Facility Compliance Agreement*, 1–2.

92. US Congress. House of Representatives. Committee on Energy and Commerce, *Environmental Compliance by Federal Agencies*, 196.

93. US Congress. Senate, *Department of Energy Fiscal Year 1986 Authorization for Defense Programs*, 35.

94. US Congress. House of Representatives. Committee on Energy and Commerce, *DOE Nuclear Facility at Fernald, Ohio*, 7, 9–10, 16.

95. US Congress. House of Representatives. Committee on Energy and Commerce, *DOE Nuclear Facility at Fernald, Ohio*, 17–18; Fluor Corporation, *Fernald at 50*, 9–14.

96. US Congress. House of Representatives. Committee on Energy and Commerce, *DOE Nuclear Facility at Fernald, Ohio*, 22–24. Quote from 24.

97. US Congress. House of Representatives. Committee on Energy and Commerce, *DOE Nuclear Facility at Fernald, Ohio*, 29–30. Quote from 30.

98. US Congress. House of Representatives. Committee on Energy and Commerce, *DOE Nuclear Facility at Fernald, Ohio*, 31–32.

99. US Congress. House of Representatives. Committee on Energy and Commerce, *DOE Nuclear Facility at Fernald, Ohio*, 34–41, 201–4.

100. US Congress. House of Representatives. Committee on Energy and Commerce, *DOE Nuclear Facility at Fernald, Ohio*, 42–46, 140–46.

101. US Congress. House of Representatives. Committee on Energy and Commerce, *DOE Nuclear Facility at Fernald, Ohio*, 48–50. Quote from 50.

102. US Congress. House of Representatives. Committee on Energy and Commerce, *DOE Nuclear Facility at Fernald, Ohio*, 50.

103. "Bomb Factories."

104. Brooks, *Restoring the Shining Waters*, 70.

105. Newman, *Love Canal*, 219.

106. Stewart and Stewart, *Fuel Cycle to Nowhere*, 36.

FIVE. GOING NATIONAL

1. "List of Week's Top-Rated TV Shows with AM-Nielsens," *Associated Press*, April 28, 1987.

2. "Accident Waiting to Happen?: ABC Show Examines Fernald," *Cincinnati Enquirer*, April 23, 1987, 52.

3. Plokhy, *Atoms and Ashes*, 223; Spears, *Rethinking*, 149–50.

4. John Corry, "TV Reviews: 'The Bomb Factories' on ABC," *New York Times*, April 23, 1987, 26.

5. Quotes from Knoblauch, *Nuclear Freeze in a Cold War*, 3, 104.

6. Harvey, *American Anti-nuclear Activism*, 55–56; Wittner, *Toward Nuclear Abolition*, 388–401; Rhodes, *Arsenals of Folly*, 275–76; Gusterson, *Nuclear Rites*, 175–76.

7. Quotes from "ABC's Alarming 'Bomb Factories,'" *Washington Post*, April 24, 1987; See also "TV Reviews; 'The Bomb Factories' on ABC"; "Accident Waiting to Happen?," 52; "No Place to Hide," *United Press International*, April 22, 1987.

8. Stewart and Steward, *Fuel Cycle to Nowhere*.

9. "History of the Military Production Network," 20th Anniversary Planning/ANA and MPN History, DG 250, Alliance for Nuclear Accountability, Acc. 2017-074, Box 19, Swarthmore College Peace Collection; Glazer and Glazer, *Environmental Crusaders*, 9; Metz, "Citizen Advisory Boards," 93.

10. "The Plutonium Challenge: An Open Letter to the President and the Congress of the United States," Plutonium Challenge, November 5, 1987, in US Congress, House of Representatives, Committee on the Budget, *Department of Energy Defense Nuclear Facilities Cleanup and Modernization*, 411.

11. Chris Sivula, "11 Arrested in N Reactor Protest," *Tri-City Herald (Kennewick, Washington)*, April 27, 1987, 1.

12. Ackland, *Making a Real Killing*, 4.

13. US Congress. Senate. Committee on Governmental Affairs, *Nuclear Protections and Safety Act of 1987*, 1.

14. Glenn and Taylor, *John Glenn*, 351.

15. US Congress. Senate. Committee on Governmental Affairs, *Nuclear Protections and Safety Act of 1987*, 3.

16. US Congress. Senate. Committee on Governmental Affairs, *Nuclear Protections and Safety Act of 1987*, 1.

17. Carlisle, *Supplying the Nuclear Arsenal*, 188.

18. US Congress. Senate. Committee on Governmental Affairs, *Nuclear Protections and Safety Act of 1987*, 1–2.

19. Carlisle, *Supplying the Nuclear Arsenal*, 188–190.

20. US Congress. Senate. Committee on Governmental Affairs, *Nuclear Protections and Safety Act of 1987*, 1–2.

21. US Congress. Senate. Committee on Governmental Affairs, *Nuclear Protections and Safety Act of 1987* 2–3.

22. US Congress. Senate. Committee on Governmental Affairs, *Nuclear Protections and Safety Act of 1987*, 3.

23. Glenn and Taylor, *John Glenn*.

24. US Congress. Senate. Committee on Governmental Affairs, *Nuclear Protections and Safety Act of 1987*, 9; Gosling and Fehner, *Closing the Circle*, 47; US Congress. Senate. Governmental Affairs Committee, *Reactor Safety Issues at Department of Energy Facilities*, 1.

25. "Nuclear Ohio," a pamphlet by Sierra Club of Northeast Ohio's Nuclear Committee, September 1988, Personal Papers of Linda Musmeci Kimball, Oxford, Ohio; Physicians for Social Responsibility, *Covering the Map*, 1; "G.A.O. Says 4 Government Reactors Operated at Unsafe Power Level," *New York Times*, March 13, 1987, 15; "They Lied to Us: Unsafe, Aging U.S. Weapons Plants are Stirring Fear and Disillusion," *Time*, October 31, 1988.

26. "The Plutonium Challenge: An Open Letter" in US Congress. House of Representatives. Committee on the Budget, *Department of Energy Defense Nuclear Facilities Cleanup and Modernization*, 174.

27. "Questions and Answers," Plutonium Challenge, [1987], 4, Personal Papers of Dave Fankhauser, Cincinnati, Ohio.

28. "The Plutonium Challenge: An Open Letter" in US Congress. House of Representatives. Committee on the Budget, *Department of Energy Defense Nuclear Facilities Cleanup and Modernization*, 177–78.

29. US Congress. House of Representatives. Committee on the Budget, *Department of Energy Defense Nuclear Facilities Cleanup and Modernization*, 175.

30. US Congress. House of Representatives. Committee on the Budget, *Department of Energy Defense Nuclear Facilities Cleanup and Modernization*, 174–77; "Questions and Answers," Plutonium Challenge, [1987], 3, Personal Papers of Dave Fankhauser.

31. "Questions and Answers," Plutonium Challenge, [1987], 2, Personal Papers of Dave Fankhauser; Makhijani, Hu, and Yih, *Nuclear Wastelands*, 207; and Plates 19–24 in Del Tredici, *At Work in the Fields of the Bomb*.

32. Lisa Crawford, interview with Fernald Living History Project, 7,; Meyer, interview.

33. "List of Participants for Colorado Meeting," and "Discussion of Concept of National Movement and Necessity for Basic Mission Statement," November 9–11, 1987, MPN Colorado Meeting 1987, Alliance for Nuclear Accountability Records, Accession 2017-074, Box 13, Swarthmore College Peace Collection.

34. Spears, *Rethinking*, 134–35; "History and Legacy," La Foret Conference and Retreat Center, https://www.laforet.org/_files/ugd/e0247f_515737a8018b4664b770d2167ef960c8.pdf.

35. Shabecoff, *Fierce Green Fire*, 231–50.

36. Newman, *Love Canal*; Blum, *Love Canal Revisited*; Gibbs, *Love Canal and the Birth of the Environmental Health Movement*.

37. McGurty, *Transforming Environmentalism*.

38. Spears, *Rethinking*, 2–3; Newman, *Love Canal*, 147.

39. Spears, *Rethinking*, 136–37.

40. Hamilton, "Convergence and Divergence," 49; "Major Victories and Organizations," November 9–11, 1987, MPN Colorado Meeting 1987, Alliance for Nuclear Accountability Records, Accession 2017-074, Box 13, Swarthmore College Peace Collection.

41. "Major Victories and Organizations"; "Emergency Drill Set April 25," *FMPC Update: An Informational Bulletin for the Fernald Community* (April 1987), Personal Papers of Linda Musmeci Kimball, Oxford, Ohio.

42. "Fact Sheet: Feed Materials Production Center," Box 7, Folder 36, John H. Glenn Archives, Senate Papers, Ohio State University; "Major Victories and Organizations."

43. "Major Victories and Organizations."

44. "Discussion of Concept of National Movement and Necessity for Basic Mission Statement," "List of Participants for Colorado Meeting," and "What Do We Need to Get There?," November 9–11, 1987, MPN Colorado Meeting 1987, Alliance for Nuclear Accountability Records, Accession 2017-074, Box 13, Swarthmore College Peace Collection; Spears, *Baptized in PCBS*.

45. "Democracy before Weaponry: A Bill of Rights for Citizens in the Shadows of America's Nuclear Weapons Production Facilities," November 9–11, 1987, MPN Colorado Meeting 1987, Alliance for Nuclear Accountability Records, Accession 2017-074, Box 13, Swarthmore College Peace Collection.

46. Longhurst, *Citizen Environmentalists*, 3–22.

47. "Democracy before Weaponry."

48. "Communications 'BUDDY' System," November 9–11, 1987, MPN Colorado Meeting 1987, Alliance for Nuclear Accountability Records, Accession 2017-074, Box 13, Swarthmore College Peace Collection.

49. "Communications 'BUDDY' System"; "History of the Military Production Network"; "Environet: Communication Link for Local Grass Roots Activists," *RACHEL's Hazardous Waste News 129* (May 16, 1989), https://www.ejnet.org/rachel/rhwn129.htm; Szasz, *Ecopopulism*, 75.

50. "BBSs Promote Environmental Awareness," *Link-Up 7*, no. 4 (July/August 1990): 11; "Environmental Issues Online," *Computers in Libraries* (April 1991): 20; "Environmentalism Goes Online: It's Only Natural," *Link-Up 11*, no. 2 (March–April 1994): 12; "Environet"; Dunaway, *Seeing Green*, 209–22.

51. "History of the Military Production Network"; "New Groups," "National Organizations," "Goals for Action for Individual Organizations and National Movement," November 9–11, 1987, MPN Colorado Meeting 1987, Alliance for Nuclear Accountability Records, Accession 2017-074, Box 13, Swarthmore College Peace Collection; Spears, *Rethinking*, 175.

52. "700-Mile Peace Trek Ends at Fernald," *Cincinnati Enquirer*, September 6, 1988, A-8; "Demonstrators to March to Fernald," *Cincinnati Enquirer*, September 1, 1988, D-2.

53. Quote from "Peace March Stops in Marion over Weekend," *Marion Star* (Marion, Ohio), August 6, 1988, 5; Harvey, *American Anti-nuclear Activism*, 153–56.

54. Harvey, *American Anti-nuclear Activism*, 153–56.

55. "700-Mile Peace Trek," A-8; "Demonstrators to March to Fernald," D-2.

56. "700-Mile Peace Trek," A-8; "Demonstrators to March to Fernald," D-2; Linda Musmeci Kimball, "Ohio Peace March Ends at Fernald," *Peace Center Press*, [1988] and unknown photographer, "Ohio Peace March for Global Nuclear Disarmament," Personal Papers of Linda Musmeci Kimball.

57. "Seven Arrested in Peace Protest at Fernald Plant: Activists Face Charges of Criminal Trespassing," *Cincinnati Post*, September 6, 1998, 1B.

58. "McCrackin, Six Others Are Arrested at Fernald," *Cincinnati Enquirer*, September 7, 1988, F-2.

59. "McCrackin, Six Others Are Arrested"; "Seven Arrested in Peace Protest," 1B.

60. "Rev. Maurice McCrackin: Minister Had Passion for Justice," *Cincinnati Post*, July 26, 1999.

61. "Seven Arrested in Peace Protest," 1B.

62. "700-Mile Peace Trek," A-8.

63. Harvey, *American Anti-nuclear Activism*, 143–67.

64. "700-Mile Peace Trek," A-8.

65. Hales, *Atomic Spaces*, 128–31.

66. "First-Ever Open House Scheduled September 17," *FMPC Update* (September 1988): 1.

67. "First-Ever Open House," 1.

68. Offenhauer, *Defense Nuclear Facilities Safety Board*, 44–67.

69. "Fernald Union Rejects Contract Offer, Sets Strike," *Cincinnati Enquirer*, October 7, 1988, E-2; Rainey, *One Hundred Miles from Home*, 109.

70. Cass Peterson, "Mission Fading for Aged A-Plant," *Washington Post*, February 28, 1988.

71. Peterson, "Mission Fading."

72. "Not[able] Fernald Reports," Series 4099, Box 2151, Fernald Controversy 10/88 File, 1–2, Governor Communications Office Information Files, 1982–1991, Ohio History Connection, Columbus, Ohio.

73. "Governor Celeste's Announcement on Feed Production Materials Center at Fernald," Memorandum, October 18, 1988, Series 4099, Box 2151, Fernald Controversy 10/88 File, 1–2, Governor Communications Office Information Files, 1982–1991, Ohio History Connection.

74. "Senators against Closing Fernald Plant," *Cincinnati Enquirer*, October 21. 1988, D-1.

75. Memorandum RE: Fernald, from Gary Falle and Becky Blood to Governor Celeste, October 21, 1988, Series 4099, Box 2151, Fernald Controversy 10/88 File, 1–2, Governor Communications Office Information Files, 1982–1991, Ohio History Connection.

76. "Donahue to Air Fernald Show," *Cincinnati Enquirer*, October 27, 1988, A16; "Fernald Furor Takes to Airwaves: Donahue Show Goes Live with Controversy," *Cincinnati Enquirer*, October 29, 1988, A-1, A-8.

77. *St. James Encyclopedia of Popular Culture*, s.v. "Phil Donahue," by Charles Coletta, accessed July 11, 2021; "Donahue to Air Fernald Show," *Cincinnati Enquirer*, October 27, 1988, A16; "Fernald Furor Takes to Airwaves," 1.

78. "Fernald Furor Takes to Airwaves" A-1, A-8.

79. "Neighbors of Uranium Plant Demand Clean-up," *Post-Crescent* (Appleton, Wisconsin), October 29, 1988, 2.

80. "Fernald Furor Takes to Airwaves," A-1, A-8.

81. "Fernald Furor Takes to Airwaves," A-1, A-8.

82. "Fernald Furor Takes to Airwaves," A-1, A-8.

83. "Fernald Furor Takes to Airwaves," A-1, A-8; *The MacNeil-Lehrer NewsHour*,

PBS, October 17, 1988, American Archive of Public Broadcasting, https://americanarchive.org/catalog/cpb-aacip_507-q814m92559.

84. *The MacNeil-Lehrer NewsHour*, PBS, October 17, 1988; US Congress. House of Representatives. Committee on Energy and Commerce, *DOE: Pollution at Fernald*, 1–2.

85. Ben Kaufman, "DOE Ignored Fernald Pollution," *Cincinnati Enquirer*, October 8, 1988, C1–C2.

86. "U.S., for Decades, Let Uranium Leak at Weapon Plant," *New York Times*, October 15, 1988. 1; Kaufman, "DOE Ignored Fernald Pollution," C1–C2.

87. *The MacNeil-Lehrer NewsHour*, PBS, October 17, 1988.

88. LaGrone, interview.

89. *The MacNeil-Lehrer NewsHour*, PBS, October 17, 1988.

90. *The MacNeil-Lehrer NewsHour*, PBS, October 17, 1988.

91. Williams, *Determining Our Environments*, 47; "They Lied to Us."

92. "They Lied to Us."

93. Clawson, interview, 1, 7–8; Beth Grace, "Ohio Facility's 1,000 Employees Face Bleak Prospects: Death, Illness Haunt Uranium Plant's Neighbors," *Los Angeles Times*, April 16, 1989.

94. Clawson, interview, 1.

95. "They Lied to Us"; Grace, "Ohio Facility's 1,000 Employees."

96. "They Lied to Us."

97. Charles Bradley Leach, "Greenhills, Ohio: The Evolution of an American New Town" (PhD diss., Case Western Reserve University, 1978), 1–2.

98. "They Lied to Us."

99. "They Lied to Us."

100. "$50 Billion Sought for Weapons Plants; 20-Year Plan Includes Relocation, Reactors," *Washington Post*, December 11, 1988, 1.

101. "$50 Billion Sought," 1.

102. Governor Richard Celeste to Secretary of Energy John Herrington, December 15, 1988, Series 4099, Box 2151, Fernald Controversy 10/88 File, Governor Communications Office Information Files, 1982–1991, Ohio History Connection; "After 37 Troubled Years, Fernald Faces the End," *Cincinnati Enquirer*, December 11, 1988, 12.

103. Lerner, *Sacrifice Zones*, 2–3; "$50 Billion Sought," 1.

104. Gosling and Fehner, *Closing the Circle*, 62–63, and Fluor Corporation, *Fernald at 50*, 21; "Remarks Prepared for Delivery by Attorney General Anthony Celebrezze Jr. for the Fernald Feed Materials Production Center News Conference," December 2, 1988, Series 4099, Box 2151, Fernald Controversy 10/88 File, Governor Communications Office Information Files, 1982–1991, Ohio History Connection; Williams, *Determining Our Environments*, 49–50.

105. "Employees End Strike at Fernald," *Cincinnati Enquirer*, December 18, 1988, B1.

106. "Employees End Strike at Fernald,", B6.

107. "Company Chief Wishes Production Would Continue," *Cincinnati Enquirer*, December 18, 1988, B1.

108. "Company Chief Wishes Production Would Continue," B6.

109. "Staff on Job at Fernald: Normal Plant Operations to Resume after Holidays," *Cincinnati Enquirer*, December 20, 1988, 1.

110. "Staff on Job at Fernald," 1, 16; "$50 Billion Sought," 1; Gosling and Fehner, *Closing the Circle*, 55.

111. Gosling and Fehner, *Closing the Circle*, 53.

112. "Glenn: Cleanup Funds Stingy," *News-Journal* (Mansfield, Ohio), January 13, 1989, 5.

113. Quote from Gosling and Fehner, *Closing the Circle*, 66.

114. Gosling and Fehner, *Closing the Circle*, 53, 55; "$50 Billion Sought," 1; "20-Year Plan Includes Relocation, Reactors," *Washington Post*, December 11, 1988, 1; LaGrone, interview.

SIX. "AMERICA'S WORST POLLUTER"

1. *Crawford v. National Lead Co., 784 F. Supp. 439*—Dist. Court, SD Ohio 1989; Dan Sewell, "U.S. Judge Who Sent Pete Rose to Prison; "Civil Rights Supporter S. Arthur Spiegel Dies in Cincinnati at Age 94," *Beacon Journal (Akron, Ohio)*, January 3, 2015, B6; Spiegel, *Trial on Its Merits*.

2. Alphonse Gerhardstein, "Goodnight, Judge Spiegel," *Cincinnati Enquirer*, January 2, 2015, A8; Spiegel, US Courts interview; Spiegel, *Trial on Its Merits*, 19-23.

3. *Crawford v. National Lead Co., 784 F. Supp. 439*—Dist. Court, SD Ohio 1989; Kenneth B. Noble, "Risk to Thousands: Documents Indicate a Decision Not to Act on Major Cleanup," *New York Times*, October 15, 1988, 1.

4. Quotes from Ankney, "But I Was Only Following Orders," 399-415; *Boyle v. United Technologies Corp. 487 U.S. 500 (1988)*.

5. Ankney, "But I Was Only Following Orders," 399-415; Noble, "Risk to Thousands," 1; Quote from Spears, *Baptized in PCBs*, 236.

6. *Crawford v. National Lead Co., 784 F. Supp. 439*—Dist. Court, SD Ohio 1989.

7. Sabin, *Public Citizens*, 35-56, 120, 166-69, 173-78; Shabecoff, *Fierce Green Fire*, 203-30; Turner and Isenberg, *Republican Reversal*.

8. Pritikin, *Hanford Plaintiffs*.

9. Quote from Kohn, "America's Worst Polluter," 37-50; John Leonard, "'Who Killed Karen Silkwood?,'" *Miami News*, November 20, 1981, 18.

10. Feinberg, "In the Shadow of Fernald," 41-46; Kuletz, *Tainted Desert*, 70-76.

11. Quote from Seager, "'Hysterical Housewives,'" 273.

12. Feinberg, "In the Shadow of Fernald," 41–46.

13. "Fear Meets Power in Courtroom: Fernald-Area Residents Face the Feds Monday," *Cincinnati Enquirer*, June 4, 1989, A-11.

14. Kuletz, *Tainted Desert*, 74.

15. "Remarks at the Swearing-In Ceremony for James D. Watkins as Secretary of Energy," March 9, 1989, Public Papers, George H. W. Bush Presidential Library and Museum, https://bush41library.tamu.edu/archives/public-papers/135.

16. Britton, interview, 1.

17. Carlisle, *Supplying the Nuclear Arsenal*, 198.

18. "Remarks at the Swearing-In Ceremony for James D. Watkins as Secretary of Energy," March 9, 1989; Gosling and Fehner, *Closing the Circle*, 55–56.

19. William Lanquette, "Plutonium—No Supply, No Demand?" in *Bulletin of the Atomic Scientists 45*, no. 10 (December 1989): 44; Glazer and Glazer, *Environmental Crusaders*, 9; DG 250, Alliance for Nuclear Accountability Records, Swarthmore College Peace Collection.

20. Lanquette, "Plutonium—No Supply, No Demand," 44; H.R. 2403 International Plutonium Control Act, 101st Congress, 1st Session, May 18, 1989, https://www.congress.gov/bill/101st-congress/house-bill/2403/text?r=4&s=1.

21. Lanquette, "Plutonium—No Supply, No Demand," 44.

22. Spears, *Rethinking*, 147.

23. Spears, *Rethinking*, 147; Sabin, *Public Citizens*, 103–8.

24. Sabin, *Public Citizens*, 73–90; "Living on Earth Profile #5: Lisa Crawford, Citizen Turned Anti-Nuclear Weapons Waste Activist," *Living on Earth*, transcript of May 26, 1995, episode, https://loe.org/shows/segments.html?programID=95-P13-00021&segmentID=4; Arjun Makhijani, "Democracy in the Nuclear Age—Remembering Bill Mitchell," *Arjun's Science and Democracy Blog*, May 2016, https://ieer.org/news/democracy-nuclear-age-remembering-bill-mitchell.

25. Lisa Crawford, "Cross-Training Questionnaire," August 1, 1989, Cross Training, DG 250, Alliance for Nuclear Accountability, Acc. 2017-074, Box 36, Swarthmore College Peace Collection.

26. "Minutes of the Military Production Network Meeting," Myrtle Beach, South Carolina, November 17–20, 1988, 7–11, DG 250, Alliance for Nuclear Accountability, Acc. 2017-074, Box 13, Swarthmore College Peace Collection; "Minutes of the Military Production Network Meeting," Harpers Ferry, West Virginia, 17–27, DG 250 Alliance for Nuclear Accountability, Acc. 2017-074, Box 24, Swarthmore College Peace Collection.

27. "Summary of the Military Production Network Meeting," September 13–17, 1989, New Market, Tennessee, MPN Meetings 1989, DG 250, Alliance for Nuclear Accountability, Acc. 2017-074, Box 24, Swarthmore College Peace Collection.

28. Spears, *Rethinking*, 134–42; Shabecoff, *Fierce Green Fire*, 231–50; Gottlieb, *Forcing the Spring*, 1–11, 162–204.

29. Makhijani, "Democracy in the Nuclear Age."

30. Glazer and Glazer, *Environmental Crusaders*, 185.

31. "Minutes of the Military Production Network Meeting," Harpers Ferry, West Virginia, 9, DG 250 Alliance for Nuclear Accountability, Acc. 2017-074, Box 24, Swarthmore College Peace Collection.

32. Lisa Crawford, interview with Fernald Living History Project, 19, ; Ken Crawford, interview.

33. Jill Lancelot and James Beard to Congress, March 28, 1989, Briefing Book, DG 250, Alliance for Nuclear Accountability, Acc. 2017-074, Box 36, Swarthmore College Peace Collection.

34. "Fernald Residents for Environmental Safety and Health," Briefing Book, DG 250, Alliance for Nuclear Accountability, Acc. 2017-074, Box 36, Swarthmore College Peace Collection.

35. Alexander, "Place of Recourse," 312.

36. Brown and Mikkelsen, *No Safe Place*; Harr, *Civil Action*.

37. Lisa Crawford, interview with the Fernald Living History Project, 10.

38. Elizabeth Neus, "Stress Issue Is Key as Fernald Trial Opens Today," *Cincinnati Enquirer*, June 5, 1989, A-10.

39. Sabin, *Public Citizens*, 93.

40. "Fear Meets Power in the Courtroom," A-1, A-11.

41. Neus, "Stress Issue Is Key," A1, A10.

42. Mindy S. Korol, "Children's Psychological Responses to a Nuclear Waste Disaster in Fernald, Ohio (PhD diss., University of Cincinnati, 1990), 1–3.

43. Korol, "Children's Psychological Responses," 3; Brown and Mikkelsen, *No Safe Place*; Neus, "Stress Issue Is Key," A1, A10.

44. Neus, "Stress Issue Is Key," A1, A10.

45. Neus, "Stress Issue Is Key," A1, A10.

46. Zaretsky, *Radiation Nation*, 13–14; Olwell, *At Work in the Atomic City*, 135–36; Longhurst, *Citizen Environmentalists*.

47. "Fear Meets Power in the Courtroom," A-11.

48. Neus, "Stress Issue Is Key," A1, A10; Zierler, *Invention of Ecocide*.

49. M. A. J. McKenna and Ben Kaufman, "Government Defense Angers Spectators," *Cincinnati Enquirer*, June 6, 1989, A-1, A-8.

50. Nash, *Inescapable Ecologies*, 196–97; Brown and Mikkelsen, *No Safe Place*, 134–36, 148–50.

51. US Congress. Senate, *Department of Energy's Nuclear Facilities*, 314–15.

52. "Government Defense Angers Spectators," A-8; "They Lied to Us," *Time*,

October 31, 1988; "Donahue Show Goes Live with Controversy," *Cincinnati Enquirer*, October 29, 1988, 1.

53. US Congress. House of Representatives. Committee on Energy and Commerce, *DOE: Pollution at Fernald, Ohio*, 100th Congress, 69–70; "Short Biography of Arjun Makhijani," Institute for Energy and Environmental Research, accessed August 21, 2022, https://ieer.org/wp/wp-content/uploads/2021/11/Short-Biography-of-Arjun-Makhijani.pdf; quote from "Alleged Fernald Dangers Are Detailed," *Beacon Journal (Akron, Ohio)*, June 7, 1989, B-3.

54. "Alleged Fernald Dangers Are Detailed," B-3.

55. "Alleged Fernald Dangers Are Detailed," B-3; US Congress. Senate. Committee on Governmental Affairs, *Management and Operation*, 281–90.

56. Al Salvato and Randy Ludlow, "Lawyer: Fernald Dangers Haunt Residents," *Cincinnati Post*, June 7, 1989, 10A.

57. Jay Mathews, "Bomb Tests Are Blamed for Cancer," *Washington Post*, October 14, 1982; George Raine, "Trial Hinges on Safety of Atom Tests," *New York Times*, September 27, 1982; Kuletz, *Tainted Desert*, 74.

58. "Chemistry Class Comes to Fernald Courtroom," *Cincinnati Enquirer*, June 10, 1989, A-12.

59. "Chemistry Class Comes to Fernald Courtroom," A-12.

60. Quote from Elizabeth Neus and Ben Kaufman, "Fernald Ailments Belittled," *Cincinnati Enquirer*, June 10, 1989, A1, A12; Randy Ludlow, "Fernald Fallout Denied," *Cincinnati Post*, June 10, 1989, 4A.

61. Neus and Kaufman, "Fernald Ailments Belittled," A1, A12.

62. American Psychiatric Association, *Diagnostic and Statistical Manual*, 248; Brown and Mikkelsen, *No Safe Place*, 87; Nixon, *Slow Violence*, 2–3; Green, Lindy, and Grace, "Psychological Effects of Toxic Contamination."

63. Neus and Kaufman, "Fernald Ailments Belittled," A1, A12.

64. Al Salvato, "Fernald Trial Likely to Set Precedent," *Cincinnati Post*, June 14, 1989, 1A, 4A.

65. Salvato, "Fernald Trial Likely to Set Precedent," 4A.

66. Alexander, "Place of Recourse," 312–13; "U-Plant Neighbors Win in Mock Trial," *Chillicothe Gazette*, June 16, 1989, 1A, 10A; "Fernald: Verdict in the Summary Trial Reflects the Public's Outrage," *Cincinnati Enquirer*, June 22, 1989, A18.

67. "Memorandum of Understanding of Settlement of Fernald Litigation," Case No. C-1-85-0149, Box 63, Folder 39, John H. Glenn Archives, Senate Papers, Ohio State University.

68. "Fernald Neighbors Offered $73 Million," *La Crosse Tribune*, July 2, 1989, 6.

69. "Fernald: Verdict in the Summary Trial," A18.

70. Kuletz, *Tainted Desert*, 74.

71. Williams, *Determining Our Environments*, 48.

72. Kuletz, *Tainted Desert*, 74; "Radiation Exposure Compensation Act," US Department of Justice, accessed May 21, 2023, https://www.justice.gov/civil/common/reca.

73. Ackland, *Making a Real Killing*, 214–16.

74. Elizabeth Neus, "Fernald Halts Production," *Cincinnati Enquirer*, July 13, 1989, 1; "Production Suspended at Fernald," *Indianapolis Star*, July 13, 1989, A4.

75. Kelley, interview, 20.

76. Al Salvato, "Federal Panels Back 1990 Fernald Closure," *Cincinnati Post*, July 28, 1989, 5A; Gosling and Fehner, *Closing the Circle*, 64–66.

77. Salvato, "Federal Panels Back 1990 Fernald Closure," 5A.

78. Quote from US Department of Energy, *Environment, Health, and Safety Compliance Assessment*, iv; Gosling and Fehner, *Closing the Circle*, 65.

79. Gosling and Fehner, *Closing the Circle*, 65; US Department of Energy, *Environment, Health, and Safety Compliance Assessment*, 16.

80. Quote from US Department of Energy, *Environment, Health, and Safety Compliance Assessment*, iv; Gosling and Fehner, *Closing the* Circle, 65.

81. US Department of Energy, *Environment, Health, and Safety Compliance Assessment*, iii–iv.

82. Gosling and Fehner, *Closing the Circle*, 67; Marshall, "Tiger Teams Draw Researchers' Snarls," 366–68.

83. Gosling and Fehner, *Closing the Circle*, 66, 71.

84. US Department of Energy, *Environment, Health, and Safety Compliance Assessment*, v; US Congress. House of Representatives. Committee on Energy and Commerce, *DOE: Pollution at Fernald, Ohio*, 101st Congress, 36.

85. Gosling and Fehner, *Closing the Circle*, 67–68, 71–72.

86. Walker, *Road to Yucca Mountain*, 182–84.

87. Quote from Gosling and Fehner, *Closing the Circle*, 69.

88. Gosling and Fehner, *Closing the Circle*, 69, 89.

89. Kirk, *Counterculture Green*, iii.

90. Office of Technology Assessment, *Complex Cleanup*, 6.

91. Gosling and Fehner, *Closing the Circle*, 69–70.

92. "Radioactive Water Found under Plant," *Cincinnati Enquirer*, October 25, 1989, E1–E2.

93. *Descriptions of 29 Sites Placed on the Final National Priorities List in November 1989*, Environmental Protection Agency, HW-8.21, November 1989, National Service Center for Environmental Publications (NSCEP).

94. Stewart and Stewart, *Fuel Cycle to Nowhere*, 36.

95. "Options Few for Tackling the Problem" and "Water," *Cincinnati Enquirer*, February 11, 1990, A-16; Williams, *Determining Our Environments*, 46.

96. "Options Few for Tackling the Problem" and "Water."

97. "Options Few for Tackling the Problem" and "Water.".

98. US Congress. House of Representatives. Committee on Energy and Commerce, *DOE: Pollution at Fernald, Ohio*, 101st Congress, 58, 62.

99. Langston, *Sustaining Lake Superior*, 53; Hamblin, *Poison in the Well*, 224–30.

100. Worster, *Nature's Economy*, 342–47; Zaretsky, *Radiation Nation*, 1–6; Spears, *Rethinking*, 70–76.

101. US Congress. House of Representatives. Committee on Energy and Commerce, *DOE: Pollution at Fernald, Ohio*, 101st Congress, 62.

102. Yocum, interview, 2; Yocum, "Community's Experience,", 56.

103. Yocum, "Community's Experience," 54.

104. Brown and Mikkelsen, *No Safe Place*.

105. Yocum, "Community's Experience," 56.

106. US Congress. House of Representatives. Committee on Energy and Commerce, *DOE: Pollution at Fernald, Ohio*, 101st Congress, 62.

107. Lisa Crawford, interview with the author.

108. US Congress. House of Representatives. Committee on Energy and Commerce, *DOE: Pollution at Fernald, Ohio*, 101st Congress, 62.

109. US Congress. House of Representatives. Committee on Energy and Commerce, *DOE: Pollution at Fernald, Ohio*, 101st Congress, 58, 62.

110. US Congress. House of Representatives. Committee on Energy and Commerce, *DOE: Pollution at Fernald, Ohio*, 101st Congress, 63.

111. US Congress. House of Representatives. Committee on Energy and Commerce, *DOE: Pollution at Fernald, Ohio*, 101st Congress, 63.

112. Peyton, "Kentucky's 'Atomic Graveyard,'" 227–28.

113. US Congress. House of Representatives. Committee on Energy and Commerce, *DOE: Pollution at Fernald, Ohio*, 101st Congress, 63.

114. "Yes, Fernald Can Be Made Right," *Cincinnati Enquirer*, August 18, 1989, 10.

115. "Yes, Fernald Can Be Made Right," 10.

116. John Glenn's Statement on Fernald's Transfer to the Office of Environmental Restoration and Waste Management, October 1, 1990, RG 57/A John Glenn Senate Papers, Box 521, Folder 20, Ohio Congressional Archives, Ohio State University; Len Ackland, "Who the Hell Will Insure Us?," *Bulletin of the Atomic Scientists 48*, no. 9 (November 1992): 25.

117. G-000-1004.7, US Department of Energy Feed Materials Production Center Community Meeting, Transcript, 6–7, 35–42, December 11, 1990, https://www.lm.doe.gov/cercla/documents/fernald_docs/CAT/106953.pdf.

118. US Department of Energy, *Secretary's Annual Report*, 377; Branham, interview, 19.

119. Britton, interview 2.

120. Branham, interview, 17.

121. "Energy Hearing Today," *Palladium-Item* (Richmond, Indiana), January 14, 1991, A3; "Fernald Cleanup Lacks Storage for Waste," *Cincinnati Enquirer*, January 14, 1991, A-7, A-8.

122. "Public Hearing Tackles Fernald Cleanup Plans," *Cincinnati Post*, January 12, 1991.

123. Longhurst, *Citizen Environmentalists*, 16.

124. Quote from Gosling and Fehner, *Closing the Circle*, 65.

125. Gosling and Fehner, *Closing the Circle*, 65; "Fernald Cleanup Lacks Storage for Waste," A-7, A-8.

126. "Fernald Cleanup Lacks Storage for Waste," A-7, A-8.

127. McClanahan, "Case for Safe and Affordable Energy," 29, 31, 55.

128. McClanahan, "Case for Safe and Affordable Energy," 80–81; "Energy Department Told to Clean Up Fernald Now," *Cincinnati Enquirer*, January 15, 1991, C1 and C2.

129. "Energy Department Told to Clean Up Fernald Now," C1, C2; Gosling and Fehner, *Closing the Circle*, 69.

130. "Fernald Neighbors Fear Cleanup Won't Come," *Dayton Daily News*, January 15, 1991, 12-B.

131. "Statement of Senators John Glenn and Howard Metzenbaum Regarding the Programmatic Environmental Impact Statement on Environmental Restoration and Waste Management at U.S. Department of Energy Facilities," January 14, 1991, RG 57/A, Box 521, Folder 35, John Glenn Senate Papers, Ohio Congressional Archives, Ohio State University.

132. "Fernald Cleanup Lacks Storage for Waste," A-7, A-8.

133. "Energy Department Told to Clean Up Fernald Now," C1, C2.

134. US Department of Energy, *Closing the Circle on the Splitting of the Atom*, 2, 25; US Department of Energy, *Linking Legacies*, 31.

135. For positive outcomes of the medical monitoring program, see Wones et al., "Medical Monitoring," 1374–83.

SEVEN. FUTURESITE

1. "'Inauguration Day' for New Mission at Fernald Site," *DOE This Month* 14, no. 9 (September 1991): 3.

2. "Fernald Has New Name and Image," *Palladium-Item* (Richmond, Indiana), August 24, 1991, 3.

3. "The Bomb Factories: Contamination Abounds at DOE's Ohio Uranium Mill," *Seattle Times*, December 15, 1986.

4. "Government Gives Plant New Name, Fernald Woes Remain, Residents Say," *Cleveland Plain Dealer*, August 19, 1991, 1C.

5. Gosling and Fehner, *Closing the Circle*.

6. Gregg Easterbrook, "James Watkins: For the Energy Department, A Man Willing to Call Them as He Sees Them," *Los Angeles Times*, August 11, 1991; Gosling and Fehner, *Closing the Circle*, 84.

7. Elizabeth Neus, "Dangerous Thorium to Be Shipped Out: DOE Approves Transfer of Radioactive Material from Fernald Plant," *Cincinnati Enquirer*, August 24, 1991, 1; Kuletz, *Tainted Desert*, 70–76.

8. Easterbrook, "James Watkins."

9. Federal Facilities Environmental Restoration Dialogue Committee, *Final Report of the Federal Facilities Environmental Restoration Dialogue Committee*, 1.

10. Walker, *Road to Yucca Mountain*, 174–186.

11. Federal Facilities Environmental Restoration Dialogue Committee, *Final Report of the Federal Facilities Environmental Restoration Dialogue Committee*, 2.

12. Quote from Rainey, *One Hundred Miles from Home*, 111.

13. Williams, *Determining Our Environments*, 35.

14. Hamilton, "Convergence and Divergence," 56–59; "On-Site Disposal Facility," DOE Office of Legacy Management, accessed September 19, 2022, https://www.energy.gov/sites/prod/files/2020/04/f74/Fernald%20Preserve%2C%20Ohio%20On-Site%20Disposal%20Facility.pdf.

15. Applegate and Sarno, "FUTURESITE," 13–27.

16. Lisa Crawford, interview with Fernald Living History Project, 23.

17. Fernald Citizens Task Force. *Final Report*, 33, accessed September 19, 2022, https://lmpublicsearch.lm.doe.gov/SiteDocs/112103.pdf#search=Fernald%20Citizens%20Task%20Force.

18. Lisa Crawford, interview with Fernald Living History Project, 23.

19. Tim Bonfield, "Cashing in on Fernald," *Cincinnati Business Courier*, July 27, 1992; "Nuclear-Cleanup Plan Criticized," *Seattle Times*, August 29, 1992.

20. Frederickson, *Cold War Dixie*; Ackland, *Making a Real Killing*; Hewlett and Duncan, *Atomic Shield*.

21. Lisa Crawford, interview with Fernald Living History Project, 25; and Branham, interview, 27.

22. General Accounting Office, *Department of Energy*, 11.

23. Williams, *Determining Our Environments*, 26.

24. "Cleaning Up on Cleanups: Environment: Industry Is Making Huge Profits by Ridding Factories, Dumps and Military Installations of Toxics. Much of the Mess was Made by the Firms Now Cashing in," *Los Angeles Times*, September 15, 1991, D1.

25. Debra K. Rubin, "DOE Picks Fluor for Fernald," *Engineering News-Record*, August 24, 1992, 9; "Nuclear-Cleanup Plan Criticized"; "Cleanup," *Sunday News* (Lancaster, Pennsylvania), September 15, 1994, 44.

26. "Cleaning Up on Cleanups," D1.

27. "Cleaning Up on Cleanups," D1.

28. "Cleaning Up on Cleanups," D1; Westad, *Cold War*, 579–616.

29. For quote, see "Cleaning Up on Cleanups," D1; "Fluor Daniel President Helps Company Diversify, Prosper," *Los Angeles Times*, March 14, 1988, 73.

30. Williams, *Determining Our Environments*, 53.

31. Stewart and Stewart, *Fuel Cycle to Nowhere*, 36.

32. "Cleaning Up on Cleanups," D1.

33. Williams, *Determining Our Environments*, 54.

34. "Fernald Union Endorses Operator," *Cincinnati Enquirer*, March 2, 1991, 24.

35. "Westinghouse Won't Seek New DOE Contract at Fernald," *PR Newswire*, January 8, 1992.

36. Elizabeth Neus, "Fernald Gets Hazardous Material Training," *Cincinnati Enquirer*, October 26, 1991, 13, 15.

37. Quotes from Neus, "Fernald Gets Hazardous Material Training," 13, 15; US Congress. House of Representatives. Committee on Commerce, *Federal Barriers to Common Sense Cleanups*, 39–40.

38. Len Ackland, "Who the Hell Will Insure Us?," *Bulletin of the Atomic Scientists* 48, no. 9 (November 1992): 25; Branham, interview, 18.

39. Ackland, "Who the Hell Will Insure Us?," 25; Power, *America's Nuclear Wastelands*, 176.

40. *Fernald Project Update*, October 1991, 11, https://lmpublicsearch.lm.doe.gov/SiteDocs/112645.pdf.

41. "Fernald Meetings and Press Conference," April 21, 1992; Bob Alvarez to Senator John Glenn, April 15, 1992, Box 29, Folder 15, John H. Glenn Archives, Senate Papers, Ohio State University.

42. Ackland, "Who the Hell Will Insure Us?," 25.

43. "Remarks by Senator John Glenn," April 22, 1992, Box 537, Folder 17, John H. Glenn Archives, Senate Papers, Ohio State University.

44. Ackland, "Who the Hell Will Insure Us?," 25; Branham, interview, 26.

45. Ackland, "Who the Hell Will Insure Us?," 25–26; Quote from "ERMC," *Tri-City Herald* (Kennewick, Washington), July 22, 1992, 2.

46. Quote from Michael Slater and Bob Alvarez to Senator John Glenn, April 21, 1992, Box 29, Folder 15, John H. Glenn Archives, Senate Papers, Ohio State University; James H. Rubin, "States May Not Fine Federal Agencies as Punishment for Pollution Violations," *Associated Press*, April 21, 1992.

47. "Talking Points on Supreme Court Decision on Fernald," Box 29, Folder 15, John H. Glenn Archives, Senate Papers, Ohio State University.

48. "The Community Perspective—Getting Started, Founding Principles, and Re-

sults," Fernald Community Alliance, accessed September 22, 2022, http://fernald communityalliance.org/pdf/The%20Community%20Perspective.pdf.

49. US Congress. Senate, *Federal Facilities Compliance Act of 1991*, 24.

50. "Fisher Pleased with Waste Vote," *Marion Star* (Marion, Ohio), September 25, 1992, 16; in 1991, the Senate passed the bill by a 94–3 bipartisan vote. See Roll Call Vote, 102nd Congress, 1st Session, H.R. 2194 Federal Facilities Compliance Act of 1992, United States Senate, accessed October 26, 2021, https://www.senate.gov/legislative/LIS/roll_call_lists/roll_call_vote_cfm.cfm?congress=102&session=1&vote=00230.

51. Turner and Isenberg, *Republican Reversal*, 115–121.

52. "Statement of Administration Policy: H.R. 1056—Federal Facilities Compliance Act," July 14, 1989, The American Presidency Project, UC Santa Barbara, https://www.presidency.ucsb.edu/documents/statement-administration-policy-hr-1056-federal-facilities-compliance-act; "Statement of Administration Policy: S. 596—Federal Facility Compliance Act," October 17, 1991, The American Presidency Project, UC Santa Barbara.

53. US Congress. Senate, *Federal Facilities Compliance Act of 1991*; "Supreme Court Rules against Ohio in Fernald Case: Fisher Vows to Seek Legislative Remedy," April 21, 1992, Box 29, Folder 15, John H. Glenn Archives, Senate Papers, Ohio State University; US Congress. Senate, *Federal Facilities Compliance Act of 1991*, 24.

54. Quote from Turner and Isenberg, *Republican Reversal*, 158; Oreskes and Conway, *Merchants of Doubt*, 190, 194.

55. "Gore Visits Fernald," *Cincinnati Post*, September 30, 1992, 1; Howard Wilkinson, "Gore Uses Fernald to Blast Bush: Candidate Tells Residents Things Will Change under Clinton," *Cincinnati Enquirer*, October 1, 1922, A-1, A-12.

56. Sharon Maloney, "Gore Rips Bush on Fernald Cleanup," *Cincinnati Post*, October 1, 1992, 10A.

57. Wilkinson, "Gore Uses Fernald to Blast Bush," A-12.

58. Maloney, "Gore Rips Bush on Fernald Cleanup," 10A; "People Trust Gore's Word on Fernald," *Cincinnati Enquirer*, November 9, 1992, 9; "Fernald's Neighbors Expect Gore to Keep Campaign Promise," *Lancaster Eagle-Gazette* (Lancaster, Ohio), November 9, 1992, 2.

59. Stewart and Stewart, *Fuel Cycle to Nowhere*, 36–38; Gosling and Fehner, *Closing the Circle*, 110–11.

60. Debra K. Rubin, "DOE Picks Fluor for Fernald," 9.

61. Debra K. Rubin, "DOE Picks Fluor for Fernald," 9; Williams, *Determining Our Environments*, 53.

62. Bonfield, "Cashing In on Fernald."

63. "People Trust Gore's Word on Fernald," 9.

64. "Residents to Monitor Fernald Nuclear Cleanup," *Dayton Daily News*, August 16, 1992, 4-B.

65. Gosling and Fehner, *Closing the Circle*, 115–16.

66. Thomas W. Lippman, "An Energetic Networker to Take Over Energy," *Washington Post*, January 19, 1993.

67. Gosling and Fehner, *Closing the Circle*, 135; Advisory Committee on Human Radiation Experiments, *Human Radiation Experiments*, xxi–xxiii; US Department of Energy, *Closing the Circle on the Splitting of the Atom*.

68. US Congress. House of Representatives, *Ecosystem Management*, 309.

69. Federal Facilities Environmental Restoration Dialogue Committee, *Interim Report*, 75, National Service Center for Environmental Publications (NSCEP), accessed November 1, 2021, https://nepis.epa.gov/Exe/ZyPDF.cgi/20011DPL.PDF?Dockey =20011DPL.PDF; Gosling and Fehner, *Closing the Circle*, 115; Lippman, "Energetic Networker."

70. Williams, *Determining Our Environments*, 33–34.

71. Federal Facilities Environmental Restoration Dialogue Committee, *Interim Report*, 6.

72. Federal Facilities Environmental Restoration Dialogue Committee, *Interim Report*, 6; Sabin, *Public Citizens*.

73. Federal Facilities Environmental Restoration Dialogue Committee, *Interim Report*, v; Depoe, "Public Involvement," 158.

74. Williams, *Determining Our Environments*, 14–15, 17–18; Longhurst, *Citizen Environmentalists*, 14–16.

75. Williams, *Determining Our Environments*, 63.

76. Williams, *Determining Our Environments*, 63; Wright et al., "In Memoriam: Eula Bingham"; Katharine Q. Seelye, "Eula Bingham, Champion of Worker Safety, Dies at 90," *New York Times*, June 22, 2020.

77. Grumbly, interview, 10.

78. Williams, *Determining Our Environments*, 63–64; Applegate, interview, 1–2.

79. Williams, *Determining Our Environments*, 63–64.

80. Linda Dono Reeves, "Fernald Cleanup Closer to 'Passing Grade,'" *Cincinnati Enquirer*, January 15, 1994, B1.

81. Quote from Reeves, "Fernald Cleanup," B1; Steve Bennish, "Management Shake-up Hits Fernald Cleanup Team," *Cincinnati Enquirer*, December 16, 1993, C2; US Congress. House of Representatives, *Contracting Problems at DOE's Fernald Site*; Fernald Citizens Task Force Minutes, November 9, 1996, 2, Department of Energy Office of Legacy Management, https://lmpublicsearch.lm.doe.gov/SiteDocs/113014.pdf#search=Fernald%20Citizens%20Task%20Force%20branham.

82. Reeves, "Fernald Cleanup," B1.

83. Ken Crawford, interview 9–10.

84. Lisa Crawford, interview with Fernald Living History Project, 18.

85. Williams, *Determining Our Environments*, 108.

86. Fernald Citizens Task Force, *Final Report*, 2–3, 14.

87. Sarno, interview, 1.

88. Sarno, "Making Cleanup Decisions," 1172.

89. Sarno, interview, 1; "Minutes from the December 9, 1993, Meeting of the Fernald Citizens Task Force," December 9, 1993, Department of Energy Office of Legacy Management Site Documents, https://lmpublicsearch.lm.doe.gov/SiteDocs/110160.pdf#search=Fernald%20citizen%20task%20force%20minutes; Fernald Citizens Task Force, *Final Report*, 14.

90. Williams, *Determining Our Environments*, 107–9, 127–31; Sarno, interview, 1–2.

91. Sarno, interview, 1–2.

92. "Clean Sites Inc.: A Touchdown or a Political Football?" *Industry Week*, July 23, 1984, 64.

93. Costle, interview; Grumbly, interview, 1–2; Sabin, *Public Citizens*.

94. Philip Shabecoff, "Common Cause: Environmentalists and Industry," *New York Times*, April 14, 1984.

95. Klacsmann, "Focusing Private-Sector Action," 188–189; Conrad MacKerron, "Clean Sites Hits Its Stride as a Super Mediator," *Chemical Week*, April 27, 1988, 20.

96. Shabecoff, "Common Cause"; Paulson and Herleikson, "From Conflict to Cleanup," 38; Halvorson, *Valuing Clean Air*, 132–62.

97. Sarno, "Making Cleanup Decisions," 1174.

98. Sarno, interview, 2; US House of Representatives, House Energy and Commerce Subcommittee on Oversight and Investigations, *Superfund Cleanup of Toxic Waste*, June 20, 1988, https://www.c-span.org/video/?3055-1/superfund-cleanup-toxic-waste.

99. Dan Herbeck, "Are Love Canal Chemicals Still Making People Sick?," *Buffalo News*, June 1, 2018, 1–2; Nancy A. Fischer, "Chemical in Line Halts Sewer Work near Love Canal," *Buffalo News*, January 21, 2011, 2.

100. Sarno, interview, 2; US House of Representatives, House Energy and Commerce Subcommittee on Oversight and Investigations, *Superfund Cleanup of Toxic Waste*.

101. Sabin, *Public Citizens*; and Halvorson, *Valuing Clean Air*.

102. Gosling and Fehner, *Closing the Circle*, 115; and Lippman, "Energetic Networker"; Douglas Frantz, "O'Leary Wins Praise amid Critical Views," *Los Angeles Times*, December 28, 1992.

103. MacKerron, "Clean Sites."

104. Williams, *Determining Our Environments*, 63; Wright et al., "In Memoriam: Eula Bingham"; Seelye, "Eula Bingham."

105. "Clean Sites Inc.," 64.

106. Sarno, "Making Cleanup Decisions," 1174.

107. Philip Shabecoff, "Chemical and Conservation Groups Form Toxic Cleanup Unit," *New York Times*, June 1, 1984, A14.

108. Williams, *Determining Our Environments*, 110; "Ohio Activist Belittles Plant

Cleanup Nominee," *Cincinnati Enquirer*, October 17, 1989; "Sierra Clubbers Join NLO Pickets," *Cincinnati Enquirer*, October 13, 1985, B2.

109. Sarno, "Making Cleanup Decisions,"1174.

110. Lisa Crawford, interview with the author.

111. "The Community Perspective," Fernald Community Alliance.

112. Applegate and Sarno, "FUTURESITE," 16.

113. Lerner, *Sacrifice Zones*, 2–3.

114. Applegate and Sarno, "FUTURESITE," 17; Daniel Roth, "Board Game Explains Fernald Cleanup Budget," *Cincinnati Enquirer*, February 23, 1994, 10.

115. Applegate and Sarno, "FUTURESITE," 17–18.

116. Applegate and Sarno, "FUTURESITE," 19–21. Quote from 21.

117. Applegate and Sarno, "FUTURESITE," 15–21.

118. Fernald Citizens Task Force. *Final Report*, 22.

119. Lisa Crawford, interview with Fernald Living History Project, 22–23.

120. Applegate and Sarno, "FUTURESITE," 22–23; Fernald Citizens Task Force. *Final Report*, 32–34.

121. Fernald Citizens Task Force. *Final Report*, 34.

122. Fernald Citizens Task Force. *Interim Report*; Applegate and Sarno, "FUTURESITE," 17.

123. Fernald Citizens Task Force. *Final Report*, 31–32.

124. "U.S. Department of Energy Environmental Justice Strategy—Executive Order 12898," Office of Legacy Management, accessed November 28, 2022, https://www.energy.gov/sites/default/files/EJStrategy_EO12898.pdf; Melosi, "Environmental Justice," 51.

125. Kuletz, *Tainted Desert*, 12–13.

126. Kuletz, *Tainted Desert*, 146–47; Grossman, *Unlikely Alliances*.

127. "Military Production Network Briefing Paper: Handling Radioactive Wastes," Nuclear Weapons Issues Briefing Kit, 1995, Fernald Preserve Visitors Center Reading Room, Hamilton, Ohio.

128. Lisa Crawford, interview with Fernald Living History Project, 23.

EIGHT. GRASSROOTS CLEANUP

1. "Girders to Be Demolished at Radioactive Plant Site," *Journal-Tribune* (Marysville, Ohio), September 9, 1994, 8; Linda Dono Reeves, "Fernald Building to Be Imploded: Demolition Blasts Will Collapse It within 7 Seconds," *Cincinnati Enquirer*, September 10, 1994, B4; Laraia, *Nuclear Decommissioning Case Studies*, 101.

2. Gerald P. Motl and Terry D. Borgman, "Lessons Learned from the D & D of Fernald Plant 7," FERMCO Fernald Environmental Management Project, January 14,

1994, University of North Texas Digital Library, Government Documents Department, https://digital.library.unt.edu/ark:/67531/metadc1385459/m2/1/high_res_d/10170118.pdf; Laraia, *Nuclear Decommissioning Case Studies*, 101; Makhijani, Hu, and Yih, *Nuclear Wastelands*, 212.

3. Quotes from Christine Wolff, "Going, Going . . . Still There!: Fernald Implosion Bombs," *Cincinnati Enquirer*, September 11, 1994, 1, 14; Christine Wolff, "Fernald Building (Finally) Falls Down: Third Try Works; Explosives Do the Job," *Cincinnati Enquirer*, September 18, 1994, B2.

4. Wolff, "Fernald Building (Finally) Falls Down," B2; Laraia, *Nuclear Decommissioning Case Studies*, 101.

5. Wolff, "Fernald Building (Finally) Falls Down," B2.

6. Reeves, "Fernald Building to Be Imploded," B4; US Department of Energy, *Final Remedial Action Report for Operable Unit 3*.

7. US Department of Energy, *Closing the Circle on the Splitting of the Atom*, v.

8. Turner and Isenberg, *Republican Reversal*, 134–35.

9. Linda Dono Reeves, "GOP Shift Could Cut into Cleanup Funds," *Cincinnati Enquirer*, November 13, 1994, B11.

10. Paul Barton, "Fernald Cleanup Costs Cut in Half: Much of Land to be Left Unusable or Restricted," *Cincinnati Enquirer*, April 4, 1995, 1.

11. Reeves, "GOP Shift Could Cut into Cleanup Funds," B11; Fernald Citizens Task Force, *Final Report*, 33.

12. Lisa Crawford, interview with Fernald Living History Project, 11.

13. Barton, "Fernald Cleanup Costs Cut in Half," A4.

14. Williams, *Determining Our Environments*, 45; "Ready for Prime Time President Bush Has Tapped Ohio's Rob Portman to Be the Nation's Top Trade Negotiator," *Cleveland Plain Dealer Sunday Magazine*, March 20, 2005.

15. Fernald Citizens Task Force, *Final Report*, 36–37.

16. Fernald Citizens Task Force, *Final Report*, 36–37.

17. Fernald Citizens Task Force, *Final Report*, 37; "Director's Final Findings and Orders," Ohio EPA, June 6, 1996, https://www.energy.gov/sites/prod/files/em/2001_Agreements/FEMP_DFFO6-6-96.pdf; Fluor Corporation, *Closing the Circle of History*, 80; Gosling and Fehner, *Closing the Circle*, 99.

18. Fernald Citizens Task Force, *Final Report*, 38.

19. Fernald Citizens Task Force, *Final Report*, 37.

20. Mitchell, interview, 12–13; Mike Gallagher and Tim Bonfield, "Audit: Fernald Cleanup Botched; Millions Wasted," *Cincinnati Enquirer*, March 19, 1997, A1, A6; Mike Gallagher, "Feds Dig Deeper at Fernald: Local Congressmen Have More Concerns," *Cincinnati Enquirer*, October 15, 1996, B1, B5; Mike Gallagher, "Faster Fernald Cleanup? 10-year Plan Given Tentative Approval," *Cincinnati Enquirer*, June 7, 1996, A1, A4.

21. Adam Bernstein, "Alvin L. Alm, 63, Dies," *Washington Post*, July 25, 2000; "Fernald Citizens Task Force Memorandum Regarding Ten-Year Vision," June 28, 1996, Department of Energy Office of Legacy Management, https://lmpublicsearch.lm.doe.gov/SiteDocs/112764.pdf#search=Fernald%20ten%2Dyear%20plan.

22. US Department of Energy, *Strategic Plan*, 26.

23. First quote from "Letter from Assistant Secretary Alvin L. Alm," July 1, 1996, US Department of Energy. Shared with the author by James Werner; Werner, interview; Second quote from "Address to Joint Session of Congress, May 25, 1961," Historic Speeches, John F. Kennedy Presidential Library and Museum, https://www.jfklibrary.org/learn/about-jfk/historic-speeches/address-to-joint-session-of-congress-may-25-1961.

24. "Letter from Assistant Secretary Alvin L. Alm," July 1, 1996, US Department of Energy. Shared with the author by James Werner.

25. Radioactive Waste Campaign, *Deadly Defense*, 117.

26. Branham, interview, 18; *New Releases* (US Nuclear Regulatory Commission) 7, no. 1 (January 6, 1987): 1.

27. US Department of Energy, *Seventh National Stakeholder Workshop Summary Report*, 38–41; Branham, interview, 17–19; *New Releases* (US Nuclear Regulatory Commission) 7, no. 1, January 6, 1987, 1.

28. Brinley Varchol and Dennis Carr, "The Fernald Closure Project—from Weapons to Wetlands," paper presented at PMI Global Congress, 2007, Atlanta, GA (Newtown Square, PA: Project Management Institute, 2007), accessed October 5, 2022, https://www.pmi.org/learning/library/fernald-closure-innovative-project-7214.

29. Varchol and Carr, "The Fernald Closure Project"; Debra K. Rubin, "DOE Picks Fluor for Fernald," *Engineering News-Record*, August 24, 1992, 9.

30. US Department of Energy, *Final Remedial Action Report for Operable Unit 1*, 8–9, 14.

31. US Department of Energy, *Final Remedial Action Report for Operable Unit 1*, 14; Rainey, *One Hundred Miles from Home*, 113–14; Williams, *Determining Our Environments*, 69; Robert Gehrke, "Utah Firm Wins Job to Cart Off Fernald Soil," *Cincinnati Enquirer*, July 3, 1998, A8; Rachel Melcer, "Fernald Waste to Ride the Rails: Plan Under Way to Empty Pits," *Cincinnati Enquirer*, May 31, 1998, A1.

32. US Department of Energy, *Final Remedial Action Report for Operable Unit 1*, 13.

33. Mark Cherry, Dave Lojek, and Con Murphy, "The Highly Successful Safe Remediation of the Fernald Waste Pits Undertaken under the Privatization Model," paper presented at the Waste Management Conference, February 23–27, 2003, Tucson, AZ, University of North Texas Digital Library, Government Documents Department, https://digital.library.unt.edu/ark:/67531/metadc734907/m2/1/high_res_d/811180.pdf.

34. US Department of Energy, *Final Remedial Action Report for Operable Unit 1*, 13;

Rachel Melcer, "Fernald Waste Will Head West by Spring, *Cincinnati Enquirer*, November 27, 1998, A1, A12

35. US Department of Energy, *Final Remedial Action Report for Operable Unit 1*, 16–17, 26.

36. US Department of Energy, *Final Remedial Action Report for Operable Unit 2*, 8, 14, 16–17.

37. US Department of Energy, *Final Remedial Action Report for Operable Unit 3*, 8, 36, 44.

38. *DOE This Month* 22, no. 4 (April 1999): 11.

39. US Department of Energy, *Final Remedial Action Report for Operable Unit 3*, 22–23.

40. "Fernald: 'Safe Shutdown' Complete," *Cincinnati Enquirer*, March 22, 1999, 4.

41. US Department of Energy, *Final Remedial Action Report for Operable Unit 4*, 3; Morgan and Stegner, "How Clean Is Clean?," 67.

42. Varchol and Carr, "Fernald Closure Project"; US Department of Energy, "Celebrating the 10th Anniversary,".

43. US Army Corps of Engineers, *Waste Disposal Options*, 2-10, 2-11; Morgan and Stegner, "How Clean Is Clean," 82–85; "Fernald Citizens Task Force Weekly Mailing of Upcoming Events and Meetings As Well As Copies of News Releases and News Clippings," March 28, 1997, Department of Energy Office of Legacy Management, https://lmpublicsearch.lm.doe.gov/SiteDocs/Revised%20234717.pdf.

44. US Army Corps of Engineers, *Waste Disposal Options*, 2-10, 2-11.

45. US Department of Energy, *Final Remedial Action Report for Operable Unit 4*, 15–16.

46. US Department of Energy, *Final Remedial Action Report for Operable Unit 4*, 16; US Army Corps of Engineers, *Waste Disposal Options*, 2-10, 2-41, 6-8.

47. Makhijani and Makhijani, *Shifting Radioactivity Risks*, 30.

48. US Department of Energy, *Interim Remedial Action Report for Operable Unit 5*, 9–10, 12–13, 16–19; "Onsite Disposal Facility for Low-level Radioactive Wastes from Fernald D & D Program," Geosyntec Consultants, accessed October 15, 2022, https://www.geosyntec.com/projects/item/3373-onsite-disposal-facility-for-low-level-radioactive-wastes-from-fernald-d-d-program.

49. US Department of Energy, *Interim Remedial Action Report for Operable Unit 5*, 8–9, 12–14, 49–51.

50. Spezio, *Slick Policy*, 13.

51. "Background on EPA's 2000 Drinking Water Regulations for Radionuclides," US Nuclear Regulatory Commission, accessed October 16, 2022, https://www.nrc.gov/docs/ML0601/ML060130112.pdf; Brettschneider, interview, 4; Fernald Citizens Task Force, *Final Report*, 27–28; US Department of Energy, *Interim Remedial Action Report for Operable Unit 5*, 8–9, 12–14, 49–51.

52. US Department of Energy, *Interim Remedial Action Report for Operable Unit 5*,

16–17, 19–22, 23–26; "Operable Unit 5 Environmental Media Factsheet," October 1994, 1–5, https://lmpublicsearch.lm.doe.gov/SiteDocs/111126.pdf.

53. Peggy O'Farrell, "After 10 Years, Fernald Cleanup Completed," *Cincinnati Enquirer*, October 31, 2006, B1.

54. Christopher Maag, "Nuclear Site Nears End of Its Conversion to a Park," *New York Times*, September 20, 2006, A20.

55. Hamilton, "Convergence and Divergence," 62–67.

56. US Department of Energy, *From Cleanup to Stewardship*, 1.

57. US Department of Energy, *From Cleanup to Stewardship*, 1.

58. US Department of Energy, *Office of Legacy Management*, 1.

59. US Department of Energy, "Celebrating the 10th Anniversary."

60. US Department of Energy, *From Cleanup to Stewardship*, vii.

61. Advisory Committee on Human Radiation Experiments, *Human Radiation Experiments*, 239–48.

62. Outreach Panel Meeting in Cincinnati, Ohio, Advisory Committee on Human Radiation Experiments, October 21, 1994, National Security Archive, George Washington University, https://nsarchive2.gwu.edu//radiation/dir/mstreet/commeet/pm01/pl1tran.txt.

63. Wones et al., "Medical Monitoring," 1374–83.

64. Wones et al., "Medical Monitoring," 1374–83; Pinney et al., "Health Effects in Community Residents," 150.

65. Wones et al., "Medical Monitoring," 1383.

66. "A Study of Former Fernald Workers," National Institute for Occupational Safety and Health, June 2013, https://www.cdc.gov/niosh/pgms/worknotify/pdfs/Fernald_Notification_FINAL-508.pdf; for the full study, see Silver et al., "Mortality and Ionizing Radiation Exposures," 453–63.

67. Szymendera, *Energy Employees Occupational Illness Compensation Program Act*.

68. Grumbly, interview, 9.

69. Werner, interview; James Werner, LinkedIn profile, accessed May 28, 2023, https://www.linkedin.com/in/jimwerner.

70. Decker, "Ecological Restoration of Native Plant Communities," 2–3; Ohio Environmental Protection Agency, *Fernald Natural Resource Trustees 2018 Annual Report to the Public*, 1.

71. Martin, *Wild by Design*, 5.

72. Fernald Citizens Advisory Board and the Perspectives Group, Inc., *Telling the Story of Fernald*, 92.

73. Fernald Citizens Advisory Board and the Perspectives Group, Inc., *Telling the Story of Fernald*, 7–8, 32.

74. Krupar, "Burying Atomic History," 48.

75. Krupar, "Disappearing Nuclear Landscape," 528.

76. Krupar, "Disappearing Nuclear Landscape," 528.

77. Brown, *Plutopia: Nuclear Families*; Hamblin, *Arming Mother Nature*; Rhodes, *Arsenals of Folly*, 306–9.

78. Krupar, "Burying Atomic History," 32.

79. Decker, "Ecological Restoration of Native Plant Communities," 1.

80. "Cleaning Up on Cleanups," D1.

81. Turner, *Charged*, 169–172.

82. Fluor Corporation, *Closing the Circle of History*, 88.

83. "Once Contaminated Site Now Restored," *Springfield News-Sun* (Springfield, Ohio), January 7, 2007, 26.

84. For the Fernald Community Alliance, see http://fernaldcommunityalliance.org.

85. Havlick, *Bombs Away*, 63–64.

86. "Fernald Preserve Fact Sheet," US Department of Energy Office of Legacy Management, accessed May 29, 2023, https://www.energy.gov/sites/default/files/2022-09/FernaldPreserveFactSheet.pdf.

87. "Fernald Preserve Fact Sheet"; Mel White, "Birding in Ohio," April 28, 2016, National Audubon Society, accessed October 25, 2022, https://www.audubon.org/news/birding-ohio.

88. Ohio Environmental Protection Agency, *Fernald Natural Resource Trustees 2021 Annual Report*, 1.

89. Cronon, *"Trouble with Wilderness,"* 69–90.

90. Nixon, *Slow Violence*, 2–3; "Leadership in Energy and Environmental Design," US Department of Energy Office of Legacy Management, accessed May 29, 2023, https://www.energy.gov/lm/articles/fernald-leed-fact-sheet; "Fernald Preserve Fact Sheet"; Hughes, *Human-Built World*, 153–74.

91. Hamblin, *Arming Mother Nature*, 10–13; Hughes, *Human-Built World*, 153–74.

92. Brown, *Plutopia*, 337–38; Zaretsky, *Radiation Nation*, 101–43.

93. Hans M. Kristensen and Matt Korda, "United States Nuclear Weapons, 2022," *Bulletin of the Atomic Scientists* 78, no. 3 (2022): 162–84.

94. US Department of Energy, *Interim Remedial Action Report for Operable Unit 5*, 20–22; Krupar, "Burying Atomic History," 58.

95. Worster, *Nature's Economy*, 342–47; "Nuclear Weapons: Who Has What at a Glance," Arms Control Association, accessed May 29, 2023, https://www.armscontrol.org/factsheets/Nuclearweaponswhohaswhat; Ellsberg, *The Doomsday Machine*, 17, 307–8, 343.

96. Vanderbilt, *Survival City*, 188–91; Krupar, "Burying Atomic History," 55–58.

CONCLUSION

1. Johnson, *Romancing the Atom*, 98–99; Winkler, *Life under a Cloud*, 195–96.
2. Johnson, *Romancing the Atom*, 98–99.
3. Johnson, *Romancing the Atom,*, 99–100, 126.
4. Johnson, *Romancing the Atom,*, 103–11, 120–25.
5. Wilson, "Fernald Project of the Atomic Energy Commission," 54–56.
6. Johnson, *Romancing the Atom*, 103–7; Plate 19. "Ingots of Fernald at Ashtabula," Plate 20. "Ashtabula Uranium Metal Extrusion Press," and Plate 24. "Back to Fernald," in Del Tredici, *At Work in the Fields of the Bomb*.
7. US Congress. Senate. Committee on Governmental Affairs, *Management and Operation*, 110.
8. Johnson, *Romancing the Atom*, 98–99.
9. Johnson, *Romancing the Atom*, 112–13; Brown, *Dispatches from Dystopia*, 57–77.
10. Government Accountability Office, *Environmental Cleanup*, 26–32; US Army Corps of Engineers, *Formerly Utilized Sites*, 6–9.
11. Government Accountability Office. *DOE Nuclear Cleanup*, 1.
12. Zaretsky, *Radiation Nation*; Crease and Bond, *Leak*.
13. Del Tredici, *At Work in the Fields of the Bomb*, ix.
14. Wellerstein, *Restricted Data*.
15. Del Tredici, *At Work in the Fields of the Bomb*, ix.
16. Power, *America's Nuclear Wastelands*; Carpenter, interview.
17. Johnson, *Romancing the Atom*, 195.
18. "Nuclear Weapons," Union of Concerned Scientists, accessed May 31, 2023, https://www.ucsusa.org/nuclear-weapons; "Nuclear Weapons: Who Has What at a Glance," Arms Control Association, accessed May 31, 2023, https://www.armscontrol.org/factsheets/Nuclearweaponswhohaswhat.
19. Higuchi, *Political Fallout*, 4–6.
20. Senators John Glen and Kirk Kempthorne to Senate Colleagues, March 21, 1995, Box 521, Folder 20, John H. Glenn Archives, Senate Papers, Ohio State University.
21. "Glenn: Cleanup Funds Stingy," *News-Journal* (Mansfield, Ohio), January 13, 1989, 5.
22. Turner and Isenberg, *Republican Reversal*, 5–8.
23. Quotes from Gottlieb, *Forcing the Spring*, 5; Alston, "The Summit."
24. Turner, *Charged*, 170.
25. Rabe, *Beyond NIMBY*, 1–3; Shabecoff, *Fierce Green Fire*, 237–38.
26. Kirk, *Counterculture Green*, 1–2.
27. Stewart Brand, interview with Victoria and Albert Museum [2016], *You Say You Want a Revolution? Records and Rebels, 1966–1970*, accessed May 31, 2023, https://www.vam.ac.uk/articles/meet-the-rebels.

28. Montrie, *Myth of Silent Spring*.

29. Turner, *Charged*, 170.

30. Lisa Crawford, interview with Fernald Living History Project, 18.

31. Brown, *Manual for Survival*, 10.

32. Brown, *Manual for Survival*, 10.

33. Boyer, *By the Bomb's Early Light*, 47–93.

34. "List of Participants for Colorado Meeting," and "Discussion of Concept of National Movement and Necessity for Basic Mission Statement," November 9–11, 1987, MPN Colorado Meeting 1987, Alliance for Nuclear Accountability Records, Accession 2017-074, Box 13, Swarthmore College Peace Collection.

35. "Elements of a Strong National Movement," November 9–11, 1987, MPN Colorado Meeting 1987, Alliance for Nuclear Accountability Records, Accession 2017-074, Box 13, Swarthmore College Peace Collection.

36. "History of the Military Production Network's Approach to Diversity," Alliance for Nuclear Accountability Records, Accession 2017-074, Box 40, Swarthmore College Peace Collection.

37. "History of the Military Production Network's Approach to Diversity," Alliance for Nuclear Accountability Records, Accession 2017-074, Box 40, Swarthmore College Peace Collection, 4; MPN Coordinating Committee to Juan Montes, April 29, 1994, MPN History, Alliance for Nuclear Accountability, Acc. 2017-074, Box 40, Swarthmore College Peace Collection.

38. "History of the Military Production Network's Approach to Diversity," Alliance for Nuclear Accountability Records, Accession 2017-074, Box 40, Swarthmore College Peace Collection, 4; MPN Coordinating Committee to Juan Montes, April 29, 1994, MPN History, Alliance for Nuclear Accountability, Acc. 2017-074, Box 40, Swarthmore College Peace Collection; Arjun Makhijani to Teresa Juarez, September 28, 1995; Damacio Lopez to MPN Management Board, November 13, 1995; Tom Goldtooth to MPN Management Board, October 12, 1995; Lance Hughes to Deehon Ferris, November 22, 1995; Vina Colley to MPN Management Board, [n.d.], Letters on Boycott and Removal of Teresa Juarez, Alliance for Nuclear Accountability Records, Accession 2017-074, Box 40, Swarthmore College Peace Collection.

39. Maria Painter to MPN Coordinating Committee, February 1, 1994, MPN History, Alliance for Nuclear Accountability, Acc. 2017-074, Box 40, Swarthmore College Peace Collection.

40. Damacio Lopez to MPN Management Board, November 13, 1995, Letters on Boycott and Removal of Teresa Juarez, Alliance for Nuclear Accountability Records, Accession 2017-074, Box 40, Swarthmore College Peace Collection.

41. "History of the Military Production Network's Approach to Diversity," Alliance for Nuclear Accountability Records, Accession 2017-074, Box 40, Swarthmore College Peace Collection.

42. Phillip Harrison to Arjun Makhijani, February 20, 1996; Arjun Makhijani to Phillip Harrison, March 15, 1996, Letters on Boycott and Removal of Teresa Juarez, Alliance for Nuclear Accountability Records, Accession 2017-074, Box 40, Swarthmore College Peace Collection.

43. Glazer and Glazer, *Environmental Crusaders*, 4–5.

44. US Department of Energy, "Celebrating the 10th Anniversary."

45. US Department of Energy, "Celebrating the 10th Anniversary."

46. Havlick, *Bombs Away*; Brown, *Manual for Survival*.

47. "Fernald Reborn," Center for Design Research and Innovation at DAAP, University of Cincinnati, 2006, Personal Papers of John Hancock, Cincinnati, Ohio.

48. Krupar, "Burying Atomic History," 40; quote from Lisa Crawford, interview with Fernald Living History Project, 27.

49. "Rare Bird Brings Flocks of Bird Watchers to Ohio," *Ideastream Public Media*, May 17, 2011, https://www.ideastream.org/2011-05-17/rare-bird-brings-flocks-of-bird-watchers-to-ohio.

50. Megan Marples and Rachel Ramirez, "What Is the Doomsday Clock?," *CNN*, January 20, 2022, https://www.cnn.com/2022/01/20/world/doomsday-clock-2022-climate-scn/index.html.

51. Hans M. Kristensen and Matt Korda, "United States Nuclear Weapons, 2022" in *Bulletin of the Atomic Scientists* 78, no. 3 (2022): 162–84.

52. Higuchi, *Political Fallout*, 1–6.

53. Intergovernmental Panel on Climate Change, *Climate Change 2023*, 5–7.

54. Higuchi, *Political Fallout*, 1–6; Jarrige and Le Roux, *Contamination of the Earth*, 286–322.

55. Spence, *Dispossessing the Wilderness*, 55–70.

56. Patrick Greenfield, "Protected Areas Don't Always Benefit Wildlife, Global Study Finds," *Guardian*, April 20, 2022, https://www.theguardian.com/environment/2022/apr/20/protected-areas-dont-always-benefit-wildlife-global-study-finds-aoe.

57. Turner, *Charged*, 172–85.

58. Lisa Crawford, interview with Fernald Living History Project, 27.

BIBLIOGRAPHY

ARCHIVES AND PERSONAL PAPERS

Alliance for Nuclear Accountability, Swarthmore College Peace Collection.
American Archive of Public Broadcasting (online).
The American Presidency Project, UC Santa Barbara (online).
Daniel Ellsberg Papers, University of Massachusetts Amherst Libraries (online).
Fankhauser, Dave (personal papers).
Fernald Community Alliance (online).
Fernald Preserve Visitors Center Reading Room, Hamilton, Ohio.
Governor Communications Office Information Files, Ohio History Connection.
Hancock, John (personal papers).
Historic Speeches, John F. Kennedy Presidential Library and Museum (online).
John H. Glenn Archives, The Ohio State University.
Kimball, Linda Musmeci (personal papers).
National Security Archive, George Washington University (online).
National Service Center for Environmental Publications, US EPA (online).
Office of Legacy Management Site Documents, Department of Energy (online).
Office of Scientific & Technical Information Technical Reports, University of North Texas (online).
Project Management Institute Learning Library (online).
Public Papers, George H. W. Bush Presidential Library and Museum (online).
Reverse the Arms Race Federation, Ohio History Connection.
Southwest District Office, Ohio EPA.

GOVERNMENT DOCUMENTS

Congressional Research Service. *The Energy Employees Occupational Illness Compensation Program Act (EEOICPA)*. R46476. Washington, DC: Congressional Research Service, February 10, 2022.

Federal Facilities Environmental Restoration Dialogue Committee. *Final Report of the Federal Facilities Environmental Restoration Dialogue Committee: Consensus Principles and Recommendations for Improving Federal Facilities Cleanup.* Washington, DC: Environmental Protection Agency, 1996.

———. *Interim Report of the Federal Facilities Environmental Restoration Dialogue Committee.* Washington, DC: Environmental Protection Agency, 1993.

Fernald Citizens Advisory Board and the Perspectives Group, Inc. *Telling the Story of Fernald: Community Based Stewardship and Public Access to Information.* Alexandria, VA: The Perspectives Group, October 2002.

Fernald Citizens Task Force. *Final Report of the Fernald Citizens Task Force, Final Review Draft,* June 26, 1995.

———. *Interim Report: Preliminary Recommendations on Future Use and Cleanup Levels for the Fernald Site,* November 1994.

General Accounting Office. *Department of Energy: National Priorities Needed for Meeting Environmental Agreements.* Washington, DC: US General Accounting Office, 1995.

———. *Environment and Workers Could Be Better Protected at Ohio Defense Plants.* RCED-86-61. Washington, DC: US General Accounting Office, 1985. https://www.gao.gov/assets/150/143998.pdf.

Gosling, F. G., and Terrence R. Fegner. *Closing the Circle: The Department of Energy and Environmental Management, 1942–1994.* Washington, DC: Department of Energy, 1994.

Government Accountability Office. *DOE Nuclear Cleanup: Clear Guidance on Categorizing Activities and an Assessment of Contract Cost Effectiveness Need.* Washington, DC: US Government Accountability Office, 2023.

———. *Environmental Cleanup: Status of Major DOE Projects and Operations.* Washington, DC: US Government Accountability Office, 2022.

Hartsock, John K. *Geologic Considerations of Waste Control at the Feed Materials Production Center, Fernald, Ohio.* Washington, DC: US Atomic Energy Commission, 1960.

Hewlett, Richard G., and Francis Duncan. *Atomic Shield: A History of the Atomic Energy Commission,* Volume II, *1947–1952.* Washington, DC: US Atomic Energy Commission, 1972.

History Associates, Inc. *History of the Production Complex: The Methods of Site Selection.* Washington, DC: US Department of Energy, 1987.

Intergovernmental Panel on Climate Change. *Climate Change 2023: Synthesis Report, Summary for Policymakers.* Geneva, Switzerland: Intergovernmental Panel on Climate Change, 2023.

Oak Ridge Incident Investigation Board. *Investigation of September–December 1984 Plant 9 Excessive Uranium Emissions.* ORO-855, Feed Materials Production Center, February 6, 1985.

Offenhauer, Priscilla. *Defense Nuclear Facilities Safety Board: The First Twenty Years.* Washington, DC: Federal Research Division, Library of Congress, 2009.

Office of Technology Assessment. *Complex Cleanup: The Environmental Legacy of Nuclear Weapons Production.* Washington, DC: US Congress, 1991.

Ohio Environmental Protection Agency. *Fernald Natural Resource Trustees 2018 Annual Report to the Public*, June 2019.

———. *Fernald Natural Resource Trustees 2021 Annual Report to the Public*, June 2022.

Sedam, Alan C. *Occurrence of Uranium in Ground Water in the Vicinity of the U.S. Department of Energy Feed Materials Production Center, Fernald, Ohio.* Open-File Report 85-099. Columbus, OH: US Geological Survey, 1984.

Szymendera, Scott D. *The Energy Employees Occupational Illness Compensation Program Act (EEOICPA)*, R46476, Congressional Research Service, February 10, 2022. https://crsreports.congress.gov/product/pdf/R/R46476.

US Army Corps of Engineers. *Formerly Utilized Sites Remedial Action Program Update, Fiscal Year 2022.* Washington, DC: US Army Corps of Engineers, 2023.

———. *Waste Disposal Options and Fernald Lessons Learned Technical Memorandum for the Niagara Falls Storage Site, Lewiston, New York.* Buffalo: US Army Corps of Engineers Buffalo District, July 2011.

US Census Bureau. *Number of Inhabitants: Ohio.* [1950?]. www2.census.gov/library/publications/decennial/1950/population-volume-1/vol-01-38.pdf.

US Congress. House of Representatives. *Contracting Problems at DOE's Fernald Site.* 103rd Congress, First Session, December 1, 1993.

———. *Ecosystem Management.* 103rd Congress, Second Session, September 20, 1994.

US Congress. House of Representatives. Committee on Commerce. *Federal Barriers to Common Sense Cleanups.* 105th Congress, First Session, February 14 and March 7, 1997.

US Congress. House of Representatives. Committee on Energy and Commerce. *DOE: Pollution at Fernald, Ohio.* 100th Congress, Second Session, October 14, 1988.

———. *DOE: Pollution at Fernald, Ohio.* 101st Congress, Second Session, July 5, 1990.

———. *DOE Nuclear Facility at Fernald, OH.* 99th Congress, Second Session, August 13, 1986.

———. *DOE Regulation of Mixed Waste.* 99th Congress, Second Session, April 10, 1986.

———. *Environmental Compliance by Federal Agencies.* 100th Congress, First Session, April 28, 1987.

US Congress. House of Representatives. Committee on the Budget. *Department of Energy Defense Nuclear Facilities Cleanup and Modernization.* 101st Congress, First Session, February 8, 1989.

US Congress. Senate. *Department of Energy's Fiscal Year 1986 Authorization for Defense Programs.* 99th Congress, First Session, March 14, 1985.

———. *Department of Energy's Nuclear Facilities*. 101st Congress, October 5 and 31 and November 13, 1989.

———. *Federal Facilities Compliance Act of 1991*. 102nd Congress. First Session, April 16, 1991.

———. *A Legislative History of the Superfund Amendments and Reauthorization Act of 1986 (Public Law 99-499): Together with a Section-by-Section Index*, vol. III. Washington, DC: US Government Printing Office, 1990.

US Congress. Senate. Committee on Governmental Affairs. *Management and Operation of the US Department of Energy's Fernald, OH, Feed Materials Production Center*. 99th Congress, First Session, April 22, 1985.

———. *Nuclear Protections and Safety Act of 1987*. 100th Congress, First Session, June 16–17, 1987.

———. *Reactor Safety Issues at Department of Energy Facilities*. 100th Congress, First Session, March 12, 1987.

US Department of Commerce. *Population and Housing Unit Counts: Ohio*. Washington, DC: US Government Printing Office, 1990.

US Department of Energy. *A Closer Look at Uranium Metal Production: A Technical Overview*. Fernald, OH: Department of Energy, March 1988.

———. *Closing the Circle on the Splitting of the Atom: The Environmental Legacy of Nuclear Weapons Production in the United States and What the Department of Energy Is Doing About It*. Washington, DC: Department of Energy Office of Legacy Management, 1995.

———. *Environment, Health, and Safety Compliance Assessment*. Feed Materials Production Center, Fernald, Ohio. Washington, DC: Department of Energy, 1989.

———. *Environmental Remediation '91: "Cleaning Up the Environment for the 21st Century."* Washington, DC: Department of Energy, 1991.

———. *Final Remedial Action Report for Operable Unit 1—Waste Pits Remedial Action Project*. Cincinnati: Fernald Closure Project, August 2006. https://lmpublicsearch.lm.doe.gov/SiteDocs/7062.pdf.

———. *Final Remedial Action Report for Operable Unit 2—Other Waste Units*. Cincinnati: Fernald Closure Project, September 2006.

———. *Final Remedial Action Report for Operable Unit 3 at the Fernald Closure Project*. Cincinnati: Fernald Closure Project, February 2007.

———. *Final Remedial Action Report for Operable Unit 4—Silos 1 through 4*. Cincinnati: Fernald Closure Project, September 2006.

———. *From Cleanup to Stewardship*. Washington, DC: Department of Energy Office of Environmental Management, 1999.

———. *Interim Remedial Action Report for Operable Unit 5*. Cincinnati: Fernald Closure Project, August 2008.

———. *Linking Legacies: Connecting the Cold War Nuclear Weapons Production Processes to Their Environmental Consequences.* Washington, DC: Department of Energy Office of Environmental Management, 1997.

———. *Office of Legacy Management: The First Five Years, FY 2004-2008.* Washington, DC: Department of Energy, 2008.

———. "Privacy Act of 1975: Amendment of System Notices and New Routine Use Statement." *Federal Register* 50, no. 35 (February 21, 1985): 7209.

———. *The Secretary's Annual Report to Congress.* Washington, DC: Department of Energy, 1991.

———. *Seventh National Stakeholder Workshop Summary Report, Chicago, Illinois, May 27-28, 1999.* Washington, DC: Department of Energy Office of Worker and Community Transition, November 1999.

———. *Strategic Plan: Providing America with Energy Security, National Security, Environmental Quality, Science Leadership.* Washington, DC: Department of Energy, September 1997.

US Environmental Protection Agency. *Descriptions of 29 Sites Placed on the Final National Priorities List in November 1989.* HW-8.21. November 1989. National Service Center for Environmental Publications.

US Environmental Protection Agency and Department of Energy. *Federal Facilities Compliance Agreement*, July 18, 1986. DOE Office of Legacy Management. https://www.lm.doe.gov/cercla/documents/fernald_docs/CAT/106532.pdf.

INTERVIEWS

Adams, Weldon. Fernald Living History Project, October 11, 1999. https://www.fernaldcommunityalliance.org/FLHPinterviews/FLHP-99Adams.pdf.

Applegate, John. Fernald Living History Project, September 30, 1999. https://www.fernaldcommunityalliance.org/FLHPinterviews/Applegate.pdf.

Branham, Gene. Fernald Living History Project, July 8, 1999. https://www.fernaldcommunityalliance.org/FLHPinterviews/Branham.pdf.

Brettschneider, Dave. Fernald Living History Project, April 26, 2000. http://fernaldcommunityalliance.org/FLHPinterviews/FLHP-105Brettschneider.pdf.

Britton, Bill. Fernald Living History Project, 2001. https://www.fernaldcommunityalliance.org/FLHPinterviews/Britton.pdf.

Carpenter, Tom. Interview with Cynthia Kelly. Atomic Heritage Foundation, September 12, 2018. https://www.manhattanprojectvoices.org/oral-histories/tom-carpenters-interview.

Chesley, Stan. Fernald Living History Project, September 9, 1999. https://www.fernaldcommunityalliance.org/FLHPinterviews/Chesley.pdf.

Clawson, Marvin. Fernald Living History Project, August 24, 1999. https://www.fernald communityalliance.org/FLHPinterviews/Clawson.pdf.

Craig, Jack. Fernald Living History Project, March 9, 2001. https://www.fernald communityalliance.org/FLHPinterviews/Craig-final.pdf.

Crawford, Ken. Fernald Living History Project, August 17, 1999. https://www.fernald communityalliance.org/FLHPinterviews/CrawfordKen.pdf.

Crawford, Lisa. Fernald Living History Project, August 17, 1999. https://www.fernald communityalliance.org/FLHPinterviews/CrawfordLisa.pdf.

Crawford, Lisa. Interview with author, August 15, 2018.

Costle, Doug. Interview with the EPA, August 4–5, 1996. https://archive.epa.gov/epa /sites/production/files/2015-11/documents/grumbly.pdf.

Davies, Paul. Fernald Living History Project, May 27, 1999. https://www.fernald communityalliance.org/FLHPinterviews/Davies.pdf.

Dillhoff, Karl. Fernald Living History Project, August 3, 1999. https://www.fernald communityalliance.org/FLHPinterviews/Dilhoff.pdf.

Dunaway, Don. Fernald Living History Project, July 8, 1999. https://www.fernald communityalliance.org/FLHPinterviews/Dunaway.pdf.

Fankhauser, Dave. Fernald Living History Project, January 25, 2001. https://www .fernaldcommunityalliance.org/FLHPinterviews/Fankhauser-final.pdf.

Finfrock, Dan. Fernald Living History Project, May 27, 1999. https://www.fernald communityalliance.org/FLHPinterviews/Finfrock.pdf.

Griffis, Matthew R. "Oral History with Jerome Wilson," *Roots of Community Project*, University of Southern Mississippi, November 19, 2016. https://aquila.usm.edu/cgi /viewcontent.cgi?article=1001&context=rocinterviews.

Grumbly, Thomas. Interview with the EPA, Superfund 25th Anniversary Oral History Project, December 22, 2005. https://archive.epa.gov/epa/sites/production/files /2015-11/documents/grumbly.pdf.

Harper, Jane. Fernald Living History Project, August 31, 1999. https://www.fernald communityalliance.org/FLHPinterviews/Harper.pdf.

Kasparek, Dick. Fernald Living History Project, January 17, 2000. https://www.fernald communityalliance.org/FLHPinterviews/Kasparek.pdf.

Kelley, Pete. Fernald Living History Project, September 16, 1999. https://www.fernald communityalliance.org/FLHPinterviews/Kelley.pdf.

Knollman, Bill. Fernald Living History Project, July 15, 1998. https://www.fernald communityalliance.org/FLHPinterviews/KnollmanB.pdf.

LaGrone, Joe. Interview with Keith McDaniel. Oak Ridge Public Library, July 29, 2011. https://oakridgetn.contentdm.oclc.org/digital/collection/p15388coll1/id/145.

Meyer, Kathy and Don. Interview with author, May 29, 2021.

Mitchell, Graham. Fernald Living History Project, September 9, 1999. https://www .fernaldcommunityalliance.org/FLHPinterviews/Mitchell.pdf.

Rathgens, Lucy. Fernald Living History Project, June 29, 1999. https://www.fernald communityalliance.org/FLHPinterviews/Rathgens.pdf.

Sarno, Doug. Fernald Living History Project, March 9, 2001. https://www.fernald communityalliance.org/FLHPinterviews/Sarno-final.pdf.

Sellet, Ruth. Fernald Living History Project, June 15, 1999. https://www.fernald communityalliance.org/FLHPinterviews/Sellet.pdf.

Sneed, Gene. Fernald Living History Project, September 30, 1999. https://www.fernald communityalliance.org/FLHPinterviews/FLHP-97Sneed.pdf.

Spiegel, S. Arthur. US Courts, June 16, 2014. https://www.uscourts.gov/news/2014 /06/16/wwii-profile-s-arthur-spiegel.

Weidner, Bob. Fernald Living History Project, June 24, 1999. https://www.fernald communityalliance.org/FLHPinterviews/Weidner.pdf.

Werner, James. Interview with author, May 5, 2023.

Wilson, Jerome. Roots of Community Project, November 19, 2016.

Yocum, Edwa. Fernald Living History Project, July 27, 1998. https://www.fernald communityalliance.org/FLHPinterviews/FLHP-F-1Yocum.pdf.

LEGAL DOCUMENTS

Boyle v. United Technologies Corp. 487 U.S. 500 1988.
Crawford v. National Lead Co., 784 F. Supp. 439 – Dist. Court, SD Ohio 1989.

NEWSPAPERS, NEWSLETTERS, AND PERIODICALS

Asbury Park Press
Associated Press
Atomizer
Beacon Journal (Akron, Ohio)
Buffalo News
Bulletin of the Atomic Scientists
Chemical Week
Chillicothe Gazette
Cincinnati Business Courier
Cincinnati Enquirer
Cincinnati Magazine
Cincinnati Post
Cleveland Plain Dealer
Cleveland Plain Dealer Sunday Magazine
CNN
Columbus Dispatch
Community Companion (Cincinnati, Ohio)
Courier-Journal (Louisville, Kentucky)
Courier-Post (Camden, New Jersey)
Daily Register (Red Bank, New Jersey)
Dayton Daily News
DOE *This Month*
Engineering News-Record
FMPC Update (US DOE)
Forbes
Friends Journal
Guardian
Ideastream Public Media
Independent Coast Observer (Gualala, California)
Indianapolis Star

Industry Week
Journal-News (Hamilton, Ohio)
Journal-Tribune (Marysville, Ohio)
La Crosse Tribune
Lancaster Eagle-Gazette (Lancaster, Ohio)
Link-Up
Los Angeles Times
Marion Star (Marion, Ohio)
Miami News (Miami, Florida)
New Releases (US NRC)
New York Times
News-Journal (Mansfield, Ohio)
News-Messenger (Fremont, Ohio)
Palladium-Item (Richmond, Indiana)
Post-Crescent (Appleton, Wisconsin)
PR Newswire
Prologue (US NARA)
RACHEL's Hazardous Waste News
Rolling Stone
Seattle Times
Springfield News-Sun (Springfield, Ohio)
Sunday News (Lancaster, Pennsylvania)
Time
Tri-City Herald (Kennewick, Washington)
UC Magazine (Cincinnati, Ohio)
United Press International
Washington Post

SECONDARY SOURCES

Abalone Alliance. "Declaration of Nuclear Resistance." In *Nuclear Reactions: Documenting American Encounters with Nuclear Energy*, edited by James W. Feldman, 204–6. Seattle: University of Washington Press, 2017.

Ackland, Len. *Making a Real Killing: Rocky Flats and the Nuclear West*. Albuquerque: University of New Mexico Press, 1999.

Advisory Committee on Human Radiation Experiments. *The Human Radiation Experiments: The Final Report of the President's Advisory Committee*. New York: Oxford University Press, 1996.

Alexander, Roberta Sue. *A Place of Recourse: A History of the U.S. District Court for the Southern District of Ohio, 1803–2003*. Athens: Ohio University Press, 2005.

———. "A Place of Recourse: The Changing Role of the Federal District Court for the Southern District of Ohio." *History of Ohio Law*. Vol. 1. Edited by Michael Les Benedict and John F. Winkler. Athens: Ohio University Press, 2004.

Alston, Dana. "The Summit." *Race, Poverty, and the Environment* 2, no. 3/4 (1991).

American Psychiatric Association. *Diagnostic and Statistical Manual of Mental Disorders*, 3rd ed. rev. Washington, DC: American Psychiatric Association, 1987.

Amundson, Michael A. *Yellowcake Towns: Uranium Mining Communities in the American West*. Boulder: University Press of Colorado, 2002.

Ankney, R. Joel. "But I Was Only Following Orders: The Government Contractor Defense in Environmental Tort Litigation." *William and Mary Law Review* 32, no. 2 (Winter 1991): 399–437.

Applegate, John, and Douglas J. Sarno. "FUTURESITE: An Environmental Remediation Game-Simulation." *Simulation & Gaming* 28, no. 1 (March 1997): 13–27.

Balogh, Brian. *Chain Reaction: Expert Debate and Public Participation in American Commercial Nuclear Power, 1945–1975*. New York: Cambridge University Press, 1991.

Blum, Elizabeth D. *Love Canal Revisited: Race, Class, and Gender in Environmental Activism*. Lawrence: University Press of Kansas, 2008.

Boyer, Paul. *By the Bomb's Early Light: American Thought and Culture at the Dawn of the Atomic Age*. New York: Pantheon Books, 1985.

Brooks, David. *Restoring the Shining Waters: Superfund Success at Milltown, Montana*. Norman: University of Oklahoma Press, 2015.

Brown, Kate. *Dispatches from Dystopia: Histories of Places Not Yet Forgotten*. Chicago: University of Chicago Press, 2015.

———. *Manual for Survival: A Chernobyl Guide to the Future*. New York: W. W. Norton and Company, 2019.

———. *Plutopia: Nuclear Families, Atomic Cities, and the Great Soviet and American Plutonium Disasters*. New York: Oxford University Press, 2013.

Brown, Phil, and Edwin J. Mikkelsen. *No Safe Place: Toxic Waste, Leukemia, and Community Action*. Berkeley: University of California Press, 1997.

Burger, Joanna. "Integrating Environmental Restoration and Ecological Restoration: Long-Term Stewardship at the Department of Energy." *Environmental Management* 26, no. 5 (2000): 469–78.

Cahn, Robert, ed. *An Environmental Agenda for the Future*. Washington, DC: Island Press, 1985.

Caldicott, Helen. "Nuclear Madness." In *Nuclear Reactions: Documenting American Encounters with Nuclear Energy*, edited by James W. Feldman, 200–203. Seattle: University of Washington Press, 2017.

Carlisle, Rodney P. *Supplying the Nuclear Arsenal*. Baltimore: Johns Hopkins University Press, 1996.

Carr Childers, Leisl. *The Size of the Risk: Histories of Multiple Use in the Great Basin*. Norman: University of Oklahoma Press, 2015.

Carson, Rachel. *Silent Spring*, 50th Anniversary Edition. Boston: Mariner Books, 2002.

Caufield, Catherine. *Multiple Exposures: Chronicles of the Radiation Age*. New York: Harper and Row, 1989.

Crease, Robert P., and Peter D. Bond. *The Leak: Politics, Activists, and Loss of Trust at Brookhaven National Laboratory*. Cambridge, MA: MIT Press, 2022.

Cronon, William. "The Trouble With Wilderness; or, Getting Back to the Wrong Nature" in *Uncommon Ground: Toward Reinventing Nature*, edited by William Cronon, 69–90. New York: W. W. Norton and Co., 1995.

Del Tredici, Robert. *At Work in the Fields of the Bomb*. New York: Harper and Row, 1987.

Depoe, Stephen P. "Public Involvement, Civic Discovery, and the Formation of Environmental Policy: A Comparative Analysis of the Fernald Citizens Task Force and the Fernald Health Effects Subcommittee." *Communication and Public Participation in Environmental Decision Making*, edited by Stephen P. Depoe, John W. Delicath, and Marie-France Aepli Elsenbeer. Albany: State University Press of New York, 2004.

Donaghy, Aaron. *The Second Cold War: Carter, Reagan, and the Politics of Foreign Policy*. Cambridge: Cambridge University Press, 2021.

Dunaway, Finis. *Seeing Green: The Use and Abuse of American Environmental Images*. Chicago: University of Chicago Press, 2015.

Egan, Michael. *Barry Commoner and the Science of Survival: The Remaking of American Environmentalism*. Cambridge, MA: MIT Press, 2007.

Ellsberg, Daniel. *The Doomsday Machine: Confessions of a Nuclear War Planner*. New York: Bloomsbury, 2017.

Elmore, Bartow J. *Seed Money: Monsanto's Past and Our Food Future*. New York: W. W. Norton and Company, 2021.

Fehner, Terrence R., and F. G. Gosling. "Coming in from the Cold: Regulating U.S. Department of Energy Facilities, 1942–96." *Environmental History 1*, no. 2 (April 1996): 5–33.

Feinberg, Kenneth R. "In the Shadow of Fernald: Who Should Pay the Victims?" *Brookings Review 8*, no. 3 (Summer 1990): 41–46.

Feldman, James W., ed. *Nuclear Reactions: Documenting American Encounters with Nuclear Energy*. Seattle: University of Washington Press, 2017.

Fluor Corporation. *Closing the Circle of History: A History of the Fernald Site . . . Its Workers and Successful Cleanup*. Fernald, OH: Fluor Corporation, n.d.

———. *Fernald at 50: From Weapons to Wetlands*. Fernald, OH: Fluor Fernald Public Affairs, [n.d.].

Frederickson, Kari A. *Cold War Dixie: Militarism and Modernization in the American South*. Athens: University of Georgia Press, 2013.

Freeman, Lindsey A. *Longing for the Bomb: Oak Ridge and Atomic Nostalgia*. Chapel Hill: University of North Carolina Press, 2015.

Gerber, Michele Stenehjem. *On the Home Front: The Cold War Legacy of the Hanford Nuclear Site*. Lincoln: University of Nebraska Press, 1992.

Gibbs, Lois Marie. *Love Canal and the Birth of the Environmental Health Movement*. Washington, DC: Island Press, 2011.

Glazer, Penina Migdal, and Myron Peretz Glazer. *The Environmental Crusaders: Confronting Disaster and Mobilizing Community*. University Park: Pennsylvania State University Press, 1998.

Glenn, John, and Nick Taylor. *John Glenn: A Memoir*. New York: Bantam Books, 1999.

Gordin, Michael D. *Red Cloud at Dawn: Truman, Stalin, and the End of the Atomic Monopoly*. New York: Farrar, Straus, and Giroux, 2009.

Gottlieb, Robert. *Forcing the Spring: The Transformation of the American Environmental Movement.* Washington, DC: Island Press, 1993.

Green, Bonnie L., Jacob D. Lindy, and Mary C. Grace. "Psychological Effects of Toxic Contamination." In *Individual and Community Responses to Trauma and Disaster: The Structure of Human Chaos*, edited by Robert J. Ursano, Brian G. McCaughey, and Carol S. Fullerton, 154–76. Cambridge: Cambridge University Press, 1994.

Grossman, Zoltán. *Unlikely Alliances: Native Nations and White Communities Join to Defend Rural Lands.* Seattle: University of Washington Press, 2017.

Gusterson, Hugh. *Nuclear Rites: A Weapons Laboratory at the End of the Cold War.* Berkeley: University of California Press, 1996.

Hacker, Barton C. *Elements of Controversy: The Atomic Energy Commission and Radiation Safety in Nuclear Weapons Testing, 1947–1974.* Berkeley: University of California Press, 1994.

Hales, Peter Bacon. *Atomic Spaces: Living on the Manhattan Project.* Urbana: University of Illinois Press, 1997.

Halvorson, Charles. *Valuing Clean Air: The EPA and the Economics of Environmental Protection.* New York: Oxford University Press, 2021.

Hamblin, Jacob Darwin. *Arming Mother Nature: The Birth of Catastrophic Environmentalism.* New York: Oxford University Press, 2013.

———. *Poison in the Well: Radioactive Wastes in the Oceans at the Dawn of the Nuclear Age.* New Brunswick, NJ: Rutgers University Press, 2008.

———. *The Wretched Atom: America's Global Gamble with Peaceful Nuclear Technology.* New York: Oxford University Press, 2021.

Hamilton, Jennifer Duffield. "Convergence and Divergence in the Public Dialogue on Nuclear Weapons Cleanup." *Nuclear Legacies: Communication, Controversy, and the U.S. Nuclear Weapons Complex*, edited by Bryan C. Taylor, William J. Kinsella, Stephen P. Depoe, and Maribeth S. Metzler. Lanham, MD: Lexington Books, 2007.

Hamm, Thomas D. *The Quakers in America.* New York: Columbia University Press, 2003.

Harr, Jonathan. *A Civil Action.* New York: Random House, 1995.

Harvey, Kyle. *American Anti-nuclear Activism, 1975–1990: The Challenge of Peace.* New York: Palgrave McMillan, 2014.

Havlick, David G. *Bombs Away: Militarization, Conservation, and Ecological Restoration.* Chicago: University of Chicago Press, 2018.

Hays, Samuel P. *Beauty, Health, and Permanence: Environmental Politics in the United States, 1955–1985.* New York: Cambridge University Press, 1987.

Higuchi, Toshihiro. *Political Fallout: Nuclear Weapons Testing and the Making of a Global Environmental Crisis.* Stanford, CA: Stanford University Press, 2020.

Hughes, Thomas P. *Human-Built World: How to Think about Technology and Culture.* Chicago: University of Chicago Press, 2004.

Humes, Edward. *Garbology: Our Dirty Love Affair with Trash*. New York: Avery, 2012.

Jarrige, François, and Thomas Le Roux. *The Contamination of the Earth: A History of Pollutions in the Industrial Age*. Cambridge, MA: MIT Press, 2021.

Johnson, Robert R. *Romancing the Atom: Nuclear Infatuation from the Radium Girls to Fukushima*. Santa Barbara, CA: Praeger, 2012.

Jundt, Thomas. *Greening the Red, White, and Blue: The Bomb, Big Business, and Consumer Resistance in Postwar America*. New York: Oxford University Press, 2014.

Kiernan, Vincent. *Atomic Bill: A Journalist's Dangerous Ambition in the Shadow of the Bomb*. Ithaca, NY: Cornell University Press, 2022.

Kirk, Andrew. *Counterculture Green: The Whole Earth Catalog and American Environmentalism*. Lawrence: University Press of Kansas, 2007.

Klacsmann, John A. "Focusing Private-Sector Action on Public Hazards." *Hazards: Technology and Fairness*. Washington, DC: National Academy Press, 1986.

Knepper, George W. *Ohio and Its People*. Kent, OH: Kent State University Press, 1989.

Knoblauch, William M. *Nuclear Freeze in a Cold War: The Reagan Administration, Cultural Activism, and the End of the Arms Race*. Amherst: University of Massachusetts Press, 2017.

Kohn, Howard. "America's Worst Polluter." In *The Rolling Stone Environmental Reader*. Washington, DC: Island Press, 1992.

Krupar, Jason. "Burying Atomic History: The Mound Builders of Fernald and Weldon Spring." *Public Historian* 29, no. 1 (Winter 2007): 31–58.

———. "The Disappearing Nuclear Landscape: Snapshots of Lost Atomic Technologies." *Technology and Culture* 61, no. 2 (2020): 512–48.

Kuletz, Valerie L. *The Tainted Desert: Environmental and Social Ruin in the American West*. New York: Routledge, 1998.

Lakshmi, Rama, and Shalini Sharma. "Building a Safe Space for Unsafe Memories: The Remember Bhopal Museum." In *Telling Environmental Histories: Intersections of Memory, Narrative, and Environment*, edited by Katie Holmes and Heather Goodall. Cham, Switzerland: Palgrave Macmillan, 2017.

Langston, Nancy. *Sustaining Lake Superior: An Extraordinary Lake in a Changing World*. New Haven, CT: Yale University Press, 2017.

Laraia, Michele. *Nuclear Decommissioning Case Studies: Accidental Impacts on Workers, the Environment and the Public*. Vol. 1. London: Academic Press, 2021.

Lear, Linda A. *Rachel Carson: Witness for Nature*. Boston: Mariner Books, 2007.

Lerner, Steve. *Sacrifice Zones: The Front Lines of Toxic Chemical Exposure in the United States*. Cambridge, MA: MIT Press, 2010.

Longhurst, James. *Citizen Environmentalists*. Medford, MA: Tufts University Press, 2010.

Makhijani, Annie, and Arjun Makhijani. *Shifting Radioactivity Risks: A Case Study of* the K-65 Silos and Silo 3 Remediation and Waste Management at the Fernald Nuclear Weapons Site. Takoma Park, MD: Institute for Energy and Environmental Research, August 2006. https://ieer.org/wp/wp-content/uploads/2006/08/ShiftingRadioactivity Risks-fullrpt.pdf.

Makhijani, Arjun, Howard Hu, and Katherine Yih. *Nuclear Wastelands: A Global Guide to Nuclear Weapons Production and Its Health and Environmental Effects.* Cambridge, MA: MIT Press, 1995.

Markowitz, Gerald E., and David Rosner. *Deceit and Denial: The Deadly Politics of Industrial Pollution.* Berkeley: University of California Press, 2003.

Marshall, Eliot. "Tiger Teams Draw Researchers' Snarls." *Science* 252 (April 19, 1991): 366–68.

Martin, Laura J. *Wild by Design: The Rise of Ecological Restoration.* Cambridge, MA: Harvard University Press, 2022.

May, Elain Tyler. *Homeward Bound: American Families in the Cold War.* New York: Basic Books, 1988.

McGurty, Eileen Maura. *Transforming Environmentalism: Warren County, PCBs, and the Origins of Environmental Justice.* New Brunswick, NJ: Rutgers University Press, 2007.

Melosi, Martin V. "Environmental Justice, Political Agenda Setting, and the Myths of History." In *Environmental Politics and Policy, 1960s–1990s,* edited by Otis L. Graham, Jr. University Park: Pennsylvania State University Press, 2000.

Metz, John J. "Citizen Advisory Boards and the Cleanup of the U.S. Nuclear Weapons Complex: Public Participation or Public Relations Ploy?" *Local Environmental Movements: A Comparative Study of the United States and Japan,* edited by Pradyumna P. Karan and Unryu Suganuma, 75–110. Lexington: University of Kentucky Press, 2008.

Montrie, Chad. *The Myth of Silent Spring: Rethinking the Origins of American Environmentalism.* Berkeley: University of California Press, 2018.

Morgan, Kenneth, and Gary Stegner. "How Clean Is Clean?: Stakeholders and Consensus-Building at the Fernald Uranium Plant." In *Stakeholders and Scientists: Achieving Implementable Solutions to Energy and Environmental Issues,* edited by Joanna Burger. New York: Springer, 2011.

Nash, Linda. *Inescapable Ecologies: A History of Environment, Disease, and Knowledge.* Berkeley: University of California Press, 2006.

Newman, Richard S. *Love Canal: A Toxic History from Colonial Times to the Present.* New York: Oxford University Press, 2016.

Nixon, Rob. *Slow Violence and the Environmentalism of the Poor.* Cambridge, MA: Harvard University Press, 2011.

Olwell, Russell B. *At Work in the Atomic City: A Labor and Social History of Oak Ridge, Tennessee.* Knoxville: University of Tennessee Press, 2004.

Oreskes, Naomi, and Erik M. Conway. *Merchants of Doubt: How a Handful of Scientists Obscured the Truth on Issues from Tobacco Smoke to Global Warming*. London: Bloomsbury Press, 2012.

Paulson, Glenn, and Cynthia Herleikson. "From Conflict to Cleanup: The Clean Sites Approach." *Journal of the Washington Academy of Sciences* 76, no. 1 (March 1986): 36–43.

Peyton, Caroline. "Kentucky's 'Atomic Graveyard': Maxey Flats and Environmental Inequity in Rural America." *Register of the Kentucky Historical Society* 115, no. 2 (Spring 2017): 223–63.

Physicians for Social Responsibility. *Covering the Map: A Survey of Military Pollution Sites in the United States*. Washington, DC: Physicians for Social Responsibility, 1993.

Pinney, Susan, Ronald W. Freyberg, Gail E. Levine, Donald E. Brannen, Lynn S. Mark, James M. Nasuta, Colleen D. Tebbe, Jeanette M. Buckholz, and Robert Wones. "Health Effects in Community Residents Near a Uranium Plant at Fernald, Ohio, USA." *International Journal of Occupational Medicine and Environmental Health* 16, no. 2 (2003): 139–53.

Plokhy, Serhii. *Atoms and Ashes: A Global History of Nuclear Disasters*. New York: W. W. Norton and Company, 2022.

Power, Max S. *America's Nuclear Wastelands: Politics, Accountability, and Cleanup*. Pullman: Washington State University Press, 2008.

Pritikin, Trisha T. *The Hanford Plaintiffs: Voices from the Fight for Atomic Justice*. Lawrence: University Press of Kansas, 2020.

Rabe, Barry G. *Beyond NIMBY: Hazardous Waste Siting in Canada and the United States*. Washington, DC: Brookings Institution, 1994.

Radioactive Waste Campaign. *Deadly Defense: Military Radioactive Landfills*. New York: Radioactive Waste Campaign, 1988.

Rainey, Carol. *One Hundred Miles from Home: Nuclear Contamination in the Communities of the Ohio River Valley: Mound, Paducah, Piketon, Fernald, Maxey Flats, and Jefferson Proving Ground*. Cincinnati: Little Miami Press, 2008.

Rhodes, Richard. *Arsenals of Folly: The Making of the Nuclear Arms Race*. New York: Vintage Books, 2007.

———. *The Making of the Atomic Bomb*. New York: Simon and Schuster, 1986.

Robey, Sarah E. *Atomic Americans: Citizens in a Nuclear State*. Ithaca, NY: Cornell University Press, 2022.

Rome, Adam. *The Bulldozer in the Countryside: Suburban Sprawl and the Rise of American Environmentalism*. New York: Cambridge University Press, 2001.

———. *The Genius of Earth Day: How a 1970 Teach-in Unexpectedly Made the First Green Generation*. New York: Hill and Wang, 2013.

Rothman, Hal K. *Saving the Planet: The American Response to the Environment in the Twentieth Century*. Chicago: Ivan R. Dee, 2000.

Sabin, Paul. *Public Citizens: The Attack on Big Government and the Remaking of American Liberalism*. New York: W. W. Norton and Co., 2021.

Sarno, Douglas J. "Making Cleanup Decisions at Hazardous Waste Sites: The Clean Sites Approach." *Journal of the Air & Waste Management Association* 41, no. 9 (1991): 1172–75.

Seaborg, Glenn T. *Journal of Glenn T. Seaborg, Chairman of the Atomic Energy Commission, 1961–1971*. Vol. 4. Berkeley: University of California Lawrence Berkeley Laboratory, 1989.

Seager, Joni. "'Hysterical Housewives' and Other Mad Women: Grassroots Environmental Organizing in the United States." In *Feminist Political Ecology: Global Issues and Local Experiences*, edited by Dianne Rocheleau, Barbara Thomas-Slayter, and Esther Wangari, 271–83. London: Routledge, 1996.

Shabecoff, Philip. *A Fierce Green Fire: The American Environmental Movement*. New York: Hill and Wang, 1993.

Silver, Sharon, Stephen J. Bertke, Misty Jena Hein, Robert D. Daniels, Donald A. Fleming, Jeri L. Anderson, Susan M. Pinney, Richard W. Hornung, and Chih-Yu Tseng. "Mortality and Ionizing Radiation Exposures among Workers Employed at the Fernald Feed Materials Production Center (1951–1985)." *Occupational and Environmental Medicine* 70, no. 7 (July 2013): 453–63.

Spears, Ellen Griffith. *Baptized in PCBS: Race, Pollution, and Justice in an All-American Town*. Chapel Hill: University of North Carolina Press, 2014.

———. *Rethinking the American Environmental Movement Post-1945*. New York: Routledge, 2019.

Spence, Mark David. *Dispossessing the Wilderness: Indian Removal and the Making of the National Parks*. New York: Oxford University Press, 1999.

Spezio, Teresa Sabol. *Slick Policy: Environmental and Science Policy in the Aftermath of the Santa Barbara Oil Spill*. Pittsburgh: University of Pittsburgh Press, 2018.

Spiegel, S. Arthur. *A Trial on Its Merits: The Life of a Federal Judge*. Cincinnati: Clerisy Press, 2009.

Stern, Sheldon M. *The Cuban Missile Crisis in American Memory: Myth versus Reality*. Stanford, CA: Stanford University Press, 2012.

Stradling, David. *Cincinnati: From River City to Highway Metropolis*. Charleston, SC: Arcadia, 2003.

———. *The Nature of New York: An Environmental History of the Empire State*. Ithaca, NY: Cornell University Press, 2010.

———. *Smokestacks and Progressives: Environmentalists, Engineers, and Air Quality in America, 1881–1951*. Baltimore: Johns Hopkins University Press, 1999.

Stradling, David, and Richard Stradling. *Where the River Burned: Carl Stokes and the Struggle to Save Cleveland.* Ithaca, NY: Cornell University Press, 2015.

Stewart, Richard Burleson, and Jane Bloom Stewart. *Fuel Cycle to Nowhere: U.S. Law and Policy on Nuclear Waste.* Nashville: Vanderbilt University Press, 2011.

Szasz, Andrew. *Ecopopulism: Toxic Waste and the Movement for Environmental Justice.* Minneapolis: University of Minnesota Press, 1994.

Titus, A. Constandina. *Bombs in the Backyard: Atomic Testing and American Politics.* Reno: University of Nevada Press, 1986.

Turner, James Morton. *Charged: A History of Batteries and Lessons for a Clean Energy Future.* Seattle: University of Washington Press, 2022.

Turner, James Morton, and Andrew C. Isenberg. *The Republican Reversal: Conservatives and the Environment from Nixon to Trump.* Cambridge, MA: Harvard University Press, 2018.

Vanderbilt, Tom. *Survival City: Adventures among the Ruins of Atomic America.* New York: Princeton Architectural Press, 2002.

Voyles, Traci Brynne. *Wastelanding: Legacies of Uranium Mining in Navajo Country.* Minneapolis: University of Minnesota Press, 2015.

Walker, J. Samuel. *Permissible Dose: A History of Radiation Protection in the Twentieth Century.* Berkeley: University of California Press, 2000.

———. *The Road to Yucca Mountain: The Development of Radioactive Waste Policy in the United States.* Berkeley: University of California Press, 2009.

———. *Three Mile Island: A Nuclear Crisis in Historical Perspective.* Berkeley: University of California Press, 2004.

Warren, Christian. *Brush with Death: A Social History of Lead Poisoning.* Baltimore: Johns Hopkins University Press, 2000.

Weart, Spencer R. *Nuclear Fear: A History of Images.* Cambridge, MA: Harvard University Press, 1988.

Wellerstein, Alex. *Restricted Data: The History of Nuclear Secrecy in the United States.* Chicago: University of Chicago Press, 2021.

Wellock, Thomas Raymond. *Critical Masses: Opposition to Nuclear Power in California, 1958–1978.* Madison: University of Wisconsin Press, 1998).

Westad, Odd Arne. *The Cold War: A World History.* New York: Basic Books, 2017.

White, Richard. "'Are You an Environmentalist or Do You Work for a Living?': Work and Nature." In *Uncommon Ground: Toward Reinventing Nature,* edited by William Cronon, 171–85. New York: W. W. Norton and Company, 1995.

Williams, Walter Lee, Jr. *Determining Our Environments: The Role of Department of Energy Citizen Advisory Boards.* Westport, CT: Praeger, 2002.

Winkler, Allan M. *Life under a Cloud: American Anxiety about the Atom.* New York: Oxford University Press, 1993.

Wittner, Lawrence S. *Toward Nuclear Abolition: A History of the World Nuclear Disarmament Movement, 1971 to the Present*. Stanford, CA: Stanford University Press, 2003.

Wolfe, Tom. *The Right Stuff*. New York: Farrar, Straus, and Giroux, 1979.

Wones, Robert, Susan M. Pinney, Jeanette M. Buckholz, Colleen Deck-Tebbe, Ronald Freyberg, and Amadeo Pesce. "Medical Monitoring: A Beneficial Remedy for Residents Living Near an Environmental Hazard Site." *Journal of Occupational and Environmental Medicine 51*, no. 12 (December 2009): 1374–83.

Worster, Donald. *Nature's Economy: A History of Ecological Ideas, 2nd ed.* New York: Cambridge University Press, 1994.

Wright, Michael, Peg Seminario, Frank Mirer, Eric Frumin, and Debbie Berkowitz. "In Memoriam: Eula Bingham, 1929–2020." *Environmental Health Perspectives 128*, no. 10 (October 2020).

Yocum, Edwa. "A Community's Experience with Environmental Health Research at the Fernald Feed Production Plant." In *Tortured Science: Health Studies, Ethics, and Nuclear Weapons in the United States*, edited by Dianne Quigley, Amy Lowman and Steve Wing, 53–67. Amityville, NY: Baywood Publishing, 2012.

Zaretsky, Natasha. *Radiation Nation: Three Mile Island and the Political Transformation of the 1970s*. New York: Columbia University Press, 2018.

Zierler, David. *The Invention of Ecocide: Agent Orange, Vietnam, and the Scientists Who Changed the Way We Think about the Environment*. Athens: University of Georgia Press, 2011.

INDEX

ABC News Closeup: The Bomb Factories, 107–8
Adams, Weldon, 27, 57, 61–64, 66, 70, 86
Advanced Sciences, Inc., 150
AEC. *See* Atomic Energy Commission
AFL-CIO, 52, 82, 88, 165
African Americans, 21–22, 68
Agent Orange, 76, 134, 140
Alba Craft, Inc., 207–9
Alexander, Jim, 58
Alliance of Ohio Universities, 172
Alm, Alvin, 189, 200
Alston, Dana, 212
Alvarez, Robert, 122, 134, 167
American Friends Service Committee, 33, 39, 52, 113. *See also* Quakers
American Ordinance Association, 23
Amoco, 171
Anthropocene, 211, 219–20
anticommunism, 31, 48, 107
antinuclear activism, 38–41, 47–48, 214, 51, 107–8. *See also* peace movement
Antioch College, 47, 54
Appalachia, 21–22
Applegate, John, 173, 175, 180, 185
Applegate, Thomas, 45–48
Arthur, Daniel J., 102–5
Ashtabula. *See* Reactive Metals, Inc.

As Low as Reasonably Achievable, 133
Association to Preserve Bodega Head, 40
Atomic Energy Act, 5, 15, 17, 63, 97
Atomic Energy Commission (AEC): and Fernald, 13–14; and radioactive waste management, 23–24, 26, 54–55; and science, 25, 64, 152
"Atoms for Peace," 37
Aveni, Virginia, 97

Babcock, Mike, 68, 86, 89
Bain, Edward, 120
Barthel, C. E., 43
Beard, Jim, 114, 117
Becker, Mark, 120
Beckett, Opal, 143
Bell, Nina, 114, 117
Bettis Atomic Power Laboratory, 93
Beverley Hills Supper Club fire, 76, 142
Bhopal disaster, 76
Bibb, William, 64–65, 67
Bierbaum, Phillip, 53
Bingham, Clyde, 26
Bingham, Eula, 173, 178–80
Bonneville Power Administration, 151
Boswell, Bruce, 121, 129, 146–47
Boyle v. United Technologies Corp., 132–33
Bradburne, John, 189
Brand, Stewart, 213

Branham, Gene, 21; and Clinton administration, 174; and labor negotiations, 88–89, 98, 189; and remediation jobs, 171; and strikes, 85–86; testimony of, 81–82
Britton, Bill, 93–94, 156
Brokaw, Pauline, 33–35, 40, 47, 99
Brookhaven National Laboratory, 151
Brooks, Paul, 30
Bulletin of the Atomic Scientists, 219
Bush, George H. W., 107, 135, 168–70
Butterfield, Amy, 126
Butters, Mary, 114

Cade, Ebb, 68
Carey, Elizabeth, 158
Carlow, Mary Ellen, 113
Carpenter, Tom, 37–42, 44–47; and Government Accountability Project, 54, 88, 99, 102; and Hanford Challenge, 210; and Trinity Day, 52–54
Carroll, Ginny, 122
Carson, Rachel, 14, 30, 32, 37
Carter, Jimmy, 63, 79, 93, 132
Castle Bravo, 29
Catalytic Construction Company, 18
Celeste, Richard, 59, 69, 122–24, 128
Celebrezze, Anthony, Jr., 59, 71, 79, 82, 129
Centers for Disease Control (CDC), 69, 141, 152
Chandler, James F., 17, 25
Chavez, Jake J., 132, 142–43
Chavis, Benjamin, 6. *See also* environmental justice
Checkoway, Harvey, 67
Chemical Manufacturers Association, 176
Chernobyl, 98, 107, 110, 122
Chesley, Stanley, 76–77, 132, 141–42, 144–45

Chicago Tribune (newspaper), 122
Cincinnati, 13, 17, 23, 27–28, 170
Cincinnati Alliance for Responsible Energy. *See* Citizens Against a Radioactive Environment
Cincinnati Enquirer (newspaper): and community relations, 98, 171; and Fernald closure, 128; and John Glenn, 79; and labor, 85; and lawsuit, 125, 139–40, 143; and peace movement, 120; and radioactive waste, 41, 56; remediation criticism by, 193; and uranium leak, 3, 58; and water contamination, 44; worker op-ed in, 154–55; and Zimmer plant, 40
Cincinnati Gas and Electric, 45–48
Cincinnati Post (newspaper), 27, 44, 69, 119, 144–45
citizen advisory boards, 161, 172
Citizens Against a Radioactive Environment (CARE), 40–42, 44, 46–48
Citizens Against Rocky Flats Contamination, 113–14
Citizens Clearinghouse for Hazardous Waste, 6, 74
Citizens Concerned about Radiation Pollution, 39
civil disobedience, 33–34, 39–40, 52, 119–21
Clawson, Doris, 126, 143
Clawson, Marvin, 75, 126
Clayton, Leslie, 33
Clean Air Act, 147, 168, 176
Clean Sites, Inc., 175–80
Clean Water Act, 147
Clinton, Bill, 168, 170, 201
Coalition for Safe Power, 114, 117
coal mining, 21–22
Coffin, Thaddeus, 33

Cold War: impact on nuclear weapons production, 16, 162–63; impact on radioactive waste management, 2, 14, 24
Colorado Committee for Environmental Information, 39
Colorado Peace Network, 114
Commoner, Barry, 14, 29–30, 32, 51
Community Resource Center, Denver, 115
compartmentalization, 26
Comprehensive Environmental Response, Compensation, and Liability Act (CERCLA): and cancer risk, 177; and environmental politics, 163–64; and Fernald, 63, 129, 147, 175; and lawsuits, 77; and National Priorities List, 151; and remediation, 188
Cone, Clayton, 15
Connor, Tim, 114
Conservation Foundation, 176
Cooke, Kerry, 140
Cornell, Si, 27
Costle, Douglas M., 176, 178
Cowdrey, Sharon, 215
Crawford, Ken, 55–56, 71–73, 75, 169
Crawford, Lisa , 71–72; and burnout, 174; and DOE, 95, 159, 174; and FRESH leadership, 4, 95, 157, 169; harassment of, 75; and lawsuit, 75–76, 134, 138–39, 145; and legacy, 220; and Military Production Network, 113, 115, 117, 136–37, 179; and NIMBYs, 161; and On-Site Disposal Facility, 184; and remediation, 171, 185–86, 203, 217; testimony of, 96–98, 151–52, 167–68; and well water, 55–56, 72–73, 77–78
Crawford v. National Lead Co., 132–33, 138–46
Critical Mass Project, 47
Crosby Township, OH, 20, 153–54, 169

Cuban Missile Crisis, 27, 36
Curtis, Nolan, 180

Daniel, Bill, 165
Danielson, Judy, 39–40
Davies, Paul, 26
Davis, Billy Joe, 64–65
Deitriech, Michael, 76
Delta Steel, 55–56
Del Tredici, Robert, 210–11
Department of Defense (DOD): and contamination, 134, 160; and human radiation experiments, 198; and military spending, 5; and nuclear propulsion, 23; and remediation, 162–63
Department of Energy (DOE): and accelerated remediation, 189, 194; culture of production at, 4, 8, 9, 26, 54–55, 91–92, 95, 102–5, 112, 158, 217; and environmental health and safety, 83, 86, 95, 91, 110; and Environmental Impact Statements, 156–58; environmental transformation of, 8, 36, 83, 101–2, 106, 115, 121, 125, 130–31, 135, 147, 149–50, 174, 197, 200–201, 203, 212; Five-Year Plan, 149; General Environmental Protection Program, 147; and media coverage, 85, 94, 99, 108–9, 133–34; and Office of Legacy Management, 8, 197–98; and public participation, 10, 206; and public relations, 82, 209–210; and radiation victims, 134–35, 142–43, 145–46; and radioactive waste, 160; and remediation, 9, 111, 127–28, 162–63, 209; and risk, 34, 45, 65, 214; and safe shutdown, 192; and Second Cold War, 5, 31; and self-regulation, 5, 15–17, 53, 78, 81–82, 97, 109
Depoe, Stephen, 202

INDEX · 291

détente, 5, 27, 31, 41
Devine, Tom, 47–48, 54
Dickerson, Robert, 119
Dingell, John, 187
DOE. *See* Department of Energy
DOE/Westinghouse School for Environmental Excellence, 155–56, 164–65
Donahue, Phil, 123–24, 141
Doomsday Clock, 219–20
Dow Chemical, 171
downwinders, 134, 142–43, 145–46
Duell, David, 78
Duffy, Leo, 149, 157–58, 160
Dunaway, Don, 62–63
Dunn, Pam, 174, 215

Earth Day, 30, 42, 94, 178
Eckert, Dennis, 167
ecological restoration, 201, 204–5, 220
Edelstein, Michael, 139–40
Efron, Sonni, 163
Egilman, David, 142
Eisenhower, Dwight, 37
Ellsberg, Daniel, 39
Energy Employees Occupational Illness Compensation Program Act, 200
Energy Research Foundation, 111, 114
Envirocare, 190, 193–94
Environmental Defense Fund, 82, 90
environmental justice: and Carter administration, 173; and Clinton administration, 183; and energy transition, 220; and Fernald, 10, 160–61, 182–84; and mainstream movement, 137; and Military Production Network boycott, 215–16; and nuclear waste, 157; and Warren County, NC, 6–7, 114
environmental movement: and antimodernism, 9, 213–14; and antiregulatory backlash, 89–90; and changing tactics, 48; and democracy, 116, 136; development of, 30, 51; diversity, equity, and inclusion in, 115, 215–16; and expertise, 15, 31–32; grassroots influence on, 6–7, 10, 74–75, 98, 114, 137, 212; impact on society, 6, 15, 43; and the internet, 117; and labor unions, 89; and nuclear threat, 7, 90, 219; and policy reform, 6, 16–17, 106; and psychological stress, 139–40, 144; and remediation, 128–29, 161; and risk, 178–79; and teach-ins, 42; and women 73, 114
Environmental Policy Institute, 88, 90, 111, 122
Environmental Protection Agency (EPA): and Clean Sites, Inc., 176; defunding of, 5; and dialogue, 160, 171; and drinking water, 42, 55, 196; and oversight, 63, 84, 101, 146–48, 188; and pollution control, 44; and public expectations, 6, 15, 175–76
Environmental Research Foundation, 117
environmental restoration management contractors, 162, 170
environmental transformation. *See* Department of Energy: environmental transformation of
epidemiology, 67–69, 141; popular, 152–53
Estes, Ray, 120

fallout, radioactive, 29–30, 143, 211
Fankhauser, Dave, 99–100, 118, 214
FATLC. *See* Fernald Atomic Trades and Labor Council
FBI, 26, 46, 146
Federal Energy Administration, 171
Federal Facilities Compliance Act, 8–9, 167–70

Federal Facilities Environmental Restoration Dialogue Committee (FFERDC), 160–61, 171–72
Federal Mine Safety and Health Act, 53
Federation of American Scientists, 111
feed materials, 2, 20, 29
Feed Materials Production Center. *See* Fernald
Fernald: and accidents, 44–45, 61, 66, 94–96, 100; and advantages for remediation, 162, 189; and closure, 127–30; and community relations, 3–4, 25–29, 31–32, 59, 64–67, 93, 98, 121–22; and demolition, 185–87, 192; deterioration of, 5, 27–28, 70, 101–5, 147; development of, 17, 20, 25; and eminent domain, 13–15; and environmental monitoring, 43, 66, 102–5, 115; first impressions of, 21, 41, 64, 79–80, 93–94, 100, 155; impact of nuclear arms race on, 5, 31, 85; and media coverage, 41, 107, 122–27; and openness initiative, 198; and radioactive waste, 2, 15, 25–26, 51, 91, 98, 100, 188, 194; remediation at, 9–10, 83, 121, 129, 150–51, 155, 159, 170–71, 175, 185–97, 205, 217; and restoration, 204–5; and shutdown, 146–47, 148–49, 192; and uranium processing, 1–2, 18–20, 100; and workforce, 20–22, 27, 94, 113, 154–56, 165, 192–93
Fernald Atomic Trades and Labor Council (FATLC): and environmental education, 164–65; and FRESH, 108; and health studies, 52, 59, 69, 142; and joint safety board, 88, 93; and lawsuit, 199–200; leadership of, 21, 81, 98; and remediation jobs, 155–56, 165–66, 171, 189–90, 192; and strikes, 85–89, 121–22, 129–30; and Trinity Day, 52–53; and worker compensation, 198
Fernald Citizens Task Force (later Fernald Citizens Advisory Board): and accelerated remediation, 188; and community representation, 179–80; founding of, 172–73; and history, 202, 217–18; and radioactive waste disposal, 161, 181–84; and risk, 214
Fernald Community Alliance, 204
Fernald Environmental Management Project, 159
Fernald Living History Project, 202
Fernald Medical Monitoring Program, 145, 199
Fernald Preserve, 10, 203–6, 217–20
Fernald Residents for Environmental Safety and Health (FRESH): and coping strategies, 139–40; and demands, 137–38, 171; and Federal Facilities Compliance Act, 167–69; and Fernald Citizens Task Force, 174, 213; and Fernald tours, 98–100; founding of, 4, 59, 72; and human radiation experiments, 198; and identity, 79, 137, 183, 188, 213; impact on antinuclear activism, 8, 109, 204, 220; and lawsuit, 75–77, 115, 199; and local control, 179; and Military Production Network, 108, 113, 115, 117, 136, 214–15; and radioactive waste, 160, 164; and unions, 87–88, 165
Fernandez, Louis, 176
FFERDC, 160–61, 171–72
Fiehrer, Paul, 18
Finfrock, Dan, 32
Fitzgerald, Barbara, 118

Fluor Daniel, Inc.: and accelerated remediation, 190, 197; and Fernald contract, 170–71; and labor relations, 174, 189–90; and remediation industry, 163, 203
Food and Drug Administration, 178
Formerly Utilized Sites Remedial Action Program (FUSRAP), 208–9
Forsberg, Randall, 48–49
Foundation for National Progress, 35
Freedom of Information Act, 44–45, 54
Freese, Kathy, 33
Freeze. *See* Nuclear Weapons Freeze Campaign
FRESH. *See* Fernald Residents for Environmental Safety and Health
Friends of the Earth, 90, 111
Fuchs, Arthur, and May, 13
Fuller (company), 18
FUTURESITE, 161, 180–81

Galbraith, Robert, 151
Gee, Edwin A., 176
General Accounting Office (GAO), 79, 91–92, 110, 193
General Advisory Committee, 14
General Electric, 23
George A. Fuller Company, 18
Geosyntec, 195
Gerdeman, Alice, 157
Gibbs, Lois, 6, 73–74, 114, 179. *See also* Love Canal
Gill, Henry A., Jr., 140, 144–45
Gillette, Robert, 122
Gingrich, Newt, 8, 187
Glenn, John: and Committee on Governmental Affairs, 80–81, 109–10, 134, 187; and environmental activism, 4, 111; and environmental impact statement, 157; and FRESH, 59, 78–80, 115; and history, 211–12; and investigations, 91; and labor, 123, 147, 165–66; and legislation, 88, 121, 167
Gomez, James M., 163
Goodyear, 33. *See also* Portsmouth Gaseous Diffusion Plant
Gorbachev, Mikhail, 107
Gore, Al, 168–70
Gorsuch, Ann, 5, 31, 177
Government Accountability Project (GAP), 47, 88, 99, 102
government contractor defense, 132–33
grassroots activism. *See* environmental movement
Greater Cincinnati Occupational Health Center, 142
Great Miami Aquifer: and radioactive contamination, 45, 55, 150–51, 153; and remediation, 194, 196–97; and site selection, 17
Great Miami River, 42, 44–45, 105, 152, 197
Green, Bonnie, 142
Greenhills, OH, 126
Greenpeace, 111, 114, 117, 179
Griten, Amy, 33
Group of Ten, 90
Grumbly, Thomas, 173–74, 178, 187, 200
Gulf General Atomic, 26

Haliburton, 170
Hamric, Phil, 185–86
Hanford Education Action League, 114
Hanford Site (Washington): and antinuclear activism, 108, 112–13; and eminent domain, 16; and environmental health and safety, 107; and Fernald,

1–2, 104, 122; and labor disputes, 166; and production reactors, 2, 41, 101, 110, 130; and remediation, 209
Hanford Watch, 114
Hardy, Beck, 114
Harper, Jane, 153–54
Harshaw Chemical Works, 18
Hartsock, John K., 55
Hatfield, Mark O., 49
Health and Environmental Advisory Committee, Fernald, 93
Health Effects Institute, 176
Heard, John, 89
Heatherton, Richard, 68
Herrington, John S., 83–84, 92, 101–2, 123
human radiation experiments, 68–69, 99, 198–99
Hutchinson, Ralph, 215

ICF Technology, Inc., 200
Idaho National Engineering Laboratory, 127, 140, 151
Indigenous peoples, 134, 183–84, 202
"informed of radiation contamination syndrome," 142–44
Institute for Defense and Disarmament Studies, 48
Institute for Energy and Environmental Research, 137, 141, 215
Institute for Policy Studies, 47
International Commission on Radiation Protection, 91
International Paper Company, 176
Irwin, Clara, 13
Irwin, Raymond, 13
Izaak Walton League, 90

Jacobs Engineering Group, Inc., 170
Janrus, Judith, 119

Johnson, Lyndon, 172
Joint Committee on Atomic Energy, 14
Juarez, Reyna, 215
Juarez, Teresa, 215

K-65 silos: and investigations, 99, 148; and radioactive contamination, 15, 25–26, 56–57; and radon venting, 95–96; and remediation, 193–94
Kane, James, 83
Karl, C. L., 23
Kaufman, Ben, 3, 56, 58
Kaufman, Nick, 174
Kelchner Environmental, 191
Kelley, William, 82–83, 146–47
Kempthorne, Dirk, 212
Kennedy, Donald, 176
Kennedy, Edward M., 49
Kennedy, John F., 189
Kerr-McGee, 117
Keystone Center, 171, 179
Keystone Committee (FFERDC), 160–61, 171–72
Kimball, Daryl, 207
Kimball, Linda Musmeci, 50–51, 207, 209–11
Kindness, Tom, 95
Kingfisher, Pamela, 215
Kirby, Darrell, 165
Kirkham, Cathy, 114, 117
Kirschenbaum, Sara, 35
Knollman, Byron, 72
Knollman, Henry, 13
Kohn, Howard, 133–34

LaGrone, Joe, 79, 124–25
Lambert, Berta, 118, 120–21
Laurence, William, 27
Lavelle, Rita, 177

Lawrence Livermore National Laboratory, 127, 148
LEAF v. Hodel, 63, 97
Lederburg, Joshua, 176
Legal Environmental Assistance Foundation, 63. See also *LEAF v. Hodel*
Life Guard Idaho, 114
Limited Nuclear Test Ban Treaty, 49, 51, 73
Lindy, Jacob, 142–44
Lippert, Dorothy, 142
Lloyd, Michael G., 154
Lockheed, 163
Los Alamos National Laboratory, 189, 209
Los Angeles Times (newspaper), 122, 163
Love Canal, 6, 73–74, 77–78, 114, 139, 177–78
Lovejoy, Sam, 38
Lown, Bernard, 207
Luken, Tom: and environmental activism, 59, 147, 169; and labor, 123; and lawsuit, 124–25; and legislation, 88; and pork-barrel spending, 27; and public meeting, 71–72; and South Plume, 151–54
Lushbaugh, Clarence, 67–69

MacNeil-Lehrer NewsHour, 124–25
Magnuson, Ed, 122
Makhijani, Annie, 194
Makhijani, Arjun, 137, 141, 194, 214–15
Male, Richard, 115
Mallinckrodt Chemical Works, 18, 25, 56, 194, 209
Maloney, Kathy, 114, 117
Manchise, Lou, 88
Manhattan Project, 16, 18, 23, 33–35
Mann, David, 185
Marshall, Donald S., 78
Martell, Ed, 39

Martins, Debbie, 65
McClain, Makini, 215
McCrackin, Maurice, 119–20
McFarland, Bill, 140–41
McFarland, Gerda, 140–41
Meadows, Eunice, 120
Merrick, Thomas, 163
Merritt, Maggie, 57
Metzenbaum, Howard, 123, 157
Meyer, Kathy, 59, 65–66, 72–73, 81, 169
Meyer, Don, 71–72, 169
Miamisburg Environmental Health and Safety, 215
Miami University, 43, 50, 118, 124, 207
Military Production Network (MPN): and boycott, 214–16; and criticism of DOE, 171; founding of, 113–17; and FRESH, 7, 179; and Lobby Days, 136; and organization, 108, 137, 214; and radioactive waste disposal, 183–84
military-to-wildlife refuges, 204
Military Toxics Project, 215
Miller, Janet, 114
Minges, Cecilia, 15
Mitchell, Bill, 114, 117, 137
Mitchell, Graham, 43–44, 77, 151
Mobil Chemical, 55
Molander, Robert, 49
Monsanto, 35, 171, 176
Montes, Juan, 215
Monticello Mill Tailings, 151
Mother Jones (magazine), 36
Mound Laboratory, 33, 35, 90, 130, 151, 189
MPN. *See* Military Production Network
Mullin, James, 120
MX (intercontinental ballistic missile), 48

Nader, Ralph, 30, 37, 176
Najarian, Thomas, 52

296 · INDEX

NASA, 23
National Academy of Sciences, 23, 25, 110
National Audubon Society, 90, 204
National Center for Atmospheric Research, 39
National Committee for a Sane Nuclear Policy (SANE), 48, 114. *See also* SANE/FREEZE
National Environmental Policy Act (NEPA), 63, 116, 147, 156
National Institute for Occupational Safety and Health (NIOSH), 36, 52–53, 67, 142, 199–200
National Institutes of Health (NIH), 90, 198
National Lead of Ohio (NLO): and bonuses, 92; and Dutch Boy paint, 29; and firing, 70–71, 85–86, 93; and labor relations, 85–88, 104; and lawsuits, 125, 132–33, 139, 141–42, 199; and metallurgy, 18; and public relations, 34, 56–59, 70, 82–83; and risk, 45, 59, 63–64, 66, 86; and security, 26, 53; and subcontractors, 208; and uranium processing, 1; and water contamination, 55–56
National Organization for Women, 120
National Parks Conservation Association, 90
National People of Color Environmental Leadership Summit, 212
National Resource Information Center, 118
"national sacrifice zones," 10, 128, 157, 180, 204
National Security Council, 127
National Wildlife Federation, 90
Native Americans for a Clean Environment, 117, 215
Natural Resources Defense Council (NRDC): and activism, 200–201; and environmental impact statements, 88; and Group of Ten, 90; and lawsuits, 63, 82, 156; Plutonium Challenge, 111; and Tiger Teams, 148
Nelson, Gaylord, 178
Neumann, John, 85
Neus, Elizabeth, 120
Nevada Test Site, 160, 192, 194
Newark Air Force Station, 33
New Brunswick Laboratory, 18
New Right, 30–31
Newsweek (magazine), 122
New York Times (newspaper): and Fernald, 82, 111, 125; and William Laurence, 27; and nuclear weapons production, 108, 122; and remediation, 197
NIMBY. *See* not-in-my-backyard (NIMBY) activism
Nixon, Richard, 43, 47, 63
Noble, Kenneth, 122
Northern States Power Company, 171
Northwest Nuclear Safety Campaign, 114, 117
not-in-my-backyard (NIMBY) activism: and criticism, 74–75, 161, 213; and Fernald, 10, 89, 213; and peace movement, 35, 38
NSC-68, 16
nuclear arms race, 5, 16, 218–19
Nuclear Fuel Services, 170
nuclear power, 2, 37, 45–46, 92
Nuclear Regulatory Commission (NRC), 42, 46–48, 110, 189
nuclear secrecy, 14, 16–17, 26–27, 63, 121, 210
nuclear weapons: in popular culture, 49; and stockpile, 112; and testing, 29, 37, 44, 65, 142–43, 145–46, 211; and World War II, 16, 107

Nuclear Weapons Freeze Campaign: and criticism, 36, 49–50; and decline, 7, 107; founding of, 48–49; and freeze rally, New York City, 49–50; and freeze resolution, 49. *See also* SANE/FREEZE

nuclear weapons production complex: and class, 105; and Cold War buildup, 16, 35, 38; and culture of production, 1–2, 4, 8–9; and deteriorating facilities, 41; and the environment, 2, 4, 102, 158; and modernization, 127, 130–31, 135; in Ohio, 35

nuclear winter, 49

Oak Ridge, TN: and eminent domain, 16; and Fernald, 3, 58, 71, 91–92, 95, 125; and laboratories, 148; and mercury releases, 58, 63, 65; and remediation, 151, 209

Oak Ridge Associated Universities (ORAU), 67–68

Oak Ridge Environmental Peace Alliance, 215

Occupational Safety and Health Act, 53

Occupational Safety and Health Administration (OSHA), 6, 15, 173, 178

O'Connor, Al, 67

OCP. *See* Oxford Citizens for Peace

Odendahl, Terry, 115

Office of Technology Assessment (OTA), 150

Ohio: and lawsuits, 71, 82, 115, 167, 201, 204–5; and nuclear weapons production, 35, 122–23; and oversight, 129; and pollution, 43

Ohio Department of Health (ODH), 44, 55, 77

Ohio Environmental Protection Agency (Ohio EPA): and Crawford well, 77; and Fernald, 77, 147, 150, 188, 205; founding of, 43; and mixed waste, 97; and peace movement, 42–43; and uranium contamination, 55, 151

Ohio Nuclear Weapons Awareness Day, 33. *See also* Trinity Day

Ohio Nuclear Weapons Freeze Campaign, 33, 35, 50–51

Ohio Peace March, 118–21

Ohio Public Interest Campaign, 66, 88, 114, 118

Ohio Public Radio, 53

Ohio River, 40, 42

Ohio Valley Citizens Concerned about Nuclear Pollution, 40

Oil, Chemical, and Atomic Workers Union, 52

O'Leary, Hazel, 171, 178, 187, 198, 200

On-Site Disposal Facility, 10, 161, 182, 191–92, 194–95, 203

Oxford Citizens for Peace (OCP), 33, 50–51, 118, 158, 207, 209

Pacey, Gilbert, 207–8

Paddy's Run (stream), 42, 44, 55, 105, 205

Paducah Gaseous Diffusion Plant, 185

Painter, Maria, 215

Pantex Plant, 16

Paul, Liz, 114

Peabody Magnaflux, 46

peace movement: and class, 120; and the environment, 51; and Fernald, 33–36, 42, 119–20; and nuclear arsenal, 211; and nuclear power, 38; and Ohio, 35, 50, 118; and resurgence, 48; and Rocky Flats, 40

Pentagon Papers scandal, 30, 39, 44

Perry, Dick, 27

Pessefall, Mike, 120

Peterson, Cass, 122

Pierce, James, 142
Pierce, Shirley, 142
Pilcher, Jen, 113
Pinellas Plant, 127
Physicians for Social Responsibility, 48, 111–12, 207
plutonium: and Fernald, 81, 104–5; and human radiation experiments, 68; and Manhattan Project, 34; surplus of, 41, 122
Plutonium Challenge, 108–9, 111–13, 117, 136
Portman, Rob, 185, 188
Portsmouth Gaseous Diffusion Plant, 33, 35, 52–53, 79, 91, 209
Portsmouth Naval Shipyard, 52

Quakers, 33–34, 45, 52, 118. *See also* American Friends Service Committee
Qualls, Roxanne, 118–19

Radford, Dan, 82
radiation, 52
Radiation Exposure Compensation Act, 145–46
radiation protection, 1, 20, 60–61, 194
radioactive contamination: and Cold War, 2, 26; and water, 42, 44, 55, 57, 66, 150–54
railroads, 39–40, 104, 190–91
Rathgens, Lucy, 94
Reactive Metals, Inc., 1, 33, 113, 208
Reagan, Ronald: and Fernald, 212; and nuclear arms race, 5, 31, 107, 112; and nuclear safety board, 121; and SARA, 105; and "Star Wars," 79. *See also* Republican Reversal
Reide, Elmer, 65
Reidy, Ellen, 13, 17
Reilly, William K., 176, 178
Reising, Johnny, 197

remediation, industry, 149–50, 159, 162–64, 177–78, 196, 203
Republican Reversal, 5–6, 212
Resource Conservation and Recovery Act (RCRA), 63, 78, 97, 129, 147, 167, 188
Rhodes, Brewster, 66
Richardson, Bill, 192
Rickover, Hyman, 93, 135
Rockwell International, 33
Rocky Flats, 16, 38–40, 130, 146, 189
Rocky Mountain Arsenal, 134
Roe, Edgar Lee, 76
Rolling Stone (magazine), 133–34
Rose, Pete, 132
Rosell, Louise, 132
Ross Township, OH, 18, 20, 169
Ruckelshaus, William, 47
Rural Alliance for Military Accountability (RAMA), 215–16

"sacrifice zones," national, 10, 128, 157, 180, 204
Saenger, Eugene, 99, 198–99
Safe Drinking Water Act, 196
Sagan, Carl, 49
Salvato, Al, 145
SANE/FREEZE, 118, 157. *See also* National Committee for a Sane Nuclear Policy; Nuclear Weapons Freeze Campaign
Sarno, Doug, 175–80
Savannah River site (South Carolina): and antinuclear activism, 112–13; and Cold War buildup, 16; environmental health and safety, 101, 107, 110; and modernization, 127; and plutonium surplus, 41; and radioactive contamination, 2; and remediation, 151
Scalia, Antonin, 133
Schauer, Hilbert, 146

Schell, Jonathon, 49
Schneider, Keith, 122
Schultz, Lisa, 114
Schwab, Bob, 189
Seaborg, Glenn T., 23–25, 152
Seattle Times (newspaper), 101
Second Cold War, 5, 31
Seitz, Frederick, 25
Shafer, Peggy, 142–43
Shank, Rick, 123
Shanker, Thom, 122
Sierra Club, 82, 88, 90, 99, 111, 179
Singer, Steve, 107
Silent Spring, 30, 37. *See also* Carson, Rachel
Silkwood, Karen, 46, 133–34
site-specific advisory boards (citizen advisory boards), 161, 172
Skitt, Gary, 33
"slow violence," 2, 90, 144, 205
Smith, George, 58
Snake River Alliance, 140
Sneed, Gene, 21–22
Snyder, Sarah, 180
Solo, Pam, 39–40
sovereign immunity, 106, 125, 132, 151, 167, 170
Spenceley, Robert, 34, 56–57, 61–64, 66, 101
Spiegel, Arthur, 132–33, 138
Stansbery, Mark, 120
Stockholm International Peace Research Institute, 48
Stokes, Lincoln, 34
Stone, Walter, 142
Superfund. *See* Comprehensive Environmental Response, Compensation, and Liability Act (CERCLA)
Superfund Amendments and Reauthorization Act (SARA), 105–6, 147–48, 151, 164

Tabor, Bob, 174
Taft, Robert A., II, 154
Taylor, Robert, 63
Theisen, Malcolm, 61, 125
Thomas, Charles A., 35
thorium, 26, 28, 98, 160
Three Mile Island nuclear power plant, 41–42, 48, 139, 142
Three Valley Conservation Trust, 204
Threlkeld, Richard, 107
Tiger Teams, 147–49
Time (magazine), 111, 122, 126–27, 141
Times Beach, MO, 139
tort litigation: and chemical industry, 177; and Fernald, 76–77, 133–34, 138; and nuclear weapons plants, 145; and psychological stress, 139–40, 142–44
Train, Russell E., 176, 178
Trinity Day, 33–36, 51, 53, 207
Trinity test, 27, 33
Truman, Harry, 16
Tuck, John, 159

Union Carbide, 18, 76
Union of Concerned Scientists, 112
unions, labor: and gender, 94; and nuclear weapons plants, 88, 166; and peace movement, 120; and radioactive contamination, 36, 52, 67–68; and the Republican party, 85, 89; and violence, 22. *See also* Fernald Atomic Trades and Labor Council
United Church of Christ, 113
United Nations, 37
University of Chicago, 34
University of Cincinnati: and antinuclear activism, 40, 42; and Fernald Citizens Task Force, 173; and human radiation experiments, 198; and medical moni-

toring, 199; and oral history, 202; and psychiatric clinic, 142
University of Findlay, 156, 164–65
University of North Carolina, 67–68
uranium: as community hazard, 126–27, 150–54, 199, 209; and drinking water, 196; and ore sources, 208; and risk, 143; as workplace hazard, 55, 67–69, 81, 86, 91, 95, 102–5, 199–200
uranium leak, 1–3, 8, 58–64
uranium processing, 1–2, 18–20, 34, 45, 100, 207–8
US Army Corps of Engineers, 13, 63, 209
US Fish and Wildlife Service, 204–5
US Geological Survey, 55, 66, 73
US Navy, 93, 135

Venice Castle, 72
Venice Pavilion, 18, 85, 89
violence, slow, 2, 90, 144, 205
vitrification, 193–94

Wald, Matthew, 122
Walker, Mary, 97, 101
Wall, Jim, 140
War Resisters League, 51
Washington Post (newspaper), 82, 122, 127
Waste Control Specialists, 194
waste pits, remediation, 190–91
Watergate scandal, 30, 44, 47
water tower, 29, 32
Watkins, James D.: and activists, 159; and Environmental Impact Statements, 156; and FBI raid, 146; and Fernald, 170; and Five-Year Plan, 149; and radioactive waste, 160; swearing-in of, 135; and Tiger Teams, 147–48
Webb, Tony, 35–36
Weidner, Bob, 62
Werner, James, 200–201
Westinghouse: and criticism, 95; and environmental management, 93, 121, 148–49; and labor relations, 129–30, 155–56; and nuclear contracts, 86, 92, 164; and public relations, 98–100; and remediation industry, 163
whistleblowers, 45–48, 102–5
Wiethe, Donetta D., 132
Wilderness Society, 90
Wilkinson, Thomas, 120
William H. Zimmer Nuclear Power Station, 40–41, 45–48, 99, 157
Wilson, Jerome, 67–69
Wirth, Tim, 165
Woburn, MA, 77, 138–39
Wolf, Barbara, 114
Women Strike for Peace, 51, 73
World Wildlife Fund, 176
Wyden, Ron, 136

Yocum, Edwa, 151–53
Young, Russell M., 132, 143
Yucca Mountain Nuclear Waste Repository, 149, 160, 183–84

Zimmer plant. *See* William H. Zimmer Nuclear Power Station
Zinser, Charles, 126–27, 141

WEYERHAEUSER ENVIRONMENTAL BOOKS

Cleaning Up the Bomb Factory: Grassroots Activism and Nuclear Waste in the Midwest, by Casey A. Huegel

Capturing Glaciers: A History of Repeat Photography and Global Warming, by Dani Inkpen

The Toxic Ship: The Voyage of the Khian Sea and the Global Waste Trade, by Simone M. Müller

People of the Ecotone: Environment and Indigenous Power at the Center of Early America, by Robert Michael Morrissey

Charged: A History of Batteries and Lessons for a Clean Energy Future, by James Morton Turner

Wetlands in a Dry Land: More-Than-Human Histories of Australia's Murray-Darling Basin, by Emily O'Gorman

Seeds of Control: Japan's Empire of Forestry in Colonial Korea, by David Fedman

Fir and Empire: The Transformation of Forests in Early Modern China, by Ian M. Miller

Communist Pigs: An Animal History of East Germany's Rise and Fall, by Thomas Fleischman

Footprints of War: Militarized Landscapes in Vietnam, by David Biggs

Cultivating Nature: The Conservation of a Valencian Working Landscape, by Sarah R. Hamilton

Bringing Whales Ashore: Oceans and the Environment of Early Modern Japan, by Jakobina K. Arch

The Organic Profit: Rodale and the Making of Marketplace Environmentalism, by Andrew N. Case

Seismic City: An Environmental History of San Francisco's 1906 Earthquake, by Joanna L. Dyl

Smell Detectives: An Olfactory History of Nineteenth-Century Urban America, by Melanie A. Kiechle

Defending Giants: The Redwood Wars and the Transformation of American Environmental Politics, by Darren Frederick Speece

The City Is More Than Human: An Animal History of Seattle, by Frederick L. Brown

Wilderburbs: Communities on Nature's Edge, by Lincoln Bramwell

How to Read the American West: A Field Guide, by William Wyckoff

Behind the Curve: Science and the Politics of Global Warming, by Joshua P. Howe

Whales and Nations: Environmental Diplomacy on the High Seas, by Kurkpatrick Dorsey

Loving Nature, Fearing the State: Environmentalism and Antigovernment Politics before Reagan, by Brian Allen Drake

Pests in the City: Flies, Bedbugs, Cockroaches, and Rats, by Dawn Day Biehler
Tangled Roots: The Appalachian Trail and American Environmental Politics,
    by Sarah Mittlefehldt
Vacationland: Tourism and Environment in the Colorado High Country,
    by William Philpott
Car Country: An Environmental History, by Christopher W. Wells
Nature Next Door: Cities and Trees in the American Northeast, by Ellen Stroud
Pumpkin: The Curious History of an American Icon, by Cindy Ott
The Promise of Wilderness: American Environmental Politics since 1964,
    by James Morton Turner
The Republic of Nature: An Environmental History of the United States, by Mark Fiege
A Storied Wilderness: Rewilding the Apostle Islands, by James W. Feldman
Iceland Imagined: Nature, Culture, and Storytelling in the North Atlantic,
    by Karen Oslund
Quagmire: Nation-Building and Nature in the Mekong Delta, by David Biggs
Seeking Refuge: Birds and Landscapes of the Pacific Flyway, by Robert M. Wilson
Toxic Archipelago: A History of Industrial Disease in Japan, by Brett L. Walker
Dreaming of Sheep in Navajo Country, by Marsha L. Weisiger
Shaping the Shoreline: Fisheries and Tourism on the Monterey Coast,
    by Connie Y. Chiang
The Fishermen's Frontier: People and Salmon in Southeast Alaska, by David F. Arnold
Making Mountains: New York City and the Catskills, by David Stradling
Plowed Under: Agriculture and Environment in the Palouse, by Andrew P. Duffin
The Country in the City: The Greening of the San Francisco Bay Area,
    by Richard A. Walker
Native Seattle: Histories from the Crossing-Over Place, by Coll Thrush
Drawing Lines in the Forest: Creating Wilderness Areas in the Pacific Northwest,
    by Kevin R. Marsh
Public Power, Private Dams: The Hells Canyon High Dam Controversy,
    by Karl Boyd Brooks
Windshield Wilderness: Cars, Roads, and Nature in Washington's National Parks,
    by David Louter
On the Road Again: Montana's Changing Landscape, by William Wyckoff
Wilderness Forever: Howard Zahniser and the Path to the Wilderness Act, by Mark Harvey
The Lost Wolves of Japan, by Brett L. Walker
Landscapes of Conflict: The Oregon Story, 1940–2000, by William G. Robbins
Faith in Nature: Environmentalism as Religious Quest, by Thomas R. Dunlap
The Nature of Gold: An Environmental History of the Klondike Gold Rush,
    by Kathryn Morse

Where Land and Water Meet: A Western Landscape Transformed, by Nancy Langston

The Rhine: An Eco-Biography, 1815–2000, by Mark Cioc

Driven Wild: How the Fight against Automobiles Launched the Modern Wilderness Movement, by Paul S. Sutter

George Perkins Marsh: Prophet of Conservation, by David Lowenthal

Making Salmon: An Environmental History of the Northwest Fisheries Crisis, by Joseph E. Taylor III

Irrigated Eden: The Making of an Agricultural Landscape in the American West, by Mark Fiege

The Dawn of Conservation Diplomacy: U.S.-Canadian Wildlife Protection Treaties in the Progressive Era, by Kurkpatrick Dorsey

Landscapes of Promise: The Oregon Story, 1800–1940, by William G. Robbins

Forest Dreams, Forest Nightmares: The Paradox of Old Growth in the Inland West, by Nancy Langston

The Natural History of Puget Sound Country, by Arthur R. Kruckeberg

WEYERHAEUSER ENVIRONMENTAL CLASSICS

Debating Malthus: A Documentary Reader on Population, Resources, and the Environment, edited by Robert J. Mayhew

Environmental Justice in Postwar America: A Documentary Reader, edited by Christopher W. Wells

Making Climate Change History: Documents from Global Warming's Past, edited by Joshua P. Howe

Nuclear Reactions: Documenting American Encounters with Nuclear Energy, edited by James W. Feldman

The Wilderness Writings of Howard Zahniser, edited by Mark Harvey

The Environmental Moment: 1968–1972, edited by David Stradling

Reel Nature: America's Romance with Wildlife on Film, by Gregg Mitman

DDT, *Silent Spring, and the Rise of Environmentalism*, edited by Thomas R. Dunlap

Conservation in the Progressive Era: Classic Texts, edited by David Stradling

Man and Nature: Or, Physical Geography as Modified by Human Action, by George Perkins Marsh

A Symbol of Wilderness: Echo Park and the American Conservation Movement, by Mark W. T. Harvey

Tutira: The Story of a New Zealand Sheep Station, by Herbert Guthrie-Smith

Mountain Gloom and Mountain Glory: The Development of the Aesthetics of the Infinite, by Marjorie Hope Nicolson

The Great Columbia Plain: A Historical Geography, 1805–1910, by Donald W. Meinig

CYCLE OF FIRE

Fire: A Brief History, 2nd edition, by Stephen J. Pyne
The Ice: A Journey to Antarctica, by Stephen J. Pyne
Burning Bush: A Fire History of Australia, by Stephen J. Pyne
Fire in America: A Cultural History of Wildland and Rural Fire, by Stephen J. Pyne
Vestal Fire: An Environmental History, Told through Fire, of Europe and Europe's Encounter with the World, by Stephen J. Pyne
World Fire: The Culture of Fire on Earth, by Stephen J. Pyne

ALSO AVAILABLE

Awful Splendour: A Fire History of Canada, by Stephen J. Pyne

www.ingramcontent.com/pod-product-compliance
Lightning Source LLC
Chambersburg PA
CBHW020327240426
43665CB00044B/724